Treating Disruptive Disorders

Treating Disruptive Disorders is a practical book for busy clinicians—psychiatrists, psychologists, mental health counselors, clinical social workers, and more—as well as students, interns, and residents in the mental health professions. It distills the most important information about combined and solitary treatments of a variety of psychological disorders characterized by disruptive behaviors, including those where disruptive aspects are part of core symptoms (like ADHD, ODD, or conduct disorder), and those where disruptive features are commonly associated with core symptoms (like mood, personality, and cognitive/developmental disorders). In addition to an analysis of the best in evidence-based practice and research, the volume also includes brief clinical vignettes to help present the material in an easily accessible, understandable, readable, and relevant format. The chapter authors are experts in the treatment of these disorders and review a wide variety of empirically supported treatments for children, adolescents, and adults.

George M. Kapalka, PhD, is the author or editor of six books, including *Pediatricians and Pharmacologically Trained Psychologists: Practitioner's Guide to Collaborative Treatment; Counseling Boys and Men With ADHD*; and *Parenting Your Out-of-Control Child* (which has been translated into eight foreign languages), as well as dozens of articles in professional journals and other peer-reviewed publications. His views and opinions have been quoted in various newspapers and magazines (including the *New York Times*), as well as on television (including NBC). He is a practicing psychologist and holds board certifications in clinical psychology and psychopharmacology.

Clinical Topics in Psychology and Psychiatry
Bret A. Moore, PsyD, Series Editor

Treating Disruptive Disorders

A Guide to Psychological, Pharmacological, and Combined Therapies

Edited by
George M. Kapalka

Routledge
Taylor & Francis Group

NEW YORK AND LONDON

First published 2015
by Routledge
711 Third Avenue, New York, NY 10017

and by Routledge
27 Church Road, Hove, East Sussex BN3 2FA

Routledge is an imprint of the Taylor & Francis Group, an informa business

© 2015 Taylor & Francis

The right of the editor to be identified as the author of the editorial material, and of the authors for their individual chapters, has been asserted in accordance with sections 77 and 78 of the Copyright, Designs and Patents Act 1988.

Library of Congress Cataloging-in-Publication Data
Treating disruptive disorders: a guide to psychological, pharmacological, and combined therapies/edited by George M. Kapalka.
p.; cm.—(Clinical topics in psychology and psychiatry)
Includes bibliographical references.
Kapalka, George M., editor. II. Series: Clinical topics in psychology and psychiatry. [DNLM: 1. Attention Deficit and Disruptive Behavior Disorders—therapy. 2. Attention Deficit and Disruptive Behavior Disorders—drug therapy. 3. Attention Deficit and Disruptive Behavior Disorders—psychology. 4. Combined Modality Therapy. 5. Psychotherapy. 6. Psychotropic Drugs—therapeutic use. WS 350.6]
RC394.A85
616.85'890651—dc23
2014037853

ISBN: 978-0-415-71959-9 (hbk)
ISBN: 978-0-415-71960-5 (pbk)
ISBN: 978-1-315-86729-8 (ebk)

Typeset in Baskerville
by Swales & Willis Ltd, Exeter, Devon, UK

MIX
Paper from
responsible sources
FSC
FSC® C013056
www.fsc.org

Printed and bound in Great Britain by
TJ International Ltd, Padstow, Cornwall

Contents

Contributors

Vincent P. Aguirre, MS, Department of Psychology, Texas A&M University, College Station, Texas, USA.

Margaret J. Areizaga, PhD, Bronxville, New York, USA.

Lia Billington, PhD, Vincent Family Medicine Center, Santa Fe, New Mexico, USA.

Elizabeth Brestan-Knight, PhD, Department of Psychology, Auburn University, Auburn, Alabama, USA.

Lara Buckley, MS, Graduate School of Psychology, California Lutheran University, Oxnard, California, USA.

Jennifer Burger, PsyD, ABPP, Department of Psychology, Wilmington College, Bexley, Ohio, USA.

Ivette M. Calles, MS, Department of Psychology, Texas A&M University, College Station, Texas, USA.

Anil K. Chacko, PhD, Department of Applied Psychology, New York University, New York, New York, USA.

Brandi L. Chew, PhD, Seattle Children's Hospital Autism Center, Seattle, Washington, USA.

Michael S. L. Ching, MD, MPH, Department of Pediatrics, Tripler Army Medical Center, Honolulu, Hawaii, USA.

David F. Curtis, PhD, Department of Pediatrics, Baylor College of Medicine, Texas Children's Hospital, Houston, Texas, USA.

Sara R. Elkins, PhD, Department of Clinical, Health, and Applied Sciences, University of Houston–Clear Lake, Houston, Texas, USA.

Nicole Feirsen, MA, Department of Psychology, Graduate School and University Center, City University of New York, Flushing, New York, USA.

Ken Fogel, PsyD, Park Ridge, Illinois, USA.

Angela A. Gorman, PhD, Hershey, Pennsylvania, USA.

Loran P. Hayes, Department of Psychology, University of Utah, Salt Lake City, Utah, USA.

Robert W. Heffer, PhD, Department of Psychology, Texas A&M University, College Station, Texas, USA.

Benjamin D. Hill, PhD, Department of Psychology, University of South Alabama, Mobile, Alabama, USA.

Michael B. Himle, PhD, Department of Psychology, University of Utah, Salt Lake City, Utah, USA.

Nicolette Howells, PhD, Center for Cognitive and Behavioral Therapy, Columbus, Ohio, USA.

Edward F. Hudspeth, PhD, Department of Counselor Education, Henderson State University, Arkadelphia, Arkansas, USA.

Sonia C. Izmirian, MA, Department of Psychology, University of Hawaii at Manoa, Honolulu, Hawaii, USA.

Heather Kirkpatrick, PhD, ABPP, Genesys Regional Medical Center, Flint, Michigan, USA.

Patricia Lopez, MA, Department of Educational and School Psychology, Alliant International University, Alhambra, California, USA.

Ashlee R. Loughan, PhD, Neurobehavioral Associates, Augusta, Georgia, USA.

Rebecca Lundeen, MA, Department of Educational Leadership, University of Southern California, Long Beach, California, USA.

Kimberly M. Matthews, MEd, Department of Leadership and Counselor Education, University of Mississippi, Booneville, Mississippi, USA.

Samantha Miller, PhD, Austin, Texas, USA.

William E. Pelham, PhD, ABPP, Department of Psychology, Florida International University, Miami, Florida, USA.

Robert Perna, PhD, RN, Department of Psychology/Neuropsychology, TIRR Memorial Hermann Hospital, Houston, Texas, USA.

Estrella Rajwan, Department of Psychology, Graduate School and University Center, City University of New York, Flushing, New York, USA.

Krishnapriya Ramanujam, Department of Psychology, University of Utah, Salt Lake City, Utah, USA.

Mimi Sa, PsyD, MSCP, Isanti, Minnesota, USA.

David Shprecher, MD, Department of Neurology, University of Utah, Salt Lake City, Utah, USA.

Angela V. Sikkenga, MA, Department of School Psychology, Chapman University, Los Angeles, California, USA.

Channing Sofko, MS, Department of Psychology, University of Southern Alabama, Mobile, Alabama, USA.

Timothy Thornberry, PhD, Department of Psychology, Morehead State University, Morehead, Kentucky, USA.

Matthew Tirrell, MS, Department of Psychological Counseling, Monmouth University, West Long Branch, New Jersey, USA.

Jennifer M. Twyford, PhD, Graduate School of Psychology, California Lutheran University, Oxnard, California, USA.

Jessy Warner-Cohen, PhD, MPH, Long Island Jewish Medical Center, Glen Oaks, New York, USA.

Dawn Wirick, PhD, School of Counseling, Walden University, Minneapolis, Minnesota, USA.

Tony Wu, PhD, ABPP, Department of Psychology, Walden University, Minneapolis, Minnesota, USA.

Amanda Zwilling, Department of Psychology, Graduate School and University Center, City University of New York, Flushing, New York.

Series Editor's Foreword

Treating Disruptive Disorders: A Guide to Psychological, Pharmacological, and Combined Therapies is the fourth book in one of Routledge's newest series, Clinical Topics in Psychology and Psychiatry (CTPP). The overarching goal of CTPP is to provide mental health practitioners with practical information that is both comprehensive and relatively easy to integrate into day-to-day clinical practice. It is multidisciplinary in that it covers topics relevant to the fields of psychology and psychiatry and appeals to both the student and the senior clinician. Books chosen for the series are authored and edited by national and international experts in their respective areas, and contributors are also highly respected clinicians. The current volume exemplifies the intent, scope, and aims of the CTPP series.

Editor George Kapalka relies on some of the nation's leading experts with regard to understanding and managing disruptive behaviors commonly encountered in clinical practice. As he and Angela A. Gorman note in Chapter 1, until relatively recent in our history, few choices were available for managing disruptive behaviors, whether it be aggressive or assaultive behavior by an individual suffering from psychosis or a third grader who was falling behind in the classroom because of impulsivity related to attention-deficit/hyperactivity disorder. It is no longer the norm to simply sedate someone who has been labeled as "difficult" or a "problem." Today, research shows us that many of the behaviors that are fueled by an individual's internal urges to say or act in ways deemed disruptive can be effectively minimized if not outright eliminated within the context of a variety of psychiatric conditions and presentations. Both medication and cognitive and behavioral therapies have a place. And, as illustrated in this volume, the approach of combining pharmacology and behavioral psychology may provide the most robust effects for many disruptive behaviors and disorders.

Although *Treating Disruptive Disorders* does not provide a step-by-step protocol for managing disruptive behavior disorders, it provides the clinician with the latest research and sound guidance for empirically guided practice. The clinician, whether novice or veteran, will recognize that she does not need to learn about new theoretical models or obscure pharmaceutical agents to successfully manage disruptive behaviors, but rather utilize therapies that are already familiar and used regularly in clinical practice. This is arguably the most useful aspect of the book.

In an area of clinical practice that has posed some of the most significant challenges for health-care providers over the centuries, it is ironic that we are only now seeing the first comprehensive guide on the subject. Kapalka has done the field a great service by compiling in one place the most effective pharmacological, psychological, and combined therapies available for disruptive behaviors.

Bret A. Moore, PsyD, ABPP
Series Editor
Clinical Topics in Psychology and Psychiatry

Preface

The term "disruptive" is a psychological construct. Like all hypothetical constructs, it lacks uniform definition and is subject to individual interpretation. When it comes to "disruptive behaviors," however, while precise definition may vary from person to person, there is significant overlap with regard to which behaviors are regarded as such by most mental health professionals. Disruptive behaviors generally interfere with many aspects of functioning and cause significant difficulties for patients, families or caretakers, and significant others involved in patients' educational, occupational, and social lives. They also pose considerable challenges for the treating professionals, as many of those behaviors may be difficult to bring under control, and in severe cases the behaviors may create danger to the patient and those around him, including the treating professionals. It is clear, therefore, that finding the most effective ways to address these behaviors is a high priority.

The nature of the specific behaviors that are regarded as disruptive may vary from person to person, but most professionals agree that a disruptive behavior is one that potentially threatens (or violates) one's physical integrity, property, space, or day-to-day functioning. Thus disruptive behaviors usually encroach on the rights of others, but they may also be self-directed. The most likely candidates for classification as disruptive are behaviors that are considered aggressive, especially when the levels of aggression become severe enough to be considered verbally or physically violent. Physical aggression may include assault on someone else or destruction of property, but it may also be self-directed and include self-mutilation or attempts at suicide. Verbal aggression is usually directed toward others and commonly includes yelling, threatening, name calling, and various forms of verbal intimidation. In sum, the aggressive behavior described above is one type of behaviors considered to be disruptive in accordance with the operational definition followed in this book.

Disruptive behaviors may not always involve aggression, however. For example, they may interfere with the ability of others to benefit from education (e.g., when one student acts out or otherwise interferes with the teacher's ability to teach in the classroom), concentrate in the workplace (such as when a coworker is not able to suppress impulses to make noises or move about excessively), feel comfortable in their surroundings (like when others around them talk excessively or otherwise become distracting), and maintain proper social interaction (e.g., when others interrupt conversations or social interactions).

Lack of appropriate impulse control often underlies disruptive behaviors. When triggers evoke reactions—for example, when a person is angered or when someone experiences the urge to move, say, or do something—most individuals are appropriately able to contain those reactions and usually do not behave disruptively unless the stimulus is of significant severity to exceed normal self-control (e.g., when a spouse discovers that the other spouse is having an affair). But some individuals possess little control over day-to-day triggers and act out many of their impulses through words and behaviors with seemingly little ability to control their internal urges. This book therefore conceptualizes disruptive behaviors as those that emanate from internal urges that most individuals would be able to suppress in a given situation, while individuals who behave disruptively seemingly cannot. Thus impulsivity and limited self-control are thought herein to underlie disruptive behaviors that may be violent or otherwise problematic.

Disruptive disorders are those disorders where disruptive features and behaviors are commonly present that are severe enough to interfere with individuals' day-to-day functioning, impairing their ability to adaptively function among others. While not an official diagnostic category, disruptive disorders are considered to be a conceptual grouping of those disorders in which disruptive behaviors are most commonly experienced. These disorders may be further classified into two categories. In some disorders, disruptive features and behaviors are core symptoms that are listed in the diagnostic criteria for those disorders. In those disorders, impulsivity and self-control problems (often including aggression) are thought to be the central aspects of the underlying psychopathology. In other cases, underlying psychopathology may not necessarily result in disruptive behaviors for all individuals, but disruptive features are commonly associated with many people diagnosed with those disorders.

In this book readers will find a review of etiological, epidemiological, diagnostic, and treatment data about disruptive disorders (categorized as such in accordance with the above operational definitions). Chapter 1 discusses, in general terms, the benefits and drawbacks of monotherapies (psychotherapy-only and medication-only treatments) versus combined treatments (medications and psychotherapy). Because both monotherapies and combined treatment approaches offer unique benefits as well as challenges, readers are encouraged to consider those issues before selecting the approach that may be most appropriate for their patients.

Chapters 2 and 3 review the etiology of disruptive disorders, focusing particularly on impulse control and aggression. Both are reviewed from the psychological as well as biological viewpoints, helping to ground readers in the factors that underlie disruptive symptoms and behaviors. Chapter 4 reviews epidemiology and course of disruptive disorders, further providing the context as well as the risks that those disorders pose to individuals, those around them, and society at large.

The chapters in Part II review treatment of disorders for which disruptive features and behaviors are considered core symptoms. Chapter 5 reviews treatment of attention-deficit/hyperactivity disorder (ADHD), Chapter 6 discusses treatment of oppositional defiant disorder (ODD), and Chapter 7 reviews treatment of conduct disorder (CD). Treatments of ODD and CD focus primarily on the pediatric population (children and adolescents), with ADHD discussed from a life span perspective, including treatment of adults. Chapter 8 reviews treatment of tic disorders (especially Tourette's disorder), and Chapter 9 discusses treatment of intermittent explosive disorder.

Part III reviews treatment of disorders in which disruptive features are not included in core symptoms but are commonly associated with patients diagnosed with those disorders. Chapter 10 discusses treatment of disruptive features associated with autism spectrum disorder and intellectual disability, Chapter 11 reviews treatment of disruptive symptoms commonly seen in select mood and personality disorders, and Chapter 12 reviews treatment of disruptive features that commonly accompany delirium and other neurocognitive disorders.

While the above list of disorders is not exhaustive and disruptive features may be associated with other disorders, space considerations dictate inclusion of only those disorders in which disruptive symptoms are most likely to occur or co-occur. I hope that this practical volume provides needed guidance to professionals who treat patients with these challenging disorders.

Part I

Etiology, Epidemiology, and Course of Disruptive Disorders

1 To Medicate or Not to Medicate

Weighing the Benefits and Challenges of Available Treatments for Disruptive Disorders

George M. Kapalka and Angela A. Gorman

Since the days of Freud and Kraeplin and well into the mid-twentieth century, we seemed to have had only two widely recognized choices to treat patients with psychological disorders: long-term institutionalization (and, mostly, significant sedation) for the most severely ill and intensive psychoanalysis for those able to function outside the psychiatric hospitals. The decision of whether to sedate or hospitalize patients was primarily made on the basis of the degree of disruption these patients caused to those around them. Those most severely disruptive (e.g., violent) were usually sedated, and those patients were most likely to be institutionalized.

Over the past five decades, significant developments changed the face of mental health treatment. A plethora of research revealed that many individuals with psychological disorders exhibit structural and functional differences in their brains. For example, functional impairments in the anterior cingulate cortex (ACC) have been identified in youth with disruptive behaviors (Gavita et al., 2012), and researchers have explored the function and role of monoamine neurotransmitters such as serotonin and dopamine, which may play key roles in the development of disruptive behaviors (Malmberg et al., 2008). In general, imbalance in activity between "hot" and "cold" brain circuitry is currently believed to underlie many disruptive symptoms and features (see Chapter 2 in this volume for a review). Stress hormones like cortisol have also been implicated. For example, an association may exist between cortisol reactivity and callous unemotional (CU) traits in boys, which are often present in youth with disruptive behavior disorders (Van De Wiel et al., 2004). This is consistent with the body of literature that highlights the correlation between the reactivity of the hypothalamic pituitary adrenal (HPA) in times of stress and disruptive/aggressive behavior (Stadler et al., 2011).

Because brain changes are likely to be reflected in feelings and behaviors, psychopharmacological approaches were developed to try to address some of the biological factors that may be responsible, at least in

part, for the symptoms. Many of these approaches have proven effective
in reducing (and sometimes eliminating) many symptoms, including disruptive behaviors, and intervening pharmacologically has been shown to
be beneficial, especially in cases where symptoms are severe and potentially dangerous.

But today many critics believe the pendulum has swung too far in the
direction of pharmacological treatments. With the US Food and Drug
Administration's loosening of restrictions on direct-to-consumer medication advertisement (the United States is one of only two countries in the
world allowing such advertisements), ads for various medications now fill
the air, seemingly most of the day and on almost every radio and television station, and medication ads similarly have infiltrated much of the
Internet. This is driving a culture where medications are seen as a quick
fix that provide improvement with little effort or cost (if one has proper
health insurance coverage), and the significant adverse effects that many
of these medications may have tend to be underemphasized. In addition,
medications are treatments and not cures, and so when the medications
are discontinued, the symptoms are likely to return.

Many nonmedical mental health professionals tend to recognize these
factors and usually seek to minimize pharmacological approaches, focusing instead on psychological treatments. Over the past five or six decades,
research on various forms of psychotherapy has exploded and many specific treatments have been developed for many specific disorders. This is a
reasonable approach, especially with children and the elderly population,
as introducing medications in these populations may result in unpredict-
able reactions and medical risks. But is it realistic for psychotherapy to
replace the need for psychotropic medications? Will symptom improvement be sufficient so that treatment with medications will not be needed?

The above questions are most appropriate in the context of disruptive symptoms and behaviors. Disruptive disorders are often-referred
disorders for psychiatric (Jensen et al., 2007) and mental health services
(Zisser & Eyberg, 2010), and most who encounter individuals with these
disorders must decide whether the referral should be to a prescriber or
a psychotherapist. On the one hand, disruptive behaviors by their very
nature require quick stabilization, because the problems that patients
and those around them experience as a result of aggressive and impulsive
actions tend to be troubling and impairing. This suggests that treatment
with medications may offer quicker improvement. But does that mean
that psychotherapeutic treatments are not as desirable? And can the benefits be maximized when combined treatment approaches (including
psychological and pharmacological treatments) are utilized? While the
contributions to this volume grapple with these questions and strive to
offer readers much-needed guidance, broad themes permeate these
reviews, and contemplating these factors while consulting the reviews will

help focus the readers on important aspects to consider when choosing the best treatment.

Pharmacological Treatment of Disruptive Disorders

Research findings reveal that many medications are effective in reducing disruptive symptoms and features. Most notably, psychostimulants have been shown to reduce impulsivity (MTA Cooperative Group, 1999), while mood stabilizers—including anticonvulsants (Stanford et al., 2001), atypical antipsychotics (Buitelaar et al., 2001), and lithium (Jones et al., 2011) as well as serotonergic antidepressants (especially selective serotonin reuptake inhibitors, or SSRIs; Coccaro et al., 2009)—have been shown to reduce propensity toward impulsive aggression and violence. Of course, medications come with risks, and various patients tolerate medications to varying degrees. Thus clinicians must frequently consider whether the benefits outweigh the risk, and, if so, which patients are best candidates for medications.

Severity of the symptoms often influences the decision of whether treatment with medications is needed. For example, milder forms of impulsivity or agitation may respond well to psychotherapy. Severe variants of these symptoms may be difficult to treat with psychological therapies, however, and intense and dangerous symptoms are likely to require psychopharmacological treatment. Therefore most clinicians find that individuals with seriously compromised self-control and significant potential for violence usually require an approach that includes pharmacological treatment. Jensen et al. (2007) confirmed, for example, that the use of psychotropic agents are usually limited to cases in which symptoms are more severe and may not be as responsive to psychological interventions alone.

When psychosocial treatment is effective, progression of improvement is gradual, requiring several sessions to become evident. Even those variants termed "brief therapy" generally require 8–15 sessions before significant improvement is expected. When disruptive symptoms debilitate patients and pose significant risks to those around them, waiting so long for improvement may not be prudent. Conversely, many pharmacological treatments produce at least some improvement within days of the onset of treatment, although a few weeks (in some cases, four to six) may be needed for more comprehensive response. Still, this is usually faster than psychological treatments, and the amount of improvement seen with medications may be greater than the improvement seen with psychotherapy over the same period of time.

In order for psychological treatments to be effective, patients need to attend sessions regularly. If rapid progress is needed, sessions need to be scheduled at least weekly. Yet driving to the therapist's office once per week, and spending an hour in the office, may be difficult for some patients (or families) with significant time obligations. When the patient is a child or adolescent, psychotherapy must be done outside of school hours, because missing school one day per week to attend psychotherapy is neither practical for the family nor beneficial to the student.

The cost of weekly psychotherapy is also likely to constitute a significant expense for many families, and few are able to cover such costs out of pocket. In the United States, most patients with health-care coverage are covered by private plans, usually purchased through an employer. The quality of this coverage varies widely. Unfortunately, mental health care is often considered to be the "step-child" of the health-care industry, and levels of coverage for mental health treatment are often much lower than they are for medical care. Although laws on the federal and state levels have been passed to close that gap, many exclusions exist, and the disparity between medical and mental health coverage continues.

Limiting the patient's access to care is one common method of containing health-care costs. Many individuals with managed health-care coverage have benefits that are primarily evident "on paper" and virtually disappear when the insured seeks treatment. Gatekeepers review the need for care, and these reviews delay sessions and interrupt the continuity of care. Gatekeepers may initially authorize four to six sessions, and additional reviews are needed for each subsequent block. It is up to the discretion of the gatekeeper to authorize further treatment, and when the gatekeeper believes that a patient has made sufficient progress, or that sufficient progress is not evident, further authorization may not be issued. Although every insurer has appeals procedures, these appeals are internal to the insurer, and patients usually have no external review to invoke if the insurer refuses to authorize continued care. To make matters worse, appeals often take months; in the meantime patients are getting no care and, in the case of disruptive symptoms, continue to pose risks to themselves and those around them.

Another challenge is that millions of children and adolescents in the United States have no health-care coverage. While federal and state authorities are striving to close this gap, there continues to be a significant portion of our society without insurance coverage that cannot afford mental health care. Various agencies exist that may service these individuals, including networks of community mental health centers (CMHCs) that provide care to those who need it, sometimes without (or with minimal) cost. In many states, however, CMHCs are overextended, and long wait times are necessary (in some cases, up to eight weeks) before the agency is able to provide care. Meanwhile, patients are suffering and are receiving no treatment. In addition, in rural states, the nearest CMHC may be a long distance away. For all of those reasons, patients and their families may need to utilize psychopharmacological treatment either instead of or in addition to psychosocial interventions.

Psychological Treatment of Disruptive Disorders

Although there are good reasons why pharmacology may be appropriate for some patients, psychological treatments clearly have their place, and much research has shown that psychosocial interventions are effective. Cognitive and behavioral interventions are most clearly supported for the treatment of disruptive disorders and tend to aim directly at the problematic thoughts and behaviors. For example, interventions that have demonstrated efficacy include problem-solving skills training (Kazdin et al., 1987b), problem-solving skills training and practice (Kazdin et al., 1989), rational emotive mental health program (Block, 1978), Triple P enhanced and Triple P standard (Sanders et al., 2000), anger control training (Lochman et al., 1993), group assertive training (Huey & Rank, 1984), incredible years child training (Webster-Stratton & Hammond, 1997), and problem-solving social skills training (Kazdin et al., 1992). In addition, combining the use of playgroups and social modeling has been effective for teaching social skills to youth with disruptive behavior disorders (Nash & Schaefer, 2011). Effective interventions that target parents include parent management training (Bernal et al., 1980; Kazdin et al., 1992), problem-solving skills training and parent management training (Kazdin et al., 1987a), helping the noncompliant child (Peed et al., 1977), incredible years parent training (Webster-Stratton & Hammond, 1997), multidimensional treatment foster care (for both children and caregivers; Chamberlain & Reid, 1998), multisystemic therapy (for both children and parents; Henggeler et al., 1992), parent–child interaction therapy (Schuhmann et al., 1998), Barkley's (1997) manual-based parent management training model, and *Parenting Your Out-of-Control Child* (Kapalka, 2007). Similar interventions have also been developed that target teachers, including *Eight Steps to Classroom Management Success* (Kapalka, 2009).

Psychological therapies may be especially well suited in situations where impairment from the symptoms does not severely impair patients or affect the safety of those around them. With some patients, introducing medications may be risky, which is especially concerning when medications are used with patient populations that are medically or developmentally vulnerable, like children, adolescents, and the elderly. Most studies that investigated the use of psychotropic medications lasted at most a few months, and therefore long-term effects of most medications are not known. In addition, improvement from medications usually lasts only as long as the medications are administered, and return of the original symptoms is likely upon discontinuation of medications. Conversely, psychosocial treatments teach patients new skills that are applicable in a wide variety of life situations that they may encounter, and at least in theory those new skills are acquired more permanently. Even after therapy terminates, the presumption is that the therapeutic benefits derived during treatment will continue.

Even in the short term, many medications have risks and adverse effects. Many of the medications utilized to diminish disruptive behaviors are sedating (psychostimulants being the notable exception), at least at first, and so they may adversely affect the patient's day-to-day functioning and ability to work or attend school. In addition, most medications carry other risks, including effects on memory and concentration, changes in appetite and sleep patterns, cardiovascular reactions, metabolic changes, and a variety of other physical and psychological reactions. While the severity of these adverse effects varies from one person to another, if symptoms are not severe enough to require immediate improvement, it may be worth it to avoid those risks and initially try psychological treatments.

While psychoanalysis usually required long-term treatment, many current psychosocial approaches are more clearly time limited and problem focused. In most cognitive and behavioral treatments at least some progress is expected after three or four sessions, and more significant improvement usually occurs over eight to fifteen sessions. When disruptive symptoms are not unusually debilitating and do not pose significant risks to those around them, this time frame may provide sufficiently rapid improvement.

Because in psychological treatments patients generally attend sessions regularly, the mental health professional usually has the opportunity to get to know the patient well. This familiarity allows the professional to monitor the patient's symptoms and clarify or change the diagnosis as further symptoms become apparent. This is especially important in the context of disruptive disorders, as comorbidity with other disorders is the rule rather than the exception. An astute mental health professional is able to tailor treatment to address all the symptoms and disorders that are becoming apparent as the treatment is unfolding.

For patients with good health-care coverage, the cost of psychotherapy may only involve copayment (especially when using in-network providers), thus limiting out-of-pocket expenses. Those without health care may be candidates for various forms of free or subsidized care available through federal, state, and local government agencies as well as various nonprofit organizations. Although availability of those programs varies widely from state to state (and often from one portion of the state to another), in some parts of the country patients may be able to access these services.

Combined Treatment of Disruptive Disorders

It is clear that each modality, pharmacotherapy, and psychological treatment offers unique benefits that address or minimize problems inherent when either approach is used as monotherapy. Medications work only as long as they are being administered, but psychological treatments offer lasting changes and acquisition of new skills. Medications may cause adverse effects, utilizing psychotherapy may (at least in theory) allow lower doses of medications to be utilized, and combined treatment offers the additional benefit of more frequent monitoring of response to medications (including both desired and adverse effects), as psychotherapists see their patients much more frequently than medication prescribers. Psychotherapists are also in the position to address other issues regarding the use of medications, such as adherence and patients' perceptions of the medications, thus maximizing the likelihood of deriving benefits from the medications.

Researchers are increasingly exploring the integration of psychotherapy and psychopharmacology as a means to treat various disruptive disorders (Kutcher et al., 2004). In fact, disruptive behavior disorders tend to be the most often referred disorders for psychiatric care (Jensen et al., 2007), and many of these referrals come from nonmedical mental health clinicians, indicating that many professionals desire to obtain combination treatment for their patients. Clinicians seek this integrative approach to enable the simultaneous treatment of biological, behavioral, cognitive, and psychosocial aspects of these disorders.

But the integrative approach to the treatment of disruptive disorders has rarely been studied. This dearth of research findings poses challenges to clinicians, as few guidelines exist about how to integrate treatments. While it makes conceptual sense that combining both treatments maximizes therapeutic benefits, the incremental validity of adding one treatment to another has rarely been investigated, and in those few instances where such a combination was explored, findings have been inconsistent. On the one hand, research findings have suggested that combining psychotherapy and pharmacotherapy in the treatment of mood and personality disorders is superior to either treatment alone (Kool et al., 2007). On the other hand, the degree of improvement of attention-deficit/hyperactivity disorder (ADHD) symptoms did not differ significantly for combined treatment or psychostimulant monotherapy, and both were statistically superior to behavioral treatment alone (MTA Cooperative Group, 1999). For oppositional symptoms, however, only the combined intervention was statistically superior. It is clear, therefore, that the incremental validity of adding one treatment to another remains unknown, and clinicians currently have no bases to gauge how much further improvement can be expected when one treatment is added to the other.

Proper sequencing of combining treatments also remains mostly unexplored. Many believe that, with the exception of the unusually severe cases, the first-line treatment for most patients should consist of cognitive or behavioral therapy, adding medications only when improvement is not sufficient. Conversely, however, the reverse sequence may also offer benefits—initial stabilization of symptoms may improve engagement in psychotherapy, further maximizing therapeutic benefits. Thus, when combined treatments are considered, the question of which modality should be used has not been answered.

Methods of integration of the two therapies also remain unknown. Will lower doses of medications be needed when the patient simultaneously participates in psychosocial treatment? Will less intensive (and less frequent) psychological treatment be sufficient when medications are also being utilized? Not only are those questions unanswered, but also it is likely that the answer to these questions may differ based on patient characteristics and the patient's response to each modality. Clinicians are thus left to use their own judgment when considering various aspects of this issue.

Access to combined treatment is also likely to pose significant challenges. Ideally, one mental health professional would administer both modalities of treatment, but in the United States the delivery of medications and psychotherapy has been highly compartmentalized, with few professionals providing both treatments. Although psychiatrist and psychiatric nurse practitioners possess some psychotherapy training at least in theory, few actually deliver these services, and most exclusively perform medication management. In addition, the United States suffers from significant shortages of psychiatric prescribers, and therefore most prescriptions for psychotropics are written by general practitioners, internists, and pediatricians who lack the training (or time) required to provide psychological treatment. Conversely, nonmedical mental health professionals do not have the ability to prescribe medications. One exception exists: some psychologists have undergone significant medical training, and two US states (New Mexico and Louisiana), the US territory of Guam, and various branches of the US government now allow these psychologists to prescribe psychotropic medications. To date, about 150 psychologists with this training prescribe medications, and the number is likely to expand; for example, Illinois just passed prescriptive authority for properly trained psychologists. But 150 providers able to deliver combined treatment is not sufficient to meet the demand, and so, at least in the near future, patients requiring both treatment modalities will usually require the services of two mental health providers. This not only strains time and financial resources but also raises issues of access to care, especially in rural areas with few practicing mental health professionals.

In the end, practitioners who consider whether to utilize pharmacotherapy, psychotherapy, or both treatments must arrive at the decision by considering various aspects of the case, and the choice will likely vary from one patient to another. The following guidelines may assist practitioners in making such a decision.

Clinical Points to Remember

1 Pharmacotherapy as monotherapy may offer easier access (as medical providers tend to be more widely available, especially in rural areas) and may be cheaper and less time consuming. On the other hand, medications are only treatments, not cures, and the symptoms will presumably return when the medications are discontinued.

2 Various categories of psychotropic medications are utilized in treatment of disruptive disorders, and risks and adverse effects vary widely. While psychostimulants and SSRI antidepressants are generally well tolerated, mood stabilizers and atypical antipsychotics generally tend to have more significant adverse effects and medical risks.

3 The use of medications has not been researched over the long term, and so long-term risks and adverse effects remain mostly unknown. This is a particular concern with vulnerable patient populations, including children, adolescents, and the elderly. Most psychotropic medications also pose significant risks during pregnancy. With those patients, use of psychological interventions is usually considered a first-line approach.

4 Psychological treatment poses fewer risks and may offer the additional benefit of long-term improvement, as changes and skills acquired in treatment may remain after treatment stops. On the other hand, improvement is likely to be gradual and usually requires at least several sessions for any noticeable changes, with full results requiring as many as 15 sessions or more. Access to providers, especially those who are trained in the best practices reviewed herein, may also be difficult to attain, especially in remote and rural areas.

5 The decision of whether to use medications is often determined in large part by symptom severity. Those patients with most severe symptoms, especially when those symptoms threaten others, are stabilized more quickly with medications.

6 At least in theory, combined treatment may offer the benefits of each modality alone, although this has not been convincingly supported with available clinical research.

7 Incremental utility of adding one treatment to another is an important consideration. Clinicians should consider how much further improvement is likely after adding the second treatment modality. Clinicians must weigh the incremental benefit against the increased need for time and resources when two providers must be utilized, as well as access to both types of providers.

8 Treatment compliance with psychotropic medications may be inconsistent, especially when medications pose significant adverse effects

that are troubling to the patient (such as sedation, memory difficulties, sexual dysfunction, etc.). In some cases, combined treatment may allow practitioners an increased opportunity to monitor medications and address any concerns and adverse effects, as both providers will be able to review patient's response to medications.

9 When combined treatment is utilized, it is necessary for both providers to remain in close contact. Both providers must support and encourage both treatment modalities. The patient must get the message from both providers that maximal improvement will result from the complementary contributions of both treatments.

10 Clinicians must ascertain and review patients' and family members' preference for either modality. Clinicians must also accept that the modality for which patients and their families express the most clearly evident preference is the one that is most likely to be adhered to, and therefore the one that will ultimately result in the greatest response. Combined treatment is most likely to be effective when patients accept that both treatments are needed for optimal symptom reduction.

References

Barkley, R. A. (1997). *Defiant children: A clinician's manual for assessment and parent training* (2nd ed.). New York: Guilford Press.

Bernal, M. E., et al. (1980). Outcome evaluation of behavioral parent training and client-centered parent counseling for children with conduct problems. *Journal of Applied Behavior Analysis, 13,* 677–691.

Block, J. (1978). Effects of a rational-emotive mental health program on poorly achieving, disruptive high school students. *Journal of Counseling Psychology, 25,* 61–65.

Buitelaar, J. K., et al. (2001). A randomized controlled trial of risperidone in the treatment of aggression in hospitalized adolescents with subaverage cognitive abilities. *Journal of Clinical Psychiatry, 62*(4), 239–248.

Chamberlain, P., & Reid, J. B. (1998). Comparison of two community alternatives to incarceration for chronic juvenile offenders. *Journal of Consulting and Clinical Psychology, 66,* 624–633.

Coccaro, E. F., et al. (2009). A double-blind, randomized, placebo-controlled trial of fluoxetine in patients with intermittent explosive disorder. *Journal of Clinical Psychiatry, 70*(5), 653–662. doi:10.4088/JCP.08m04150

Gavita, O. A., et al. (2012). Anterior cingulate cortex findings in child disruptive behavior disorders: A meta-analysis. *Aggression and Violent Behavior, 17,* 507–513.

Henggeler, S. W., et al. (1992). Family preservation using multisystemic therapy: An effective alternative to incarcerating serious juvenile offenders. *Journal of Consulting and Clinical Psychology, 60,* 953–961.

Huey, W. C., & Rank, R. C. (1984). Effects of counselor and peer-led group assertive training on black-adolescent aggression. *Journal of Counseling Psychology, 31,* 95–98.

Jensen, P. S., et al. (2007). Management of psychiatric disorders in children and adolescents with atypical antipsychotics: A systematic review of published clinical trials. *European Child and Adolescent Psychiatry, 16*, 104–120.

Jones, R. M., et al. (2011). Efficacy of mood stabilizers in the treatment of impulsive or repetitive aggression: Systematic review and meta-analysis. *British Journal of Psychiatry, 198*(2), 93–98. doi:10.1192/bjp.bp.110.083030

Kapalka, G. M. (2007). *Parenting your out-of-control child.* Oakland, CA: New Harbinger.

Kapalka, G. M. (2009). *Eight steps to classroom management success.* Thousand Oaks, CA: Corwin.

Kazdin, A. E., et al. (1987a). Effects of parent-management training and problem-solving skills training combined in the treatment of antisocial child behavior. *Journal of the American Academy of Child and Adolescent Psychiatry, 26*, 416–424.

Kazdin, A. E., et al. (1987b). Problem-solving skills and relationship therapy in the treatment of antisocial behavior. *Journal of Consulting and Clinical Psychology, 55*, 76–85.

Kazdin, A. E., et al. (1989). Cognitive behavior therapy and relationship therapy in the treatment of children referred for antisocial behavior. *Journal of Consulting and Clinical Psychology, 57*, 522–536.

Kazdin, A. E., et al. (1992). Cognitive problem-solving skills training and parent management training in the treatment of antisocial behavior in children. *Journal of Consulting and Clinical Psychology, 60*, 733–747.

Kool, S., et al. (2007). Treatment of depressive disorder and comorbid personality pathology: Combined therapy versus pharmacotherapy. *Tijdschrift voor Psychiatrie, 49*(6), 361–372.

Kutcher, S., et al. (2004). International consensus statement on attention-deficit/ hyperactivity disorder (ADHD) and disruptive behavior disorders (DBDs): Clinical implications and treatment practice suggestions. *European Neuropsychopharmacology, 14*, 11–28.

Lochman, J. E., et al. (1993). Effectiveness of a social relations intervention program for aggressive and non-aggressive, rejected children. *Journal of Consulting and Clinical Psychology, 61*, 1053–1058.

Malmberg, K., et al. (2008). ADHD and disruptive behavior scores—Associations with MAO-A and 5-HTT genes and with platelet MAO-B activity in adolescents. *BMC Psychiatry, 8*(28). doi:10.1186/1471-244X-8-28

MTA Cooperative Group (1999). A 14-month randomized clinical trial of treatment strategies for attention-deficit/hyperactivity disorder. *Archives of General Psychiatry, 56*, 1073–1086.

Nash, J. B., & Schaefer, C. E. (2011). Social skills play groups for children with disruptive behavior disorders: Integrating play and group therapy approaches. In A. A. Drewes, S. C. Bratton, & C. E. Schaefer (Eds.), *Integrative play therapy.* Hoboken, NJ: John Wiley & Sons.

Peed, S., et al. (1977). Evaluation of the effectiveness of a standardized parent training program in altering the interaction of mothers and their noncompliant children. *Behavior Modification, 1*, 323–350.

Sanders, M. R., et al. (2000). The Triple P positive parenting program: A comparison of enhanced, standard, and self-directed behavioral family intervention for parents of children with early-onset conduct problems. *Journal of Consulting and Clinical Psychology, 68*, 624–640.

14   *George M. Kapalka and Angela A. Gorman*

Schuhmann, E. M., et al. (1998). Efficacy of parent-child interaction therapy: Interim report of a randomized trial with short-term maintenance. *Journal of Clinical Psychology, 27*, 34–45.

Stadler, C., et al. (2011). Cortisol reactivity in boys with attention-deficit/hyperactivity disorder and disruptive behavior problems: The impact of callous unemotional traits. *Psychiatry Research, 187*, 204–209.

Stanford, M. S., et al. (2001). A double-blind placebo-controlled crossover study of phenytoin in individuals with impulsive aggression. *Psychiatry Research, 103*(2–3), 193–203.

Van De Wiel, N., et al. (2004). Cortisol and treatment effect in children with disruptive behavior disorders: A preliminary study. *Journal of the American Academy of Child and Adolescent Psychiatry, 43*, 1011–1018.

Webster-Stratton, C., & Hammond, M. (1997). Treating children with early-onset conduct problems: A comparison of child and parent training interventions. *Journal of Consulting and Clinical Psychology, 65*, 93–109.

Zisser, A., & Eyberg, S. M. (2010). Parent-child interaction therapy and the treatment of disruptive behavior disorders. In J. R. Weisz & A. E. Kazdin (Eds.), *Evidence-based psychotherapies from children and adolescents* (2nd ed., pp. 179–193). New York: Guilford Press.

2 Brain Structure and Function Involved in Self-Control, Impulsivity, and Disruptive Behaviors

Ken Fogel

Humans typically view themselves as being "above" the rest of the animal kingdom, which can mainly be attributed to the development (of sophistication) of the human brain. The substantial increase in size and complexity of the cerebral cortex in relation to the rest of the brain has allowed humans to maintain a tight equilibrium or homeostasis among numerous areas at once. The "lower" (i.e., subcortical) areas of the brain are held in check by downward inhibitory control.

While this viewpoint is overly simplistic, the metaphor of a hierarchy of functioning is helpful for understanding human behavior, especially when aspects of behavior become problematic for the person or society. For example, the orbitofrontal cortex (OFC) and its connections to lower brain regions have been linked to controlling social behavior and monitoring reactive aggression ever since an accidental explosion blasted this area of Phineas Gage's brain (Brodal, 2010). Problems are overtly manifested via disorders of self-control, impulse-control, or disruptive behaviors.

This chapter attempts to parse the complexity of disruptive behavior disorders by summarizing neurobiological findings in two broad domains: impulsivity/self-control and aggression. It concludes with a brief synopsis of the disorders most influenced by these domains. To start, a brief overview and review of relevant neurobiological concepts and terms help set the context.

Key Brain Areas and Neurotransmitters

Although a gross oversimplification, one metaphor likens the nervous system to an intricate and interconnected wiring network, which is often the most effective explanation to use with patients. In this metaphor, the brain comprises multiple "nodes" and bundled "cables" of wires, each of which plays roles in various aspects of behavior. In the above example of Phineas Gage, the OFC is a node that plays a role in integrating emotional behaviors and furnishing emotional information toward decision making (Fuster, 2008).

Other brain areas (and some of their roles) that are especially relevant for the discussion in this chapter include: anterior cingulate cortex (ACC; organizing/initiating goal-directed behavior, monitoring processes, detecting/focusing on errors, choosing behavior in conflicting task); ventromedial prefrontal cortex (VMPFC; emotional memory for limbic regulation, suppressing untimely actions); dorsolateral prefrontal cortex (DLPFC; planning, working memory, cognitive flexibility); inferior frontal cortex (IFC; inhibiting motor responses, cognitive switching, selective and sustained attention; Fuster, 2008); basal ganglia (motor learning, automating behavioral habits); amygdala (emotional coloring of learned experiences, emotional alarm, conditioned fear); and ventral striatum/nucleus accumbens (emotional component of motivation, positive emotion, reward; Brodal, 2010).

In contrast with the wires that send electricity through our homes, relatively few brain-based neurons are "fused together." Instead, neural connections are more akin to "joints," where the gap—or synapse—demarcates the zone of neurotransmitter traffic that represents the flow of information. The primary relevance, however, is that many medications exert most of their influence at the level of the synapse and neurotransmitters.

Of the numerous neurotransmitters inhabiting the central nervous system, the key players in this narrative are dopamine, serotonin, and norepinephrine. Each of these molecules plays multiple roles in the system, depending on the brain area and pathway, because each has been linked with several receptors to which they bind to convey information. Dopamine has been associated with experiences of reward, motivation, attention, motor control, and learning; serotonin with mood, sleep, appetite, sexual behavior, and learning; and norepinephrine with arousal, behavioral activation, and sleep (Fogel & Kapalka, 2012). In terms of the focus of this chapter, as will be apparent from the cited research, the most important of the three is dopamine.

At the simplest neuronal level, the outcome of any aspect of communication of a message is contingent on the temporal and spatial summation of inhibitory and excitatory stimuli. A preponderance of inhibitory inputs regulates information flow. A similar process governs the activity of networks, such that inhibitory pathways regulate the efferent output of brain areas unless outweighed by an influx of excitatory input (Fogel & Kapalka, 2012).

Inputs that ultimately result in behavioral action appear to exert an impact based on whether they arrive faster than competing messages. The more immediate or relevant to survival the behavior, the more likely the neural machinery is subcortical and thus out of voluntary control. In particular, the basal ganglia play the most influential role in motor output of automatic behaviors. Models of "neuronal races" have been postulated for many years, and studies have focused on the subcortical pathways that undergird the "race" that occurs between prompts to engage in or stop any given action (Schmidt et al., 2013). At the risk of reifying the system, this idea makes conceptual sense; a neural "inner conflict" occurs as someone is faced with a choice of actions.

Many behavioral sequences that involve planned action and regulation by feedback make use of circuits or loops between the frontal cortex and subcortical areas (Marsh et al., 2009). In particular, prefrontal cortical areas project in parallel to basal ganglia, then to midbrain, to thalamus, and back to cortex. Errors or dysfunction along these circuits are responsible for a variety of disorders, including obsessive compulsive disorder, Tourette's disorder, and attention-deficit/hyperactivity disorder (ADHD).

Some researchers characterize the diverse symptom patterns in behavioral disorders according to systems of "cold" or "hot" executive functions (EFs) based on the underlying neural circuitry (Rubia, 2011). In this case, "heat" refers to the extent to which motivational or emotional forces are involved, but neither is considered to operate independently. Again, while these summary concepts are overly simplified, they are nonetheless useful as an explanatory tool, especially in the service of differential diagnosis. While ADHD is typically conceptualized as a "cold" EF disorder (i.e., symptoms reflect cognitive dysregulation), for example, the extent to which a person manifests dysfunction in limbic (amygdala, ventral striatum) or corticolimbic (OFC, VMPFC) areas could indicate additional symptoms of emotional dysregulation (Shaw et al., 2014). Such a case might present as a diagnostic conundrum but can be reasonably explained from the standpoint of neurobiological principles and findings.

Impulsivity

Researchers of impulsivity have long considered that the phenomenon is a multifactorial construct, including several behaviors such as hyperexcitability, disinhibition, low sensitivity to the impact of negative consequences, reacting rapidly before adequate planning, and minimal concern about longer-term consequences (Moeller et al., 2001). It does not require a neurosurgeon to see the life problems such behaviors would cause.

One widely used characterization for the behavioral phenomena of impulsivity distinguishes choice from action (Winstanley et al., 2006). Impulsive choice reflects a distorted evaluation (cognition) of consequences and a preference for immediate over delayed rewards, despite foreknowledge that the future rewards are greater. By contrast, impulsive action reflects a failure in response inhibition—the capacity to inhibit a response for which there is a powerful (prepotent) drive

(Reynolds et al., 2006). Part of the strength in categorizing impulsivity by these two broad concepts stems from neuroanatomical evidence of common and distinct neurobiological pathways modulating impulsive choice and impulsive action (Chambers et al., 2009). Note that in both of these cases animal behaviors will tend toward one side: immediate rewards and minimal response inhibition. Human adults, by contrast, are expected to consider delayed gratification and inhibiting responses that are inappropriate in a given context.

Delay discounting or delay avoidance refers to a preference for immediate rewards; however, this is clinically significant only when delayed rewards are larger. People described as impulsive display a greater tendency toward delay discounting (Kirby et al., 1999). This is a normative feature of children, but it becomes problematic and excessive in cases of ADHD, the hallmark disorder of youth impulsivity (Sonuga-Barke, 2005). Defining the border between normal and abnormal in this area represents an ongoing concern, one that reflects broader issues in psychiatry and mental health, and one that neurobiology has not been able thus far to help solve.

In the case of children with ADHD, difficulties with delays might be more severe than indicated by the terms "discounting" and "avoidance." Studies point to the likelihood of delay aversion, where affected children cannot tolerate delays because of the aversive experience of the passage of time (Wilbertz et al., 2013).

Neurobiological Factors Contributing to Impulsivity

Research on the neural substrates of impulsivity has focused on response inhibition. There is increased activity in the prefrontal cortex when adolescents are engaged in performance of tasks that require behavioral inhibition (Marsh et al., 2006). With respect to the time related to delaying a choice, the VMPFC is selectively activated during an immediate choice, whereas a longer delay activates the DLPFC (McClure et al., 2004). This finding suggests that an immediate choice is associated with a more emotional response. Findings have also been relatively consistent regarding reduced activity in the striatum and ACC (Tamm et al., 2004). One overall behavioral consequence of this combination of functional patterns is problematic self-regulation, as children engage in poorly planned behaviors without the capacity to shift tasks when necessary.

In addition to frontostriatal circuits, reward processing has been shown to play a role in several facets of impulse control. Impulsive choice strongly involves the reward pathway, which appears to track the subjective value of rewards whether delayed or not (Monterosso & Luo, 2010). The ventral striatum decreases in activity in response inhibition and reward anticipation (Carmona et al., 2011), the dorsal caudate nucleus and amygdala increase in activity during delayed rewards (Plichta et al., 2009), and the OFC and VMPFC links to ventral striatal and limbic areas decrease during efforts at motivation control (Cubillo et al., 2012). The overall conclusion that can be drawn from these studies is that delaying rewards, exerting behavioral control, and inhibiting potent responses is experienced as aversive (one might go so far as to say "unnatural").

Several individual brain areas thus contribute to behavioral inhibition, but converging evidence has pointed to the IFC, especially in the right hemisphere, as a common area across numerous studies of goal-directed behavior (Dodds et al., 2011). Furthermore, two circuits appear particularly relevant to characteristics of impulsivity (Grant & Kim, 2013): a reward-discounting circuit and a motor-control circuit involved in response inhibition. The first of these appears to be modulated by both dopamine and serotonin, while the latter is modulated more by norepinephrine (Grant & Kim, 2013).

Researchers have provided evidence for the dopaminergic system's involvement in impulsivity through specific transporter and receptor gene variants in ADHD (Baumgaertel et al., 2008). Dopamine plays a key role in the development and ongoing functionality of frontostriatal circuits, as well as in value-based decision making and the capacity for delaying rewards (Volkow et al., 2009). The behavioral manifestation of choosing or switching to alternatives is associated with a dopaminergic phasic "burst" (Oades, 1985), which links the reward pathway to impulsive choice. At the same time, dopamine helps in attention processes by focusing on salient aspects of the environment (Rubia et al., 2009).

Research has consistently demonstrated a direct inverse relationship between impulsive behavior and levels of serotonin (Moeller et al., 2001). Substantial research has also supported the role of serotonin in various aspects of ADHD, with potential differences between the predominantly inattentive and predominantly hyperactive-impulsive type (Oades, 2008). Given the sheer number and variety of serotonin receptors, however, some of which have opposing effects (Fineberg et al., 2014), the relationship of impulsive behavior to serotonergic tone is complex. Furthermore, serotonergic and dopaminergic influences on behavioral manifestation and control are interrelated, but these interactions have not been studied in much detail in comparison to the individual pathways (Oades, 2008).

Aggression

Just as impulsivity is not unitary, aggression defies simple definition. In many cases, aggression can be viewed along a spectrum, between planned, proactive, or instrumental on one hand and impulsive, affective, or reactive on the other. One common theme for the first type is goal-directed behavior, similar to predatory behavior, not typically caused by frustration.

Conversely, impulsive aggression typically arises in response to perceived stress, which involves the autonomic nervous system as well as emotional processing centers of the brain (Siever, 2008).

Neurobiological Factors Contributing to Aggression

Environmental and historical factors play a significant role in the development of proclivity toward reactive or impulsive aggression, especially early physical abuse, inconsistent parenting, or reduced parental monitoring (Patterson et al., 2000). But even with the powerful influence of parenting on childhood behaviors, some of the variance of parental behavior can be explained in terms of responsiveness to the child's underlying genetically determined temperament (Larsson et al., 2008). In any case, these findings highlight a stark contrast to proactive aggression, which longitudinal research has found to be primarily mediated by genetic factors (Tuvblad et al., 2009).

In the realm of impulsive aggression, one of the more consistent findings links low levels of serotonin with increased likelihood of aggressive behavior—most strikingly in the case of completed suicides—although binding to different serotonin receptors results in opposite effects (Siever, 2008). For example, the influence of serotonin in aggressive behaviors has been well established in people diagnosed with ADHD (Flory et al., 2007) and intermittent explosive disorder (IED; Coccaro & McCloskey, 2010), especially in association with limbic areas.

When frustration associated with the negative consequences of impulsive choice reaches a certain threshold, it can devolve into aggression. For example, adolescents identified as aggressive already manifest relatively low baseline levels of serotonin. When faced with a response inhibition task, which further lowers their serotonin levels, they are far more likely to respond impulsively and aggressively (LeMarquand et al., 1998).

In cases of impulsive aggression, limbic structures engage behavioral responses via pathways throughout the lower central nervous system. Prefrontal cortical areas—such as the medial OFC, anterior insula, and ACC—send inhibitory connections to modulate this emotional expression. As an example of the neuronal "race" described above, people who respond with impulsive aggression have been found to demonstrate overactivity in the limbic areas, dysfunction in the inhibitory brain areas, or low serotonergic tone (New et al., 2002).

Instrumental aggression in youth, on the other hand, has been linked to the subsequent development of psychopathic traits (Pardini & Frick, 2013). Among various findings, one common theme is reduced physiological arousal and activity in the emotion processing centers (Siever, 2008). The decreased activity in the amygdala in response to negative emotions in others suggests a greater likelihood of antisocial behavior to obtain goals (Passamonti et al., 2010). This finding has also corresponded to a decreased likelihood of improvement in therapy (Pardini & Frick, 2013). In contrast to reactive aggression, serotonin levels have not been found to relate; however, some findings indicate the possible role of decreased levels of norepinephrine, which have been correlated with responsiveness to aversive cues (Stedler et al., 2010).

Psychopathology

Impulsivity and aggression both cut across several categories of psychiatric disorder, including personality, mood, disruptive behavior, and substance abuse disorders. In the current edition of the *Diagnostic and Statistical Manual of Mental Disorders* (DSM-5; American Psychiatric Association [APA], 2013), one of the many changes from previous editions involves the reorganization of the section on disruptive behavior disorders. One of the organizing principles, stated explicitly by DSM-5 working groups in their preliminary discussions (Charney et al., 2002), was orienting criteria and diagnostic groupings along neurobiological lines.

Although reliable diagnostic classification by neurobiological substrate will require much more research, the DSM-5 seems to have succeeded in some respects, given the research on differences among the disruptive behavior disorders (Clark et al., 2000). In the fourth edition of the manual (DSM-IV-TR), ADHD, oppositional defiant disorder (ODD), and conduct disorder (CD) were lumped together on the basis of the externalizing nature of the behavioral problems (APA, 2000) and separated from other impulse-control disorders. By contrast, DSM-5 separates ADHD into its own category and emphasizes the aggression underlying the latter two diagnoses.

Disruptive behavior disorders have been viewed as related based on the nature of their underlying psychopathology, and converging evidence points to common genetic factors (Arcos-Burgos et al., 2012). Research examining the genetic and environmental influences in the development of disruptive behavior disorders has demonstrated a significant impact of parental history of substance use and antisocial personality disorder (Dick et al., 2005). Rather than distinguishing a specific genetic factor that implies a hereditary link between parental substance abuse and antisocial personality disorder and specific disruptive behavior disorders, however, studies point to a "general liability" that leaves children vulnerable to developing subsequent behavioral problems (Bornovalova et al., 2010).

Attention-Deficit/Hyperactivity Disorder

Substantial time and resources have been devoted to identifying the neurobiological substrates of ADHD. The general lack of consistent findings has perpetuated the view among some that ADHD is "not a real disorder." But a more reasonable explanation reflects the heterogeneity of the disorder (Baumgaertel et al., 2008). The most commonly found structural volume reductions associated with ADHD are in the frontal lobes, basal ganglia, and cerebellum (Valera et al., 2007).

Comparing healthy controls to youth with ADHD has highlighted the role of cool EF frontostriatal networks in mediating attention (Rubia, 2011). Imaging studies of neural pathways reveal deficits in the connections between frontal areas and striatum, cingulate, parietal lobe, and cerebellum, as well as between parietal and occipital lobes (Konrad & Eickhoff, 2010). In particular, as noted previously, one specific prefrontal area that has appeared most frequently across imaging studies of ADHD is the IFC (Dodds et al., 2011). Thus it is possible that underactivation of the IFC can serve as a biomarker for the disorder.

Additional evidence points to inefficient connectivity between the amygdala and the OFC in children with ADHD (Plessen et al., 2006), which could explain poor cortical self-regulation on emotional processing mediated by the amygdala, especially with respect to delay aversion. The behavioral manifestation of this particular lack of self-regulation might start to look like ODD or even CD (Rubia et al., 2009). Such a finding is relatively common, given the extent of comorbidity across these disorders.

Overall, cerebellar volume has been linked to symptoms of ADHD and detailed analysis of cerebellar structures, especially the superior cerebellar vermis (Mackie et al., 2007). While several functions beyond motor coordination have been assigned to the cerebellum, the function of particular interest in the context of impulsivity is time perception (Nigg & Casey, 2005). A common thread connecting the variety of behavioral problems that characterize children with ADHD is difficulty in acting according to appropriate or efficient temporal sequencing.

A consistent finding in the accumulated literature on ADHD is the altered functioning and availability of norepinephrine and dopamine (Baumgaertel et al., 2008). In general, norepinephrine modulates inhibitory control by the IFC network, whereas delayed choice is more in the domain of the OFC, and modulated by dopamine (Fineberg et al., 2014). More specifically, balanced levels of both of these neurotransmitters are required for proper functioning of their circuits. Prefrontal cortical functioning can be hampered by either excessive (e.g., as found in bipolar disorder) or insufficient (e.g., as found in ADHD) dopamine or norepinephrine receptor stimulation (Arnsten, 2006).

One way of conceptualizing the relationship is in terms of "signal and noise" modulation and "gate switching," where norepinephrine activity addresses the former and dopamine the latter (Oades, 1985). Norepinephrine, in both ventromedial and lateral prefrontal areas, functions as an arousal modulator and provides stimulation to engage the attention system (Arnsten, 2006). When environmental stress increases and triggers the autonomic nervous system, however, norepinephrine levels increase, arousal levels rise, and attention suffers. Similarly, a basal level of dopamine is needed for focusing on a specific environmental stimulus; otherwise, attention "wanders." But excess dopamine leads to inflexible focus (Arnsten, 2006). In this context, stimulant medications target ADHD symptoms through amplifying signal information while helping "tune out" excess noise, but only if the dosage is in the correct range (Arnsten, 2006).

Oppositional Defiant Disorder

Oppositional defiant disorder as a single diagnosed disorder is relatively rare and almost always presents as comorbid, often with another disruptive behavior disorder (Greene, 2006). This finding has consequently limited the research on the "pure" disorder, especially neurobiological aspects. Some conceptualize ODD as being characterized more by negative emotionality than impulsivity (APA, 2013), which suggests involvement of limbic circuits. A recent preliminary functional neuroimaging study of the neural correlates of inhibitory control in pure ODD found reduced activation in the right IFC (Zhu et al., 2014), which is consistent with other studies of poor impulse control, but increased activation in areas adjacent to it, which suggests that behaviors might result from the connections between them. The results were not robust, however, and the study was limited by a small sample size. Overall, ODD seems to be a less impairing and less distinctive disorder in relation to ADHD and CD, and the limited research conducted thus far appears to support the World Health Organization's (1992) approach of considering ODD as a milder subtype of CD (Stedler et al., 2010).

Conduct Disorder

Neurodevelopmental theorists previously differentiated between child- and adolescent-onset CD on the basis of distinct biological vulnerabilities in the former and social causation in the latter (Moffitt, 1993). Yet studies have since identified structural abnormalities believed to contribute to behavior problems regardless of the age of the person (Fairchild et al., 2011). More recent attempts to elucidate the developmental pathways of CD have focused on callous-unemotional (CU) traits and anger dysregulation (Pardini & Frick, 2013). CU traits have gained increasing attention as a distinguishing factor in CD for multiple reasons. Not only is the prevalence significant (10%–50%; Kahn et al., 2012), but also the longitudinal clinical implications are more severe than for youth without this trait. The developmental pathway to early-onset CD characterized by severe problems with anger regulation highlights the strong link to ODD as a presyndrome.

The high frequency of comorbidity between CD and ADHD has hindered efforts to disentangle the neurobiological pathways underlying each disorder (Rubia, 2011). Nevertheless, it is possible to differentiate ADHD from CD on the basis of differences between those networks associated with specific executive function tasks. As noted above, ADHD appears to be characterized by deficits in cool EF pathways, resulting in reduced top-down response inhibition and control of attention. On the other hand, CD involves underactivation of hot EF cortical structures (ACC) in regulating subcortical structures (amygdala) that mediate motivation and affect (Decety et al., 2009).

Tic Disorders

Tic disorders are by definition disorders of movement and thus involve the motor pathways of the nervous system. Most research has identified the striatum as "the major pathophysiologic site in Tourette syndrome" (Harris & Singer, 2006, p. 679) and has highlighted the role of cortico-striatal-thalamo-cortical (CSTC) loops in the expression and suppression of tics (Marsh et al., 2009). The inclusion of the striatum/basal ganglia underlies the automaticity of the behavior. In addition to the DLPFC, basal ganglia, and thalamic components of this circuit, tics can result from dysregulation in other brain areas, including the cerebellum and insula (Towbin, 2009). Their roles in the disorder are less clear and consistent, but they might be related to the sensory perception that accompanies the experience (Marsh et al., 2009).

In terms of neurochemistry, several neurotransmitters appear to influence tic disorders, although dopaminergic pathways exert the most substantial impact (Towbin, 2009). This is consistent with dopamine's well-known role not only in modulating all levels of the motor CSTC loop, but also in motivation and attention. One of the proposed mechanisms by which tics overcome suppression reflects the established finding of dual (tonic-phasic) release of dopamine into the synapse. Research has supported the possibility of low tonic (baseline) release of dopamine, as well as increased phasic or "burst" release, to explain the manifestation of tics (Harris & Singer, 2006).

Notwithstanding the odd nature of some tics, especially complex ones, the disorder can be diagnostically confusing because the behavior is not entirely involuntary (APA, 2013). Are these impulsive behaviors? A reported subjective feeling of a buildup of tension preceding a tic appears similar to other impulse-control disorders. This apparent confusion clears up when considering the abovementioned neural pathways, which reflect another version of balance between "higher" and "lower" centers. To the extent that the DLPFC and other prefrontal areas are active, the tics can more likely be stifled (Marsh et al., 2009). But heightened stress or emotional intensity is associated with increasing frequency and intensity of tics (Towbin, 2009), which suggests greater subcortical influence.

While aggression is not typically associated with tic disorders, people who suffer from chronic tic disorder or Tourette's disorder can manifest aggressive, impulsive, or other disruptive behaviors as part of the symptom picture (Towbin, 2009). These additional behavioral problems are more likely in the case of comorbid diagnoses, especially ADHD. The underlying neurobiological details have not been definitively clarified, but the involvement of CSTC circuits is highly likely. For comorbid ADHD and Tourette's disorder, the DLPFC circuit has been implicated because of its role in executive functions (Wright et al., 2012).

Intermittent Explosive Disorder

Intermittent explosive disorder is typically a diagnosis of exclusion of other clinical reasons for the explosive episodes of anger that characterize its presentation (APA, 2013). "Soft signs" of a neurological disorder can nonetheless underlie the disorder. As the DSM-5 description suggests, IED anchors the continuum of problems with self-control as a result of emotional dysregulation (APA, 2013). Furthermore, IED is associated with negative feelings or consequences, which suggests that the aggressive behavior is impulsive. There is a failure of top-down pathways in controlling excessive bottom-up influence. In a sense, this is one of the most clear-cut examples of "problems with the heat" in terms of neurobiological function. For example, patients with IED manifest increased amygdala activity and decreased OFC activity when viewing angry faces (Coccaro & McCloskey, 2010).

Bipolar Disorder

The neurobiological basis of bipolar disorder (BD) remains inconclusive, although results of research point to some common themes. The complexity of the disorder is reflected in the range of neurotransmitters and pathways in which dysfunction results in symptoms. As is the case with the other disorders described in this chapter, the recurrent theme of balance between prefrontal and subcortical regions also applies to BD, but the pathological manifestation of such imbalance is emotional dysregulation and mood episodes.

Impulsive behavior is a hallmark feature of mania and may be especially problematic because of the increased risk for suicide (APA, 2013). Neuroimaging studies have shown that impulsivity is a trait-like feature of

BD (Trost et al., 2014). The OFC is the prefrontal area that has received the most empirical support for involvement in suicidal behavior in BD (Mahon et al., 2012). The OFC's connections to the amygdala, basal ganglia, ACC, and temporal lobe highlight its roles in decision making, impulse control, and regulation of emotional expression. Substantial research has found abnormal size and functioning of the OFC in BD (Mahon et al., 2012). In addition, Trost et al. (2014) found evidence of problems in prefrontal regulation of the ventral striatum, which translated to a reduced ability in patients with BD to delay responses to obtain greater long-term rewards.

Children diagnosed with BD and a comorbid disruptive behavior disorder are at an increased risk for aggressive behavior (Kohn & Asnis, 2003). In contrast to the finding of decreased amygdala activity in adolescents with CD with CU features, children with BD manifest a heightened amygdala response to pictures of neutral faces (Rich et al., 2006). Thus their aggression is much more likely to be reactive or affective than instrumental. Aggressive behaviors in BD tend to more commonly manifest in mixed (rather than manic or depressed) states, reflecting greater disorganization in limbic areas (Kohn & Asnis, 2003).

Personality Disorders

Impulsive and emotionally reactive behaviors, usually associated with negative interpersonal consequences, represent a key feature of Cluster B personality disorders (PDs). Two of these disorders, antisocial personality disorder (APD) and borderline personality disorder (BPD), are the only ones where impulsivity and aggression are included in the diagnostic criteria (APA, 2013).

Personality disorders tend not to be considered "neurobiological" in terms of conceptualization and treatment, but some features are nonetheless more driven by neural networks or neurotransmitter pathways. Furthermore, substantial evidence links traits in adolescence and adulthood to temperament in childhood (Clonninger & Svrakic, 2000). Although not inherently negative, the extreme novelty-seeking temperament can result in feelings of boredom, impulsivity, and angry outbursts, followed later by disruptive behavior disorders and interpersonal problems.

Impulsive behavior has been correlated with severity of APD, but not impulsive choice (Swann et al., 2009). As with findings of the brains of conduct-disordered youth, structural imaging studies of neural correlates of APD have established a primary role of the prefrontal cortex, especially the OFC (Huebner et al., 2008). Other areas of interest include the amygdala, insula, and striatum (Passamonti et al., 2010). Problems in connectivity between prefrontal cortex and hippocampus in adults with APD can account for the inability to learn from experience, especially contextual cues, and can culminate in impulsive reactions with little to no remorse (Getz, 2014). This combination of findings emphasizes structures in the hot EF pathway and highlights the developmental progression from CD to APD (Rubia, 2011). When healthy controls view pictures of intentional versus accidental harm, for example, they manifest increased connectivity between VMPFC and amygdala, which suggests a response of controlling reactions of intense negative affect (Decety et al., 2009). In contrast, youth with a history of severe aggressive behavior display significantly more intense response in limbic and somatosensory brain areas, without the prefrontal activation and connectivity that would indicate behavioral modulation of the negative affect.

In patients with BPD, emotional dysregulation is the hallmark feature, often manifested as impulsive aggression (APA, 2013). Although questions remain about some the details, neurobiological findings have consistently demonstrated frontolimbic dysfunction, specifically networks involving the ACC, OFC, DLPFC, amygdala, and hippocampus (Leichsenring et al., 2011). In particular, excessive amygdala activation occurs in response to emotional triggers, in tandem with decreased prefrontal activation, which is thus inadequate to control the heightened emotional response. The result tends to be unstable or erratic behavior. Impulsivity and instability that becomes aggressive have been linked more specifically to dysfunctional activity in the OFC (Getz, 2014).

Other Disorders

Other clinical disorders can be characterized by episodes of aggression or impulsivity, even though such symptoms are not necessarily prototypical. For example, aggressive and impulsive behaviors are associated with delirium, dementia, and substance-related disorders (APA, 2013). In general, the extent to which such behaviors are observed in these disorders will be evident upon neurological or neuropsychological evaluation. The findings are almost always consistent with those presented in the bulk of this chapter. Patients with Alzheimer dementia who exhibit problems with inhibiting behaviors, for example, demonstrate decreased activity in OFC, DLPFC, and ACC compared to Alzheimer disease patients with no overt behavioral problems (Lane et al., 2011).

The increased likelihood of disruptive behaviors in developmental disorders, such as intellectual disabilities or autism spectrum disorder, reflects more overarching or diffuse deficits in neurological functioning (Lecavalier et al., 2011). This is reflected in the inconsistencies in imaging and neurochemistry research (Getz, 2014). Consequently, while impulsivity and aggression are not necessarily considered key associated features of developmental disorders, such behaviors can erupt, seemingly "from out of nowhere" in individual cases.

Summary and Conclusions

Mental health professionals face the daunting but central task of "drawing the line" between normal and abnormal behavior. Behaviors like impulsiveness and aggression can appear relatively straightforward to place on the "abnormal" side of the fence. But these behaviors must be contextualized socially and culturally, and, more broadly speaking, evolutionarily. Humans engage in response inhibition, delayed gratification, and long-term planning to an extent not matched by any other species, a reflection of highly developed cortical control. But clearly some moments call for "animal responses," like competitive sports, creative arts, and romantic relationships. These tendencies always exist in balance, one with varying degrees of neurobiological involvement.

In treating people who manifest disorders of impulse control, disruptive behaviors, or aggression, emphasizing that balance is central to treatment decisions. This chapter has explored aspects of disruptive behavior disorders that demonstrate a more substantial biological etiology. Of these, ADHD, bipolar disorder, IED, and tic disorders appear to be the most influenced by physiological origin, which is reflected in their treatment protocols. On the other hand, research on etiology of ODD, CD, and antisocial and borderline personality disorders is more equivocal. Clinicians are thus more likely to engage such clients with psychological treatments, except in the most severe cases.

References

APA. American Psychiatric Association. (2000). *Diagnostic and statistical manual of mental disorders* (4th ed.). Washington, DC: Author.

APA. American Psychiatric Association. (2013). *Diagnostic and statistical manual of mental disorders* (5th ed.). Washington, DC: Author.

Arcos-Burgos, M., et al. (2012). A common genetic network underlies substance use disorders and disruptive or externalizing disorders. *Human Genetics, 131,* 917–929.

Arnsten, A. F. T. (2006). Stimulants: Therapeutic actions in ADHD. *Neuropsychopharmacology, 31,* 2376–2383.

Baumgaertel, A., et al. (2008). Disruptive behavior disorders. In S. H. Fatemi & P. J. Clayton (Eds.), *The medical basis of psychiatry* (pp. 301–333). Totowa, NJ: Humana Press.

Bornovalova, M. A., et al. (2010). Familial transmission and heritability of childhood disruptive disorders. *American Journal of Psychiatry, 167,* 1066–1074.

Brodal, P. (2010). *The central nervous system: Structure and function* (4th ed.). Oxford: Oxford University Press.

Carmona, S., et al. (2011). Response inhibition and reward anticipation in medication-naïve adults with attention deficit/hyperactivity disorder: A within subject case control neuroimaging study. *Human Brain Mapping, 33,* 2350–2361.

Chambers, C. D., et al. (2009). Insights into the neural basis of response inhibition from cognitive and clinical neuroscience. *Neuroscience and Biobehavioral Reviews, 33*, 631–646.

Charney, D. S., et al. (2002). Neuroscience research agenda to guide development of a pathophysiologically based classification system. In D. J. Kupfer, M. B. First, & D. A. Regier (Eds.), *A research agenda for DSM-V* (pp. 31–83). Washington, DC: American Psychiatric Association.

Clark, C., et al. (2000). Do executive function deficits differentiate between adolescents with ADHD and oppositional defiant/conduct disorder? A neuro-psychological study using the Six Elements Test and Hayling Sentence Completion Test. *Journal of Abnormal Child Psychology, 28*, 403–414.

Clonninger, C. R., & Svrakic, D. M. (2000). Personality disorders. In B. J. Kaplan & V. A. Sadock (Eds.), *Comprehensive textbook of psychiatry* (Vol. 1, 7th ed., chap. 24). Philadelphia: Lippincott Williams & Wilkins.

Coccaro, E. F., & McCloskey, M. S. (2010). Intermittent explosive disorder: Clinical aspects. In E. Aboujaoude & L. M. Koran (Eds.), *Impulse control disorders* (chap. 20). Cambridge: Cambridge University Press.

Cubillo, A., et al. (2012). A review of fronto-striatal and fronto-cortical brain abnormalities in children and adults with attention deficit hyperactivity disorder (ADHD) and new evidence for dysfunction in adults with ADHD during motivation and attention. *Cortex, 48*, 194–215.

Decety, J., et al. (2009). Atypical empathic responses in adolescents with aggressive conduct disorder: A functional MRI investigation. *Biological Psychology, 80*, 203–211.

Dick, D. M., et al. (2005). Understanding the covariation among childhood externalizing symptoms: Genetic and environmental influences on conduct disorder, attention deficit hyperactivity disorder, and oppositional defiant disorder symptoms. *Journal of Abnormal Child Psychology, 33*, 219–229.

Dodds, C. M., et al. (2011). Dissociating inhibition, attention, and response control in the frontoparietal network using functional magnetic resonance imaging. *Cerebral Cortex, 21*, 1155–1165.

Fairchild, G., et al. (2011). Brain structure abnormalities in early-onset and adolescent-onset conduct disorder. *American Journal of Psychiatry, 168*, 624–633.

Fineberg, N. A., et al. (2014). New developments in human neurocognition: Clinical, genetic, and brain imaging correlates of impulsivity and compulsivity. *CNS Spectrums, 19*, 69–89.

Flory, J. D., et al. (2007). Serotonergic function in children with attention deficit hyperactivity disorder: Relationship to later antisocial personality disorder. *British Journal of Psychiatry, 190*, 410–414.

Fogel, K., & Kapalka, G. (2012). Neuroscience. In M. Muse & B. A. Moore (Eds.), *Handbook of clinical psychopharmacology for psychologists* (pp. 45–105). Hoboken, NJ: Wiley.

Fuster, J. M. (2008). *The prefrontal cortex* (4th ed.). London: Academic Press.

Getz, G. E. (2014). *Applied biological psychology.* New York: Springer.

Grant, J. E., & Kim, S. W. (2013). Brain circuitry of compulsivity and impulsivity. *CNS Spectrums, 19*, 21–27. doi:10.1017/S109285291300028X

Greene, R. W. (2006). Oppositional defiant disorder. In M. Hersen & J. C. Thomas (Eds.), *Comprehensive handbook of personality and psychopathology* (Vol. 3). *Child psychopathology* (pp. 285–298). Hoboken, NJ: John Wiley & Sons.

Harris, K., & Singer, H. S. (2006). Tic disorders: Neural circuits, neurochemistry, and neuroimmunology. *Journal of Child Neurology, 21,* 678–689.

Huebner, T., et al. (2008). Morphometric brain abnormalities in boys with conduct disorder. *Journal of the American Academy of Child and Adolescent Psychiatry, 47,* 540–547.

Kahn, R. E., et al. (2012). The effects of including a callous-unemotional specifier for the diagnosis of conduct disorder. *Journal of Child Psychology and Psychiatry, 53,* 271–282. doi:10.1111/j.1469-7610.2011.02463.x

Kirby, K. N., et al. (1999). Heroin addicts have higher discount rates for delayed rewards than non-drug-using controls. *Journal of Experimental Psychology: General, 128,* 78–87.

Kohn, S. R., & Asnis, G. M. (2003). Aggression in psychiatric disorders. In M. Mattson (Ed.), *Neurobiology of aggression: Understanding and preventing violence* (pp. 135–149). Totowa, NJ: Humana Press.

Konrad, K., & Eickhoff, S. B. (2010). Is the ADHD brain wired differently? A review on structural and functional connectivity in attention deficit hyperactivity disorder. *Human Brain Mapping, 31,* 904–916.

Lane, S. D., et al. (2011). Neuropsychiatry of aggression. *Neurologic Clinics, 29,* 49–64.

Larsson, H., et al. (2008). Relationships between parental negativity and childhood antisocial behavior over time: A bidirectional effects model in a longitudinal genetically informative design. *Journal of Abnormal Child Psychology, 36,* 633–645.

Lecavalier, L., et al. (2011). Autism spectrum disorders and intellectual disability. In J. L. Matson & P. Sturmey (Eds.), *International handbook of autism and pervasive developmental disorders* (pp. 37–51). New York: Springer Science & Business Media.

Leichsenring, F., et al. (2011). Borderline personality disorder. *Lancet, 377,* 74–84.

LeMarquand, D. G., et al. (1998). Tryptophan depletion, executive functions, and disinhibition in aggressive, adolescent males. *Neuropsychopharmacology, 19,* 333–341.

Mackie, S., et al. (2007). Cerebellar development and clinical outcome in attention deficit hyperactivity disorder. *American Journal of Psychiatry, 164,* 647–655.

Mahon, K., et al. (2012). Relationship between suicidality and impulsivity in bipolar disorder: A diffusion tensor imaging study. *Bipolar Disorder, 14,* 80–89.

Marsh, R., et al. (2006). A developmental fMRI study of self-regulatory control. *Human Brain Mapping, 27,* 848–863.

Marsh, R., et al. (2009). Functional disturbances within frontostriatal circuits across multiple childhood psychopathologies. *American Journal of Psychiatry, 166,* 664–674.

McClure, S. M., et al. (2004). Separate neural systems value immediate and delayed monetary rewards. *Science, 306,* 503–507.

Moeller, F. G., et al. (2001). Psychiatric aspects of impulsivity. *American Journal of Psychiatry, 158,* 1783–1793.

Moffitt, T. E. (1993). Adolescence-limited and life-course-persistent antisocial behavior: A developmental taxonomy. *Psychological Review, 100,* 674–701.

Monterosso, J. R., & Luo, S. (2010). An argument against dual valuation system competition: Cognitive capacities supporting future orientation mediate rather than compete with visceral motivations. *Journal of Neuroscience, Psychology, and Economics, 3,* 1–14.

New, A. S., et al. (2002). Blunted prefrontal cortical 18-fluorodeoxyglucose positron emission tomography response to meta-chlorophenylpiperazine in impulsive aggression. *Archives of General Psychiatry, 59,* 621–629.

Nigg, J. T., & Casey, B. J. (2005). An integrative theory of attention-deficit/hyperactivity disorder based on the cognitive and affective neurosciences. *Development and Psychopathology, 17,* 785–806.

Oades, R. D. (1985). The role of noradrenaline in tuning and dopamine in switching between signals in the CNS. *Neuroscience and Biobehavioral Reviews, 9,* 261–283.

Oades, R. D. (2008). Dopamine-serotonin interactions in attention-deficit/ hyperactivity disorder (ADHD). *Progress in Brain Research, 172,* 543–565.

Pardini, D., & Frick, P. J. (2013). Multiple developmental pathways to conduct disorder: Current conceptualizations and clinical implications. *Journal of the Canadian Academy of Child and Adolescent Psychiatry, 22,* 20–25.

Passamonti, L., et al. (2010). Neural abnormalities in early-onset and adolescence-onset conduct disorder. *Archives of General Psychiatry, 67,* 729–738.

Patterson, G. R., et al. (2000). Hyperactive and antisocial behaviors: Comorbid or two points in the same process? *Developmental Psychopathology, 12,* 91–106.

Plessen, K. J., et al. (2006). Neuroimaging of tic disorders with coexisting attention-deficit/hyperactivity disorder. *European Child and Adolescent Psychiatry, 16*(Suppl. 1), 60–70.

Plichta, M. M., et al. (2009). Neural hyporesponsiveness and hyperresponsiveness during immediate and delayed reward processing in adult attention-deficit/ hyperactivity disorder. *Biological Psychiatry, 65,* 7–14.

Reynolds, B., et al. (2006). Dimensions of impulsive behavior: Personality and behavioral measures. *Personality and Individual Differences, 40,* 305–315.

Rich, B. A., et al. (2006). Limbic hyperactivation during processing of neutral facial expressions in children with bipolar disorder. *Proceedings of the National Academy of Sciences, 103,* 8900–8905.

Rubia, K. (2011). "Cool" inferior frontostriatal dysfunction in attention-deficit/ hyperactivity disorder versus "hot" ventromedial orbitofrontal-limbic dysfunction in conduct disorder: A review. *Biological Psychiatry, 69,* e69–e87.

Rubia, K., et al. (2009). Disorder-specific dissociation of orbitofrontal dysfunction in boys with pure conduct disorder during reward and ventrolateral prefrontal dysfunction in boys with pure ADHD during sustained attention. *American Journal of Psychiatry, 166,* 83–94.

Schmidt, R., et al. (2013). Canceling actions involves a race between basal ganglia pathways. *Nature Neuroscience, 16,* 1118–1124.

Shaw, P., et al. (2014). Emotional dysregulation in attention-deficit/hyperactivity disorder. *American Journal of Psychiatry, 171,* 276–293.

Siever, L. J. (2008). Neurobiology of aggression and violence. *American Journal of Psychiatry, 165,* 429–442.

Sonuga-Barke, E. J. S. (2005). Causal models of attention-deficit/hyperactivity disorder: From common simple deficits to multiple developmental pathways. *Biological Psychiatry, 57,* 1231–1238.

Stedler, C., et al. (2010). The heterogeneity of disruptive behavior disorders: Implications for neurobiological research and treatment. *Frontiers in Psychiatry.* doi:10.3389/fpsyt.2010.00021

Swann, A. C., et al. (2009). Trait impulsivity and response inhibition in antisocial personality disorder. *Journal of Psychiatric Research, 43,* 1057–1063.

Tamm, L., et al. (2004). Event-related fMRI evidence of frontotemporal involvement in aberrant response inhibition and task switching in attention-deficit/hyperactivity disorder. *Journal of the American Academy of Child and Adolescent Psychiatry, 43,* 1430–1440.

Towbin, K. E. (2009). Tic disorders. In M. K. Dulcan (Ed.), *Dulcan's textbook of child and adolescent psychiatry* (pp. 417–433). Washington, DC: American Psychiatric Association.

Trost, S., et al. (2014). Disturbed anterior prefrontal control of the mesolimbic reward system and increased impulsivity in bipolar disorder. *Neuropsychopharmacology, 39*(8), 1914–1923. doi:10.1038/npp.2014.39

Tuvblad, C., et al. (2009). Genetic and environmental stability differs in reactive and proactive aggression. *Aggressive Behavior, 35,* 437–452.

Valera, E. M., et al. (2007). Meta-analysis of structural imaging findings in attention-deficit/hyperactivity disorder. *Biological Psychiatry, 61,* 1361–1369.

Volkow, N. D., et al. (2009). Imaging dopamine's role in drug abuse and addiction. *Neuropharmacology, 56*(Suppl. 1), 3–8.

Wilbertz, G., et al. (2013). Neural and psychophysiological markers of delay aversion in attention-deficit hyperactivity disorder. *Journal of Abnormal Psychology, 122,* 566–572.

Winstanley, C. A., et al. (2006). Behavioral models of impulsivity in relation to ADHD: Translation between clinical and preclinical studies. *Clinical Psychology Review, 26,* 379–395.

World Health Organization. (1992). *The ICD-10 classification of mental and behavioral disorders: Clinical descriptions and diagnostic guidelines.* Geneva: Author.

Wright, A., et al. (2012). Impulse control disorders in Gilles de la Tourette syndrome. *Journal of Neuropsychiatry and Clinical Neuroscience, 24,* 16–27.

Zhu, Y., et al. (2014). Differences in functional activity between boys with pure oppositional defiant disorder and controls during a response inhibition task: A preliminary study. *Brain Imaging and Behavior.* doi:10.1007/s11682-013-9275-7

3 Psychological and Developmental Understanding of Self-Control, Impulsivity, and Disruptive Behaviors

Matthew Tirrell and George M. Kapalka

Disruption of adaptive, prosocial behaviors typically occurs with poor modulation of urges and emotion dysregulation (Arsenio & Lemerise, 2010). There are several avenues by which the control of urges may result in behavioral dysfunction. For example, some individuals have difficulties controlling the normal range of urges (as seen in attention-deficit/hyperactivity disorder, or ADHD), others experience extreme urges outside the expected range (as seen in intermittent explosive disorder), and some may exhibit a combination of both (as seen in tic disorders). Poorly modulated disruptive urges and limited emotion regulation (such as irritability and low frustration tolerance) impair one's ability to self-regulate behavior, which is a key component of disruptive disorders.

Degrees of self-control and aggression are well established to be the fundamental dimensions in disruptive disorders (Broidy et al., 2003) based on the premise that disruptive disorders are a product of a failure of self-control, an expression of aggressive behavior, or a combination of aggression and impaired self-control. To understand the psychological aspects of disruptive disorders, an examination of the development of self-control and aggression is warranted.

Self-Control

Many social scientists define self-control as the extent to which a person is able to resist impulses, inhibit or overcome urges, and delay gratification (Vazsonyi & Huang, 2010). Gailliot et al. (2007) further declare self-control as a component of an individual's personality that enables the restraint of thoughts, feelings, and behaviors to maximize rewards and comply with cultural norms. Individuals who are able to exercise appropriate self-control are likely to improve their goal attainment and experience desirable outcomes, including social acceptance, interpersonal growth, cognitive stability, and personal, career, and academic achievements.

Conversely, impaired self-control may be associated with a range of dysfunctional cognitive expressions such as inattention or distractibility, or may be expressed through dysfunctional behaviors such as hyperactivity and tics. Problems with executive functions (language, memory, and planning) may also be associated with these difficulties (Barkley, 1997; Fischer et al., 1990). Disruptive urges are experienced universally and the spectrum of disruptive behaviors can range widely; only a small portion of the population possesses such limited self-control that diagnostic levels of disruptive behaviors become apparent.

The life span developmental perspective sheds light on the acquisition and course of self-control and its relation to disruptive disorders. Self-control typically becomes evident in the first year of life and gradually increases through the toddler years until solidifying in early childhood (Barkley, 1997). This developmental sequence is directly related to language, memory, and attention, all of which develop concurrently in the formative years (Berk, 2008). Supported or impeded by environmental and psychosocial influences, the developmental course of self-control remains relatively stable through adolescence into adulthood (Broidy et al., 2003).

It is essential to acknowledge the role that individual differences play in the acquisition and development of self-control. According to Vazsonyi and Huang (2010), while many factors contribute to the development and progression of self-control, a certain degree of variance is expected in children and may be a result of innate predispositions. These differences in emotion regulation, coping strategies, willful effort, personal motivations, and bonding may mediate the integration of self-control as a prosocial behavior (Gilliom et al., 2002). According to Barkley (1997), "individual differences in inhibition appear to be an even greater determinant of performance in delayed-response tasks than is age or general development level" (p. 210). In addition to inherent differences, however, the etiology and development of self-control throughout the life span are explained in cognitive, behavioral, and social learning models.

Intrapersonal Factors Influencing Self-Control

Cognitive and behavioral perspectives add to our understanding of the pathogenesis of disruptive disorders through impaired self-control. In his seminal research on self-control, Russell Barkley (1997) formulates self-control as a cognitively driven behavioral response by an individual that is directed toward the self in order to inhibit a poor response over a significant period of time, thus increasing the likelihood of a more desired goal. Modern social learning theoretical models similarly emphasize the powerful role of cognitions; individuals are not merely responders to environmental stimuli but active perceivers and thoughtful contributors to their environments (Bandura, 1977). Cognitive-behavioral themes such as frustration tolerance, personality structures, distortions, and emotion regulation all contribute to the acquisition and development of self-control (Patterson & Newman, 1993). Comparable definitions of frustration tolerance among theorists center on delayed gratification; however, Mischel's (1986) thorough explanation of frustration tolerance can be aptly summarized as a cognitive technique for directing one's own behaviors in response to environmental stimuli.

A key component of frustration tolerance is locus of control. In general, when individuals perceive that the environment controls or delays an outcome, they often become frustrated, but those who delay responding tend to develop self-control (Mischel, 1986). Eisenberger et al. (1985) suggest that the amount of effort one puts forth to delay reward via internal locus of control can mediate frustration tolerance. Individuals with low frustration tolerance typically react impulsively to environmental stressors for the sake of immediate gratification, whether it is to achieve a desired goal or to avoid a negative outcome. Accordingly, individuals with poor levels of self-control (either because of neurobiological predispositions or environmental and social influences) may acquire better impulse control through cognitive-behavioral training by resisting small rewards with little volitional effort to gradually attain higher rewards with greater cognitive effort. Barkley's (1997) research on executive functions supports this perspective by contending that low frustration tolerance is linked to impulsivity (as seen in ADHD) and comorbid cognitive deficits confound receptivity to effortful cognitive-behavioral training. Impaired cognitive-behavioral mastery of frustration tolerance has wide implications for mental health clinicians who must specifically target the client's aptitude for delaying gratification, distress tolerance, and emotion regulation across myriad psychosocial dimensions in the treatment of disruptive disorders.

Personality structures and temperament also play a role in the development of self-control. Nigg et al. (2002) reviewed five personality dimensions in relation to the impulsive and hyperactive symptoms of ADHD and discovered a high correlation between ADHD and neuroticism and low correlations with openness, agreeableness, extraversion, and conscientiousness. Patterson and Newman (1993) confirmed this finding but also found extraversion to be highly correlated with disruptive behaviors, implying that stable personality traits that persist into adulthood are linked to disruptive disorders, including ADHD. In addition, Patterson and Newman contend that individuals who lack introspection and self-reflection on personal gains and losses react quickly to frustration and develop poor self-control because of their failure to associate negative outcomes with disinhibition. Nigg et al. similarly suggest that impulsivity is highly correlated with a negative temperament and poor mood regulation. Implications from these findings call for the thorough assessment of personality structures and temperament characteristics that accompany impulse-control deficits.

In their exploration of the relationship between anger regulation and self-control, Gilliom et al. (2002) discovered that successful emotion regulation depends largely on an individual's proclivity to employ coping strategies in response to external stimuli. Children who utilized adaptive techniques to distract themselves from stressful tasks, for example, were able to consistently reduce the intensity of their anger. While there were individual differences in the techniques the children exercised, ranging from shifting attention to seeking parental attachment, their use of emotion regulation skills was found to improve overall self-control efficacy. This finding confirms that emotion regulation is related to self-control and reveals that various strategies may be effective to address deficits in this area.

The influence of goal orientation on impulsivity appears to be equally meaningful. While comparing adolescents and young adults with varying future goals, Chen and Vazsonyi (2011) found that self-control was highest in individuals whose perspective was oriented toward the future with a positive outlook on goal attainment. Barkley (1997) asserts that the role of cognizance about future consequences is central to the development of self-control in association with the primary executive functions, whereby self-control is increased through a continuous feedback loop between self-directed, inhibitory speech and successful attainment of rewards. Similarly, Patterson and Newman (1993) contend that the ability to focus on consequences, facilitated by the executive functions of planning and reasonable judgment, initiates and reinforces the adaptive coping skill of self-control. Alternatively, individuals with poorly modulated impulses fail to learn from negative events, reflect on consequences, or develop anticipatory insights into the risks of impulsive behavior. Therefore it is important for mental health practitioners to recognize and explore an individual's goal orientation, intrapersonal insight, and emotion regulation skills in order to redirect potential for impulsivity and other disruptive behaviors.

Interpersonal Factors Influencing Self-Control

Human beings and their environments affect each other in profound ways, whereby individuals learn, change, and grow through their experiences with the phenomenological world. "Social learning theory approaches the explanation of human behavior in terms of a continuous reciprocal interaction between cognitive, behavioral, and environmental determinants" (Bandura, 1977, p. vii). This dynamic exchange may either promote or inhibit self-control, depending on an individual's neurological makeup and response to life experiences. Barkley (1997) affirms that innate executive functioning and the maturation process largely induce individual capabilities and tendencies for self-control, and social norms and expectations shape the development of self-control over time. Vazsonyi and Huang (2010) suggest that self-control develops from positive socialization experiences with parents, caregivers, schools, and civic organizations, especially through modeling, rewarding of prosocial behaviors, and providing opportunities to learn discipline and delay gratification. The data from their long-term studies reinforce the consensus that patterns of impulsivity remain stable over time in the absence of adaptive or therapeutic interventions.

Families of origin, especially parents and guardians, largely influence the acquisition and development of self-control (Berk, 2008; Bradley & Corwyn, 2007). Parental influence on self-control begins early in life and has a sustained effect over time. As early as the toddler stage, parental warmth and sensitivity induce the development of self-control via reinforcement of compliant behavior (Berk, 2008). Parental warmth and involvement are fundamental resources for developing self-control through bonding, mutual respect, rule adherence, structured routines, and supervised activities (Bradley & Corwyn, 2007). Parents and caregivers employ numerous adaptive techniques to promote self-control in early childhood, including responding sensitively to the child's needs, encouraging linguistic expression, providing opportunities for autonomy and attention building, and praising compliance (Berk, 2008).

Accordingly, parental behaviors and family dynamics can have deleterious effects on the development of self-control. Harsh parental control, excessive punishment, and abuse have been linked to poor self-regulation and a host of externalizing behaviors seen in several disruptive disorders (Bradley & Corwyn, 2007). Similarly, coercive and impulsive parenting styles that utilize inconsistent rules and disciplinary practices may reduce self-control in children by disempowering them and impeding self-efficacy (Bornovalova et al., 2013). Contrasting child-rearing styles among parents are incongruent with adaptive co-parenting skills that strengthen impulse control in children, often resulting in family conflicts and disruptive behaviors, delinquency, and inattention in the child (Bornovalova et al., 2013). Children who do not learn to self-regulate their impulsive emotions and behaviors from their family of origin are likely to experience social, academic, and occupational problems in the future (Fischer et al., 1990).

The quality of the adult and parent–child relationships within the home can negatively impact the development of self-control. Discord between adults may lead to maladaptive child-rearing practices and separation or divorce, and the environmental instability that ensues often increases the likelihood that children will develop problematic impulsive behaviors (DeKlyen, 1996). An inadequate parental unit impairs the development of self-regulatory skills through poor modeling, which may alter a child's sense of security and adaptive socialization. Disruptive behaviors are common when the parent–child relationship is interrupted by parental mental illness or other deficiencies such as lack of affection, poor limit setting, or inattention to the child (DeKlyen, 1996). In those situations, clinicians must consider working with the parents and families of individual clients to address such deficiencies in the family unit.

Parental criminality is also related to disruptive behaviors in children. Antisocial parents are more likely than prosocial parents to divorce, experience marital dysfunction, and employ maladaptive child-rearing styles such as physical punishment, all of which are established determinants of poor self-control in children. Additionally, the poor parent–child attachment in families with an antisocial parent predicts disruptive, antisocial behavior in children and adolescents (Bornovalova et al., 2013). Lahey et al. (1989) suggest that maternal antisocial personality traits mediate impulsive behavior, as seen in ADHD and other disruptive disorders, and McCarty and McMahon (2003) correlate being reared by a depressed mother with disruptive pathology in adolescent boys. Implications for children reared in such environments may include the perpetuation of impulsive, antisocial, and aggressive behaviors into adulthood. Accordingly, clinicians must specifically address parental temperament, child-rearing practices, and attachment issues in the treatment setting.

In addition to the family of origin, social influences on the development of self-control originate from a variety of sources. While family and peers remain primary influences, institutions, communities, media, and socioeconomic conditions also moderate social learning at the individual level. Bronfenbrenner's (1994) ecological model best captures the dynamics between these interpersonal factors, explaining how social exchanges of an individual with every facet of society affect individual development. Community environments such as schools, places of worship, and local neighborhoods provide opportunities for the acquisition or suppression of adaptive self-regulation skills through successful or failed peer interactions (Bradley & Corwyn, 2007). Involvement by peers, teachers, employers, and community leaders in reinforcing rewards for individual effort is a robust predictor of self-control in children and adolescents (Eisenberger et al., 1985). Mass media is also a salient factor in the acquisition and maintenance of self-control (Bandura, 1977). Bandura asserts that modeling the representations in mass media programs can change the way individuals respond to observed stimuli, altering their emotional regulation and distractibility. Each of the aforementioned paradigms has strong implications for mental health clinicians to consider regarding the development of self-control in at-risk populations.

Socioeconomic status (SES) is another significant variable, as research has shown that low SES and poor living conditions contribute to impulsivity and disruptive behaviors (Johnson et al., 1999). Low parental income, education, and occupational status are predictive factors for impulse control, mood, and personality disorders, and are linked to myriad disruptive disorders (Johnson et al., 1999). Poverty is linked with poor self-regulation skills (including emotional dysregulation and linguistic deficits) in children of various ages (Bradley & Corwyn, 2007). Low socioeconomic conditions directly and indirectly influence the development of self-control by simultaneously impeding an individual's opportunities for adaptive skill building and creating harsh conditions for families to rear children (Baum et al., 1985). Low socioeconomic environments impede the development of adaptive coping strategies, such as shifting one's attention away from stressful situations, leaving people vulnerable to chronic stress (Gilliom et al., 2002). Clinicians must consider the influences of all levels of community, SES, media, and peer groups as pertinent factors in the development of disruptive behaviors and other mental health problems.

Aggression

As with self-control, a clear understanding of aggression is salient to any discussion of disruptive disorders. Researchers tend to define aggression as behaviors that intend to harm, with underlying components of poor self-control and anger dysregulation (Geen, 1990). While there are many types of aggression—instrumental, physical, verbal, and relational— underlying each of them is harmful behavior directed at others (Berk, 2008). Bandura and Walters (1959) highlight the component of harm in their contention that aggression is tantamount to antisocial behavior that is harmful and disruptive to other people or property. When expressed as an overt physical act of anger, aggression can be considered synonymous with violence. Please note that our discussion of self-control intentionally precedes that of aggression to underscore the inherent presence of impulsivity in aggression.

Aggression may also be viewed as an emotionally driven response to environmental stressors, especially in reaction to frustration. Bandura and Walters (1959) define frustration as "the occurrence of conditions that prevent or delay the attainment of a goal-response" (p. 89). Frustration is similarly described as an emotional state resulting from goal deflection, which often precedes aggressive behavior (Baum et al., 1985). Affect regulation is linked to aggression—primarily as an antecedent—whereby individuals with aggressive tendencies tend to react impulsively to emotional stressors (Geen, 1990). The delay of gratification, then, is a deterrent to disruptive, aggressive urges.

A plethora of maladaptive outcomes may result from impaired frustration tolerance over an individual's life span. Loeber and Stouthamer-Loeber (1998) document the high rates of youth in treatment centers and schools receiving services for disruptive, violent behavior. As they age into adulthood, delinquent youth are at risk for many psychosocial problems, including substance use, divorce, unemployment, and legal difficulties (Loeber & Stouthamer-Loeber, 1998). Similarly, adolescent aggression has been found to correlate significantly with adult depressive symptoms (Diamantopoulou et al., 2011). In addition, poor frustration tolerance may contribute to rejection from peers when individuals engage in impulsive, aggressive acts in social settings (Coie et al., 1992). These factors propel the course of the development of disruptive and aggressive behaviors, and aggression is found to remain relatively stable (especially in the most severely impaired) over time (Loeber & Stouthamer-Loeber, 1998). These findings suggest that mental health clinicians must address clients' abilities to tolerate frustration, delay gratification, and regulate emotions in order to reduce aggressive behaviors.

It is important to recognize characterological traits underlying aggressive behaviors. Potegal and Knutson (1994) suggest that irritability and emotional susceptibility are key mediators of aggression. Geen (1990) recognize a host of additional factors that affect the development of aggression, including sex differences (male), cognitive development (low), and alcohol use (high). All of these variables should be considered because they play a significant role in moderating the acquisition and progression of aggressive behaviors.

Intrapersonal Factors Influencing Aggression

Cognitive-behavioral theoretical framework prioritizes internal experience over external stimuli. The development of aggression is thus understood by examining the role of individual interpretation or perception of an event and assigning negative meaning to it (Geen, 1990). In fact, an individual's perception of a situation is more salient than the situation itself; therefore a stimulus only evokes aggression when perceived by the individual as hostile or threatening (Zahn-Waxler et al., 1986).

In the cognitive-behavioral approach, one's internal dialogue drives intrapersonal emotional experience, and subjective intrapersonal experience results in the development and expression of aggression through various mechanisms. Ellis (2001) emphasizes the role of one's irrational belief system in the formation of unhealthy responses to neutral stimuli, thereby instigating a negative reciprocal dynamic that can elevate emotional symptoms to diagnostic levels. Similarly, Beck suggests that individuals contribute to their own emotional discomfort by creating negative intellectual paradigms through the automatic thought processes they initiate upon a triggering event (Alford & Beck, 1997). It is this skewed perception that may compel an individual to react aggressively to an otherwise dispassionate event, fueled by distorted, biased, or personalized feelings about the situation. The statements made to oneself about an experience may increase and reinforce one's negative assumptions and result in maladaptive behaviors, such as violence or abuse. In order to reduce the potential for aggression, counselors must assist clients in gaining insight into their subjective psychological experiences by identifying irrational beliefs, distorted automatic reactions, and negative self-statements.

Anger is a significant intrapersonal construct involved in the development of aggression. Negative affect, especially anger, tends to precipitate (although not necessitate) aggressive behavior, typically based on a perceived threat or injustice (Tangney et al., 1996). According to Berkowitz (1990), internal psychological processes associate anger with negative ideas, perceptions, ruminations, and hostile inclinations. The methods by which people manage anger and related cognitions vary widely and directly affect subsequent behaviors (Tangney et al., 1996). For those devoid of adaptive coping strategies, for example, aggressive behaviors may provide an escape from the unpleasant psychological and somatic experiences connected with anger (Berkowitz, 1990). According to Tangney et al., the level of insight into one's emotional state and the importance one places on the triggering event directly correlate with the expression of aggressive behavior. Aggressive individuals tend to perceive their hostility, resentment, and irritability as self-protective, and therefore they exhibit less regard for the long-term consequences on recipients of their aggressive acts (Tangney et al., 1996). Developing adaptive coping skills to improve positive self-management (especially in situations invoking anger) and increasing the intrapersonal awareness and evaluation of anger are critical components of cognitive-behavioral treatment of disruptive disorders.

Capacity for empathy, problem solving, and role reversibility moderate intrapersonal experiences of social interactions (including aggression), so deficits in any of these predispose vulnerability to aggression (Zahn-Waxler et al., 1986). In addition, low IQ, learning disabilities, and negative temperament have been found to correlate highly with disruptive behaviors because these are associated with cognitive deficiencies that impair judgment, forestall a sense of consequences, and make one more suggestible (Bandura & Walters, 1959). Aggression is most likely to be developed and strengthened when reinforced by positive outcomes, that is, achieving desired goals (Mischel, 1986). Any perceived expectation of a reward for aggressive behavior is likely to increase the probability of such behavior. Consequently, mental health professionals should explore executive skills, empathy, and role reversal when evaluating and treating aggressive and disruptive behaviors.

Ample consideration must also be given to the psychological construct of intentionality as a fundamental intrapersonal component of aggression.

Baum et al. (1985) explain that while intent to harm underlies all acts of aggression, society does not shun all forms of aggression. For example, athletes, caregivers, and authority figures regularly engage in acceptable aggressive behaviors whenever they make a tackle, get children to comply (e.g., by taking toys away from them), or make an arrest. In addition, intentionality is a broad concept—regardless of whether the behavior is fully realized, the intent to induce harm qualifies an act as aggressive. For instance, unsuccessful attempts are considered as aggressive as those that come to fruition.

Social information processing (SIP) models further examine the sequence of cognitive encoding, interpretation, and response in the development of aggressive behaviors. Zahn-Waxler et al. (1986) contend that specific aggressive outcomes—such as anger, hostility to others, or hyperarousal to stimuli—are the result of breaches in this information processing sequence. Clinicians must identify and target these breaches (such as faulty encoding and misinterpretation) in order to arrest the development and progression of aggressive urges.

Interpersonal Factors Influencing Aggression

As Arsenio and Lemerise (2010) suggest, no single source can unilaterally account for the creation of aggression; rather, aggression likely arises from a complementary amalgam of psychological, environmental, and social factors. While disruptive urges, including aggression, may to some extent be innate, social learning theorists contend that aggression is mediated by empirical experiences and, more immediately, individual cognitions (Berk, 2008), and the greatest influence on the development of aggression is not biological drives but experiential learning from external sources (Bandura, 1977). Imitation and reinforcement are fundamental principles that promote social learning, and imitation involves the direct observation and modeling of environmental stimuli, while reinforcement involves the promotion or extinguishment of behaviors through rewards or punishments. Individuals learn through experiencing, observing, and perceiving the mutually influential interactions with their environment, becoming exposed to their family, community, socioeconomics, and the media as sources for learning and developing aggression.

An individual's family appears to be the primary influence on learned behaviors. A wide body of research findings reports a robust link between family experiences and aggressive behavior (Shaver & Mikulincer, 2011). Peters et al. (1992) found that residing with an antisocial father, depressed mother, or an alcoholic parent is a contributing factor to the development of aggressive or violent behavior. Similarly, parents' negative views of their own families of origin have been found to mediate the development of aggression in their children (DeKlyen, 1996). Current parenting styles are informed by the parenting styles of previous generations, and maladaptive child-rearing practices instill aggression and delinquency in children primarily through lack of warmth and maternal rejection. Accordingly, clinicians should review multigenerational family systems to uncover the possible presence of these underlying factors of aggression.

Maladaptive parent–child interactions are well-documented determinants of aggression in children (Bornovalova et al., 2013): "harsh treatment by parents may serve as a model for aggressiveness and may contribute to coercive styles of parent–child conflict" (Bradley & Corwyn, 2007, p. 1391). Harsh treatment that compels aggressive responses in children may specifically entail spontaneous physical punishment, neglect, rejection, abuse, excessive displays of anger, and withholding love and nurturance (Lefkowitz et al., 1977). Clinicians should screen for these factors because they significantly influence the development of aggression and disruptive behaviors in children.

Socialization of youth reaches beyond the family into local and larger communities. Such environments serve as resources for developing aggressive tendencies, whether by direct contact or observed through media (Baum et al., 1985). Environments filled with violence, crime, or maltreatment of others provide modeling opportunities for individuals vulnerable to aggressive predispositions. For example, a well-documented significant relationship exists between aggression and harsh environments such as low-income housing and overcrowded day care centers (Peters et al., 1992). Additionally, life in low-income urban communities tends to contain high levels of stress and additional deviant influences that promote aggression (Gilliom et al., 2002). Loeber and Stouthamer-Loeber (1998) point out that aggression tends to rise and fall on the basis of the presence or absence of other aggressive peers. Some researchers even suggest that environmentally propagated aggressive behaviors, as seen in delinquency, serve as a protective measure against urban environmental stressors (Baum et al., 1985), thus reinforcing the development of aggression. Though these factors are beyond clinicians' control, mental health practitioners must be sensitive to an individual's environment to identify and address its impact on aggressive tendencies.

Socialization through mass media also promotes the development of aggression, primarily by providing suggestive material ripe for potential imitation (Lefkowitz et al., 1977) as well as exposure to societal cues for aggressive behavior, such as permissiveness, revenge, relatability to aggressors, and justification of violence (Geen, 1990). Media images appear to have long-term effects on the development of aggression, often promoting aggression through desensitization to violence. Baum et al. (1985) suggest that violence in the media instigates aggressive behavior in boys that follows them through adolescence and into adulthood. In addition, the content of media images appears to matter in the socialization process, as modeling of violence (via graphic displays of weapons, crimes, and fighting) begets aggression in boys, while the absence of female aggressors moderates the media impact on girls (Lefkowitz et al., 1977). According to Berk (2008), the media's influence on aggression is wide reaching owing to its habituating effects over time; children become more aggressive as they fail to link long-term consequences with violent images that are fantastical in nature (as in cartoons or video games). While counselors cannot limit the influence of media in the development of aggression, clinicians can actively focus on ways in which individuals interact with and perceive their environmental and psychosocial influences in order to develop strategies for overcoming or reducing these negative influences.

Self-Control, Aggression, and Disruptive Disorders

Although many psychological and developmental factors mediate the acquisition and course of self-control and aggression, specific patterns of these influences separate various disruptive disorders.

Attention-Deficit/Hyperactivity Disorder

The primary symptoms of ADHD are developmentally excessive levels of impulsivity and inattention. ADHD is diagnosed as either inattentive type or hyperactive-impulsive type, with diagnostic criteria that center on distractibility or failure to maintain self-controlled behaviors, respectively (American Psychiatric Association [APA], 2013). Failure to regulate self-control is central to the diagnosis of ADHD. While aggression is not a core symptom of this disorder, aggressive outbursts often accompany the core symptoms, especially in young children. Individuals with ADHD exhibit wide variability in their abilities to regulate attention and impulse control across different settings (Barkley, 1997). For instance, children, adolescents, or adults with ADHD may be able to play a video game for sustained periods of time but have difficulties remaining on task in school or at work. Cognitive deficits often underlie problems with self-control evident in many individuals with ADHD, and environmental factors (such as coercive interaction between parents and children) further contribute to the development of disruptive behaviors (Nigg et al., 1998).

Oppositional Defiant Disorder

The core symptoms of oppositional defiant disorder (ODD) include anger, irritability, vindictiveness, and defiant behavior (APA, 2013). These behaviors stem from impulsivity, aggression, and, more specifically, verbal aggression. Impaired self-control in ODD is seen as a function of a failure to regulate emotions effectively, often resulting in excessive displays of anger and defiance. Except for temper outbursts, individuals with ODD do not act violently, nor do they violate the rights of others. Instead, verbal or covert acts of aggression are more typical, as seen in resentful behavior or intentionally annoying outbursts. In addition, ODD tends to frequently co-occur with ADHD, further underscoring the underlying aspect of impulsivity as symptom of both disorders stemming from difficulties resisting disruptive urges. As with ADHD, cognitive deficits and coercive parental interactions are frequently associated with symptoms of ODD (Lahey et al., 1989).

Conduct Disorder

Individuals with conduct disorder (CD) typically engage in overt aggressive acts, including physical assault, theft, or destruction of property (APA, 2013). Indifference to societal norms and violation of personal rights of others are defining characteristics of CD (APA, 2013). While impulsivity may potentiate CD, violent physical aggression is the dominant feature of this disorder. Research suggests that parental personality and rearing style are strong predictors of CD (Lahey et al., 1989). Similarly, CD is a primary predictor of adult antisocial personality disorder (APA, 2013), and those with conduct disorder often exhibit poor prognoses and treatment outcomes; therefore, environmental (such as residential or legal) interventions may be needed.

Tic Disorders

Automatic motor movements or vocalizations define all tic disorders, including Tourette's disorder, the most severe of the four tic disorders (APA, 2013). Symptoms of tic disorders worsen under stress, and environmental and psychosocial stimuli mediate the disruptive urges underlying these diagnoses. Impaired self-control underlies the impulsive nature of tics, and the strength of the impulsive urges as well as lack of awareness of physical and cognitive precipitants to the urges influence the degree of symptom expression.

Intermittent Explosive Disorder

Both impulsivity and aggression characterize intermittent explosive disorder (IED). The symptoms include infrequent yet volatile outbursts of physical harm to people or property disproportionate to any perceived trigger (APA, 2013). Outside of the isolated outbursts of violence, individuals with IED usually appear calm, and following the outbursts they typically express regret for their actions. While violent and physically aggressive in nature, the destructive episodes are a result of the failure to regulate self-control. In select situations, individuals with IED may experience extreme urges beyond the expected range, thus overwhelming their coping and inhibitory skills. Social cues, prior learning, and environmental factors (such as level of stress) are common associated features.

Mood Disorders

Some mood disorders include symptoms of irritability and may be characterized by disruptive urges and behaviors secondary to irritability. In particular, symptoms of disruptive mood dysregulation disorder (DMDD), which shares some commonalities with IED, include a combination of low self-control and presence of physical or verbal aggression (APA, 2013). These are expressed through explosive temperamental outbursts as well as the irritable moods that persist between episodes. Cognitive deficits underlying limited frustration tolerance and impaired modulation of anger are associated with DMDD. Because this diagnosis is reserved for children and adolescents (primarily to assuage the overdiagnosis of pediatric bipolar disorder), individuals with DMDD are particularly vulnerable to social and environmental influences on disruptive urges, including family dynamics and parenting styles associated with low self-control and increased aggression. Peer factors often exacerbate the severity of symptoms (Pope & Bierman, 1999).

People with bipolar disorders may also exhibit features of both impulsivity and aggression. Disruptive behaviors associated with impaired self-control often characterize symptoms of mania in particular—as exemplified by rapid/unrestrained speech and reckless decisions that may include overspending or hypersexuality—and psychomotor agitation, which may stem from the hostility and anger driven by intense mood swings, and can result in harm to self or others (APA, 2013). Though genetic factors are strongly associated with bipolar disorders, environmental and psychosocial risk factors often exacerbate symptoms and may affect individuals' responses to situational triggers. For example, deficient cognitive structures underlying poor impulse control and cognitive distortions often preceding aggressive responses are likely to interact with biological factors when producing disruptive symptoms and behaviors. In addition, because symptoms of bipolar disorder often include suicide attempts, and completed suicides are associated with a diagnosis of bipolar disorder more so than with any other disorder described by the APA (2013), it is critical for clinicians to specifically address the impulsive and aggressive aspects of the bipolar disorders.

Personality Disorders

Two personality disorders are most associated with dysregulated disruptive urges: antisocial and borderline personality disorders. Impulsivity is a core symptom of both of these disorders, and aggression is a core symptom of antisocial personality disorder (APA, 2013). Antisocial individuals tend to be irritable and impulsive, and they often disregard the rights of others while they aggressively seek satisfaction of their own needs. Deficient cognitive structures are evident in individuals with APD, as they usually fail to consider the consequences of their behaviors on others. Parental and socioeconomic deficits are strong predictors of APD, so these factors need to be assessed. Lack of empathy and callousness may result in violence and other criminal behaviors, and legal and residential (such as correctional) interventions are often needed.

Borderline personality disorder is characterized by significant problems with impulsivity linked to severe emotional dysregulation (APA, 2013). This is primarily a psychosocial disorder with fear of abandonment and interpersonal distress at its core. Faulty interpretation of environmental triggers often results in feelings of despair, triggering poorly modulated and intense behaviors aimed at reducing the feelings of abandonment and perceived rejection. Patterns of parental instability and dysfunction in close romantic relationships are commonly associated with this disorder, and consequently interventions involving family members or significant others may be needed.

Other Disorders with Disruptive Features

Neurocognitive disorders, intellectual disabilities, and autism spectrum disorders warrant inclusion because individuals with these disorders often exhibit aspects of impaired self-control and potential for aggression. Individuals with delirium, neurocognitive disorder (formerly referred to as dementia in the fourth edition of the *Diagnostic and Statistical Manual of Mental Disorders*), and autism spectrum disorders have the potential to display varying degrees of aggression when highly symptomatic (APA, 2013). Examples of aggression may include lashing out verbally, exposing oneself publicly, or shoplifting. Pathogenesis of these disorders may vary, but impaired cognitive structures needed to utilize self-control are often associated with the severity of the outbursts. Because individuals with these disorders often reside with family members or in supportive environments, consideration of environmental factors is crucial.

Summary and Conclusions

This chapter reviewed the underlying psychological and developmental factors associated with disruptive disorders. The fundamental concepts of self-control (poor impulse control) and aggression emerge as primary underpinnings of disruptive urges and behaviors. While various theoretical perspectives may help understand these factors, the cognitive-behavioral approach has most frequently been used to conceptualize the psychopathology underlying disruptive behaviors. Many environmental, cognitive, and social factors have been shown to mediate the acquisition, development, and course of self-control and aggression, especially including familial instability, parental discord, harsh child-rearing practices, abusive experiences, socioeconomic deficits, antisocial peer relations, deviant reinforcements and rewards, cognitive-perceptual distortions, and information processing deficiencies. Individual differences in the predispositions and responses to such stimuli are evident, compelling clinicians to review these factors as they pertain to each individual case. In addition, because of space limitations, this chapter did not review other associated factors (such as gender and cultural determinants). Clinicians are encouraged to follow a broad view to understand the psychological and developmental influences on poor self-control and aggression, and to use that broad understanding to inform a comprehensive approach to the treatment of the symptoms of disruptive disorders.

References

Alford, B., & Beck, A. (1997). *The integrative power of cognitive therapy.* New York: Guilford Press.

APA. American Psychiatric Association. (2013). *Diagnostic and statistical manual of mental disorders* (5th ed.). Washington, DC: Author.

Arsenio, W. F., & Lemerise, E. A. (2010). *Emotions, aggression, and morality in children: Bridging development and psychopathology.* Washington, DC: American Psychological Association.

Bandura, A. (1977). *Social learning theory.* Englewood Cliffs, NJ: Prentice-Hall.

Bandura, A., & Walters, R. H. (1959). *Adolescent aggression.* New York: Ronald Press.

Barkley, R. A. (1997). *ADHD and the nature of self-control.* New York: Guilford Press.

Baum, A., et al. (1985). *Social psychology.* New York: Random House.

Berk, L. E. (2008). *Lifespan development.* New York: Pearson Education.

Berkowitz, L. (1990). On the formation and regulation of anger and aggression. *American Psychologist, 45*(4), 494–503.

Bornovalova, M. A., et al. (2013). Disentangling the relative contribution of parental antisociality and family discord to child disruptive disorders. *Personality Disorders, 4*(3), 239–246. doi:10.1037/a0028607

Bradley, R. H., & Corwyn, R. F. (2007). Externalizing problems in fifth grade: Relations with productive activity, maternal sensitivity, and harsh parenting from infancy through middle childhood. *Developmental Psychology, 43*(6), 1390–1401. doi:10.1037/0012-1649.43.6.1390

Broidy, L. M., et al. (2003). Developmental trajectories of childhood disruptive behaviors and adolescent delinquency: A six-site, cross-national study. *Developmental Psychology, 39*(2), 222–245. doi:10.1037/0012-1649.39.2.222

Bronfenbrenner, U. (1994). Ecological models of human development. In *International encyclopedia of education* (Vol. 3, 2nd ed.). Oxford: Elsevier.

Chen, P., & Vazsonyi, A. T. (2011). Future orientation, impulsivity, and problem behaviors: A longitudinal moderation model. *Developmental Psychology, 47*(6), 1633–1645. doi:10.1037/a0025327

Coie, J. D., et al. (1992). Predicting early adolescent disorder from childhood aggression and peer rejection. *Journal of Consulting and Clinical Psychology, 60*(5), 783–792.

DeKlyen, M. (1996). Disruptive behavior disorder and intergenerational attachment patterns: A comparison of clinic-referred and normally functioning preschoolers and their mothers. *Journal of Consulting and Clinical Psychology, 64*(2), 357–365.

Diamontopoulou, S., et al. (2011). Gender differences in the development and adult outcome of co-occurring depression and delinquency in adolescence. *Journal of Abnormal Psychology, 120*(3), 644–655. doi:10.1037/a0023669

Eisenberger, R., et al. (1985). Effort training increases generalized self-control. *Journal of Personality and Social Psychology, 49*(5), 1294–1301.

Ellis, A. (2001). *Overcoming destructive beliefs, feelings, and behaviors: New directions for rational emotive behavior therapy.* Amherst, NY: Prometheus.

Fischer, M., et al. (1990). The adolescent outcome of hyperactive children diagnosed by research criteria: II. Academic, attentional, and neuropsychological status. *Journal of Consulting and Clinical Psychology, 58*(5), 580–588.

Gailliot, M. T., et al. (2007). Self-control relies on glucose as a limited energy source: Willpower is more than a metaphor. *Journal of Personality and Social Psychology, 92*(2), 325–336. doi:10.1037/0022-3514.92.2.325

Geen, R. G. (1990). *Human aggression.* Pacific Grove, CA: Brooks/Cole.

Gilliom, M., et al. (2002). Anger regulation in disadvantaged preschool boys: Strategies, antecedents, and the development of self-control. *Developmental Psychology, 38*(2), 222–235. doi:10.1037//0012-1649.38.2.222

Johnson, J. G., et al. (1999). A longitudinal investigation of social causation and social selection processes involved in the association between socioeconomic status and psychiatric disorders. *Journal of Abnormal Psychology, 108*(3), 490–499.

Lahey, B. B., et al. (1989). Personality characteristics of the mothers of children with disruptive behavior disorders. *Journal of Consulting and Clinical Psychology, 57*(4), 512–515.

Lefkowitz, M. M. (1977). *Growing up to be violent: A longitudinal study of the development of aggression.* New York: Pergamon Press.

Loeber, R., & Stouthamer-Loeber, M. (1998). Development of juvenile aggression and violence. *American Psychologist, 53*(2), 242–259.

McCarty, C. A., & McMahon, R. J. (2003). Mediators of the relation between maternal depressive symptoms and child internalizing and disruptive behavior disorders. *Journal of Family Psychology, 17*(4), 545–556. doi:10.1037/0893-3200.17.4.545

Mischel, W. (1986). *Introduction to personality: A new look* (4th ed.). New York: Holt, Rinehart, and Winston.

Nigg, J. T., et al. (1998). Neuropsychological correlates of childhood attention-deficit/hyperactivity disorder: Explainable by comorbid disruptive behavior or reading problems? *Journal of Abnormal Psychology, 107*(3), 468–480.

Nigg, J. T., et al. (2002). Big five dimensions and ADHD symptoms: Links between personality traits and clinical symptoms. *Journal of Personality and Social Psychology, 83*(2), 451–469. doi:10.1037//0022-3514.83.2.451

Patterson, C. M., & Newman, J. P. (1993). Reflectivity and learning from aversive events: Toward a psychological mechanism for the syndromes of disinhibition. *Psychological Review, 100*(4), 716–736.

Peters, R. D., et al. (1992). *Aggression and violence throughout the lifespan.* Newbury Park, CA: Sage.

Pope, A. W., & Bierman, K. L. (1999). Predicting adolescent peer problems and antisocial activities: The relative roles of aggression and dysregulation. *Developmental Psychology, 35*(2), 335–346.

Potegal, M., & Knutson, J. F. (1994). *The dynamics of aggression: Biological and social processes in dyads and groups.* Hillsdale, NJ: Lawrence Erlbaum.

Shaver, P. R., & Mikulincer, M. (2011). *Human aggression and violence.* Washington, DC: American Psychological Association.

Tangney, J., et al. (1996). Assessing individual differences in constructive versus destructive responses to anger across the lifespan. *Journal of Personality and Social Psychology, 70*(4), 780–796.

Vazsonyi, A. T., & Huang, L. (2010). Where self-control comes from: On the development of self-control and its relationship to deviance over time. *Developmental Psychology, 46*(1), 245–257. doi:10.1037/a0016538

Zahn-Waxler, C., et al. (1986). *Altruism and aggression: Biological and social origins.* Cambridge, MA: Cambridge University Press.

4 Epidemiology and Course of Disruptive Disorders

Jessy Warner-Cohen, Jennifer M. Twyford, and Lara Buckley

Disruptive behavior disorders (Dbds), by their very nature, can interrupt the functioning of the individual, family, community, and society as a whole. For example, Copeland et al. (2011) found, as part of the Great Smokey Mountain Study, that males overall had a greater chance of being diagnosed with any mental health disorder, and that difference was accounted for by gender differences in rates of disruptive behavior. There are also significant monetary costs associated with these disorders. Pelham et al. (2007) has estimated that the average annual cost of treating each child with attention-deficit/hyperactivity disorder (ADHD) is $2,636, another $4,900 in educational costs, and $7,040 in crime and delinquency costs, for a total of $14,576 per child with ADHD per year. De Graaf et al. (2008) noted an average of 22.1 annual excess lost days among adults across 10 countries. The cost is high and the impact is great. This chapter reviews the epidemiology and course of these disorders in order to better understand the scope of impact of these disorders and how they affect people across the life span.

Prevalence

Disruptive behavior, as described throughout this chapter, nearly always begins its course in childhood. But before discussing the prevalence of childhood disruptive behavior disorders, one should be aware of the limitations of this area of research, as there are specific challenges to assessing pediatric psychiatric epidemiology. One challenge is the paucity of appropriately sensitive and specific measures. Measures to assess mental health disorders on a large scale, such as those needed in epidemiological surveys, have often been developed on an adult population and may not capture the developmental shifts associated with these disorders in youth (Costello et al., 2005). Costello et al. (2005) also note that using disability-adjusted life-years (DALYs) would more appropriately measure the burden of childhood psychiatric issues, but in practice DALYs are rarely calculated and reported. Only in the past 15 years or so have pediatric psychiatric issues even been measured in epidemiological studies (Costello et al., 2005). Even so, the following information should therefore be viewed as a reasonable estimate, given the above limitations.

One prominent DBD is ADHD. In a community sample of adolescents, Roberts et al. (2007) found a 12-month prevalence of ADHD of 2.06%. Merikangas et al. (2010), using the 2001–2004 National Health and Nutrition Examination Survey data, found a higher 12-month prevalence of ADHD among children 8-15 years old, noting a rate of 7.8%. It is possible that these differences reflect differences among age groups. Willcutt (2012) conducted a meta-analysis and estimated a combined childhood and adolescent prevalence of 5.9%. Any of these estimates indicate a sizable proportion of youths with problems regulating attention and behavior.

But ADHD is disproportionally distributed among population demographics. Barkley (2003), citing his previous research, noted what appeared to be increased rates of ADHD among African Americans. He explains, however, that these rates may be deceptive in that they were based solely on teacher behavioral reports. He also notes that, when controlling for comorbid conditions, socioeconomic status (SES) does not play a significant role in ADHD prevalence (Barkley, 2003). Using more recent data, Schieve et al. (2012) utilized the National Health Interview Survey from years 2006–2010 to look at the demographics of children with ADHD. Over two-thirds of respondents with ADHD were reported to be male. Of those with ADHD, the majority identified as non-Hispanic white, and their mothers were more likely to have greater than a high school education. Russell et al. (2013), using the British Millennium Cohort Study, found that among those with ADHD, children were more likely to be male, have lower cognitive ability, younger gestational age at birth, and younger maternal age. The prominence of ADHD among males persists through adulthood. Cumyn et al. (2009) found significantly greater numbers of males than females with ADHD even in adulthood. The burden of illness therefore seems to rest heavily on certain segments of the population.

There is considerable variability in estimates of oppositional defiant disorder (ODD). Boylan et al. (2007) conducted a meta-analysis of prevalence of ODD among youths. Rates ranged from 1.8% to 15.4%, although it was not indicated if these were 12-month or lifetime prevalence estimates (Boylan et al., 2007). Roberts et al. (2007) found a 12-month prevalence of 2.77% within a community sample. Merikangas et al. (2010), based on NHANES data, had a similar result and found a 12-month prevalence of 2.1% among 8- to 15-year-olds. Nock et al. (2007) found a lifetime prevalence of 10.2%. These ranges in prevalence estimates may reflect differences in methods of calculating prevalence estimates (i.e., surveying teachers vs. parents, calculating 12-month vs. lifetime prevalence) and differences in measurement tools. Although there are some reports of

ODD being more common in males (Quy & Stringaris, 2012), large-scale epidemiological data indicate no significant gender differences (Nock et al., 2007). Those with ODD are more likely to come from lower SES backgrounds and to have experienced a coercive form of parenting (Quy & Stringaris, 2012).

Similar rates were found among those with conduct disorder (CD). Nock et al. (2006), based on the National Comorbidity Study Replication, noted a lifetime CD prevalence of 9.5%. In a community sample of adolescents, Roberts et al. (2007) found the 12-month prevalence to be 3.32%. The likelihood of being diagnosed with CD in one's lifetime is associated with "young age, male gender, low educational attainment, being separated or divorced, residing in the Western U.S., and residing in urban settings" (Nock et al., 2006, p. 5).

There are mixed results on whether there are gender differences within ODD or CD. Roberts et al. (2007) found that there were significantly higher rates of ODD or CD among males than females, although when looking at demographics associated with ODD, Nock et al. (2007) found no significant difference between males and females. Maughan et al. (2004), examining ODD and CD on a national level in England, found that CD was significantly more prevalent in boys than girls, and rates showed a linear trend over time, with greater rates with increasing age in both genders. ODD was similarly more common in boys than girls (Maughan et al., 2004). These mixed findings warrant further investigation.

There is also a temporal quality to ODD/CD diagnosis. For ODD, the median age of onset is estimated to be 12.0 (Nock et al., 2007). Those in the lowest age groups were found to be significantly less likely to have ODD or CD than those in middle childhood or teen years (Roberts et al., 2007). Additionally, those with ODD or CD were significantly less likely to have married parents (Roberts et al., 2007).

The prevalence of two other disruptive behavior disorders, Tourette's disorder and Intermittent Explosive Disorder (IED), has been measured as well. The Centers for Disease Control and Prevention estimates that three per 1,000 youths aged 6–17 have a parent report a lifetime diagnosis of Tourette's disorder. Among those with diagnosed Tourette's disorder, boys outnumbered girls by three to one, and those diagnosed were twice as likely to be older, rather than younger, youths (Centers for Disease Control and Prevention, 2009). When surveying adolescents as part of the National Comorbidity Survey Replication, McLaughlin et al. (2012) found a lifetime prevalence of IED of 5.3%, and similar results were found with adults (Kessler et al., 2006). The average number of attacks over the course of a month was 11.8 (Kessler et al., 2006).

With the publication of the fifth edition of the *Diagnostic and Statistical Manual of Mental Disorders* (DSM-5), a new disruptive disorder, disruptive mood dysregulation disorder (DMDD), was introduced. This disorder describes children with severe emotional and behavioral disturbance and nonepisodic irritability. The research is limited for this disorder, but prevalence can be extrapolated from existing data sets. Copeland et al. (2013) utilized existing surveys and pulled out those with symptoms consistent with DMDD. Of the three studies utilized, rates of DMDD ranged from 0.8% (Caring for Children in the Community study) to 3.3% (Duke Preschool Anxiety Study). Among those with symptoms of DMDD, there were significantly greater impairments in parental and teacher relations, more school suspensions, greater service use both in mental health and medical settings, higher levels of poverty, and more likelihood of being raised in a single-parent family and having parents with low levels of education (Copeland et al., 2013). Because DMDD has been added to the DSM, additional research will likely be conducted in the future.

Disruptive behaviors can also appear as a part of other disorders. Behavior disturbance—especially irritability, aggression, and rage—is a core feature of bipolar disorder, but these symptoms often overlap with comorbid disorders such as ODD and ADHD (Hammen & Rudolph, 2003). Children with autism spectrum disorders have been noted to demonstrate disruptive behaviors such as self-injury, decreased need for sleep (Klinger et al., 2003), tantrums, impatience, and stubbornness (Brereton et al., 2006). According to measures of disruptive behavior, children with autism spectrum disorders fall in the 66th percentile compared to those with intellectual disability (Brereton et al., 2006).

Patients with personality disorders, especially borderline personality disorder (BPD) and antisocial personality disorder (ASPD), often demonstrate disruptive behaviors as part of the disorder. The prevalence of BPD is estimated to be 1.4% of the US population and ASPD 0.6% (Lenzenweger et al., 2007). When examined on a population level, there is a trend indicating greater likelihood of males diagnosed with ASPD (Lenzenweger et al., 2007), and about 75% of those diagnosed with BPD are females (American Psychiatric Association [APA], 2013). Self-mutilation is a diagnostic feature of BPD, with such behavior occurring in up to 80% of those diagnosed, and individuals with BPD exhibit an increased risk of intimate partner violence (as cited in Sansone & Sansone, 2012).

Disruptive behaviors can range across an individual's life span. Among those diagnosed with dementia, 45.1% have been found to have at least one disruptive behavioral symptom, significantly more than those diagnosed with mild cognitive impairment (Chan et al., 2005). Disruptive disorders should be considered across the life span.

Comorbid Conditions

As expected, DBDs often do not occur in isolation. Research has been conducted on youth with generalized conduct issues. Polier et al. (2012)

studied children with parent-identified general conduct or internalizing problems. In this community sample, 10.6% were found to have some sort of conduct problem, with 3.7% having an overlapping internalizing problem. This degree of overlap was less than in a comparison clinical sample, which utilized more specific diagnostic criteria and severity guidelines, in which 25.8% had comorbid externalizing and internalizing disorders. Within the community and clinical samples there was greater severity of social problems for those with conduct and internalizing problems as compared to those only having conduct problems (Polier et al., 2012). Therefore internalizing and externalizing disorders often co-occur and may share similar etiologies.

Individuals with ADHD are more likely than those without ADHD to have learning disorders. A significant portion (41.3%) of youths with ADHD, based on the National Health Interview Survey, also had a comorbid learning disorder (Schieve et al., 2012). Larsson et al. (2012) found significantly increased risk of learning disorders among those with ADHD. Learning disorders may contribute to patients acting out in the school and vocational settings, as those with undiagnosed learning disabilities often become frustrated, fueling the symptoms of their comorbid disruptive behavior disorders.

There is also increased risk of anxiety and depression among those with ADHD. Larsson et al. (2012) found significantly higher risk of anxiety and depression among those with ADHD. Similarly, among adults with ADHD, compared to those without, there were significantly higher rates of ADHD-specific phobia, social phobia, panic disorder, and major depressive disorder (Cumyn et al., 2009). These comorbid disorders additionally have the potential to exacerbate the existing disruptive behavior disorder and thus should be assessed when examining a person and their behavioral presentation.

In addition, ADHD may co-occur with a developmental disorder. Larsson et al. (2012) found increased risk of autism spectrum disorder among children with ADHD. Those with both disorders may exhibit an additive effect in the severity of the symptoms. Gadow et al. (2006) looked at the role of ADHD among children with autism spectrum disorders and found that those with both disorders had greater severity of symptoms and were more likely to be on medications.

There is also increased risk for co-occurrence of disruptive behavior disorders. Larsson et al. (2012) found increased risk for conduct disorder and Tourette's disorder. Significantly higher rates of past (but not present) clinically significant symptoms of conduct disorder and antisocial personality disorder also existed among adults (Cumyn et al., 2009). Increased risk of substance use also appears to occur among adults with ADHD. Van Emmerik-van Oortmerssen et al. (2012) conducted a meta-analysis on the prevalence of ADHD in substance abuse patients and found that 23.1% of patients in the substance abuse group had comorbid ADHD. Potential behavioral disturbance seen in those with substance abuse issues thus may be the manifestation of comorbid ADHD. Overall, owing to the high rates of comorbid conditions with ADHD, one should diagnostically consider the range of potential diagnoses when regarding a person's behavioral profile.

There is significantly higher risk of comorbidity of ODD with other disorders, especially mood disorders, anxiety disorders, impulse control disorders, or substance abuse disorders. Of note, only 42.5% of those with ODD went on to develop CD, and 25% had comorbid ADHD (Nock et al., 2007). The prevalence of comorbid depression with ODD ranged from 2.4% to 45.4%, and nearly all studies indicated significantly greater odds ratio of depression compared to youths without ODD. Prevalence of comorbid anxiety disorder ranged from 7.1% to 55.3%, with similarly increased odds ratios compared to those without ODD (Boylan et al., 2007). Research has also been conducted on youth with more than one disruptive behavior disorder. Among those with CD, after accounting for age and the presence of other disorders, there were significantly increased odds of comorbid ADHD in boys and girls and depression in boys. Among those with ODD, similar results were found, and additionally there were increased odds of comorbid anxiety (Maughan et al., 2004). With such high odds ratios, especially in terms of ADHD, the clear but unanswered question is whether these disorders represent distinct disorders, or is the overlap so great that the symptoms represent a spectrum of the same disorder. This consideration has diagnostic implications, and research on the prevalence and course of disruptive disorders should take this possibility into account.

Beyond ADHD, ODD, and CD, other DBDs also have high rates of comorbid conditions. Those with Tourette's disorder had high rates of comorbidity with ADHD, other conduct or behavioral disorder, anxiety disorder, depression, or developmental delay (Centers for Disease Control and Prevention, 2009). Adolescents with IED were found to be significantly more likely than the general population to have been diagnosed with a phobia, panic disorder, separation anxiety disorder, or drug abuse or dependence. When looking at the more severely impaired versus those with fewer episodes of IED, the more impaired group was significantly more likely to exhibit drug abuse or dependence (McLauglin et al., 2012).

Individuals with bipolar disorder have high rates of comorbid disruptive behavior disorders such as ADHD (34.7% of those with bipolar), ADD (24.3%), disruptive behavior disorder not otherwise specified (18.1%), and CD (4.2%; Youngstrom et al., 2005). Therefore these disorders tend to be highly comorbid with one another.

The role of genetic overlap between disorders is an emerging field of study. Faraone et al. (2012) conducted a meta-analysis of ADHD and

Bipolar I probands and found significantly increased risk of ADHD among those with genetic risk of Bipolar I (risk ratio = 2.6), including off-spring, siblings, and parents. There was similarly increased risk of Bipolar I in those with increased genetic risk of ADHD. These findings suggest that one does not need to have a relative with a specific disorder, and even the genetic risk of a disorder can raise the likelihood of developing another disorder.

Course of Disruptive Disorders

Multiple casual pathways can lead to the development of specific DBDs throughout one's life span (Farris et al., 2011; Frick, 2012). An understanding of the developmental course of DBDs informs treatment selection and aids in the development of early intervention and prevention programs. Individuals may vary in the onset and course of a DBD (Farris et al., 2011) and may display a wide range from minor symptoms of one disorder to many complex symptoms of several disorders. The domain of externalizing behaviors is far from unidimensional because of the array of behaviors, from inattention to impulsivity/hyperactivity to oppositionality to physical aggression (Hinshaw, 2002).

ADHD

Childhood and Adolescence

A developmental progression of behavioral disinhibition characterizes ADHD. On average, the onset of ADHD symptoms often occurs during the preschool years, typically at 3 to 4 years of age (Wilens & Spencer, 2010), although some symptoms have been reported earlier. Hyperactive motor behavior, such as excessive movement during sleep, has been noted to appear by age 1 to 1.5 years (Loeber et al., 2000). Other hyperactive-impulsive motor behaviors, observed in children 3 to 5 years old, include excessive climbing, excessive running inside, difficulty playing quietly, poor frustration tolerance, and deficits in adaptive behaviors (Vierhile et al., 2009). At home and at school, these children are seen as more impulsive, aggressive, and demanding of adult's time, and as having poorer social skills (DeWolfe et al., 2000; Egger & Angold, 2006). When excessive hyperactive motor behaviors and inattentive behaviors are observed for more than a year during preschool, these children are highly likely to become diagnosed with ADHD in childhood and adolescence (Reef et al., 2011).

Beginning in the elementary school years, at ages 6–12, additional ADHD behaviors begin to develop. School-age children with ADHD may develop problems with aggression (Hinshaw, 2002). Childhood ADHD has also been identified as a precursor for conduct problems in adolescence and early adulthood (Mannuzza et al., 2004; Mordre et al., 2011). By late childhood (approximately 12 years of age), executive functioning problems associated with ADHD begin to significantly affect self-regulation (Barkley et al., 2001) and adaptive functioning (Barkley et al., 1996). As a result, children with ADHD may demonstrate additional problems with social impairments and emotional well-being (Wehmeier et al., 2010). When interacting with their peers, children and adolescents with ADHD may experience difficulties with cooperation, turn taking, and sharing, or they may act in self-centered, impulsive, or hostile ways. As a result, children with ADHD have an increased likelihood of being rejected by their peers (Becker et al., 2012; Hoza, 2007). Families with a child with ADHD experience increased child–parent conflict, which may be due to the child's behavior, disregard for rules, or difficulty with communication (Wehmeier et al., 2010). As a result, the child with ADHD may experience significant emotional distress (Escobar et al., 2005), such as depression (Daviss et al., 2009) and self-esteem (Klimkeit et al., 2006), which in turn may further increase the likelihood of disruptive behaviors.

The majority of children with ADHD will likely continue to have this disorder into adolescence (Biederman et al., 2000). When children with ADHD develop into adolescents though, the severity of their symptoms may decline. In particular, the hyperactive-impulsive behaviors have shown the most significant decrease; however, inattentive behaviors tend to be the most persistent and problematic in adolescence (Biederman et al., 2000; Loeber et al., 2000). Many factors appear to contribute to the persistence of ADHD from childhood into adolescence, including the degree of childhood hyperactive-impulsive behaviors, conduct problems, oppositional behaviors, hostility, and parent–child conflicts (Barkley, 2003; Taylor et al., 1996). These factors are also important predictors for comorbid oppositional and conduct disorder for adolescents with a history of childhood ADHD (Hart et al., 1995; Mannuzza et al., 2004; Taylor et al., 1996; Yoshimasu et al., 2012). The presence of hyperactivity, inattention, and the lack of impulse control have been shown to be highly correlated predictors for future of antisocial behaviors (Herpertz et al., 2001; Hinshaw et al., 1993; Holmes et al., 2001; Mandel, 1997). Children with ADHD with predominantly hyperactive-impulsive symptoms have a greater likelihood to later develop CD and ODD and to sustain antisocial behaviors into adulthood than children with predominantly inattentive symptoms (Caspi et al., 1995; Dykman & Acherman, 1993; Holmes, 2001). Among 25-year-olds, ADHD diagnosis in childhood is associated with increased likelihood of continued and increased psychosocial and mental health impairments, including bipolar disorder, conduct disorder (Mannuzza et al., 2004), and major depression (Biederman et al., 2009).

Adulthood

Remission rates for ADHD in adulthood have been noted to be as high as 60%, with significant decline across diagnostic subcategories (Biederman et al., 2000). Clinically, adults diagnosed with ADHD may present as being impulsive, inattentive, and restless, much like the children and adolescents who carry the same diagnosis (Biederman et al., 2000, 2009), but in many adults the hyperactivity may decrease significantly in comparison to the severity of childhood, although the inattention and impulsivity symptoms tend to persist (Koumoula, 2012). The symptoms of ADHD in adulthood can have a significant impact on the professional, economic, social, and emotional well-being of adults with ADHD, including decreased financial resources, lower educational attainment, poor job performance, and more social isolation (Brod et al., 2012). ADHD symptoms typically decrease during later adulthood (Jacobs et al., 2007; Kessler et al., 2005).

Conduct and Oppositional Defiant Disorders

Childhood and Adolescence

Across the life span, the course of ODD and CD is fairly consistent and predictable, although the specific topography of the behaviors changes with development (Hinshaw & Lee, 2003). Defiance and temper tantrums in preschoolers precede physical aggression in middle and late childhood and the theft, lying, property destruction, and possible sexual assault in adolescence. Many propose a developmental relationship between ODD and CD, with ODD as the developmental precursor to CD (Burke et al., 2010; Loeber et al., 2000), although the two remain separate disorders (Rowe et al., 2010) and may be diagnosed concurrently. For example, ODD diagnosis in youth 4 to 6 years old is predictive of early-onset CD in 79% of cases (Burke et al., 2010), and no boys with CD with low levels of oppositional behavior were found in a longitudinal cluster analysis of DBD (Loeber et al., 2000). Even when controlling for ADHD and socioeconomic factors, boys with ODD have an increased risk of diagnosis with CD later in life (Loeber et al., 2000). But not all adolescents who have a history of childhood ODD develop CD (Burke et al., 2010; Rowe et al., 2010).

As with ADHD, symptoms of ODD and CD are observed in children as young as preschool age. One of the first symptoms is a disregard for rules, which is a hallmark trait of both ODD and CD (Petitclerc et al., 2009). In a 3-year-old child, it can be difficult to distinguish developmentally inappropriate oppositional behavior from developmentally appropriate behavior testing of limits and control. Egger and Angold (2006) suggest developmentally appropriate cutoffs to define the DSM criterion of *often* to distinguish developmentally appropriate preschool-age behavior from conduct problems: losing temper with adults (two to three times per day), arguing with adults (two times per week), actively defying adults (five times per day), deliberately annoying others (five times per week), blaming others (once per week), and acting angry and resentful (one time per day; Egger & Angold, 2006; Wakschlag et al., 2012). According to Egger and Angold (2006), children who exceed these thresholds may be displaying behavioral problems consistent with ODD.

Behaviors associated with ODD and CD also progress developmentally. The approximate average age of ODD symptom onset is 6 years old, and 9 years old for CD (Hinshaw & Lee, 2003). Children aged 4 to 6 with ODD (but without CD) may show a decline in ODD symptoms in six to seven years, but they may still exhibit high levels of functional impairment (Burke et al., 2010). In a longitudinal study of DBD in boys, Loeber et al. (2000) found that, regardless of whether symptoms begin earlier in childhood (7 to 9 years old) or later in childhood (10 to 12 years old), the onset of conduct behavior problems is typically proceeded by oppositional behavior, then progresses to cruelty to animals, lying at home, fire setting, shoplifting, and then fighting (Loeber et al., 2000). Physical fighting predicts the onset of CD more than any other symptom (Loeber et al., 1995). In adolescence, common behaviors with less severe consequences, such as frequent truancy and running away from home (Loeber et al., 2000), are frequently observed. In more severe cases of adolescents with CD and significant callous-unemotional traits, symptoms are likely to begin in childhood (Frick, 2012). The younger the child at onset of behaviors, the more quickly the behaviors progress from less serious to most serious (Loeber et al., 1992; McMahon et al., 2010). Furthermore, the earlier the onset of the behavior, the more severe and uncommon the later antisocial behavior, such as robbery, rape, and breaking and entering (Loeber et al., 2000).

Adulthood

Antisocial behaviors (ASBs) usually refer to behaviors of adolescents or young adults who demonstrate APD traits but do not meet the full requirement for a diagnosis of APD (i.e., no previous diagnosis of CD; Goldstein et al., 2012). Individuals who develop ASB later in adolescence tend to show fewer cognitive deficits, higher IQ scores, better academic performance, and better ability to emotionally self-regulate (Frick, 2012; Moffitt & Caspi, 2001; Walters & Knight, 2010). Although adolescents with ASB are also likely to be associated with delinquent peer groups, adolescents with later-onset ASB may additionally have higher rates of parental involvement and supervision, lower rates of experienced abuse and parental substance abuse, and higher SES (Frick, 2012; Moffitt &

Caspi, 2001). For them, the onset of ASB may be associated with the onset of puberty (Moffitt & Caspi, 2001). The earlier the onset of symptoms and criminality, the more likely that individual is to persist in disordered behavior (Walters & Knight, 2010). That is, those who have a later onset of symptoms are less likely to persist in criminality or antisocial behaviors.

Many adolescents with CD persistently exhibit ASB into adulthood (Burke et al., 2010; Khalifa et al., 2012). However, just as some children diagnosed with ODD do not progress into the more antisocial symptoms of CD (Burke et al., 2010), not all youth with CD will persist exhibiting ASB into adulthood (Holmes et al., 2001). Although the risk factors for ODD and CD (Goldstein et al., 2012; Khalifa et al., 2012) are similar to those with APD (Lahey and Loeber, 1997; Simonoff et al., 2004), adolescents with CD and later-onset APD (without ODD symptoms in childhood) tend to have greater difficulties processing negative emotionality, fear, and signs of distress in others. They also appear to be more fearless and thrill seeking, exhibit lower levels of anxiety, have fewer cognitive deficits, be more aggressive and rejecting of conventional values, and respond poorly to punishment. Those without symptoms of ADD, however, are less likely to progress into adulthood pathology (Frick, 2012; Frick & White, 2008). Youth with CD are also at increased risk for early-onset alcohol abuse (Howard et al., 2011; Khalifa et al., 2012).

Personality Disorders

The symptoms of APD typically appear to decrease with age (Goldstein et al., 2012). Despite this fact, APD usually last a lifetime. Studies have shown that adults who carry the diagnosis of APD are more likely to become parents during the teen years or at a young age; be susceptible to poverty; have increased levels of substance abuse, suicidality, mortality, difficulty maintaining employment, higher rates of divorce and relational issues, reported use of government assistance programs, and lower perceived quality of life; and be sentenced to multiple years in prison (Farris et al., 2011; Goldstein et al., 2012; Olino et al., 2010; Walters & Knight, 2010).

Symptoms of BPD and related impairment tend to be highly variable from one individual to another, with most affective instability and impulse dyscontrol clearly evident by early adulthood. Symptoms tend to become less impairing with age, and suicide risks similarly decline as individuals with BPD progress into middle and late adulthood. The majority of individuals with BPD attain greater stability in functioning by the third and fourth decades of their life (APA, 2013). Those diagnosed with BPD who receive some degree of treatment show some positive outcomes. Among adults who had been psychiatrically hospitalized and diagnosed with BPD, 88% showed remission of symptoms over 10 years, with nearly half

(39.3%) improving within two years after being discharged from the hospital. Remission is more likely among those diagnosed and treated earlier in adulthood and fewer childhood traumas (Zanarini et al., 2006).

Other Disorders

Generally, disruptive behaviors appear to decrease over time. Among those diagnosed with an autism spectrum disorder, behavioral disturbance appears to diminish over adolescence and adulthood. It has been noted that specific maladaptive behaviors such as unusual or repetitive habits and inattentive behavior show significant decreases as the person ages, and the perception of general disruptiveness shows a downward trend. Behavioral improvement is more likely among those with fewer negative behaviors when entering adolescence and those without comorbid intellectual disability (Shattuck et al., 2007). Similarly, those with Tourette's disorder will often experience a significant decrease in disruptive symptoms over time, with over one-third experiencing full remission (Bloch & Leckman, 2009).

These are disorders in which disruptive behavior does not diminish in adulthood. Although symptoms of IED usually begin before age 40, the core features tend to persist for many years (APA, 2013), although some decrease of symptomatology over time may be evident (Kessler et al., 2006).

Among those with more severe intellectual disability, especially those with comorbid mental health disorders, disruptive behavior continues to be a significant issue and especially relevant with regard to the need for residential placement (McIntyre et al., 2002). Among those with bipolar disorder, there is an increase in rate of psychiatric hospitalizations due to bipolar disorder in adulthood compared to pediatric hospitalizations, although the disruptive symptomatology tends to become less traditionally manic behaviors and more psychotic behaviors (Bladder & Carlson, 2007). As DMDD is a new disorder, there is currently no research on its progression into adulthood.

Summary and Conclusions

Disruptive behaviors are not uncommon and can persist throughout an individual's life span. Most of these disorders have some basis in childhood with considerable comorbidity between disorders. The symptoms of many, although not all, of these disorders tend to show some progressive remission in adulthood, although those with more severe symptoms in childhood tend to exhibit more persistent symptoms in adulthood. Overall, when considering the symptoms, development, and course of these disorders, it is important to consider the severity and interrelatedness of these disorders as a guide to understanding the prevalence, course, and treatment needs for those who exhibit disruptive behaviors.

References

APA. American Psychiatric Association. (2013). *Diagnostic and statistical manual of mental disorders* (5th ed.). Washington, DC: Author.

Barkley, R. A. (2003). Attention-deficit/hyperactivity disorder. In E. J. Mash & R. A. Barkley (Eds.), *Child psychopathology* (pp. 75–143). New York: Guilford Press.

Barkley, R. A., et al. (1996). Psychological adjustment and adaptive impairments in young adults with ADHD. *Journal of Attention Disorders, 1,* 41–54.

Barkley, R. A., et al. (2001). Executive functioning, temporal discounting, and sense of time in adolescents with attention deficit hyperactivity disorder and oppositional defiant disorder. *Journal of Abnormal Child Psychology, 29*(6), 541–556.

Becker, S. P., et al. (2012). Co-occurring mental health problems and peer functioning among youth with attention-deficit/hyperactivity disorder: A review and recommendations for future research. *Clinical Child and Family Psychology Review, 15,* 279–302. doi:10.1007/s10567-012-0122-y

Biederman, J., et al. (2000). Age-dependent decline of symptoms of attention deficit hyperactivity disorder: Impact of remission definition and symptom type. *American Journal of Psychiatry, 157,* 816–818.

Biederman, J., et al. (2009). Are cognitive deficits in attention deficit/hyperactivity disorder related to the course of the disorder? A prospective controlled follow-up study of grown up boys with persistent and remitting course. *Psychiatry Research, 170*(2–3), 177–182.

Bladder, J., & Carlson, G. (2007). Increased rates of bipolar disorder diagnoses among U.S. child, adolescent, and adult inpatients, 1996–2004. *Biological Psychiatry, 62,* 107–114.

Bloch, M., & Leckman, J. (2009). Clinical course of Tourette syndrome. *Journal of Psychosomatic Research, 67,* 497–501.

Boylan, K., et al. (2007). Comorbidity of internalizing disorders in children with oppositional defiant disorder. *European Child and Adolescent Psychiatry, 16*(8), 484–494.

Brereton, A. V., et al. (2006). Psychopathology in children and adolescents with autism compared to young people with intellectual disability. *Journal of Autism Developmental Disorders, 36*(7), 863–870.

Brod, M., et al. (2012). ADHD burden of illness in older adults: A life course perspective. *Quality of Life Research, 21,* 795–799.

Burke, J. D., et al. (2010). Predictive validity of childhood oppositional defiant disorder and conduct disorder: Implications for the DSM-V. *Journal of Abnormal Psychology, 119*(4), 739–751.

Caspi, A., et al. (1995). Temperamental origins of child and adolescent behavior problems: From age 3 to age 15. *Child Development, 66,* 55–68.

Centers for Disease Control and Prevention. (2009). Prevalence of diagnosed Tourette syndrome in persons aged 6–17 years—United States, 2007. *Morbidity and Mortality Weekly, 58,* 581–585.

Chan, D.-C., et al. (2005). Prevalence and correlates of behavioral and psychiatric symptoms in community dwellers with dementia or mild cognitive impairment: The Memory and Medical Care Study. *International Journal of Geriatric Psychiatry, 18,* 174–182.

Copeland, W., et al. (2011). Cumulative prevalence of psychiatric disorders by young adulthood: A prospective cohort analysis from the Great Smoky Mountains Study. *Journal of American Academy of Child and Adolescent Psychiatry, 50*(3), 252–261.

Copeland, W. E., et al. (2013). Prevalence, comorbidity, and correlates of DSM-5 proposed disruptive mood dysregulation disorder. *American Journal of Psychiatry, 170*(2), 173–179.

Costello, E. J., et al. (2005). 10-year research update review: The epidemiology of child and adolescent psychiatric disorders: I. Methods and public health burden. *Journal of American Academy of Child and Adolescent Psychiatry, 44*(10), 972–986.

Cumyn, L., et al. (2009). Comorbidity in adults with attention-deficit hyperactivity disorder. *Canadian Journal of Psychiatry, 54*(10), 673–683.

Daviss, W., et al. (2009). Associations of lifetime depression with trauma exposure, other environmental adversities, and impairment in adolescents with ADHD. *Journal of Abnormal Child Psychology, 37*(6), 857–871.

de Graaf, R., et al. (2008). The prevalence and effects of adult attention-deficit/hyperactivity disorder (ADHD) on the performance of workers: Results from the WHO World Mental Health Survey Initiative. *Occupational and Environmental Medicine, 65,* 835–842.

DeWolfe, N., et al. (2000). ADHD in preschool children: Parent-rated psychosocial correlates. *Developmental Medicine and Child Neurology, 42*(12), 825–830.

Dykman, R. A., & Acherman, P. T. (1993). Behavioral subtypes of attention deficit disorder. *Exceptional Children, 60,* 132–141.

Egger, H. L., & Angold, A. (2006). Common emotional and behavioral disorders in preschool children: Presentation, nosology, and epidemiology. *Journal of Child Psychology and Psychiatry, 47,* 313–337.

Escobar, R., et al. (2005). Worse quality of life for children with newly diagnosed attention-deficit/hyperactivity disorder, compared with asthmatic and healthy children. *Pediatrics, 116,* 364–369.

Faraone, S. V., et al. (2012). Examining the comorbidity between attention deficit hyperactivity disorder and bipolar I disorder: A meta-analysis of family genetic studies. *American Journal of Psychiatry, 169*(12), 1256–1266.

Farris, J. R., et al. (2011). Onset and progression of disruptive behavior problems among community boys and girls: A prospective longitudinal analysis. *Journal of Emotional and Behavioral Disorders, 19*(4), 233–246.

Frick, P. J. (2012). Developmental pathways to conduct disorder: Implications for future directions in research, assessment, and treatment. *Journal of Clinical and Adolescent Psychology, 41,* 378–389.

Frick, P. J., & White, S. F. (2008). Research review: The importance of callous-unemotional traits for developmental models of aggressive and antisocial behavior. *Journal of Child Psychology and Psychiatry, 49,* 359–375.

Gadow, K. D., et al. (2006). ADHD symptom subtypes in children with pervasive developmental disorder. *Journal of Autism and Developmental Disorders, 36*(2), 271–283.

Goldstein, R. B., et al. (2012). Antisocial behavioral syndromes and 3-year quality-of-life outcomes in United States adults. *Acta Psychiatrica Scandinavia, 126,* 137–150.

Hammen, C., & Rudolph, K. (2003). Childhood mood disorders. In E. J. Mash & R. A. Barkley (Eds.), *Child psychopathology* (pp. 233–278). New York: Guilford Press.

Hart, E. L., et al. (1995). Developmental changes in attention-deficit hyperactivity disorder in boys: A four-year longitudinal study. *Journal of Abnormal Child Psychology, 23,* 729–750.

Herpertz, S. C., et al. (2001). Psychophysiological responses in ADHD boys with and without conduct disorder: Implications for adult antisocial behavior. *Journal of the American Academy of Child and Adolescent Psychiatry, 40*(10), 1222–1230.

Hinshaw, S. P. (2002). Process, mechanism, and explanation related to externalizing behavior in developmental psychopathology. *Journal of Abnormal Child Psychology, 30*(5), 431–446.

Hinshaw, S. P., & Lee, S. S. (2003). Conduct and oppositional defiant disorders. In E. J. Mash & R. A. Barkley (Eds.), *Child psychopathology* (pp. 144–198). New York: Guilford Press.

Hinshaw, S. P., et al. (1993). Issues of taxonomy and comorbidity in the development of conduct disorder. *Development and Psychopathology, 5,* 31–49.

Holmes, S. E., et al. (2001). Risk factors that lead to the development of conduct disorder and antisocial personality disorder. *Child Psychiatry and Human Development, 31*(3), 183–193.

Howard, R., et al. (2011). Adolescent-onset alcohol abuse exacerbates the influence of childhood conduct disorder on late adolescent and early adult antisocial behavior. *Journal of Forensic Psychiatry and Psychology, 23,* 7–22. doi:10.1080/1478 9949.2011.641996

Hoza, B. (2007). Peer functioning in children with ADHD. *Journal of Pediatric Psychology, 32,* 655–663. doi:10.1016/j.ambp.2006.04.011

Jacobs, C. P., et al. (2007). Co-morbidity of adult attention-deficit/hyperactivity disorder with focus on personality traits and related disorders in a tertiary referral center. *European Archives of Psychiatry and Clinical Neurosciences, 257,* 309–317.

Kessler, R. C., et al. (2005). Lifetime prevalence and age-of-onset distributions of DSM-IV disorders in the National Comorbidity Survey Replication. *Archives of General Psychiatry, 62*(6), 593.

Kessler, R. C., et al. (2006). The prevalence and correlates of DSM-IV intermittent explosive disorder in the National Comorbidity Survey Replication. *Archives of General Psychiatry, 63*(6), 669–678.

Khalifa, N., et al. (2012). The relationship between childhood conduct disorder and adult antisocial personality disorder is partially mediated by early-onset alcohol abuse. *Personality Disorders: Theory, Research, and Treatment, 3*(4), 423–432.

Klimkeit, E., et al. (2006). Children should be seen and heard: Self-report of feelings and behaviors in primary-school-age children with ADHD. *Journal of Attention Disorders, 10,* 181–191.

Klinger, L., et al. (2003). Autistic disorders. In E. J. Mash & R. A. Barkley (Eds.), *Child psychopathology* (pp. 144–198). New York: Guilford Press.

Koumoula, A. A. (2012). The course of attention deficit hyperactivity disorder (ADHD) over the life span. *Psychiatriki, 23*(Suppl. 1), 49–59.

66   *Jessy Warner-Cohen et al.*

Lahey, B. B., & Loeber, R. (1997). Attention-deficit/hyperactivity disorder, oppositional defiant disorder, conduct disorder, and adult antisocial behavior: A life span perspective. In D. M. Stoff, J. Breiling, & J. D. Maser (Eds.), *Handbook of antisocial behavior* (pp. 51–59). New York: John Wiley & Sons.

Lahey, B. B., et al. (2005). Predicting antisocial personality disorder in males from a clinical assessment in childhood. *Journal of Consulting and Clinical Psychology, 73*(3), 389–399. doi:10.1037/0022-006X.73.3.389

Larsson, H., et al. (2012). Childhood attention-deficit hyperactivity disorder as an extreme of a continuous trait: A quantitative genetic study of 8,500 twin pairs. *Journal of Child Psychology and Psychiatry, 53*(1), 73–80.

Lenzenweger, M. F., et al. (2007). DSM-IV personality disorders in the National Comorbidity Survey Replication. *Biological Psychiatry, 62*(6), 553–564.

Loeber, R., et al. (1992). Developmental sequences in the age of onset of disruptive child behaviors. *Journal of Child and Family Studies, 1*(1), 21–41.

Loeber, R., et al. (1995). Which boys will fare worse? Early predictors of the onset of conduct disorder in a six-year longitudinal study. *Journal of the American Academy of Child and Adolescent Psychiatry, 34*, 499–509.

Loeber, R., et al. (2000). Findings on disruptive behavior disorders from the first decade of the Developmental Trends Study. *Clinical Child and Family Psychology Review, 3*(1), 37–60.

Mandel, H. P. (1997). *Conduct disorder and under-achievement: Risk factors, assessment, treatment, and prevention.* New York: John Wiley & Sons.

Mannuzza, S., et al. (2004). Significance of childhood conduct problems to later development of conduct disorder among children with ADHD: A prospective follow-up study. *Journal of Abnormal Child Psychology, 32*, 565–573.

Maughan, B., et al. (2004). Conduct disorder and oppositional defiant disorder in a national sample: Developmental epidemiology. *Journal of Child Psychology and Psychiatry, 45*(3), 609–621.

McIntyre, L., et al. (2002). Behaviour/mental health problems in young adults with intellectual disability: The impact on families. *Journal of Intellectual Disability Research, 46*, 239–249.

McLaughlin, K. A., et al. (2012). Intermittent explosive disorder in the National Comorbidity Survey Replication Adolescent Supplement. *Archives of General Psychiatry, 6*, 1131–1139.

McMahon, R. J., et al. (2010). Predictive validity of callous-unemotional traits measured early in adolescence with respect to multiple antisocial outcomes. *Journal of Abnormal Psychology, 199*, 752–763.

Merikangas, K. R., et al. (2010). Prevalence and treatment of mental disorders among US children in the 2001–2004 NHANES. *Pediatrics, 125*(1), 75–81.

Moffit, T. E., & Caspi, A. (2001). Childhood predictors differentiate life-course persistent and adolescent-limited antisocial pathways among males and females. *Development and Psychopathology, 13*, 355–375.

Mordre, M., et al. (2011). The impact of ADHD and conduct disorder in childhood on adult delinquency: A 30 years follow-up study using official crime records. *BMC Psychiatry, 11*, 57.

Nock, M. K., et al. (2006). Prevalence, subtypes, and correlates of DSM-IV conduct disorder in the National Comorbidity Survey Replication. *Psychological Medicine, 36*(5), 699–710.

Nock, M. K., et al. (2007). Lifetime prevalence, correlates, and persistence of oppositional defiant disorder: Results from the National Comorbidity Survey Replication. *Journal of Child Psychology and Psychiatry, 48*(7), 703–713.

Olino, T. M., et al. (2010). Conduct disorder and psychosocial outcomes at age 30: Early adult psychopathology as a potential mediator. *Journal of Abnormal Child Psychology, 38*, 1139–1149. doi:10.1177/1063426610370746

Pelham, W., et al. (2007). The economic impact of attention-deficit/hyperactivity disorder in children and adolescents. *Journal of Pediatric Psychology, 32*, 711–727.

Petitclerc, A., et al. (2009). Disregard for rules: The early development and predictors of a specific dimension of disruptive behavior disorders. *Journal of Child Psychology and Psychiatry, 50*(12), 1477–1484.

Polier, G. G., et al. (2012). Comorbidity of conduct disorder symptoms and internalizing problems in children: Investigating a community and a clinical sample. *European Child and Adolescent Psychiatry, 21*(1), 31–38.

Quy, K., & Stringaris A. (2012). Oppositional defiant disorder. In J. M. Rey (Ed.), *IACAPAP e-textbook of child and adolescent mental health*. Geneva: International Association for Child and Adolescent Psychiatry and Allied Professions.

Reef, J., et al. (2011). Developmental trajectories of child to adolescent externalizing behavior and adult DSM-IV disorder: Results of a 24-year longitudinal study. *Social Psychiatry and Psychiatric Epidemiology, 46*(12), 1233–1241.

Roberts, R. E., et al. (2007). Rates of DSM-IV psychiatric disorders among adolescents in a large metropolitan area. *Journal of Psychiatric Research, 41*(11), 959–967.

Rowe, R., et al. (2010). Developmental pathways in oppositional defiant disorder and conduct disorder. *Journal of Abnormal Psychology, 119*(4), 726–738.

Russell, G., et al. (2013). Prevalence of parent-reported ASD and ADHD in the UK: Findings from the millennium cohort study. *Journal of Autism and Developmental Disorders, 44*(1), 31–40.

Sansone, R., & Sansone, L. (2012). Borderline personality and externalized aggression. *Innovations in Clinical Neuroscience, 9*, 23–26.

Schieve, L. A., et al. (2012). Concurrent medical conditions and health care use and needs among children with learning and behavioral developmental disabilities, National Health Interview Survey, 2006–2010. *Research in Developmental Disabilities, 33*(2), 467–476.

Shattuck, P., et al. (2007). Change in autism symptoms and maladaptive behaviors in adolescents and adults with an autism spectrum disorder. *Journal of Autism and Developmental Disorders, 37*, 1735–1747.

Simonoff, E., et al. (2004). Predictors of antisocial personality: Continuities from childhood to adult life. *British Journal of Psychiatry, 184*, 118–127.

Taylor, E., et al. (1996). Hyperactivity and conduct problems as risk factors for adolescent development. *Journal of the American Academy of Child and Adolescent Psychiatry, 35*, 1213–1226.

van Emmerik-van Oortmerssen, K., et al. (2012). Prevalence of attention-deficit hyperactivity disorder in substance use disorder patients: A meta-analysis and meta-regression analysis. *Drug and Alcohol Dependence, 122*(1–2), 11–19.

Vierhile, A., et al. (2009). Attention-deficit/hyperactivity disorder in children and adolescents: Closing diagnostic, communication, and treatment gaps. *Journal of Pediatric Health Care, 23*(Suppl. 1), 5–23.

Wakschlag, L. S., et al. (2012). Defining the developmental parameters of temper loss in early childhood: Implications for developmental psychopathology. *Journal of Child Psychology and Psychiatry, 53*(11), 1099–1108.

Walters, G. D., & Knight, R. A. (2010). Antisocial personality disorder with and without antecedent childhood conduct disorder: Does it make a difference? *Journal of Personality Disorders, 24*(2), 233–246.

Wehmeier, P. M., et al. (2010). Social and emotional impairment in children and adolescents with ADHD and the impact on quality of life. *Journal of Adolescent Health, 46*(3), 209–217. doi:10.1016/j.jadohealth.2009.09.009

Wilens, T., & Spencer, T. (2010). Understanding attention-deficit/hyperactivity disorder from childhood to adulthood. *Postgraduate Medicine, 122*(5), 97–109.

Willcutt, E. G. (2012). The prevalence of DSM-IV attention-deficit/hyperactivity disorder: A meta-analytic review. *Neurotherapeutics, 9*(3), 490–499.

Yoshimasu, K., et al. (2012). Childhood ADHD is strongly associated with a broad range of psychiatric disorders during adolescence: A population-based birth cohort study. *Journal of Child Psychology and Psychiatry, 53*(10), 1036–1043.

Youngstrom, E., et al. (2005). Bipolar diagnoses in community mental health: Achenbach Child Behavior Checklist profiles and patterns of comorbidity. *Biological Psychiatry, 58*, 569–575.

Zanarini, M., et al. (2006). Prediction of the 10-year course of borderline personality disorder. *American Journal of Psychiatry, 163*, 827–832.

Part II

Disorders With Disruptive Behaviors as Core Symptoms

5 Attention-Deficit/Hyperactivity Disorder

Anil K. Chacko, Nicole Feirsen, Estrella Rajwan, Amanda Zwilling, William E. Pelham, and George M. Kapalka

Attention-deficit/hyperactivity disorder (ADHD) is characterized by developmentally inappropriate levels of inattention, overactivity, and impulsivity, resulting in significant impacts on various areas of daily life functioning (e.g., family interactions, peer relationships, academic achievement). According to the fifth edition of the *Diagnostic and Statistical Manual of Mental Disorders* (DSM-5; American Psychiatric Association [APA], 2013) criteria for ADHD in youth require the presence of several inattentive or hyperactive/impulsive symptoms occurring prior to 12 years of age, in at least two settings, and interfering with or reducing the quality of social, academic, or occupational functioning. DSM-5 defines ADHD as consisting of three types: combined presentation, predominantly inattentive presentation, and predominantly hyperactive/impulsive presentation. In addition, DSM-5 requires specification of the severity of ADHD (i.e., mild, moderate, or severe).

Diagnostic Considerations

Attention-deficit/hyperactivity disorder is often comorbid with other psychiatric disorders, making the presentation of ADHD from one person to the next potentially quite different. For instance, 50%–60% of youth with ADHD meet criteria for oppositional defiant disorder, 30% present with comorbid conduct disorder, and up to 25% present with anxiety or mood disorders (Jensen et al., 2001). In addition, it appears that the symptoms of ADHD present developmentally; predominantly hyperactive/impulsive presentation appears to occur most often in preschool-aged youth, while the predominantly inattentive presentation is most often diagnosed as youth become older (Lahey et al., 2005).

Prevalence and Course

Considered one of the most prevalent psychiatric disorders of childhood, ADHD affects 5% of school-age youth worldwide (Faraone et al., 2003), with up to three times higher diagnostic rates for males than females in community-based samples (Barkley, 2006). Moreover, ADHD is now considered a chronic condition, affecting many youths as they become adults. Given the changing presentation of ADHD in youth over time and the commonly observed comorbid psychiatric conditions and chronic nature of ADHD, treatment is often multimodal and requires the active involvement of multiple treatment providers and key individuals in the person's life. The focus of this chapter is to provide an overview of the literature about pharmacological, psychosocial, and combined approaches for the treatment of ADHD in children, adolescents, and adults.

Pharmacological Solitary Treatments

According to standards provided by the American Academy of Pediatrics (AAP) Committee on Quality Improvement and Subcommittee on Attention-Deficit/Hyperactivity Disorder (AAP, 2011), primary care clinicians are encouraged to treat ADHD as a chronic condition and should recommend stimulant medication as part of an appropriate treatment management plan in addition to select psychosocial treatments. Stimulant medication use is now recognized as gold standard evidence-based treatment for children with ADHD, and there are myriad studies supporting this status. More recently, several new classes of drugs have emerged as alternative treatment options for the management of ADHD symptoms. Over the past 15 years, there has been a growing and robust literature on pharmacological treatments for adolescents and adults with ADHD.

Stimulant Medications

Stimulants are currently the first-line pharmacological treatment option for ADHD in school-age youth. Approximately 70% of children taking stimulant medications demonstrate symptom improvement, making it the most commonly prescribed treatment (AAP, 2011). In particular, methylphenidate (MPH) is the most frequently used stimulant (Mohammadi & Akhondzadeh, 2011). MPH was originally only available in a short-term immediate-release (IR) form (Ritalin). While this formulation was shown to be efficacious and superior to other drugs with significant effects in preschool-aged children (Greenhill et al., 2006a), school-aged children (Abikoff et al., 2004), adolescents (Evans et al., 2001), and adults (Retz et al., 2011), its short half-life was a significant drawback. Accordingly, extended-release formulations were developed to reduce the compliance barrier of multiple daily administrations (Wolraich et al., 2001).

There are currently multiple extended-release formulations of MPH. OROS-MPH (Concerta), for example, is a once-a-day osmotic controlled-release oral dosage that was created to maintain drug efficacy throughout a 12-hour period (Wolraich et al., 2001). Similarly, Ritalin LA (ER-MPH using Spheroidal Oral Drug Absorption System technology) mimics a twice-daily MPH-IR regimen, and Metadate CD (MPH using Diffucaps technology) delivers 30% of the drug immediately and the remaining 70% throughout the day. While each of these drugs varies in pharmacokinetic properties, they all contain the same active ingredient, MPH, and work by providing sustained periods of increased MPH plasma concentrations via time-release technology. Several randomized controlled trials of have shown this class of drug to be an effective, safe, and tolerable for school-aged children, adolescents, and adults with ADHD (Spencer et al., 2011; Wilens et al., 2006a; Wolraich et al., 2001), although effects seem attenuated in adolescent and adult samples relative to younger children (Bitter et al., 2012). Extended-release oral MPH formulations are generally well tolerated. Common side effects include headache, abdominal pain, anorexia, insomnia, and lethargy. These adverse events were largely reported as being mild and occurring in less than 10% of study participants (Wolraich et al., 2001).

Methylphenidate is also available in a transdermal formulation (Daytrana). It is currently approved by the US Food and Drug Administration for use in children ages 6–12 with ADHD, with studies demonstrating benefits of the transdermal formulation (e.g., Pelham et al., 2005). To our knowledge, one study (Findling et al., 2010) found that transdermal MPH was effective for adolescents with ADHD based on improvements in clinician-rated ADHD symptoms. Marchant et al. (2011X) also found significant benefits of transdermal MPH for adults with ADHD. Interestingly, this study found that transdermal MPH was equally effective among adults with ADHD alone, ADHD plus emotional dysregulation, ADHD plus oppositional defiant disorder, and those with ADHD plus emotional dysregulation and oppositional defiant disorder. The dose is delivered through a patch over the course of up to eight hours (Chavez et al., 2009). One advantage of this delivery method is that it is an alternative option for children who cannot swallow large pills. Additionally, the duration of therapeutic effect is linked to the amount of time that the patch is worn, which offers flexibility in the duration of effect (Wilens et al., 2008). But disadvantages of the transdermal formulation include its slower onset of action and risk of causing skin irritation (McGough et al., 2005). Other reported side effects are similar to those of all other MPH formulations, including decreased appetite, headache, and insomnia.

Finally, MPH is also available in a synthetically modified version of the drug called dexmethylphenidate (d-MPH; Focalin). MPH is a mixture of two isomers: dextro (d)-threo-methylphenidate and levo (l)-threo-methylphenidate. The l-isomer may theoretically contribute less to the therapeutic effect of MPH than the d-isomer, thus administering the d-isomer in isolation may allow for lower doses with the same efficacy rates (Chavez et al., 2009; Mohammadi & Akhondzadeh, 2011). It is FDA approved for use in children with ADHD above the age of 6 and is available in an extended-release form (d-MPH-ER), which has a quick onset of action and is well tolerated. Randomized controlled trials have shown d-MPH-ER to be superior to placebo (Childress et al., 2009); it has also been demonstrated that d-MPH-ER has a quicker onset of action than OROS-MPH (Muniz et al., 2008; Silva et al., 2008). Again, the side-effect profile is similar to that of other MPH formulations.

Mixed amphetamine salts (MAS; Adderall) are another commonly prescribed medication for the treatment of ADHD in school-aged children, adolescents, and adults. MAS are available in an extended-release once-daily formulation, and randomized controlled trials have demonstrated the superiority of MAS to placebo in reducing symptom severity and impairment in school-age youth (Biederman et al., 2002), adolescents (Spencer et al., 2006), and adults (Adler et al., 2011). Common side effects include sad mood, insomnia, appetite suppression, and stomachache.

Lisdexamfetamine (LDX; Vyvanse) is a stimulant prodrug and has been shown to be superior to placebo in reducing core ADHD symptoms and improving classroom behavior and academic performance in school-aged children (Biederman et al., 2007a, 2007b) and adolescents (Findling et al., 2011). Studies have also shown that LDX improves ADHD symptoms and related impairments in college students (DuPaul et al., 2012X) and older adults with ADHD (Wigal et al., 2010). Prior to ingestion the compound is chemically inactive, but after oral ingestion the prodrug is broken down into l-lysine and active d-amfetamine, which produces the therapeutic effect (Mohammadi & Akhondzadeh, 2011). LDX is currently FDA approved for use in children between the ages of 6 and 12. Because of its pharmacological properties, it is believed to have a lower potential for abuse than other stimulant drugs and a reduced risk for toxicity (May & Kratochvil, 2010). LDX is generally well tolerated, with a side-effect profile similar to that of other stimulant drugs.

Nonstimulant Medications

Atomoxetine (ATX; Strattera) is a nonstimulant selective norepinephrine reuptake inhibitor that is FDA approved for use in treating ADHD in children, adolescents, and adults. Unlike most stimulant agents, the potential for abuse is low, so ATX is not categorized as a controlled substance. ATX has been proven to be superior to placebo in large randomized controlled trials of children, adolescents, and adults with ADHD on measures of ADHD symptoms and related impairments (Brown et al., 2011; Kratochvil et al., 2011; Michelson et al., 2001; Wilens et al., 2006b), with maintenance of treatment gains observed for up to two years of treatment in youth and adult samples (Kratochvil et al., 2006; Marchant et al., 2011b; Michelson et al., 2004). Evidence has been mixed with regard to its comparable efficacy with MPH. Some studies have shown that ATX also produces similar efficacy rates (in terms of both core symptoms and neuropsychological performance) as MPH, albeit in the context of potentially greater side effects (Hazell et al., 2011), whereas others have found ATX to produce inferior response rates (Newcorn et al., 2008). For adults, stimulants have greater efficacy than ATX for the treatment of ADHD (Bitter et al., 2012). ATX is generally well tolerated, and side effects have largely been described as mild to moderate in severity. Importantly, ATX has been associated with elevated heart rate and blood pressure as well as acute liver damage. In youth, there have been reports of increased risk of suicidal thinking/behavior, which led to an FDA black box warning on prescription ATX for youth. More common side effects include abdominal pain, nausea, fatigue, headache, increases in pulse, and aggression.

Guanfacine-XR (Intuniv), an α_2-adrenoreceptor agonist, has also been FDA approved for treatment of pediatric ADHD. Compared to placebo, guanfacine-XR has been shown to be efficacious in reducing core ADHD symptoms, comorbid oppositional behaviors, and general functioning in school-aged children (Biederman et al., 2008; Sallee et al., 2012). Data suggest, however, that guanfacine does not result in improved outcomes relative to placebo in adolescents (Biederman et al., 2008; Sallee et al., 2009). But guanfacine-XR is often used as an adjunct to psychostimulant treatment, and it has been shown to be efficacious as a supplement for those who do not respond to stimulant monotherapy (Wilens et al., 2012). Common side effects include somnolence, sedation, headache, and abdominal pain.

Clonidine-XR (Kapvay) is also available as a second-line treatment and is FDA approved for use in children with ADHD as both an adjunctive treatment and a monotherapy. It has been primarily used in the context of adjunctive therapy to enhance stimulant treatment for ADHD, particularly in cases in which aggression is a significant symptom, with largely positive empirical results (Kollins et al., 2011). As a monotherapy, clonidine-XR has been shown to be superior to placebo in reducing ADHD core symptom severity and improving global functioning (Jain et al., 2011), although it is unclear whether these effects are generalizable to adolescents, as these trials enroll relatively lower percentages of adolescents, and efficacy data are not reported separately by age group. Side effects commonly associated with clonidine include drowsiness, dizziness, and irritability.

Modafinil has also been reported to alleviate ADHD-related symptoms in school-aged children. It is currently approved for use in treating narcolepsy, as it has been proven efficacious in promoting wakefulness. It is not currently FDA approved for treating ADHD. Because it has relatively few adverse effects and is not likely to cause problems with addiction, it is not considered to be a controlled substance. Randomized controlled trials (RCTs) have demonstrated modafinil to be superior to placebo in improving ADHD symptoms in both home and school settings (Greenhill et al., 2006b). To our knowledge, only one study has directly compared modafinil to MPH, and it found similar results in terms of efficacy in symptom reduction between the two medications (Amiri et al., 2008). Side effects of modafinil commonly include insomnia, decreased appetite, and headache.

Benefits and Limitations of Pharmacotherapy as Sole Treatment

With multiple options of extended-release formulations, medication as the sole treatment for ADHD is appealing because it is time and cost effective. Individuals take one dose at the start of the day and benefit throughout the entire day. Moreover, medication treatments alone have proven efficacious in terms of reducing core symptoms, enhancing school and work functioning, and improving quality of life (Huang & Tsai, 2011; Surman et al., 2013). Arguably, pharmacotherapy may be more cost effective than no therapy or therapy alone (Wu et al., 2012), at least in the short term.

However, 10%–30% of children who take medications for the treatment of ADHD symptoms experience adverse effects, including decreased appetite, headache, weight loss, insomnia, somnolence, growth retardation, and increased blood pressure (Huang & Tsai, 2011). Adherence to medication regimens is also frequently suboptimal (Chacko et al., 2010). Although medication use is associated with improvement on standardized tests, it has not been associated with consistent improvement in school grades, nor has it been linked to normalization in academic functioning (Langberg & Becker, 2012). Additionally, parents often prefer behavioral treatments to medication treatments alone, and combined behavioral and medication treatments have been demonstrated as superior to unimodal treatment (Pelham, 1999), particularly for complex ADHD presentations (Hinshaw & Arnold, 2014). Lastly, there are no compelling data supporting the longer-term benefits of pharmacological approaches for the treatment of ADHD in youth. For adolescents and adults with ADHD, medication adherence is particularly challenging (Chacko et al., 2010; Olfson et al., 2007), and residual impairments requiring additional treatment often remain.

Psychological Solitary Treatments

Given the poor long-term maintenance of effects following the discontinuation of pharmacological treatment (Hoza et al., 2005), the significant number of people who experience adverse effects as a result of medication treatment for ADHD (see Chacko et al., 2010), residual impairments following pharmacological treatment, and public concerns over the unknown long-term impact of ongoing stimulant medication use, there is a critical need for evidence-based psychosocial treatments for the treatment of ADHD. These concerns are particularly salient, given the growing number of cases of preschool ADHD, and the literature reflects a growing interest in interventions for this population (Rajwan et al., 2012).

We adopt a classification system employed by Evans et al. (2014) that categorizes interventions into behavioral management interventions (interventions that teach individuals other than the patient skills to modify the patient's behavior in context), training interventions (interventions that teach/focus directly on the target patient to improve their skills), as well as combinations of these interventions. Behavior management interventions primarily include behavioral parent training, behavioral classroom management, and behavioral peer interventions, all of which are primarily used with preschool- through school-age youth with ADHD. Training interventions include an array of interventions, including traditional social skills training, organizational skills training, neurocognitive treatments, and cognitive-behavioral skills-based interventions, which have been studied in school-age youth through adults with ADHD. A review of outcomes from the most recent RCTs, when available, for each psychosocial intervention type is provided below, spanning preschool-age children through adults with ADHD.

Finally, interventions aimed at spouses/partners of adults with ADHD may also have a place in the psychosocial treatment of ADHD. Although these interventions have not been as widely researched and no RCTs exist to date of which we are aware, 40%–60% of children and adolescents with ADHD continue to exhibit significant symptoms of ADHD and associated difficulties throughout adulthood, and therefore clinicians who treat adults with ADHD may regularly encounter situations where such interventions may be beneficial.

Behavioral Management Interventions

Behavioral Parent Training

Behavioral parent training (BPT) is an intervention focused on assisting parents of a preschool- or school-age child with ADHD to understand the function of a problematic behavior (e.g., noncompliance, difficulties completing chores, etc.), and subsequently to learn specific methods to modify antecedents and consequences associated with the occurrence of the problematic target behaviors, in an effort to improve the frequency and severity of these target behaviors. As an example, antecedent-focused methods include establishing house rules as well as utilizing effective commands, while consequence-focused methods include specific labeled praise, planned ignoring, and time out from positive reinforcement. Additionally, there are methods that employ both antecedent- and consequence-focused methods. A daily report card (DRC), for example, is a monitoring and treatment system that is often employed in BPT and serves as a school–home communication system to improve school behavior. A DRC focuses on identifying and operationally defining target behaviors and intermediate goals, providing a menu of rewards when a child attains intermediate goals as well as consequences for not attaining intermediate goals. Importantly, key adults (parents and teachers) consistently monitor progress toward attaining goals, and intermediate goals are modified on the basis of responses to the DRC intervention. BPT methods have often been taught through a collaborative model where the therapist works with a parent to discuss the BPT method and how to tailor the method to meet the unique circumstances of the family. BPT has been delivered in various formats, including group, therapist–parent dyadic format, and therapist–parent–child triads. Most manualized BPT interventions are one- to two-hour sessions held weekly for about eight to twelve weeks. BPT interventions often employ multiple methods to support parents' learning of the BPT methods, including direct instruction, discussions, videotaped instruction, modeling of methods by the therapist, role-play with parents, as well as direct practice of BPT methods with the child during the session. Many BPT programs that focus on a variety of problem behaviors are widely available, and some are specifically designed to address behavior problems frequently associated with the symptoms of ADHD (e.g., Barkley, 2013; Kapalka, 2007).

Randomized clinical trials consistently indicate that BPT is one of the most efficacious psychosocial interventions for ADHD in terms of acute treatment effects on key outcomes (Pelham & Fabiano, 2008). RCTs of various BPT programs demonstrate reductions in ADHD symptoms and functional impairments (Anastopoulos et al., 1993; Chacko et al., 2009; Fabiano et al., 2012). Although most BPT programs are evaluated as a whole, Kapalka's (2007) has been researched with separate RCTs examining the effectiveness of each sequential step of the program (for a review, see Kapalka, 2010). Most BPT programs encourage all caretakers in the home to participate in the program, as treatment gains are most likely to be evident in such situations.

In addition, current research on BPT has focused on modifications to evidence-based treatments, resulting in improved access and engagement to treatment for higher-risk populations (e.g., single mothers, Chacko et al., 2009; fathers, Fabiano et al., 2009, 2012). In addition, BPT was shown to reduce parental stress (Chacko et al., 2009), improve parental self-esteem (Anastopoulos et al., 1993), and improve parenting behavior

(Chacko et al., 2009; Fabiano et al., 2012). For adolescents, parent–teen collaboration, rather than directly working with parents to manipulate environmental contingencies via BPT, has proven to be a promising approach for improving family conflict. In this approach, parents and adolescents learn communication skills, identify existing ineffective communication behaviors, and work toward resolving issues while systematically using effective communication skills (Barkley et al., 2001).

Behavioral Classroom Management

Behavioral classroom management interventions are other well-established treatments for preschool- and school-aged children with ADHD (Pelham & Fabiano, 2008). Similar to BPT, the focus of behavioral classroom management intervention is to understand the function of problematic school/classroom behaviors and to modify antecedents and consequences associated with the occurrence of identified target behaviors. In line with what is taught in BPT with parents, teachers are often supported in using antecedent-focused methods (e.g., classroom rules, effective commands) as well as consequence-focused methods (e.g., labeled praise, time-out from positive reinforcement). Importantly, effective implementation of behavioral classroom management interventions requires close collaboration between therapist and teachers. Classrooms vary in terms of size, number of students with behavioral challenges, and resources. As is the case when a therapist works with a parent in BPT, effective collaboration and tailoring intervention methods to meet the unique needs of the teacher and the classroom setting are essential to successful implementation of and response to behavioral classroom management interventions.

Behavioral classroom management interventions specifically developed for problems associated with ADHD include the abovementioned daily report card as well as structured programs similar to BPT programs developed for parents (e.g., Kapalka, 2009). These have been utilized in regular classroom settings (Kapalka, 2010; Miranda et al., 2002), special classroom settings (Fabiano et al., 2010), and summer program classroom settings (Fabiano et al., 2004). Data from studies suggest that these interventions result in significant improvements in ADHD symptoms as rated by parents and teachers (Miranda et al., 2002); however, these outcomes are not always seen (Fabiano et al., 2010). Non-ADHD-specific disruptive behaviors show more consistent improvement across studies, with children receiving contingency management showing significant improvements in adherence to class rules, increased attainment of behavioral goals (Fabiano et al., 2010), significant reductions in frequency and severity of disruptive behaviors (obsessive compulsive disorder/conduct disorder; Fabiano et al., 2004, 2010; Kapalka, 2010;), and aggression (Fabiano et al., 2004). Some studies have demonstrated improvements in academic productivity

(Fabiano et al., 2010), reductions in learning problems, and improved performance in math and science (Miranda et al., 2002); however, behavioral contingency management often does not significantly improve academic performance. Of note, a recent meta-analysis of school-based treatment for children with ADHD found that these interventions yield moderate to large effects for both behavioral and academic outcomes, and concluded that school-based interventions should be a first-line treatment for students with ADHD (DuPaul et al., 2012a).

Behavioral Peer Interventions

Behavioral contingency management has also shown promise for significantly improving peer relations, which is an area of significant impairment for youth with ADHD. In a recent study conducted by Mikami et al. (2012), teachers implemented behavioral management including praise, individual attention, and messages of acceptance to others with the goal of improving peer acceptance of children with ADHD within a classroom of same-aged peers without ADHD. While there was minimal change in behavior problems, children with ADHD in the experimental condition were significantly less rejected by their peers, had more reciprocated friendships, and received more positive messages by peers at the end of the program as compared to their control group ADHD peers. This suggests that behavioral management techniques implemented by teachers could ameliorate poor peer relationships. Similarly, Mikami et al. (2010) trained parents to become social coaches for their children, whereby parents implemented contingencies to their child for prosocial behavior. Compared to those in the no-treatment control group, those receiving treatment showed significant improvements on parent ratings of social skills and quality of play, and teachers, who were unaware of treatment assignment, also reported improved peer liking and acceptance. This study demonstrated gains in social skills outside of the treatment setting, and that changes are reported by those unaware of treatment.

Training Interventions

Skill-Based Interventions

In this section we review "skill-based" interventions that focus directly on teaching the patient specific skills to address key areas of functional impairments (social problems, disorganization, driving difficulties, etc.). These interventions focus on breaking complicated functional areas into discrete tasks/skills and then employing techniques to teach the patient discrete skills through various methods (e.g., therapist modeling, role-play, etc.). Frequent feedback, monitoring of skills in natural contexts (e.g., school, home, community), and reinforcement are often important aspects of ensuring skills are effectively implemented. Results from a variety of studies focusing on skill-based training have found mixed results depending upon the focus on the intervention.

Traditional social skills interventions often involve specific instruction to the child on various aspects of social skills (e.g., eye contact, appropriate personal space during conversations, assertiveness, etc.). Based on the current literature on traditional social skills training, it is considered to have questionable efficacy (Pelham & Fabiano, 2008). The lack of robust empirical evidence for this type of intervention may be related to variations in length or duration of the treatment as well as the intensity and content of the intervention itself across studies.

Abikoff et al. (2012) developed an organizational skills training intervention for school-age youth with ADHD. The intervention focused on teaching children to use new tools and routines to record assignments, organize school materials, more effectively monitor the amount of time involved in completing assignments, and break larger tasks into smaller, more manageable ones. Parents and teachers were taught to praise children for efforts to use the organizational skills. Results of a randomized clinical trial suggest that, relative to a wait-list control, those receiving the intervention received significantly better ratings of organization as reported by parents and teachers as well as improved academic functioning, homework, and family conflict.

There has also been considerable effort at teaching skills to older youth and adolescents with ADHD for specific functional impairments. As an example, Langberg et al. (2012) adapted an organization intervention for middle school children with ADHD, with results demonstrating significant improvements at posttreatment and at three-month follow-up in parent ratings of organization, homework, and family conflict. Moreover, studies have focused on teaching driving skills to teens (Fabiano et al., 2011) and improving academic readiness (Meyer & Kelley, 2008; Sibley et al., 2013). Importantly, for adolescents with ADHD, key adults (e.g., parents or teachers) must collaborate and support adolescents in the settings in which these youth are to utilize the skills they have learned. Skills-based interventions for specific impairments are indeed a promising intervention modality, particularly for older school-age youth and adolescents with ADHD.

Cognitive-behavioral skills-based intervention (CBSBI) appears to be a promising approach for adults with ADHD (Knouse & Safren, 2013). In CBSI, clear operationally defined treatment goals are identified, followed by a functional analysis to understand how problems arise that impede upon the patient's ability to successfully achieve their goals. A functional analysis should result in selecting strategies to address the barriers to achieving the patient's goals. Attempts to utilize the identified strategy also require the therapist to identify and address the often-observed negative cognitions (e.g., attributions for success/failure, all or none things, etc.) and emotions (e.g., anger) that accompany efforts by a patient to utilize a new skill. Additionally, CBSBI includes psychoeducation about ADHD, efforts at supporting the adult with ADHD to adhere to medication regimens, utilizing significant others (when appropriate) to help support skill implementation, and addressing relapse.

Data from two randomized clinical trials provide support for the CBSBI approach to treating ADHD in adults. Safren et al. (2010) compared an individually delivered CBSBI intervention to relaxation training and educational support for 86 adults with ADHD. Results demonstrated that the CBSBI intervention led to greater improvements in ADHD symptoms, which were maintained at 12-month follow-up assessment. Solanto et al. (2010) compared a group-based CBSBI intervention to a support group for 88 adults with ADHD and also found that the CBSBI intervention resulted in greater improvements in ADHD symptoms. Collectively, findings from these two large randomized clinical trials suggest that CBSBI is viable treatment of ADHD in adults.

There have also been efforts at studying other skill-based interventions for adults with ADHD. Mindfulness-based interventions focus on improving recognition of internal states, allowing individuals greater control over their behaviors/reactions. For adults with ADHD, it is hypothesized that greater recognition of internal states would allow for greater control over attention, impulsivity, and the often co-occurring issues commonly found in adults with ADHD (e.g., mood). Zylowska et al. (2008) and Philipsen et al. (2007) evaluated interventions that focus on mindfulness training in two open clinical trials. Data from these studies suggest that these types of intervention can improve ADHD symptoms in adults, but, given their study design, more rigorous investigation is needed.

In addition to mindfulness-based interventions, ADHD coaching has become an often-utilized approach. The National Resource Center on ADHD describes coaching as "when one person (the coach) provides objective feedback and guidance in an organized and methodical fashion to help another person (the client) address a problem or achieve identified goals" (http://www.help4adhd.org/living/coaching). Although several open trials of ADHD coaching alone (e.g., Kubik et al., 2010;) and coaching with CBSBI (e.g., Stevenson et al., 2003) have been completed, with preliminary results supporting its effects on some areas of functional impairments associated with ADHD, a more rigorous evaluation of ADHD coaching is clearly required.

Neurocognitive Treatments

Given the increasing recognition of the neurocognitive deficits experienced by youth with ADHD and the role of these factors in the longer-term course of ADHD (Halperin and Shultz, 2006), there has been a growing interest in neurocognitive training for the treatment of ADHD. Cogmed Working Memory Training (CWMT) has gained particular interest from the research and clinical community, given the number of randomized clinical trials investigating this intervention for the treatment of ADHD in youth (see Chacko et al., 2013, for a review of these studies). Multiple RCTs have demonstrated some benefit of CWMT, primarily on parent-rated ADHD symptoms and working memory tasks that closely resemble the CWMT training tasks (i.e., near-transfer outcomes). No RCT study of CWMT has demonstrated improvements in ratings from blind raters. In a recently completed RCT, Chacko et al. (2014), utilizing a more rigorously controlled placebo condition, found no differential effects of CWMT on parent/teacher reports of ADHD symptoms, objective measures of attention, impulsivity and activity, or academic achievement outcomes. The lack of significant effects of CWMT is in keeping with the general outcomes found across studies of neurocognitive interventions for youth (school age through adolescence) with ADHD (Rapport et al., 2013). Rapport et al., in a meta-analysis on neurocognitive interventions for youth with ADHD, found that these interventions had no effect on ADHD outcomes. To our knowledge, only three studies have assessed the impact of neurocognitive training in adults with ADHD (Stern et al., 2014; Virta et al., 2010; White & Shah, 2006). In general, these studies find some benefit of the neurocognitive intervention on select neurocognitive outcomes, but no generalization of effects to ADHD symptoms or related impairments in daily life functioning have been found. Collectively, there is much promise that a neurocognitive intervention would alter the underlying pathophysiology of ADHD, resulting in more enduring effects of treatment. This remains a fruitful area of investigation; however, the data suggest that current neurocognitive interventions should not be considered as first- or second-line treatments of ADHD in youth or adults.

Neurofeedback training has also received considerable attention as an intervention for the treatment of ADHD. Although there are numerous uncontrolled trials of neurofeedback, few well-controlled RCTs have been conducted. In a relatively recently completed RCT, Gevensleben et al. (2009) found significant benefits of neurofeedback on parent ratings of ADHD, ODD, and aggression, and teacher ratings of ADHD symptoms. Importantly, there were no significant effects of neurofeedback on social, academic, and home functioning, and the effects of neurofeedback appear to be considerably smaller than what is found for both pharmacological and behavioral approaches to treatment of ADHD. Similarly, Steiner et al. (2014a, 2014b) found benefits of neurofeedback for school-age youth with ADHD, but, similar to Gevensleben et al. (2009), effects were smaller than what has been observed for both psychosocial and pharmacological approaches to treatment of ADHD. Interestingly, however, in a follow-up assessment, youth who were assigned to receive neurofeedback had sustained improvements in functioning relative to those youth assigned to the cognitive training or control conditions. This sustained effect is important, given that ADHD is considered a chronic condition, and interventions that result in improvements over time are essential to treating ADHD. Neurofeedback has also been studied in adults with ADHD; however, with the exception of one group-based uncontrolled study (e.g., Mayer et al., 2012), the extant literature includes only case studies. Although promising, further investigation is warranted before fully appreciating the role of neurofeedback as a treatment for ADHD. Neurofeedback is likely best considered a possibly efficacious second-line treatment for ADHD in youth. For adults, no conclusion can be made regarding the appropriateness of neurofeedback as a treatment option.

Interventions with Spouses/Partners

Spouses/partners of adults with ADHD often encounter significant stress and frustration when dealing with the multitude of daily living problems associated with symptoms of ADHD. Murphy and Barkley (1996) reported that severe marital dissatisfaction is common in couples where one partner has been diagnosed with ADHD. The spouses often felt confused, angry, and frustrated, and complained that their partners were poor listeners, messy, forgetful, unreliable, self-centered, insensitive, and irresponsible. Barkley (2006) suggested that because so many of these behaviors may be directly related to symptoms of ADHD, spouses need to learn that many of these problems may not be secondary to "willful misconduct" (p. 699). Instead, partners of individuals with ADHD need to understand the world from their spouses' perspective, stop blaming them, and align together to fight a "common enemy" (symptoms of ADHD). If both spouses/partners develop a mutual understanding of how symptoms of ADHD affect the relationship, what each partner needs from the other, and that working together greatly improves the relationship, the chances of a positive outcome are enhanced (Dixon, 1995). Although few resources for clinicians specifically address these techniques, some have recently become available (e.g., Kapalka, 2010; Ramsay & Rostain, 2008).

Few studies to date have empirically researched the benefits of these interventions, but some research findings suggest that marital or couple counseling improves core symptoms of ADHD in the "identified patient" and reduces stress on the entire family. Nadeau (1995) recommends the inclusion of couple treatment in the comprehensive management of ADHD, and Hallowell (1995) found that including the spouse improved the overall outcome in treatment of adults with ADHD. In fact, Ratey et al. (1995) reported that couple counseling contributed to symptom reduction, stress reduction, and increased closeness in families where one of the partners was diagnosed with ADHD.

Benefits and Limitations of Psychotherapy as Sole Treatment

Overall, the current state of research in psychosocial treatments for ADHD supports behavioral parent training, behavioral contingency management, and behavioral peer interventions as effective interventions for the treatment of ADHD in preschool- and school-age youth. Some training interventions appear to be gaining considerable efficacy for older youth and adolescents (i.e., organizational skills training) and adults (CBSBI), while some remain promising (i.e., neurofeedback), others have not withstood closer empirical scrutiny (i.e., neurocognitive interventions), and others clearly need more rigorous evaluation (e.g., coaching).

Psychosocial treatments have the benefit of teaching crucial skills to key adults (i.e., parents and teachers) as well as to youth and adults who may reduce the impairment associated with ADHD symptoms. Once these skills are learned, they can theoretically be applied in various settings over time. Importantly, there are no potential health risks associated with psychosocial interventions, although some iatrogenic effects have been reported. As an example, Barkley et al. (2001) found that 10% of parent–adolescent dyads assigned to BPT experienced worsening of functioning following treatment. This finding highlights the importance of applying treatments in a developmentally informed manner and for monitoring treatment progress. Parents strongly prefer psychosocial interventions for the treatment of ADHD (Pelham, 1999), making it a first-line intervention from the perspective of many parents.

Limitations to using psychosocial treatment as a sole approach, however, are that treatment requires ongoing implementation and is relatively intense (interventions must be administered several hours a week) and, arguably, expensive (relative to pharmacological interventions). Similar to pharmacological approaches, there are no data to suggest that acute doses of behavioral interventions have longer-lasting effects on outcomes for youth affected with ADHD, although studies have shown that benefits may last several months after termination of treatment (Barkley, 2006) and treatment may also be associated with long-term reductions in stress evident in the home. Longer-term outcomes of psychosocial treatments for adolescents and adults are limited. But interventions such as neurocognitive training and neurofeedback may offer the opportunity for sustained improvements following treatment. This remains speculative and requires further study. A significant limitation, as noted by AAP (2011), is that in some communities there is a scarcity of practitioners well versed in behavioral interventions for youth with ADHD, making it difficult for families to obtain these evidence-based interventions. This is likely the case as well for psychosocial treatments (i.e., CBSBI) for adults with ADHD.

Combined Treatments

Theoretically, many assert that a combined pharmacological and psychosocial intervention provides the most efficacious treatment for ADHD (Pelham et al., 2000). A number of major studies have been conducted to systematically evaluate combined pharmacological and psychosocial treatments—exclusively in school-age children with ADHD. To our knowledge, unfortunately, there are no systematic evaluations of combined pharmacological and psychosocial treatments for adolescents or adults with ADHD.

Klein et al. (2004) studied 7- to 9-year-old children diagnosed with ADHD without comorbid learning or conduct disorders. Children were divided into three treatment conditions: MPH alone, MPH plus intensive multimodal psychosocial treatment (MPT), and MPH plus attention control psychosocial treatment (ACT). For inclusion, all children were medication-free at the time of enrollment and achieved meaningful improvement in a five-week trial of MPH. In MPT, children, parents, and teachers were involved in treatment. Children received individualized academic assistance, organization and social skills training, and individual psychotherapy. Parents participated in BPT and counseling, and teachers completed daily progress report cards for school behaviors and academic performance. In ACT, children completed individual and group-based nonacademic projects, as well as engaged in open-ended play sessions instead of receiving academic and organizational skills training. Children received general homework assistance, but individualized assessments of academic skills were not assessed, nor were strategies for improving academics discussed (Klein et al., 2004).

One-year outcomes suggested that no differential effects of treatment group were found on any measures of symptoms, functioning, impairment, or threshold of symptoms (Abikoff et al., 2004) as well as academic achievement, homework behavior, or emotional stress (Hechtman et al., 2004a) between treatment groups. Further, after year one, all children were reported to relapse when switched from MPH to placebo, regardless of treatment group. Lastly, Hechtman et al. (2004b) reported on differential treatment effects on parenting practices. Results demonstrated that the MPH plus MPT group had significantly greater improvement in knowledge of behavioral principles, and thus a significant advantage in accomplishing educational goals, compared with the MPH-alone group or the MPH plus ACT group. But no differential treatment effects were found on parent practices scales or children's perception of parental practices in year one. In year two, mothers of children in the MPH plus MPT group rated themselves as having significantly better knowledge of behavioral principles than mothers of children in the MPH plus ACT group; mothers in the MPH-alone group did not differ significantly from those in MPH plus MPT group. Further, no differential treatment effects on parent practices scales or children's perception of parental practices were found. Overall, no evidence was found of superiority of MPH plus MPT over MPH alone with regard to parenting practices. Limitations of this study include the fact that parents, teachers, and psychiatrists were not blinded to treatment in this study, and, given that all youth were required to be MPH responders to be included in the study, it is likely that these outcomes represent more robust effects of MPH than what can be seen in a more general population of youth with ADHD.

The MTA study (MTA Cooperative Group, 1999) is considered a landmark study in ADHD treatment research in youth. Researchers assessed children ages 7–9.9 years (n = 579) diagnosed with ADHD–combined type. Participants were assigned to one of four groups: MPH alone, psychosocial treatment alone, combined MPH plus psychosocial treatment, or standard community care (which often involved stimulant medication). With respect to medication, children were initially treated with various dosages of MPH, and medication was then adjusted to match patients' needs. In the psychosocial conditions, participants received 27 group sessions and 8 individual sessions of BPT over the course of 8 weeks and a summer treatment program (Pelham et al., 2000). Similarly, school-based treatment consisted on 10–16 biweekly teacher sessions focused on classroom behavior management strategies, and 12 weeks of individual behavioral work with child to provide school-based feedback.

Findings have been reported in numerous publications. In general, combined treatment and MPH-alone interventions did not differ clinically or statistically with regard to degree of improvement of ADHD symptoms, and both were statistically superior to behavioral treatment alone and community care. For other outcomes—such as oppositional symptoms, internalizing symptoms, social skills, parent–child relationships, and academic functioning—only the combined intervention was statistically superior to the community control condition on some outcomes (MTA Cooperative Group, 1999). Secondary analyses showed that the combined treatment was significantly better than the other treatments, with comparable effect sizes ranging from 0.28 to 0.7 for MPH alone and community control groups, respectively.

There has been considerable debate regarding the interpretation of the MTA findings, given the clinical implications. For instance, Greene and Ablon (2001) reported differences in the degree to which pharmacological and psychosocial treatments were adjusted to match the needs of children. With respect to medication, children were initially treated with various dosages of MPH, and medication was then adjusted to match patients' needs. In the psychosocial conditions, however, most aspects remained the same regardless of assessed need; all participants received the same behavioral intervention package. Moreover, Pelham (1999) notes that the main 14-month outcomes of the MTA study compared active MPH to a faded behavioral intervention package (i.e., the intensity of behavioral interventions were considerably reduced at the immediate posttreatment assessment). As such, the 14-month post-MTA analyses are not an accurate assessment comparing active MPH to active behavioral intervention. Moreover, when considering the dosage of interventions being compared, the immediate posttreatment findings suggest that faded behavioral interventions can provide quite robust effects. The fact that there were no differences between the behavioral intervention treatment arm and the standard community practice (many of whom received MPH), for example, suggests that behavioral intervention, even when not acutely administered, can have equivalent effects to actively administered MPH in the community setting. Interestingly, in other studies assessing combined pharmacological and psychosocial interventions, there are greater nuances that shed light on combined approaches to treatment of ADHD. Others have demonstrated that, when intensive behavioral interventions are in place, there are limited benefits of MPH on outcomes (Pelham et al., 2005), or MPH can be significantly reduced when utilized in the context of ongoing behavioral interventions (Chacko et al., 2005), which may be important when considering long-term treatment for youth with ADHD.

Benefits and Limitations of Combined Treatments

Combined treatments (i.e., select pharmacological and behavioral interventions) offer complementary effects on ADHD symptoms and associated impairments in school-age youth with ADHD. A combined approach also offers the benefits that each modality offers (e.g., skill building, effects on various domains of functioning, etc.). Combined approaches provide an opportunity to reduce the intensity of both pharmacological and behavioral interventions, thereby providing a more feasible model for implementation over time.

As with any multimodal intervention package, however, complexity is a limitation to its widespread use. Providing the type of intensive behavioral intervention implemented in the studies reviewed requires a team of professionals, coordinating services across settings and time, and involvement by multiple stakeholders (i.e., parents, teachers, and the affected youth). The ability of routine service providers and settings to implement these types of treatment regimens is a critical yet understudied issue.

Summary and Recommendations

The literature on ADHD intervention is substantial and ever growing. Although the field has identified a select number of interventions, there is continued interest in developing and evaluating alternative interventions, given that no intervention has resulted in generalized and sustained effects on all relevant functional outcomes that are often impaired in individuals with ADHD. In this regard, future research should continue to evaluate promising interventions (e.g., neurofeedback, coaching, couples counseling), address limitations of interventions that have the high potential to treat ADHD but have yet to be shown to be effective (e.g., neurocognitive training), and study further the combination of interventions that may have complementary or augmentative effects on functional outcomes. In particular, the combined treatment literature for the treatment of adolescents and adults with ADHD requires systematic evaluation.

Clinically, it appears that for preschool- and school-age children, pharmacological and psychosocial—specifically behaviorally focused— treatments are available that offer clear and robust effects on ADHD symptoms and related impairments, at least over the short term when treatment is being actively implemented. Which intervention modality to begin treatment with (pharmacological or psychosocial or both), at what intensity/ dose, and for how long treatment should last are important decisions that require active collaboration between the patient, key adults in the patients' life (e.g., parents, teachers, spouses/partners), and the treating professionals. In particular, understanding adult preferences and attitudes for implementing behaviorally focused interventions is critical, given the substantial involvement by these adults to implement treatment. For adolescents, the literature suggests that skill-based behaviorally oriented interventions that focus intensely on specific areas of functional impairment (e.g., homework completion, organization, etc.) and support the adolescent in learning specific skills and approaches to use collaboratively with the monitoring and support of adults (i.e., parent and teachers) constitute an effective approach. Similarly, CBSBI is a first-line intervention for adult ADHD, and treatment manuals for CBSBI are now commercially available. Pharmacological interventions are also effective for both adolescents and adults with ADHD, but adherence (particularly over the longer term) to medication is a notable challenge in these populations, suggesting that if pharmacological treatment is being utilized in these age groups, efforts must be made to identify barriers to medication adherence and collaborative efforts.

Thomas was a 5-year-old Caucasian male diagnosed with ADHD– combined type and oppositional defiant disorder. Kyle was experiencing significant difficulty in both home settings (mother and father were divorced and shared custody) and at school. In accordance with guidelines for the treatment of ADHD in young children (AAP, 2011) and the parents' own preferences, a course of BPT and

(continued)

(continued)

behaviorally based school consultation were implemented as first-line interventions. BPT consisted of a nine-week group-based intervention focusing on common BPT content (e.g., positive attending, planned ignoring, incentive systems, time-out from positive reinforcement, school–home daily notes, etc.). Behaviorally based school consultation consisted of six individual teacher–therapist consultation meetings, which implemented a behavioral tracking and reinforcement system (i.e., DRC with school and home-based contingent rewards based on school goals). Ongoing monitoring of response was done by utilizing the DRC. As described above, the DRC is a behavioral intervention tool *and* an assessment measure that targets specific areas of impairment that a child demonstrates in a particular setting. The DRC is developed by collaborating with the key figures in each child's setting to determine what specific difficulties a child is having and establishing behavioral criteria for success for each behavior. This behavioral criterion is determined by taking baseline rates of the specific behavior plus or −30% to encourage improvement. Separate DRCs were developed for Thomas when he was at his mother's home, his father's home, and at school. The DRC represents a simple, flexible tool that should be utilized as a standard component of behaviorally focused treatment for youth with ADHD.

Across all three settings, Thomas was exhibiting significant ADHD symptoms, including distractibility, interrupting, and hyperactivity. Additionally, significant oppositional behaviors (rule breaking, arguing, noncompliance) were evident in both home settings. As a first step in behaviorally focused treatment, the therapist collaborated with the parents and teacher on identifying how the symptoms of ADHD and ODD were impairing Thomas's functioning. Objectively defined functional outcomes (e.g., completing independent seatwork at school within a certain number of reminders, completing bedtime routine within a certain number of reminders) were incorporated into a DRC. Across all settings, the baseline DRC suggested that Thomas was attaining only approximately 10% of identified goals. Following behavioral parent training and school consultation, Thomas was attaining his goals over 60% of the time at school and at his mother's home. Attainment of DRC goals did not improve at the father's home, but this is not surprising, given that the father attended few BPT treatment sessions. Despite Thomas's significant improvements, particularly on child-specific targets of functional impairments (i.e., DRC goals), parents hoped for further incremental benefits and requested a trial of medication.

A stimulant medication treatment is often completed under the close supervision of a physician. One may assume that there is little role for a therapist in the assessment of medication. But pharmacological treatment for ADHD is often administered by a primary care physician (AAP, 2011) who may not have the time or resources to efficiently monitor treatment progress and obtain objective information on the effects of medication across various settings. In this regard, a behaviorally focused therapist plays an important role in collaborating with the primary care physician, the family, and the teacher to provide important information on the efficacy of pharmacological treatment for ADHD. As discussed, a DRC is a useful and flexible tool for ongoing assessment and treatment monitoring. It is equally effective when used to monitor medication response. In particular, we have found that utilizing a DRC allows for assessing the specific effects of medication on important, operationally defined functional outcomes across various key settings. This type of information is helpful for parents when working with a primary care physician to help decide whether medication is an appropriate treatment and at what dose.

In collaboration with the family, teacher, and prescribing physician, various doses of stimulant medications (i.e., Adderall-XR) within the context of ongoing behavioral intervention were assessed using a DRC as a monitoring tool. Based on the DRC, an interesting pattern of data emerged that reflected the effect of this combined treatment approach. The DRC data across settings indicated a beneficial effect of medication, with the 5-mg dose maximizing success with little incremental benefit of higher doses at school and the mother's home setting. But the DRC data suggested that a 10-mg dose was necessary to maximize treatment benefits in the father's home setting. Given this information, the 5-mg dose of medication was recommended for Thomas, and instead of increasing medications, Thomas's father committed to participate in a trial of BPT to attempt to obtain the same types of benefits evinced in the school and the mother's home setting. Ultimately, the longer-term treatment consisted of a BPT for Thomas's father, monthly ongoing support at school, support for Thomas's mother to continue to implement behavioral interventions, and maintenance of 5 mg of Adderall-XR. Six-month follow-up data suggested that there was maintenance of treatment gains across the mother's home setting and school and improvements in the father's home setting following the father's successful completion of BPT. As such, these outcomes represent the effect of combined evidence-based psychosocial and pharmacological treatment.

Herein we described a case of a preschool child where a combined treatment approach including both behavioral interventions (school and home based) and, subsequently, stimulant medication

(continued)

(continued)

was utilized. Combined (and sequenced) treatment was utilized to address parent preferences for prioritizing the treatment of functional impairments with further consideration for stimulant medication based on response to behavioral interventions. We have found that prioritizing parent preference for which evidence-based treatment to utilize is important given the relationship between patient preference, adherence to treatment, and efficacy of treatment. Additionally, there is often a need to address insufficient response following a unimodal treatment regimen. As such, medication was utilized, and optimal response resulted from administering combined psychosocial and pharmacological treatments.

References

Abikoff, H., et al. (2004). Symptomatic improvement in children with ADHD treated with long-term methylphenidate and multimodal psychosocial treatment. *Journal of the American Academy of Child and Adolescent Psychiatry, 43*(7), 802–811. doi:10.1097/01.chi.0000128791.10014.ac

Abikoff, H., et al. (2012). Remediating organizational functioning in children with ADHD: Immediate and longterm effects from a randomized controlled trial. *Journal of Consulting and Clinical Psychology, 81*, 113–128.

Adler, L. A., et al. (2011). Medication adherence and symptom reduction in adults treated with mixed amphetamine salts in a randomized crossover study. *Postgraduate Medicine, 123*, 71–79.

American Academy of Pediatrics Committee on Quality Improvement and Subcommittee on Attention-Deficit/Hyperactivity Disorder. (2011). ADHD: Clinical practice guideline for the diagnosis, evaluation, and treatment of attention-deficit/hyperactivity disorder in children and adolescents. *Pediatrics, 128*, 1–16.

Amiri, S., et al. (2008). Modafinil as a treatment for attention-deficit/hyperactivity disorder in children and adolescents: A double blind, randomized clinical trial. *Progress in Neuropsychopharmacology and Biological Psychiatry, 32*, 145–149.

Anastopoulos, A. D., et al. (1993). Parent training for attention deficit hyperactivity disorder: Its impact on parent functioning. *Journal of Abnormal Child Psychology, 21*, 581–596.

APA. American Psychiatric Association. (2013). *Diagnostic and statistical manual of mental disorders* (5th ed.). Washington, DC: Author.

Barkley, R. A. (2006). *Attention-deficit hyperactivity disorder: A handbook for diagnosis and treatment* (3rd ed.). New York: Guilford Press.

Barkley, R. A. (2013). *Taking charge of ADHD.* New York: Guilford Press.

Barkley, R. A., et al. (2001). The efficacy of problem-solving communication training alone, behavior management training alone, and their combination for parent–adolescent conflict in teenagers with ADHD and ODD. *Journal of Consulting and Clinical Psychology, 69*, 926–941.

Biederman, J., et al. (2002). A randomized, double-blind, placebo-controlled, parallel-group study of SLI381 (Adderall XR) in children with attention-deficit/hyperactivity disorder. *Pediatrics, 110*, 258–266.

Biederman, J., et al. (2007a). Lisdexamfetamine dimesylate and mixed amphetamine salts extended-release in children with ADHD: A double-blind, placebo-controlled, crossover analog classroom study. *Biological Psychiatry, 62,* 970–976.

Biederman, J., et al. (2007b). Efficacy and tolerability of lisdexamfetamine dimesylate (NRP-104) in children with attention-deficit/hyperactivity disorder: A phase III, multicenter, randomized, double-blind, forced-dose, parallel-group study. *Clinical Therapeutics, 29,* 450–463.

Biederman, J., et al. (2008). A randomized, double-blind, placebo-controlled study of guanfacine extended release in children and adolescents with attention-deficit/hyperactivity disorder. *Pediatrics, 121*(1), e73–84.

Bitter, I., et al., (2012). Pharmacological treatment of adult ADHD. *Current Opinion in Psychiatry, 25,* 529–534.

Brown, T. E., et al. (2011). Effect of atomoxetine on executive function impairments in adults with ADHD. *Journal of Attention Disorders, 15,* 130–138.

Chacko, A., et al. (2005). Stimulant medication effects in a summer treatment program among young children with attention-deficit/hyperactivity disorder. *Journal of the American Academy of Child and Adolescent Psychiatry, 44,* 249–257.

Chacko, A., et al. (2009). Enhancing traditional behavioral parent training for single mothers of children with ADHD. *Journal of Clinical Child and Adolescent Psychology, 38,* 206–218.

Chacko, A., et al. (2010). Improving medication adherence in chronic pediatric health conditions: A focus on ADHD in youth. *Current Pharmaceutical Design, 16,* 2416–2423.

Chacko, A., et al. (2013). Cogmed working memory training for youth with ADHD: A closer examination of efficacy utilizing evidence-based criteria. *Journal of Clinical Child and Adolescent Psychology, 42,* 769–783. doi:10.1080/15374416.2013.787622

Chacko, A., et al. (2014). A randomized clinical trial of Cogmed Working Memory Training in school-age children with ADHD: A replication in a diverse sample using a control condition. *Journal of Child Psychology and Psychiatry, 55,* 247–255. doi:10.1111/jcpp.12146

Chavez, B., et al. (2009). An update on central nervous system stimulant formulations in children and adolescents with attention-deficit/hyperactivity disorder. *Annals of Pharmacotherapy, 43,* 1084–1095.

Childress, A. C., et al. (2009). Efficacy and safety of dexmethylphenidate extended-release capsules administered once daily to children with attention-deficit/hyperactivity disorder. *Journal of Child and Adolescent Psychopharmacology, 19,* 351–361.

Dixon, E. B. (1995). Impact of adult ADD on the family. In K. Nadeau (Ed.), *A comprehensive guide to attention deficit hyperactivity disorder in adults* (pp. 236–259). New York: Brunner/Mazel.

DuPaul, G. J., et al. (2012a). The effects of school-based interventions for attention deficit hyperactivity disorder: A meta-analysis 1996–2010. *School Psychology Review, 41,* 387–412.

DuPaul, G. J., et al. (2012b). Double-blind, placebo-controlled, crossover study of the efficacy and safety of lisdexamfetamine dimesylate in college students with ADHD. *Journal of Attention Disorders, 16,* 202–220.

Evans, S.,W., et al. (2001). Dose–response effects of methylphenidate on ecologically valid measures of academic performance and classroom behavior in adolescents with ADHD. *Experimental and Clinical Psychopharmacology, 9,* 163–175.

Evans, S. W., et al. (2014). Evidence-based psychosocial treatments for children and adolescents with attention-deficit/hyperactivity disorder. *Journal of Clinical Child and Adolescent Psychology, 43*(4), 527–551.

Fabiano, G. A., et al. (2004). An evaluation of three time out procedures for children with attention-deficit-hyperactivity disorder. *Behavior Therapy, 35*, 449–469.

Fabiano, G. A., et al. (2009). A meta-analysis of behavioral treatments for attention deficit/hyperactivity disorder. *Clinical Psychology Review, 29*, 129–140.

Fabiano, G. A., et al. (2010). Enhancing the effectiveness of special education programming for children with attention deficit hyperactivity disorder using a daily report card. *School Psychology Review, 39*, 219–239.

Fabiano, G. A., et al. (2011). The Supporting a Teen's Effective Entry to the Roadway (STEER) program: Feasibility and preliminary support for a psychosocial intervention for teenage drivers with ADHD. *Cognitive and Behavioral Practice, 18*, 267–280.

Fabiano, G. A., et al. (2012). A waitlist-controlled trail of behavioral parent training for fathers of children with ADHD. *Journal of Clinical Child and Adolescent Psychology, 41*, 337–345.

Faraone, S. V., et al. (2003). The worldwide prevalence of ADHD: Is it an American condition? *World Psychiatry, 2*(2), 104.

Findling, R. L., et al. (2010). A randomized, double-blind, multicenter, parallel-group, placebo-controlled, dose-optimization study of the methylphenidate transdermal system for the treatment of ADHD in adolescents. *CNS Spectrum, 15*, 419–430.

Findling, R. L., et al. (2011). Efficacy and safety of lisdexamfetamine dimesylate in adolescents with attention-deficit/hyperactivity disorder. *Journal of the American Academy of Child and Adolescent Psychiatry, 50*, 395–405.

Gevensleben, H., et al. (2009). Distinct EEG effects related to neurofeedback training in children with ADHD: A randomized controlled trial. *International Journal of Psychophysiology, 74*, 149–157.

Greene, R. W., & Ablon, J. S. (2001). What does the MTA study tell us about effective psychosocial treatment for ADHD? *Journal of Clinical Child Psychology, 30*, 114–121.

Greenhill, L., et al. (2006a). Efficacy and safety of immediate-release methylphenidate treatment for preschoolers with ADHD. *Journal of the American Academy of Child and Adolescent Psychiatry, 45*, 1284–1293.

Greenhill, L., et al. (2006b). A randomized, double-blind, placebo-controlled study of modafinil film-coated tablets in children and adolescents with attention-deficit/hyperactivity disorder. *Journal of the American Academy of Child and Adolescent Psychiatry, 45*, 503–511.

Hallowell, E. M. (1995). Psychotherapy of adult attention deficit disorder. In K. Nadeau (Ed.), *A comprehensive guide to attention deficit hyperactivity disorder in adults* (pp. 144–167). New York: Brunner/Mazel.

Halperin, J. J., & Schulz, K. P. (2006). Revisiting the role of the prefrontal cortex in the pathophysiology of attention-deficit/hyperactivity disorder. *Psychological Bulletin, 132*, 560–581.

Hazell, P. L., et al. (2011). Core ADHD symptom improvement with atomoxetine versus methylphenidate: A direct comparison meta-analysis. *Journal of Attention Disorders, 15*, 674–683.

Hechtman, L., et al. (2004a). Academic achievement and emotional status of children with ADHD treated with long-term methylphenidate and multimodal psychosocial treatment. *Journal of the American Academy of Child and Adolescent Psychiatry, 43*, 812–819.

Hechtman, L., et al. (2004b). Children with ADHD treated with long-term methylphenidate and multimodal psychosocial treatment: Impact on parental practices. *Journal of the American Academy of Child and Adolescent Psychiatry, 43,* 830–838.

Hinshaw, S. P., & Arnold, L. E. (2014). Attention-deficit hyperactivity disorder, multimodal treatment, and longitudinal outcome: Evidence, paradox, and challenge. *WIREs Cognitive Science.* doi:10.1002/wcs.124

Hoza, B., et al. (2005). Peer-assessed outcomes in the Multimodal Treatment Study of children with attention deficit hyperactivity disorder. *Journal of Clinical Child and Adolescent Psychology, 34,* 74–86.

Huang, Y. S., & Tsai, M. H. (2011). Long-term outcomes with medications for attention-deficit hyperactivity disorder: Current status of knowledge. *CNS Drugs, 25,* 539–554.

Jain, R., et al. (2011). Clonidine extended-release tablets for pediatric patients with attention-deficit/hyperactivity disorder. *Journal of the American Academy of Child and Adolescent Psychiatry, 50,* 171–179.

Jensen, P. S., et al. (2001). Findings from the NIMH multimodal treatment study of ADHD (MTA): Implications and applications for primary care providers. *Developmental and Behavioral Pediatrics, 22,* 60–73.

Kapalka, G. M. (2007). *Parenting your out-of-control child.* Oakland, CA: New Harbinger.

Kapalka, G. M. (2009). *Eight steps to classroom management success.* Thousand Oaks, CA: Corwin.

Kapalka, G. M. (2010). *Counseling boys and men with ADHD.* New York: Routledge.

Klein, R. G., et al. (2004). Design and rationale of controlled study of long-term methylphenidare and multimodal psychosocial treatment in children with ADHD. *Journal of the American Academy of Child and Adolescent Psychiatry, 43,* 792–801.

Knouse, L. E., & Safren, S. A. (2013). Psychosocial treatment for adult ADHD. In C. Surman (Ed.), *ADHD in adults: A practical guide to evaluation and management* (pp. 119–136). New York: Humana Press.

Kollins, S. H., et al. (2011). Clonidine extended-release tablets as add-on therapy to psychostimulants in children and adolescents with ADHD. *Pediatrics, 127,* e1406–1413.

Kratochvil, C. J., et al. (2006). Effects of long-term atomoxetine treatment for young children with attention-deficit/hyperactivity disorder. *Journal of the American Academy of Child and Adolescent Psychiatry, 45,* 919–927.

Kratochvil, C. J., et al. (2011). A double-blind, placebo-controlled study of atomoxetine in young children with ADHD. *Pediatrics, 127,* e862–868.

Kubik, J. A. (201). Efficacy of ADHD coaching for adults with ADHD. *Journal of Attention Disorders, 13,* 442–453.

Lahey, B. B., et al. (2005). Instability of the DSM-IV subtypes of ADHD from preschool through elementary school. *Archives of General Psychiatry, 62*(8), 896–902.

Langberg, J. M., & Becker, S. P. (2012). Does long-term medication use improve the academic outcomes of youth with attention-deficit/hyperactivity disorder? *Clinical Child and Family Psychology Review, 15*(3), 215–233.

Langberg, J. M., et al. (2012). Evaluation of the homework, organization, and planning skills (HOPS) intervention for middle school students with attention deficits hyperactivity disorder as implemented by school mental health providers. *School Psychology Review, 41,* 342–364.

Marchant, B. K., et al. (2011a). Methylphenidate transdermal system in adult ADHD and impact on emotional and oppositional symptoms. *Journal of Attention Disorders, 15,* 295–304.

Marchant, B. K., et al. (2011b). Long-term open-label response to atomoxetine in adult ADHD: Influence of sex, emotional dysregulation, and double-blind response to atomoxetine. *Journal of Attention Disorders, 3,* 237–244.

May, D. E., & Kratochvil, C. J. (2010). Attention-deficit hyperactivity disorder: Recent advances in paediatric pharmacotherapy. *Drugs, 70*(1), 15–40.

Mayer, K., et al. (2012). Neurofeedback for adult attention-deficit/hyperactivity disorder: Investigation of slow cortical potential neurofeedback—Preliminary results. *Journal of Neurotherapy, 16,* 37–45.

McGough, J. J., et al. (2005). Long-term tolerability and effectiveness of once-daily mixed amphetamine salts (Adderall XR) in children with ADHD. *Journal of the American Academy of Child and Adolescent Psychiatry, 44,* 530–538.

Meyer, K., & Kelley, M. L. (2008). Improving homework in adolescents with attention-deficit/hyperactivity disorder: Self vs. parent monitoring of homework behavior and study skills. *Child and Family Behavior Therapy, 29,* 25–42.

Michelson, D., et al. (2001). Atomoxetine in the treatment of children and adolescents with attention-deficit/hyperactivity disorder: A randomized, placebo-controlled, dose-response study. *Pediatrics, 108,* E83.

Michelson, D., et al. (2004). Relapse prevention in pediatric patients with ADHD treated with atomoxetine: A randomized, double-blind, placebo-controlled study. *Journal of the American Academy of Child and Adolescent Psychiatry, 43,* 896–904.

Mikami, A. Y., et al. (2010). Parental influence on children with attention-deficit/ hyperactivity disorder: II. Results of a pilot intervention training parents as friendship coaches for children. *Journal of Abnormal Child Psychology, 38,* 737–749.

Mikami, A. Y., et al. (2012). A randomized trial of a classroom intervention to increase peers' social inclusion of children with attention-deficit/hyperactivity disorder. *Journal of Consulting and Clinical Psychology, 81,* 100–112.

Miranda, A., et al. (2002). Effectiveness of a school-based multicomponent program for the treatment of children with ADHD. *Journal of Learning Disabilities, 35,* 546–562.

Mohammadi, M., & Akhondzadeh, S. (2011). Advances and considerations in attention-deficit/hyperactivity disorder pharmacotherapy. *Acta Medica Iranica, 49,* 487–498.

MTA Cooperative Group. (1999). A 14-month randomized clinical trial of treatment strategies for attention-deficit/hyperactivity disorder. *Archives of General Psychiatry, 56,* 1073–1086.

Muniz, R., et al. (2008). Efficacy and safety of extended-release dexmethylphenidate compared with d,l-methylphenidate and placebo in the treatment of children with attention-deficit/hyperactivity disorder: A 12-hour laboratory classroom study. *Journal of Child and Adolescent Psychopharmacology, 18,* 248–256.

Murphy, K., & Barkley, R. A. (1996). Attention deficit hyperactivity disorder in adults. *Comprehensive Psychiatry, 37,* 393–401.

Nadeau, K. G. (Ed.). (1995). *A comprehensive guide to attention deficit hyperactivity disorder in adults.* New York: Brunner/Mazel.

Newcorn, J. H., et al. (2008). Atomoxetine and osmotically released methylphenidate for the treatment of attention deficit hyperactivity disorder: Acute comparison and differential response. *American Journal of Psychiatry, 165,* 721–730.

Olfson, M., et al. (2007). Continuity in methylphenidate treatment of adults with attention-deficit/hyperactivity disorder. *Journal of Managed Care Pharmacy, 13,* 570–577.

Pelham, W. E. (1999). The NIMH multimodal treatment study for attention-deficit hyperactivity disorder: Just say yes to drugs alone? *Canadian Journal of Psychiatry, 44,* 981–990.

Pelham, W. E., & Fabiano, G. A. (2008). Evidence-based psychosocial treatments for attention deficit/hyperactivity disorder. *Journal of Clinical Child and Adolescent Psychology, 37*, 184–214.

Pelham, W. E., et al. (2000). Behavioral versus behavioral and pharmacological treatment in ADHD children attending a summer treatment program. *Journal of Abnormal Child Psychology, 28*, 507–525.

Pelham, W. E., et al. (2005). Transdermal methylphenidate, behavioral, and combined treatment for children with ADHD. *Experimental and Clinical Psychopharmacology, 13*, 111–126.

Philipsen, A., et al. (2007). Structured group psychotherapy in adults with attention deficit hyperactivity disorder: Results of an open multicentre study. *Journal of Nervous and Mental Disease, 195*, 1013–1019.

Rajwan, E., et al. (2012). Non-pharmacological intervention for preschool ADHD: State of the evidence and implications for practice. *Professional Psychology: Research and Practice, 43*, 520–526.

Ramsay, J. R., & Rostain, A. L. (2008). *Cognitive-behavioral therapy for adult ADHD: An integrative psychosocial and medical approach.* New York: Routledge.

Rapport, M. D., et al. (2013). Do programs designed to train working memory, other executive functions, and attention benefit children with ADHD? A meta-analytic review of cognitive, academic, and behavioral outcomes. *Clinical Psychology Review, 33*(8), 1237–1252.

Ratey, J. J., et al. (1995). Relationship dilemmas for adults with ADD. In K. Nadeau (Ed.), *A comprehensive guide to attention deficit hyperactivity disorder in adults* (pp. 218–235). New York: Brunner/Mazel.

Retz, W., et al. (2011). Pharmacological treatment of adult ADHD in Europe. *World Journal of Biological Psychiatry,* Suppl. 1, 89–94.

Safren, S. A., et al. (2010). Cognitive behavioral therapy vs. relaxation with educational support for medication-treated adults with ADHD and persistent symptoms. *Journal of the American Medical Association, 304*, 857–880.

Sallee, F. R., et al. (2009). Guanfacine extended release in children and adolescents with attention-deficit/hyperactivity disorder: A placebo-controlled trial. *Journal of the American Academy of Child and Adolescent Psychiatry, 48*, 155–165.

Sallee, F. R., et al. (2012). Efficacy of guanfacine extended release in the treatment of combined and inattentive only subtypes of attention-deficit/hyperactivity disorder. *Journal of Child and Adolescent Psychopharmacology, 22*, 206–214.

Sibley, M. H., et al. (2013). A pilot trial of Supporting Teens' Academic Needs Daily (STAND): A parent-adolescent collaborative intervention for ADHD. *Journal of Psychopathology and Behavioral Assessment, 35*, 436–449.

Silva, R., et al. (2008). Treatment of children with attention-deficit/hyperactivity disorder: Results of a randomized, multicenter, double-blind, crossover study of extended-release dexmethylphenidate and D,L-methylphenidate and placebo in a laboratory classroom setting. *Psychopharmacology Bulletin, 41*, 19–33.

Solanto, M. V., et al. (2010). Efficacy of metacognitive therapy for adult ADHD. *American Journal of Psychiatry, 167*, 958–968.

Spencer, T. J., et al. (2006). Efficacy and safety of mixed amphetamine salts extended release (Adderall XR) in the management of attention-deficit/hyperactivity disorder in adolescent patients: A 4-week, randomized, double-blind, placebo-controlled, parallel-group study. *Clinical Therapeutics, 28*, 266–279.

Spencer, T. J., et al. (2011). A randomized, single-blind, substitution study of OROS methylphenidate (Concerta) in ADHD adults receiving immediate release methylphenidate. *Journal of Attention Disorders, 15,* 286–294.

Steiner, N. J., et al. (2014a). Neurofeedback and cognitive attention training for children with attention-deficit hyperactivity disorder in schools. *Journal of Developmental and Behavioral Pediatrics, 35*(1), 18–27.

Steiner, N. J., et al. (2014b). In-school neurofeedback training for ADHD: Sustained improvements from a randomized control trial. *Pediatrics, 133*(3), 483–492.

Stern, A., et al. (2014). The efficacy of computerized cognitive training in adults with ADHD: A randomized controlled trial. *Journal of Attention Disorders.* doi:10.1177.1087054714529815

Stevenson, C. S., et al. (2003). A self-directed psychosocial intervention with minimal therapist contact for adults with attention deficit hyperactivity disorder. *Clinical Psychology and Psychotherapy, 10,* 93–101.

Surman, C. B. H., et al, (2013). Do stimulants improve functioning in adults with ADHD? A review of the literature. *European Neuropsychopharmacology, 23,* 528–533.

Virta, M., et al. (2010). Short cognitive behavioral therapy and cognitive training for adults with ADHD—A randomized controlled pilot study. *Neuropsychiatric Disease and Treatment, 6,* 443–453.

White, H. A., & Shah, P. (2006). Training attention-switching ability in adults with ADHD. *Journal of Attention Disorders, 10,* 44–53.

Wigal, T. E., et al. (2010). Randomized, double-blind, placebo controlled, cross-over study of the efficacy and safety of lisdexamfetamine dimesylate in adults with attention-deficit/hyperactivity disorder: Novel findings using a simulated adult workplace environment design. *Behavior and Brain Functioning, 6,* 34–45.

Wilens, T. E., et al. (2006a). Multisite controlled study of OROS methylphenidate in the treatment of adolescents with attention-deficit/hyperactivity disorder. *Archives of Pediatrics and Adolescent Medicine, 160,* 82–91.

Wilens, T. E., et al. (2006b). Long-term atomoxetine treatment in adolescents with attention-deficit/hyperactivity disorder. *Journal of Pediatrics, 149,* 112–119.

Wilens, T. E., et al. (2008). Varying the wear time of the methylphenidate transdermal system in children with attention-deficit/hyperactivity disorder. *Journal of the American Academy of Child and Adolescent Psychiatry, 47,* 700–708.

Wilens, T. E., et al. (2012). A controlled trial of extended-release guanfacine and psychostimulants for attention-deficit/hyperactivity disorder. *Journal of the American Academy of Child and Adolescent Psychiatry, 51,* 74–85.e72.

Wolraich, M. L., et al.(2001). Randomized, controlled trial of oros methylphenidate once a day in children with attention-deficit/hyperactivity disorder. *Pediatrics, 108,* 883–892.

Wu, E. Q., et al. (2012). Cost effectiveness of pharmacotherapies for attention-deficit hyperactivity disorder: A systematic literature review. *CNS Drugs, 26,* 581–600.

Zylowska, L., et al. (2008). Mindfulness meditation training in adults and adolescents with ADHD: A feasibility study. *Journal of Attention Disorders, 11,* 737–746.

6 Oppositional Defiant Disorder

David F. Curtis, Sara R. Elkins,
Samantha Miller, Margaret J. Areizaga,
Elizabeth Brestan-Knight, and
Timothy Thornberry

Oppositional defiant disorder (ODD) is a behavioral condition, occur-ring predominantly in children and adolescents, that consists of strongly embedded patterns of negative reactions to authority, willful noncompli-ance, irritable mood, and negative attention-seeking behaviors (Steiner et al., 2007; Stringaris et al., 2010). The current *Diagnostic and Statistical Manual of Mental Disorders*, 5th edition (DSM-5; American Psychiatric Association [APA], 2013) reports that ODD affects approximately 3.3% of all children and adolescents, with a lifetime prevalence of 12.6%. In addi-tion, problems related to ODD are often severely impairing and co-occur with attention-deficit/hyperactivity disorder (ADHD), anxiety disorders, and mood-related conditions (Martel et al., 2012). Because of their dis-ruptive nature and high comorbidity with other conditions, ODD-related problems have a negative effect not only on individuals' daily functioning but also upon their relationships with peers, family members, teachers, and other caregivers (Greene et al., 2002). Consequently, effective evalu-ation and determination of appropriate treatment targets for ODD can be challenging and complex clinical endeavors.

Diagnostic Considerations

There are currently two primary symptom categories used to diagnose ODD: externalizing behavior problems and negative emotions (Frick & Nigg, 2012). ODD was first included in DSM-III in 1980, at that time requiring at least two of the following behaviors: minor rule violations, temper tantrums, argumentativeness, provocative behavior, or stubborn-ness (APA, 1980). Empirical examination of these problems has subse-quently led to an expanded description of symptoms over time (Angold & Costello, 1996; Stringaris et al., 2010). There are currently eight symp-toms of ODD listed in the DSM-5 that include: (1) arguing with author-ity figures or adults; (2) actively defying or refusing to comply with rules/requests from authority figures; (3) deliberately annoying others; (4) blaming others for own mistakes or misbehaviors; (5) prone to being touchy, irritable, or easily annoyed; (6) easily losing temper; (7) often being angry and resentful; and (8) being spiteful or vindictive at least twice within six months (APA, 2013, p. 462). For a diagnosis of ODD to be considered, the presence of four or more symptoms is required for a period of at least six months. Symptoms also must present with a frequency and persistence that exceed similar behaviors in typically developing peers (i.e., contribute to significant distress and impaired social, educational, or occupational functioning). Further, the primary problems associated with ODD are distinct from other conditions in that they frequently violate the rights of others.

While ODD symptoms do not necessarily need to be pervasive across settings, new to the DSM-5 diagnosis is a specifier of symptom severity that is based upon the cross-situational nature of impairments (Frick & Nigg, 2012). ODD diagnoses are thus further qualified as mild (limited to one primary setting), moderate (present across at least two settings), and severe (presenting in three or more settings; APA, 2013).

Prevalence and Course

Disruptive behavior disorders such as ODD are considered to be the most prevalent childhood psychiatric conditions in need of psychological services (Olfson et al., 2014). Though generally a high base rate condition overall, the prevalence of ODD reported across clinical studies varies widely (1%–11%). Data from community samples suggest that its prevalence may reach as high as 15.6% in some populations (Munkvold et al., 2011). Studies of outpatient settings report a high proportion of clinical presentations of ODD, owing to its high rate of referral, ranging from 28% to 65% (Boylan et al., 2007). There are also notable differences in the presentation of ODD based upon age, gender, and environmental factors.

With regard to age, ODD symptoms typically arise during preschool years and seldom present later than adolescence. Though researchers believe that individual child temperament influences ODD, there are no known biological or genetic predictors specific to the disorder (Loeber et al., 2009). Although ODD symptoms often present early, the nature and severity of these symptoms often change in adolescence and early adulthood. In fact, a distinct developmental relationship has been established between ODD and both conduct disorder (CD) and depression (Burke et al., 2010; Rowe et al., 2010).

Reported gender differences in ODD suggest that boys meet criteria more frequently than girls (1.4:1 in preschool and elementary school years; APA, 2013). But gender differences appear to dissipate in adolescence and beyond (Munkvold et al., 2011). While girls appear to be at greater risk for later developing depression after experiencing ODD (Burke et al., 2010), boys show a greater proclivity for developing CD (Rowe et al., 2010).

Environmental factors known to contribute to the emergence of ODD include higher family conflict and parenting stress as well as multiple socioeconomic variables (Cunningham & Boyle, 2002; Lavigne et al., 2012). The evidence to date suggests that ODD symptoms are most directly accounted for by families' reports of parenting stress and poorer family functioning overall (Lavigne et al., 2012). The relation between these contextual factors and the development of ODD dates to Gerald Patterson's (1982) descriptions of "coercive family processes." Patterson depicts a gradual development of ODD symptoms that are brought about by an interaction between a difficult child temperament and reactive, authoritarian, and inconsistent parenting.

The developmental course of ODD symptoms often reveals a consistent increase in severity over time that frequently progresses to diagnoses of CD, depression, or other major mental health concerns. Comorbidity with other conditions also frequently complicates the developmental course of ODD. In fact, this appears to be the rule rather than the exception, with nearly 50% of all ODD cases presenting co-occurring ADHD (Martel et al., 2012; Willcutt et al., 2012), 40% reporting significant anxiety symptoms (Drabick et al., 2010; Greene et al., 2002), and 12% being diagnosed with depression (Stoep et al., 2012). When depression later follows childhood onset of ODD, it is best predicted by the prominence of ODD-related negative affect. Likewise, children presenting more dominant symptoms of defiance and antagonistic behaviors frequently progress from ODD to later symptoms more representative of CD. There is an estimated 0.81 correlation between the symptoms of ODD and CD, which ultimately reflects an extremely high degree of symptom comorbidity (Boden et al., 2010; Loeber et al., 2009). Despite the strong evidence supporting ODD as a predictor of future behavioral and emotional problems, it remains unclear if its role is causal, prodromal, or simply a precursor to future concerns (Burke & Loeber, 2010).

Finally, it is important to differentiate the primary symptoms and developmental course of ODD from those of a newly introduced condition, disruptive mood dysregulation disorder (DMDD). Generally, more profound and persistent negative mood and more frequent and severe temper outbursts characterize DMDD rather than ODD (APA, 2013). Leibenluft (2011) suggests, however, that 84.9% of DMDD youths also meet DSM criteria for lifetime ODD. A primary treatment implication for distinguishing between these two conditions relates to treatment choices, as psychosocial interventions are generally preferred for ODD while psychopharmacological interventions may need to be considered for DMDD.

Pharmacological Solitary Treatments

Pharmacological research dedicated exclusively to the treatment of ODD is limited. These interventions are difficult to study because core symptoms are often conflated with those of CD (Loeber et al., 2009). Consequently, many pharmacological studies examine ODD/CD symptoms of aggression and emotional dysregulation, collapsing the separate diagnoses to instead focus upon specific, impairing symptoms. A second reason for the dearth of literature is related to the high comorbidity of ODD with other conditions such as ADHD or anxiety and mood disorders (AMDs). Although many of the medications used to treat these comorbid conditions may also help ameliorate the externalizing symptoms of ODD, the evidence and the biological mechanisms for improving oppositional behaviors remain unclear.

Because few studies are devoted to pharmacological treatments for ODD and strong evidence exists to support psychosocial intervention, the clinical practice parameters established by the American Academy of Child and Adolescent Psychiatry (AACAP) assert that "medications for youth with ODD are mostly considered to be adjunctive, palliative, and noncurative" and "should not be the sole intervention in ODD" (Steiner et al., 2007, p. 137). Similarly, international consensus statements on ODD recommend that pharmacological management of ODD in the absence of psychiatric comorbidity be cautious and limited to patients who (1) have not first benefited from psychosocial interventions or (2) exhibit extreme levels of aggression or destructive behaviors (Kutcher et al., 2004; Steiner et al., 2007).

Efficacy studies of pharmacological treatment exclusively for children with ODD have examined divalproex sodium (Depakote), lithium salts (Lithobid), or atypical antipsychotics such as risperidone (Risperdal). One randomized clinical trial and two open-label studies of divalproex sodium (DVPX) demonstrated significant reductions in "hostility" among children of average intelligence with ODD (Donovan et al., 1997, 2000; Saxena et al., 2010). Lithium salts have been used extensively in the treatment of aggression over the past 35 years; however, they have primarily been intended for pediatric-onset bipolar disorder. Only a handful of controlled trials have examined the efficacy of lithium salts for child and adolescent conduct problems and aggression (Campbell et al., 1995; Malone et al., 2000; Rifkin et al., 1997), with none specifically for ODD. Atypical antipsychotics have received greater empirical support for treating ODD, particularly for aggressive symptoms. Risperidone has been the most studied of these atypicals (Pappadopolous et al., 2006), although most investigations of "pure" ODD (i.e., without comorbidity) have been limited to children with below-average intelligence (Aman et al., 2002; Synder et al., 2002). Though providing some support for improving conduct, these studies also report significant confounds (e.g., low IQ, short treatment duration, questionable follow-up phases, use of combined medication treatments) and a high rate of adverse events (98%; Aman et al., 2002; Snyder et al., 2002).

Approximately half of children diagnosed with ODD present comorbid ADHD (Kutcher et al., 2004). Psychostimulant medication, considered the first-line treatment for ADHD, also presents potential benefits for treating comorbid externalizing symptoms of ODD (Swanson et al., 2001). Methylphenidate has been particularly well supported in both open-label (e.g., Serra-Pinheiro et al., 2004) and controlled studies (e.g., Kolko et al., 1999; Pliszka et al., 2000) for reducing disruptive behaviors and aggression in addition to improving core symptoms of ADHD. More recent studies also suggest that atomoxetine, a selective norepinepherine reuptake inhibitor (NRI), may be effective for ODD symptoms when comorbid with ADHD (Bangs et al., 2008; Dell'Agnello et al., 2009; Dittmann et al., 2011). A major advantage of atomoxetine treatment compared to stimulant therapy is the longer duration of effects, thus potentially addressing symptoms occurring during early morning and evening periods when stimulant effects have typically subsided. After methylphenidate and atomoxetine, alpha-2 adrenergic receptor agonists such as clonidine and guanfacine may be considered second-line medications for treating comorbid symptoms of ODD and ADHD. Clinical trials of clonidine or guanfacine alone or in combination with stimulant treatments have been shown to reduce oppositionality in children with comorbid ADHD (e.g., Connor et al., 2010; Palumbo et al., 2008); however, significant caution is also warranted owing to serious overdose potential (Hazell, 2010). Nonetheless, international treatment guidelines currently support the clinical use of alpha-2 agonists for children with ADHD and comorbid CD, severe ODD, or tic disorder, as well as those with comorbid ADHD and ODD who fail to respond favorably to either stimulant or atomoxetine treatment (Turgay, 2009).

Pharmacological treatments for ODD with comorbid AMDs have also been examined, though to a lesser extent. Two recent studies suggest promising support for selective serotonin reuptake inhibitor (SSRI) treatment among youth with ODD and comorbid anxiety and mood disorders (Jacobs et al., 2010; Kodish et al., 2011). But current AACAP clinical practice parameters for ODD indicate that there is insufficient evidence at this time to support the use of SSRIs for treating ODD symptoms alone (Steiner et al., 2007). With the introduction of the new diagnostic category of DMDD, now used to reflect these kinds of presenting problems, SSRI prescriptions are more likely to be directed toward the DMDD population rather than to a subset of children with comorbid ODD and AMD (Leibenluft, 2011).

Benefits and Limitations of Pharmacotherapy as Sole Treatment

Pharmacological treatments should not be considered first-line interventions for ODD, but rather secondary treatment options provided only after evidence-based psychosocial interventions or when comorbid conditions require stabilization. Though studies have examined the effects of several medications for treating ODD, few have exclusively examined ODD in the absence of co-occurring conditions. The evidence to date suggests that risperidone may offer the most potential benefits for ameliorating aggression, but with few benefits for improving symptoms of noncompliance or other conduct issues. Studies of risperidone have been limited to children with intellectual disabilities, however, and frequent negative side effects such as somnolence, extrapyramidal effects, and weight gain suggest the need for extreme caution.

When comorbid with ADHD, the strongest empirical evidence supports the combined use of stimulants and atomoxetine for treating ODD. Methylphenidate is the most supported for use with potentially substantial benefits for reducing noncompliance and reactive aggression associated with ADHD. Atomoxetine should be limited to those considered to be minimal responders to stimulants or for those experiencing negative side effects. Alpha-2 agonists such as clonidine and guanfacine currently have the least support for treating comorbid ADHD and ODD. When comorbid with anxiety and mood-related problems, pharmacological treatment data for ODD suggest benefits for judicious use of SSRIs.

Psychological Solitary Treatments

Evidence-based psychosocial interventions are recommended as the gold standard treatment approach for children with ODD. The interventions in this section have all been supported by well-conducted randomized controlled trials (RCTs) and found superior to no-treatment or waitlist control conditions. Consequently, these psychosocial treatments are all designated as either probably efficacious or well established on the basis of the criteria initially established by the APA's Task Force for Empirically Supported Treatments (Chambless & Hollon, 1998). In addition to demonstrating robust positive treatment outcomes, these programs have demonstrated longitudinal and generalized effects, proving to be both effective and durable interventions (McNeil et al., 1991). Parent training programs, especially those targeting younger children, are among the most extensively studied treatments for children with behavioral problems such as ODD and are recommended as the first-line approach (Eyberg et al., 2008). Interventions for youth in middle childhood and adolescence generally focus on individual or group sessions with the child. Children in these stages of development present a greater capacity to benefit from cognitive-behavioral approaches in which they are primary agents of change. Given that maladaptive parenting behaviors, family conflict, and family instability are associated with the development and maintenance of disruptive behaviors in children (Frick et al., 1992; Patterson, 1982), however, child-focused interventions often include a parent training component. Below is an overview of the evidence-based manualized interventions that have received the greatest research support for treating ODD, as well as additional programs that emphasize the same evidence-based practice principles.

Parent Training Programs

Parent–Child Interaction Therapy (PCIT) is a behavioral parent training program for children ages 2 to 7 (McNeil & Hembree-Kigin, 2010). The typical PCIT structure consists of weekly 60-minute therapy sessions in which the therapist, usually behind a one-way mirror, coaches a parent on their use of skills with their child. There are two stages in PCIT: child-directed interaction (CDI) and parent-directed interaction (PDI). CDI sessions focus on coaching positive attending and active ignoring skills. During PDI, limit setting and discipline techniques are emphasized to help parents follow through with behavioral strategies in a consistent and predictable manner. Parents learn to balance their warmth and responsiveness with demands and discipline. PCIT therapists code parent–child interactions to measure a parents' skill progression and to determine mastery of skills. "Graduation" from PCIT depends on parents' mastery of the specific skills taught, their self-reported confidence in handling child behaviors, and their ratings of disruptive behavior on the Eyberg Child Behavior Inventory (ECBI) falling within normal limits (Eyberg & Pincus, 1999).

Helping the Noncompliant Child (HNC) is a program for children ages 3 to 8 (McMahon & Forehand, 2003). The parent and child are seen together for sessions of 60–90 minutes held once or twice weekly over the course of approximately 10 weeks. HNC skills are achieved through therapist modeling, parent–therapist role-play, and live practice with the child in the clinic and at home. Therapist coaching occurs within the therapy room or from behind a one-way mirror. Similar to PCIT, the HNC program consists of two treatment phases. During the first phase (differential attention), parents learn skills to increase child prosocial behaviors (using positive verbal and physical attention) and to reduce minor misbehaviors (utilizing positive reinforcement and ignoring strategies). The second phase (compliance training) focuses on teaching parents to give clear instructions and follow through consistently with effective consequences (e.g., time-out or loss of privileges) for noncompliance.

Incredible Years (IY) Training Series is a set of three training programs: the child program (IY-CT, ages 3 to 8), the parent program (IY-PT, ages 2 to 10), and the teacher program for children up to age 12 (Webster-Stratton & Reid, 2003). Each IY program is delivered by a trained facilitator and carried out in a group format. Parent and child programs are typically delivered in conjunction with one another over a course of 12–22 weeks, with sessions lasting 2–3 hours. Sessions incorporate videotaped vignettes tailored to the specific target audience (e.g., parent, teacher, or child groups). Vignettes include common challenging situations followed by group discussions comparing ineffective and effective ways of dealing with the problem situations.

Triple P—Positive Parenting Program is a treatment designed for children from birth to age 12, with extensions for ages 13 to 16, and focuses on enhancing parenting confidence and skills (Sanders, 1999). Triple P can be delivered in individual, group, self-directed, or in a combination of these formats. Triple P is multileveled (Levels 1 through 5), and families participate in a specific level depending on the severity of child behavioral problems. Level 4 (Standard Triple P) and Level 5 (Enhanced Triple P) have received the most empirical support (Eyberg et al., 2008). Standard Triple P involves ten individual or eight group parent sessions on topics such as differential attention, effective commands, logical consequences, quiet time, and time-out. Level 5 is an enhanced version that incorporates home visits and three to five additional sessions designed to address family stressors (e.g., parental depression, marital conflict; Sanders et al., 2003).

Parent Management Training-Oregon Model (PMTO) is supported for use with the widest age range of children (3 to 12; Patterson et al., 1975). PMTO can be provided in group or individual formats. Individual family sessions are 60 minutes, held weekly for approximately 25–30 weeks. Group sessions are 90 minutes and are held weekly for 14 weeks. Treatment also includes midweek calls from the therapist to encourage successful implementation of home procedures and skill generalization. The therapist teaches parents via role-play and modeling of skills across five content areas: skill encouragement (e.g., incentive chart and rewards for positive behaviors), limit setting, monitoring, problem solving, and positive involvement. The order of skill content and time allocated to each skill varies depending on the family's presenting needs and level of child participation in sessions. Parent mastery of skill encouragement is a prerequisite to learning discipline strategies such as giving effective directions and consistent and calm use of consequences (e.g., time-out, privilege removal) for noncompliance.

Child-Focused Individual and Group Interventions

Problem Solving Skills Training (PSST) uses cognitive restructuring and problem-solving skills (e.g., identifying the problem, generating solutions, evaluating solutions, and perspective taking) to help youth with ODD cope with interpersonal difficulties (Kazdin, 2010). Treatment is designed for children ages 7 to 13 and consists of 12 weeks of individual child therapy sessions that last 30–50 minutes. The therapist employs interactive exercises, games, modeling, and role-play of different scenarios often encountered by the child, and uses a token economy system with response cost. Initial sessions focus on child participation, but parents are more actively included in later sessions in order to practice challenging daily scenarios and to assist the child in generalizing skills to use at home (Kazdin, 2010).

Anger Control Training (ACT) is a school-based group intervention that targets negative, defiant, and hostile behavior toward school authority figures (Larson & Lochman, 2002). Eighteen (60–90 minute) weekly sessions for children ages 8–12 focus on cognitive coping strategies, awareness of physiological cues, perspective taking, and problem-solving skills. Following skill-building sessions, participants watch videos of other children experiencing interpersonal difficulties and then discuss alternative appropriate social responses. Children participate in role-play rehearsal of alternative skill choices, using strategies introduced through the program. Final sessions provide children with opportunities to act out real-life situations and apply new skills instead of reacting with defiance or aggression. Similarly, Coping Power is a clinic-based program that was developed as an extension of ACT. Coping Power offers individual sessions for children as well as a behavioral parent training component (Lochman et al., 2010).

Programs Emphasizing Evidence-Based Practice Principles

While the aforementioned programs have received the greatest empirical support, there are also many interventions that are based exclusively upon the evidence-based principles that define these programs—for example, Barkley's (2013) *Defiant Children*, Kapalka's (2007) *Parenting Your Out-of-Control Child*, Kazdin and Rotella's (2009) *The Kazdin Method for Parenting the Defiant Child*, and Greene's (2010) *The Explosive Child*. Each program emphasizes using positive reinforcement to promote appropriate behaviors, increasing the effectiveness of commands, setting consistent limits, and using nonphysical/nonpunitive discipline techniques. However, each program also adds strategies that may be a focus of a family's treatment. For example, Barkley's (2013) 10-session program provides both proactive and reactive strategies for addressing negative behavior (e.g., contingency management, time-out, problem prediction, and school collaboration). Kazdin and Rotella's (2009) PMT incorporates behavioral shaping in sessions, teaching parents to create clear definitions of behavioral goals and reinforcing successive approximations toward desired outcomes. In addition to managing argumentative and defiant behaviors, Kapalka (2007) emphasizes strategies for managing emotional dysregulation and "out-of-control" behaviors, specifically for common problem situations such as transitions between activities, during homework, and while in public places. Similarly, Greene's (2010) *Explosive Child* program highlights difficulties related to emotion regulation as well as cognitive inflexibility among children who become explosive. Greene's approach teaches parents to recognize the warning signs of a meltdown, to remove parent behaviors that may be fueling a meltdown, and gradually to "downshift" to allow the child to consider options when they are frustrated.

Benefits and Limitations of Psychotherapy as Sole Treatment

Intervening early with an evidence-based psychosocial intervention for ODD proves not only cost effective but also potent as the best clinical practice. Positive treatment outcomes have been demonstrated for these interventions in RCTs, providing a strong evidence base for their use in the treatment of ODD (e.g., Webster-Stratton et al., 2004). In follow-up studies, these interventions also demonstrate maintenance of treatment gains for years after treatment has ended (e.g., Forgatch et al., 2009). Given the posttreatment durability of positive therapeutic effects, psychosocial interventions are considered the gold standard for children with ODD and are an especially attractive option for families, communities, and prescribing physicians alike as first-line intervention (Edidin et al., 2012).

Psychosocial interventions for ODD focus on the child and authority figure(s) learning techniques that will create new healthy patterns of interacting and interrupt the negative coercive cycle that results in defiant behavior (Patterson, 1982). The skills learned in treatment can then be applied whenever necessary after treatment has ended, with follow-up care done on an as-needed basis. By comparison, maintenance of a psychotropic medication regimen requires careful monitoring and consistent maintenance over time for the duration of medication use. In addition, medications obviously do not teach skills to change child or caregiver patterns of interactions and are therefore not viable long-term solutions. In addition, medications produce highly variable outcomes for children with disruptive behavior disorder depending on their age and comorbidities.

Combined Treatments

There is a dearth of research related to combined psychosocial and pharmacological interventions in the treatment of ODD. This stems largely from the fact that psychosocial approaches are preferred as front-line interventions, whereas medications are often used as adjuncts to treat comorbidities or to help manage aggression (Steiner et al., 2007; Turgay, 2009). Despite the lack of research for pharmacotherapy for ODD, clinical practice parameters set by the AACAP (Steiner et al., 2007) still suggest that multimodal treatment is often needed to successfully treat ODD. Further, AACAP recommends that clinicians develop individualized treatment plans for children and adolescents, as any given modality of treatment may vary in effectiveness from patient to patient (Steiner et al., 2007).

At present, existing data regarding the combined treatment of ODD must be extrapolated from studies focused primarily on other disruptive behavior disorders, namely, ADHD (MTA Cooperative Group, 1999; Swanson et al., 2001). The MTA study compared the efficacy of various treatment modalities for ADHD (MTA Cooperative Group, 1999). A subset of this study's sample was identified as having comorbid ODD, and secondary analyses found that medication combined with behavioral treatment is significantly more effective than medication alone, although the effect was small (Swanson et al., 2001). Swanson et al. add that the seemingly small effect of psychosocial intervention may be partially attributable to variability in treatment fidelity and effectiveness across sites. Some sites found moderate to large positive effects for psychosocial treatment, while others found small to large negative effects (p. 177). More combined studies are needed that use standardized manualized behavioral treatments to show incremental clinical utility above the effects of medications for children with comorbid ADHD and ODD (as well as children with "pure" ODD).

Benefits and Limitations of Combined Treatments

There are no recent studies addressing the use of combined pharmacologic and psychosocial treatments exclusively for the ODD population. Perhaps this is for good reason, given that effective family-based behavioral treatments are available for ODD. Owing to the absence of evidence to support pharmacological intervention and the strong body of evidence for parenting interventions and child-focused skill-building interventions (see Edidin et al., 2012, for a review), psychosocial interventions are clearly the most effective treatments for ODD. Because few pharmacological studies to date have even attempted to specifically treat ODD, more research is needed to explore the efficacy of adding pharmacological support to first-line psychosocial intervention.

Current practice parameters may suggest the addition of stimulants, alpha-2 agonists, or even atypical antipsychotics to psychosocial therapies to address child behaviors that are significantly aggressive, destructive, or nonresponsive to evidence-based behavior therapy. But these guidelines are based upon clinical expert consensus rather than empirical data from RCTs or even open-label trials. Pharmacological treatments should therefore be considered with caution when addressing symptoms of "pure" ODD, given the unanswered questions about their long-term effectiveness and safety with this population. Adverse events related to the use of medications (e.g., fatigue, nausea, tics, weight gain, and over-dose potential) may outweigh benefits for many children, so practitioners should carefully discuss these issues with families. From a practical standpoint, titration needs for medications may also present significant challenges owing to the relative lack of research or published medication algorithms for this population. Finally, the use of these medications for ODD is considered off label, with US Food and Drug Administration approval only granted for comorbid conditions such as ADHD, thus further prompting the need for caution (Charach et al., 2011).

Before RCTs of combined treatment strategies can be conducted with children with ODD, more studies are needed to analyze the effects of various psychotropic medications on specific symptoms of ODD, either studied in isolation or with statistical controls for the effects of comorbid symptoms (e.g., ADHD). Once these lines of research expand to study ODD in isolation or as the primary target of treatment, researchers will then be able to analyze various medications' relative efficacy alone and in combination with preferred psychosocial interventions mentioned elsewhere in this chapter.

Summary and Recommendations

Oppositional defiant disorder is a high base rate condition that causes significant behavioral, emotional, and interpersonal difficulties for the individual diagnosed as well as for family, teachers, and friends. Without treatment, ODD symptoms tend to persist and worsen over time (Shaw et al., 2005), often evolving from childhood disruptive behavior to an adolescence and adulthood marked by emotional problems or antisocial behaviors such as crime and violence. Fortunately, children and adolescents with ODD have been shown to respond positively to intervention, both during treatment and in long-term follow-up studies. More encouraging is the notion that psychosocial treatments are evidenced to be most effective for ODD, thus not requiring pharmacotherapy. In fact, pharmacological intervention studies to date are so few and unclear in their findings that medication is not even recommended as an option for combined treatment of ODD unless risks or comorbid symptoms suggest the need for additional support (Steiner et al., 2007). There are many behavior therapies available for first-line intervention, composed of either parent training or child-focused psychotherapies delivered in individual and group formats. An example of best-practice behavior therapy for a child with ODD is presented in the vignette below.

Brandon, age 4, was referred for behavioral intervention by his pediatrician, having recently been dismissed from preschool because of frequent aggressive and noncompliant behaviors. Brandon's parents reported a long history of externalizing behaviors, including argumentativeness, defiance toward adults, irritability, and aggression. Brandon's pediatrician conducted a physical exam and reviewed parent and teacher ratings of disruptive behaviors on standardized screening forms. Because no physiological concerns were noted and rating scales did not indicate significant problems with inattention, hyperactive/impulsive behaviors, or mood, Brandon's pediatrician deferred a medication trial pending a full psychological evaluation.

Brandon and his parents subsequently sought diagnostic evaluation with a child and adolescent psychologist who conducted parent and child clinical interviews, reviewed broad- and narrow-band parent and teacher rating scales, and observed their parent–child interactions. Following the evaluation and diagnostic feedback, the psychologist diagnosed Brandon with ODD and referred him for outpatient behavior therapy.

Brandon's therapist conducted an initial family interview to establish a working therapeutic alliance, identify target behaviors for intervention, and provide consultation to the family about what to expect for their participation in therapy. The therapist observed how Brandon's parents issued commands as well as how Brandon responded and interacted with them during a play observation. The therapist elicited possible patterns of situational antecedents and consequences associated with problem behaviors and recorded their frequency, duration, and parent and child responses. Finally, the therapist encouraged Brandon's parents to observe and record the frequency of his oppositional symptoms prior to each session.

The therapist also provided an overview of the structure of each session for Brandon's family, outlining the following steps:

1   The therapist models new parenting skills for Brandon's parents via role-play.
2   Brandon's parents practice behavioral techniques in role-play situations with the therapist playing the part of the child.
3   The therapist explains all activities, roles, and behavioral expectations to Brandon and enlists him to repeat them before rehearsing procedures (with the therapist).
4   Brandon's parents practice new skills using the "Child's Game/ Special Time" (Phase 1) or the "Parent's Game/Effective Commands" (Phase 2). The therapist provides in vivo feedback or via "bug-in-the-ear" (if observing behind a mirror or closed-circuit television).
5   Home therapy assignments are introduced for the family to practice new strategies at home.

(continued)

(continued)

Treatment Phase 1: Differential Attention/Child-Directed Interaction

Brandon's first phase of therapy aimed to increase his parents' effectiveness in (1) reinforcing the desired behaviors he displays and (2) taking their attention away from his oppositional, noncompliant, and disruptive behaviors. The therapist introduced three differential attending skills: attending, rewarding, and ignoring behaviors. The goal of this phase was to increase the rate and proportion of positive interactions with Brandon. In addition, Brandon's parents were encouraged to avoid using commands, redirections, corrections, and questions to discourage parental control and facilitate *child*-directed interactions. This served to strengthen the parent–child relationship and shift parent–child interactions from mostly negative to predominantly positive.

Attending strategies were introduced and practiced within the context of child-directed play, incorporating strategies modeled within "Child's Game" for HNC (McMahon & Forehand, 2003) and "Special Time" for PCIT (Eyberg, 1998). The therapist first demonstrated child-directed play by inviting Brandon to select an interactive, noncompetitive, and non-rule-based toy such as a train set, building blocks, or dinosaur landscape. The therapist described the adult role as similar to a "sportscaster," simply attending to Brandon's activities, observing and emulating his play, and narrating. Examples of these comments may include "It looks like you are building a house. I noticed that you were sitting cross-legged when you were building the walls to your house." For the remainder of the session, Brandon's parents practiced this activity while the therapist provided feedback. Brandon's family was encouraged to schedule a predictable time each day for 15–20 minutes of home rehearsal of child-directed play. The family was provided a worksheet to record the days, times, and activities performed during child-directed play. In addition, the therapist provided the family with star stickers for Brandon to add his ratings after each playtime as a one-, two-, or three-star experience.

The next session emphasized the use of three types of rewards: physical rewards, unlabeled verbal rewards/general praise, and labeled verbal rewards/specific praise. Physical rewards consisted of nonverbal attending behaviors like smiles, pats on the back, and thumbs-up as well as use of verbal praise. The rationale for this was to encourage Brandon's parents to become more attuned to his positive behaviors and prepared to deliver more specific labeled praise instead of general or unlabeled positive comments.

The third skill introduced within the first treatment phase was active ignoring for obnoxious, nondangerous, or negative behaviors. The importance of ignoring minor misbehaviors was highlighted along with the benefits of differential reinforcement of other (DRO) more productive behaviors. The therapist also explored "what if" situations, such as Brandon continuing to display negative behaviors or escalating these behaviors when ignored. The therapist discussed "extinction bursts," or initial increases in the frequency or intensity of disruptive behaviors that aim to fulfill the attention-seeking function of the problem behavior. His parents were encouraged to continue active ignoring in these situations, and shift to reinforcement of other behaviors immediately when he stops. Brandon's parents were also prepared to stop child-directed play or impose a time-out if his disruptive behaviors continued to escalate or pose physical risks or damage to the room. While actively employing these strategies during scheduled periods of child-directed play, the therapist also encouraged Brandon's parents to extend their use of differential attention to behaviors they observe throughout his typical day.

Phase 2: Compliance Training/Parent-Directed Interaction

The second phase of Brandon's therapy built upon the increased frequency of positive parent–child interactions established in Phase 1 by incorporating more directive parenting techniques. Key objectives for Phase 2 included improving parents' effective use of commands and effective implementation of time-outs.

The first session focused on commands and began with a discussion of antecedent contingencies that either detract from or enhance the effectiveness of parent commands. The therapist discussed qualities of effective commands, specifically encouraging Brandon's parents to use commands that are simple, clear, direct, and delivered only one at a time. Key word prompts such as "I'm giving you an instruction" or "Brandon, I need you to show me you are listening" were also suggested in order to prime Brandon to receive the command. In addition to the family's continued home practice of child-directed play, Brandon's parents were invited to practice use of effective commands with particular emphasis placed upon controlling antecedents that may affect their commands.

The next session highlighted the importance of differential attention skills learned in Phase 1. The therapist provided Brandon's

(continued)

(continued)

parents with instructions for using specific verbal rewards at the first sign of his compliance (e.g., "I am so proud of you for following my instruction right away!") and then again at the task's completion (e.g., "Nice job putting the game in the toy chest!"). Furthermore, Brandon's parents were encouraged to prioritize attending to Brandon's behavioral compliance and not necessarily his attitude when responding to commands. For instance, Brandon responded to an instruction to put his game away by stomping and slamming his game into the toy chest. Brandon's parents were advised to attend to his compliance with statements like "I appreciate you putting your game away the first time I asked." They thus ignored the negative attitude, specifically praised the target behavior, and thereby increased the likelihood of future compliance by making his response a less aversive/more rewarding experience. Since time-outs had not yet been introduced, noncompliance was temporarily addressed by instructing Brandon's parents to use hand-over-hand guidance to physically direct him to complete the task when failing to respond appropriately to commands within five seconds. If Brandon displayed a tantrum or aggression, his parents were instructed to ignore his negative behavior and carry out the task without his participation. Finally, Brandon's parents were encouraged to conduct compliance training in session and at home using what Barkley (2013) refers to as "fetch commands," giving frequent, single-step commands during low-demand times (i.e., outside of daily transitions such as getting ready for school) to give Brandon a high rate of rewards for compliance.

The final objective addressed in Phase 2 of Brandon's therapy was time-out. By then, the quality of parent–child interactions had proportionally shifted in favor of his family having far more positive than negative experiences. The therapist began by explaining that "time-out from reinforcement" is a more extreme use of differential attention, noting the importance of excluding Brandon from any attention from others (verbal and nonverbal engagement). His parents were encouraged to designate a time-out location in their home such as a chair facing the corner in a low-traffic room. The effectiveness of time-out was maximized by establishing clear child expectations, which included: (1) a brief explanation of why time-out is being used (e.g., "you are going to time-out because you did not follow my instructions"); (2) the rules for time-out (e.g., "the rules for time-out are for you to sit here and to be quiet"); (3) consequences for violating the rules of time-out (e.g., "if you break the rules, time-out will start over"); and (4) an explanation of how time-out will end (e.g., "when you have followed the rules of time-out, I will tell you to come out of time-out. If you ask to come out, time-out will start over"). Though durations typically recommended for time-out include 30 seconds to one minute per year of life, the therapist emphasized the minimum time needed for a steady period of compliance (longer than one minute).

The therapist noted that time-out will now be introduced when Brandon refuses to comply with a parental command. Instead of Brandon's parents imposing hand-over-hand physical prompting after five seconds of their command, they are instructed to issue an "if-then" warning (e.g., "if you do not follow my instruction, then you will have to go to time-out."). When he complied with the initial command, his parents proceeded with verbal rewards and ignored his initial display of noncompliance. When he failed to comply within five seconds, his parents directed him to the time-out location. The therapist instructed Brandon's parents to physically return him to time-out the first time he left and were encouraged to remain with him during time-out in case he attempted to elope again.

After Brandon's parents demonstrated proficiency in using time-out at home, along with all of the preceding contingency management methods, termination of therapy was discussed. The therapist reviewed all behavioral techniques introduced to date and encouraged Brandon's parents to predict any potential barriers to future implementation of these skills (e.g., planned business travel for one parent, extended family members visiting). The therapist then engaged in active problem solving with the family to prevent problems with implementation adherence or fidelity. Observations of Brandon's behavioral improvements as well as his parents' implementation efforts and skills were highlighted, emphasizing the family's competency for independently maintaining a high level of family well-being. Brandon's parents were encouraged to utilize a weekly parent conference in place of their weekly therapy appointment in order to sustain a priority for managing Brandon's weekly behavioral needs. Finally, the therapist provided parent and teacher rating scales and invited the family to return in one month for a booster session to review posttreatment outcomes, continue implementation of home behavioral strategies, and discuss any ongoing treatment needs.

References

Aman, M. G., et al. (2002). Double-blind, placebo-controlled study of risperidone for the treatment of disruptive behaviors in children with subaverage intelligence. *American Journal of Psychiatry, 159*, 1337–1346.

Angold, A., & Costello, E. J. (1996). The relative diagnostic utility of child and parent reports of oppositional defiant behaviors. *International Journal of Methods in Psychiatric Research, 6*, 253–259.

APA. American Psychiatric Association. (1980). *Diagnostic and statistical manual of mental disorders* (3rd ed.). Washington, DC: Author.

APA. American Psychiatric Association. (2013). *Diagnostic and statistical manual of mental disorders* (5th ed.). Washington, DC: Author.

Bangs, M. E., et al. (2008). Atomoxetine for the treatment of attention-deficit/hyperactivity disorder and oppositional defiant disorder. *Pediatrics, 121*, e314–e320.

Barkley, R. A. (2013). *Defiant children: A clinician's manual for assessment and parent training* (3rd ed.). New York: Guilford Press.

Boden, J. M., et al. (2010). Risk factors for conduct disorder and oppositional/defiant disorder: Evidence from a New Zealand birth cohort. *Journal of the American Academy of Child and Adolescent Psychiatry, 49*, 1125–1133.

Boylan, K., et al. (2007). Comorbidity of internalizing disorders in children with oppositional defiant disorder. *European Child and Adolescent Psychiatry, 46*, 1200–1210.

Burke, J., & Loeber, R. (2010). Oppositional defiant disorder and the explanation of the comorbidity between behavioral disorders and depression. *Clinical Psychology: Science and Practice, 17*, 319–326.

Burke, J. D., et al. (2010). Dimensions of oppositional defiant disorder as predictors of depression and conduct disorder in preadolescent girls. *Journal of the American Academy of Child and Adolescent Psychiatry, 49*, 484–492.

Campbell, M., et al. (1995). Lithium in hospitalized aggressive children with conduct disorder: A double-blind and placebo-controlled study. *Journal of the American Academy of Child and Adolescent Psychiatry, 34*, 445–453.

Chambless, D. L., & Hollon, S. D. (1998). Defining empirically supported therapies. *Journal of Consulting and Clinical Psychology, 66*, 7–18.

Charach A., et al. (2011). *Attention deficit hyperactivity disorder: Effectiveness of treatment in at-risk preschoolers; long-term effectiveness in all ages; and variability in prevalence, diagnosis, and treatment.* Comparative Effectiveness Review 44. AHRQ Publication No. 12-EHC003-EF. Rockville, MD: Agency for Healthcare Research and Quality. Retrieved from www.effectivehealthcare.ahrq.gov/reports/final.cfm.

Connor, D. F., et al. (2010). Effects of guanfacine extended release on oppositional symptoms in children aged 6–12 years with attention-deficit hyperactivity disorder and oppositional symptoms. *CNS Drugs, 24*, 755–768.

Cunningham, C. E., & Boyle, M. H. (2002). Preschool at risk for attention-deficit hyperactivity disorder and oppositional defiant disorder: Family, parenting, and behavioral correlates. *Journal of Abnormal Child Psychology, 30*, 555–569.

Dell'Agnello, G., et al. (2009). Atomoxetine hydrochloride in the treatment of children and adolescents with attention-deficit/hyperactivity disorder and comorbid oppositional defiant disorder: A placebo-controlled Italian study. *European Neuropsychopharmacology, 19*, 822–834.

Dittmann, R., et al. (2011). Atomexetine versus placebo in children and adolescents with attention-deficit/hyperactivity disorder and comorbid oppositional defiant disorder: A double-blind, randomized, multicenter trial in Germany. *Journal of Child and Adolescent Psychopharmacology, 21*, 97–110.

Donovan, S. J., et al. (1997). Divalproex treatment of disruptive adolescents: A report of 10 cases. *Journal of Clinical Psychiatry, 58*, 12–15.

Donovan, S. J., et al. (2000). Divalproex treatment for youth with explosive temper and mood lability: A double-blind, placebo-controlled crossover design. *American Journal of Psychiatry, 157*, 818–820.

Drabick, D. A. G., et al. (2010). Co-occurrence of ODD and anxiety: Shared risk processes and evidence for a dual-pathway model. *Clinical Psychology: Science and Practice, 17*, 307–318.

Edidin, J. P., et al. (2012). Disruptive behavior disorders. In W. M. Klykylo and J. Kay (Eds.), *Clinical child psychiatry* (3rd ed.). Chichester: John Wiley & Sons.

Eyberg, S. M. (1998). Parent-child interaction therapy: Integration of traditional and behavioral concerns. *Child and Family Behavior Therapy, 10*, 33–46.

Eyberg, S. M., & Pincus, D. (1999). *Eyberg child behavior inventory and Sutter-Eyberg student behavior inventory: Professional manual*. Odessa, FL: Psychological Assessment Resources.

Eyberg, S. M., et al. (2008). Evidence-based treatments for child and adolescent disruptive behavior disorders. *Journal of Clinical Child and Adolescent Psychology, 37*, 213–235.

Forgatch, M. S., et al. (2009). Testing the Oregon delinquency model with 9-year follow-up of the Oregon divorce study. *Development and Psychopathology, 21*, 637–660.

Frick, P. J., & Nigg, J. T. (2012). Current issues in the diagnosis of attention deficit hyperactivity disorder, oppositional defiant disorder, and conduct disorder. *Annual Review of Clinical Psychology, 8*, 77–107.

Frick, P. J., et al. (1992). Familial risk factors to oppositional defiant disorder and conduct disorder: Parental psychopathology and maternal parenting. *Journal of Consulting and Clinical Psychology, 60*, 49–55.

Greene, R. W. (2010). *The explosive child: A new approach for understanding and parenting easily frustrated, "chronically inflexible", children* (4th ed.). New York: HarperCollins.

Greene, R. W., et al. (2002). Psychiatric comorbidity, family dysfunction, and social impairment in referred youth with oppositional defiant disorder. *American Journal of Psychiatry, 159*, 1214–1224.

Hazell, P. (2010). Review of attention-deficit/hyperactivity disorder comorbid with oppositional defiant disorder. *Australasian Psychiatry, 18*, 556–559.

Jacobs, R. H., et al. (2010). Treating depression and oppositional behavior in adolescents. *Journal of Clinical Child and Adolescent Psychology, 39*, 559–567.

Kapalka, G. (2007). *Parenting your out-of-control child*. Oakland, CA: New Harbinger.

Kazdin, A. E. (2010). Problem-solving skills training and parent management training for oppositional defiant disorder and conduct disorder. In A. E. Kazdin & J. R. Weisz (Eds.), *Evidence-based psychotherapies for children and adolescents* (2nd ed., pp. 211–226). New York: Guilford Press.

Kazdin, A. E., & Rotella, C. (2009). *The Kazdin method for parenting the defiant child: With no pills, no therapy, no contest of wills*. Boston: Houghton Mifflin.

Kodish, I., et al. (2011). Pharmacotherapy for anxiety disorders in children and adolescents. *Dialogues in Clinical Neuroscience, 13*, 439.

Kolko, D. J., et al. (1999). Methylphenidate and behavior modification in children with ADHD and comorbid ODD or CD: Main and incremental effects across settings. *Journal of the American Academy of Child and Adolescent Psychiatry, 38*, 578–586.

Kutcher, S., et al. (2004). International consensus statement on attention-deficit/hyperactivity disorder (ADHD) and disruptive behaviour disorders (DBDs): Clinical implications and treatment practice suggestions. *European Neuropsychopharmacology, 14*, 11–28.

Larson, J., & Lochman, J. E. (2002). *Helping school children cope with anger: A cognitive-behavioral intervention*. New York: Guilford Press.

Lavigne, J. V., et al. (2012). A multi-domain model of risk factors for ODD symptoms in a community sample of 4-year-olds. *Journal of Abnormal Child Psychology, 40*, 741–757.

Leibenluft, E. (2011). Severe mood dysregulation, irritability, and the diagnostic boundaries of bipolar disorder in youths. *American Journal of Psychiatry, 168*, 129–142.

Lochman, J. E., et al. (2010). Anger control training for aggressive youths. In A. E. Kazdin & J. R. Weisz (Eds.), *Evidence-based psychotherapies for children and adolescents* (2nd ed., pp. 227–242). New York: Guilford Press.

Loeber, R., et al. (2009). Development and etiology of disruptive and delinquent behavior. *Annual Review of Clinical Psychology, 5*, 291–310.

Malone, R. P., et al. (2000). A double-blind placebo-controlled study of lithium in hospitalized aggressive children and adolescents with conduct disorder. *Archives of General Psychiatry, 57*, 649–654.

Martel, M. M., et al. (2012). Diversity in pathways to common childhood disruptive behavior disorders. *Journal of Abnormal Child Psychology, 40*, 1223–1236.

McMahon, R. J., & Forehand, R. (2003). *Helping the noncompliant child: Family-based treatment for oppositional behavior* (2nd ed.). New York: Guilford Press.

McNeil, C. B., & Hembree-Kigin, T. L. (2010). *Parent-child interaction therapy* (2nd ed.). New York: Springer.

McNeil, C. B., et al. (1991). Parent-child interaction therapy with behavior problem children: Generalization of treatment effects to the school setting. *Journal of Clinical Child Psychology, 20*, 140–151.

MTA Cooperative Group. (1999). A 14-month randomized clinical trial of treatment strategies for attention-deficit/hyperactivity disorder. *Archives of General Psychiatry, 56*, 1073–1086.

Munkvold, L. H., et al. (2011). Oppositional defiant disorder—Gender differences in co-occurring symptoms of mental health problems in a general population of children. *Journal of Abnormal Child Psychology, 39*, 577–587.

Olfson, M., et al. (2014). National trends in the mental health care of children, adolescents, and adults by office-based physicians. *JAMA Psychiatry, 71*, 81–90.

Palumbo, D. R., et al. (2008). Clonidine for attention-deficit/hyperactivity disorder: I. Efficacy and tolerability outcomes. *Journal of the American Academy of Child and Adolescent Psychiatry, 47*, 180–188.

Pappadopulos, E., et al. (2006). Pharmacotherapy of aggression in children and adolescents: Efficacy and effect size. *Journal of the Canadian Academy of Child and Adolescent Psychiatry, 15*, 27–39.

Patterson, G. R. (1982). *Coercive family process.* Eugene, OR: Castalia.

Patterson, G. R., et al. (1975). *A social learning approach to family intervention: Families with aggressive children* (Vol. 1). Eugene, OR: Castalia.

Pliszka, S. R., et al. (2000). A double-blind, placebo-controlled study of Adderall and methylphenidate in the treatment of attention-deficit/hyperactivity disorder. *Journal of the American Academy of Child and Adolescent Psychiatry, 39*, 619–626.

Rifkin, A., et al. (1997). Lithium treatment of conduct disorders in adolescents. *American Journal of Psychiatry, 154*, 554–555.

Rowe, R., et al. (2010). Developmental pathways in oppositional defiant disorder and conduct disorder. *Journal of Abnormal Psychology, 119*, 726–738.

Sanders, M. R. (1999). Triple P-Positive Parenting Program: Towards an empirically validated multilevel parenting and family support strategy for the prevention of behavior and emotional problems in children. *Clinical Child and Family Psychology Review, 2,* 71–90.

Sanders, M. R., et al. (2003). The development, evaluation and dissemination of a training program for general practitioners in evidence-based parent consultation skills. *International Journal of Mental Health Promotion, 5,* 13–20.

Saxena, K., et al. (2010). Divalproex sodium-ER in outpatients with disruptive behavior disorders: A three month open label study. *Child Psychiatry and Human Development, 41,* 274–284.

Serra-Pinheiro, M. A., et al. (2004). The effect of methylphenidate on oppositional defiant disorder comorbid with attention deficit/hyperactivity disorder. *Archives of Neuropsychiatry, 62,* 399–402.

Shaw, D. S., et al. (2005). Developmental trajectories of conduct problems and hyperactivity from ages 2 to 10. *Journal of Child Psychology and Psychiatry, 46,* 931–942.

Snyder, R., et al. (2002). Effects of risperidone on conduct and disruptive behavior disorders in children with subaverage IQs. *Journal of the American Academy of Child and Adolescent Psychiatry, 41,* 1026–1036.

Steiner, H., et al. (2007). Practice parameter for the assessment and treatment of children and adolescents with oppositional defiant disorder. *Journal of the American Academy of Child and Adolescent Psychiatry, 46,* 126–141.

Stoep, A. V., et al. (2012). Identifying comorbid depression and disruptive behavior disorders: Comparison of two approaches used in adolescent studies. *Journal of Psychiatric Research, 46,* 873–881.

Stringaris, A., et al. (2010). What's in a disruptive disorder? Temperamental antecedents of oppositional defiant disorder: Findings from the Avon Longitudinal Study. *Journal of the American Academy of Child and Adolescent Psychiatry, 49,* 474–483.

Swanson, J., et al. (2001). Clinical relevance of the primary findings of the MTA: Success rates based on severity of ADHD and ODD symptoms at the end of treatment. *Journal of the American Academy of Child and Adolescent Psychiatry, 40,* 168–179.

Turgay, A. (2009). Psychopharmacological treatment of oppositional defiant disorder. *CNS Drugs, 23,* 1–17.

Webster-Stratton, C. H., & Reid, M. J. (2003). The incredible years parents, teachers, and children training series: A multifaceted treatment approach for young children with conduct disorders. In A. E. Kazdin & J. R. Weisz (Eds.), *Evidence-based psychotherapies for children and adolescents* (pp. 224–240). New York: Guilford Press.

Webster-Stratton, C. H., et al. (2004). Treating children with early-onset conduct problems: Intervention outcomes for parent, child, and teacher training. *Journal of Clinical Child and Adolescent Psychology, 33,* 105–124.

Willcutt, E. G., et al. (2012). Validity of DSM-IV attention-deficit/hyperactivity disorder symptom dimensions and subtypes. *Journal of Abnormal Psychology, 121,* 991–1010.

7 Conduct Disorder

Tony Wu, Nicolette Howells, Jennifer Burger,
Patricia Lopez, Rebecca Lundeen, and
Angela V. Sikkenga

Accurate diagnoses and evidence-based interventions are essential to the treatment of psychological disorders. Evidence-based strategies can help patients who suffer from a multitude of psychological disorders, including conduct disorder (CD). Using interventions that lack scientific evidence is likely to be detrimental to patients, the field of psychology, and society, as response to treatment becomes less likely. Thus clinicians must learn about treatments that have proven efficacy and effectiveness in order to success-fully address patients' symptoms and improve patient's daily functioning.

The use of traditional psychotherapy to treat specific psychological conditions has received significant attention in past and current research literature; however, other treatment modalities, such as evidence-based programs and intervention with psychotropic medication, have not received as much attention, especially regarding treatment of CD. With that in mind, the purpose of this chapter is to review the best treatment methods for CD, including the use of psychotropic medications. A case study will also illustrate treatment considerations.

Diagnostic Considerations

In a comprehensive literature review, Wu (2011) noted that children with CD displayed consistent aggressive or rule-breaking behaviors toward others. These behaviors included bullying, threatening, fighting, using weapons, forcing others into sexual activity, and other socially inappro-priate behaviors. In general, biological and environmental factors each played a role in the development of CD in children. For example, children's risk of developing CD increased when their caregivers had antisocial per-sonality disorder and when siblings had severe emotional or behavioral problems. Children with CD had poor prognoses in later years; they were also more likely to have criminal histories, histories of domestic violence, mental and medical problems, financial difficulties, lower cognitive abili-ties, poor temperaments, and lower socioeconomic status (SES), and they were likely to abuse alcohol and drugs.

In most cases, CD presented in preschool children as irritable temperament and inattentiveness, and some hypothesized these traits may have resulted from poor maternal-child attachment (Sanders & Schaechter, 2007). As they aged, children with CD in elementary school came to demonstrate quick, angry temperaments and poor social skills, and tended to blame the victim in scenarios involving physical aggression. In middle and high school, children with CD commonly broke rules, overreacted emotionally, and typically did not take responsibility for their actions. Research has shown that people with childhood-onset CD, known as "early starters," are likely to exhibit antisocial personality disorder (APD) as adults (Kimonis & Frick, 2010). In general, children with CD are also more likely to have co-occurring depression, anxiety, learning disabilities, impulse-control problems, and addictions.

Prevalence and Course

Depending on the samples and methods used in the studies, the prevalence of CD has been estimated to be between 2% and 16% (Wu, 2011). Pardini and Frick (2013) noted that adolescents with conduct problems stemming from childhood were more likely to have pervasive and persistent criminal problems into adulthood. Children with childhood-onset CD displayed severe behaviors and tended to have maladjusted outcomes (Brennan & Shaw, 2013). According to Hinshaw et al. (1993), childhood-onset CD often began with oppositional defiant disorder (ODD) behaviors. In fact, 80% of boys with childhood-onset CD had been previously diagnosed with ODD (Lahey & Loeber, 1994). Typical symptoms of this are temper tantrums, defiance, irritability, argumentativeness, and annoying behaviors. The earlier-onset cases also had a strong genetic component alongside the behavioral indicators (difficult temperament, emotional dysregulation, impulsivity), the cognitive indicators (neurological impairments, deficits in verbal intelligence and executive functioning), and the social indicators (poor parenting practices, low SES; Brennan & Shaw, 2013). As adults, early starters tended to have more criminal convictions, incarcerations, and other legal involvements than their adolescent-onset counterparts. In fact, between one-third and one-half of these children were diagnosed with disorders characterized by antisocial behaviors (Loeber et al., 2002).

Compared to early starters, individuals with adolescent-onset CD tended to be less aggressive and violent. This population tended to have fewer cognitive, neuropsychological, and behavioral deficits than early starters. (Interestingly, the age of onset for girls was typically later than that of boys; Farrington, 2004.) Furthermore, individuals with adolescent-onset CD tended to have stable family units that used effective parenting strategies more often than did those with early-onset CD.

However, later-onset individuals were at a greater risk for continued substance abuse problems (Odgers et al., 2007). Interestingly, adolescents with both CD and alcohol abuse problems had a much greater risk of displaying antisocial behaviors, which speaks to the comorbid nature of CD with other mental disorders (Howard et al., 2012).

Pharmacological Solitary Treatments

Pharmacological interventions for CD have been used for decades; however, they are mostly used in conjunction with psychotherapy. Studies on pharmacological interventions for CD are often further complicated by the presence of comorbid disorders such as attention-deficit/hyperactivity disorder (ADHD), anxiety, major depression, substance use, and other related impulse-control problems. Overall, there are five classes of medications commonly prescribed to children and adolescents with CD: antipsychotics, mood stabilizers, antidepressants, stimulants, and adrenergic agents (Tcheremissine & Lieving, 2006). Each class of medication will be discussed in detail pertaining to randomized control trials, efficacy, and commonly experienced side effects in the following section.

Antipsychotics

Historically, antipsychotics have been the medications most commonly prescribed to adolescents with CD (Kaplan, 1994). Randomized controlled trials of typical antipsychotic medications for CD revealed a decrease in behavioral symptoms. In a double-blind study of 31 hospitalized children with aggressive behavior between the ages of 6 and 11, for example, the effects of molindone and thioridazine were examined over an 8-week period (Greenhill, 1985). The results, on standardized rating scales, did indicate a decrease in aggressive behaviors, but the researchers did not use a placebo control group, so these conclusions are not definitive. In addition, these medications often cause significant adverse effects, including extrapyramidal symptoms (EPSs) caused by a dopamine blockade or depletion in the basal ganglia (Blair, 1992). Other side effects of typical antipsychotics include acute dyskinesia and dystonic reactions, tardive dyskinesia, Parkinsonism, akinesia, akathisia, and a risk of neuroleptic malignant syndrome.

Atypical antipsychotics—including risperidone, aripiprazole, quetiapine, and olanzapine—may offer the benefits of decreased behavioral aggression without the EPSs. Risperidone blocks dopamine and serotonin receptors and decreases aggressive behavior in children with CD, as demonstrated in a 10-week trial on 20 outpatient children ages 5 to 15. The outcome, measured on the Rating of Aggression Against People and/ or Property (RAAP) scale, showed a decrease in aggressive behavior over the placebo group. Additionally, there were no EPSs reported during the study. These results were replicated in two additional double-blind placebo-controlled studies with small sample sizes: one with children with borderline intellectual functioning (Van Bellinghem, 2001) and the other with children with borderline intellectual functioning or mild mental retardation (Buitelaar, 2001).

Aripiprazole has been found to be effective and well tolerated in adolescents (Findling, 2009). Safety, dosage, and effectiveness were evaluated in 23 children and adolescents between the ages of 6 and 17 with CD. The participants showed improved scores on the RAAP and the Clinical Global Impressions–Severity scales. During the study the dosages had to be reduced as a result of vomiting and sedation, but after doing so the aripiprazole was generally well tolerated and improvements in aggressive behavior were noted.

Quetiapine was assessed as a treatment for CD in a seven-week randomized double-blind placebo-controlled pilot study (Conner, 2008). Nineteen children were assessed weekly using primarily the clinician-assessed Clinical Global Impressions Severity and Improvement Scales and the parent-assessed Quality of Life Scale, Overt Aggression Scale, and the Conduct Problems subscale of the Conners' Parent Rating Scales. The study demonstrated that quetiapine is superior to placebo on all clinician-assessed measures and on the parent-assessed quality of life rating scale, but found no differences on the other measures. One patient on quetiapine developed akathisia, but no other EPSs were observed. However, weight gain and metabolic disturbances are significant risks with this medication.

Finally, olanzapine, an atypical antipsychotic used in the treatment of CD, has fewer empirical studies supporting its effectiveness; however, preliminary findings were promising (Masi, 2006). In a retrospective study of 23 adolescents diagnosed solely with CD and treated with olanzapine, the participants responded well to this medication. However, as with quetiapine, risk of significant weight gain and Type II diabetes are major concerns with this medication and may limit its utility.

Mood Stabilizers

Lithium has been evaluated in three randomized controlled trials and once in a retrospective study. Campbell (1995) conducted a double-blind placebo-controlled clinical trial with 50 children diagnosed with CD. After a two-week placebo baseline period, the participants were randomly assigned lithium or placebo for six weeks and then returned to two weeks of placebo. The outcome was measured on the Global Clinical Judgments (Consensus) Scale, the Children's Psychiatric Rating Scale, Conners' Teacher Questionnaire, the Parent–Teacher Questionnaire, and the Profile of Mood States. The results indicated that lithium is superior to placebo in decreasing aggression, but only a modest effect was noted on some of the measures. A second double-blind randomized controlled trial, conducted by Rifkin (1997), evaluated 33 adolescents in an inpatient setting. Subjects were randomly assigned after one week of placebo, and in total 26 subjects completed the study. Primary outcome measures include the Behavior Rating Scale, the Hamilton Rating Scale for Depression, the Treatment-Emergent Side Effects Scale, and Conners' Teacher Rating Scales. After two weeks of treatment, it was concluded that lithium did not improve aggression symptoms. Because lithium poses significant risks of weight gain and thyroid disturbances, its limited efficacy may not outweigh concerns over serious adverse effects.

The effectiveness of anticonvulsant mood stabilizers in treating CD has also been investigated. Donovan (1997) evaluated the use of divalproex sodium in a two-part investigation. Donovan initially examined it as an open-label treatment in 10 adolescents with disruptive behavior disorder and observed significant improvement. The author then conducted a double-blind placebo-controlled study to replicate these findings. A sample of 20 children and adolescents aged 10 to 18 with CD or ODD and mood lability were evaluated in a crossover-design study. In Phase 1, the subjects were randomly assigned to divalproex sodium or placebo for six weeks, after which the drug was switched to the alternate group for six weeks. The results demonstrated clinically significant improvements after six weeks, thereby replicating the results of the initial open-label treatment study.

Another study by Steiner (2003) evaluated the efficacy of divalproex sodium in 71 youth with CD. All subjects were adolescent males with at least one criminal conviction. A seven-week randomized control trial was carried out in which participants were randomized to high- and low-dose groups. Participants in the low-dose group were administered a dose of 125 mg/day, and those in the high-dose group received a dose of 1,000 mg/day. The results indicated that divalproex sodium produced significant dose-dependent improvements in the impulse-control and self-restraint measures completed by the clinicians and subjects. A more recent study utilized the same sample to examine weekly slopes of emotions and cognitions of varying degrees of complexity (Khanzode, 2006). By measuring more basic states such as anger, depression, happiness, and anxiety as well as complex states such as impulse control, consideration of others, responsibility, and self-esteem, the researchers attempted to evaluate varying levels of psychopathology for youth with CD. The outcome of this study was mixed and indicated that further studies were warranted, however.

Another mood stabilizer, carbamazepine, has also been used as a treatment for aggressive behavior in children. Kafantaris (1992) completed a pilot study of carbamazepine in 10 hospitalized aggressive and explosive children diagnosed with CD. This study showed that the use of carbamazepine is associated with clinically and statistically significant reductions in the target symptoms of aggressiveness and explosiveness. These results were promising and suggested that a critical assessment of the efficacy and safety of carbamazepine was warranted under double-blind and placebo-controlled conditions in this population.

The common side effects of anticonvulsant mood stabilizers often include nausea, vomiting, diarrhea, weight gain, drowsiness, hives, rashes, confusion, slurred speech, and in rare cases Stevens-Johnson syndrome and liver damage. These risks must carefully be weighed against any potential clinical benefits.

Antidepressants

This category of psychotropic medications has been used in adolescents for a variety of disorders—including depression, anxiety, and obsessive compulsive disorders—and aggressive and impulsive symptoms of CD are often targeted with antidepressants (Soller, 2006), specifically serotonin-based medications (Armenteros, 2002). For example, Zubieta and Alessi (1992) evaluated trazadone, a serotonin agonist and reuptake inhibitor, for efficacy in children with disruptive behavior disorders. Their sample consisted of 22 inpatient children between the ages of 5 and 12. After treatment, 13 of the children demonstrated a decrease in aggressive behavior, and follow-up interviews with parents showed continued positive effects. Another antidepressant, fluoxetine, was evaluated in a randomized controlled trial of 126 adolescents with CD, major depressive disorder, and substance use disorder. The outcomes were promising in that the medication improved the participants' symptoms (Riggs, 2007). Citalopram, another selective serotonin reuptake inhibitor, was evaluated in an open-label study by Armenteros. In the study, impulsive aggression was defined as a pattern of aggressive behavior over the preceding six months including at least three acts of aggression within one week of the study screening. Twelve subjects aged 7 to 15 with impulsive aggression received citalopram for six weeks. Eleven subjects completed the study; one subject withdrew because of hyperactivity, which required additional pharmacotherapy. The results indicated that citalopram produces a clinically significant decrease in impulsive aggression on all outcome measures. No significant adverse effects of the medication were reported. Researchers concluded that this medication was effective and well tolerated in this sample of children and adolescents.

Finally, as previously discussed, comorbid diagnoses are commonly observed in children with CD. Aggressive behavior is often targeted in treatment alongside ADHD. Two antidepressant medications, buproprion and reboxetine (which are currently not available in the United States, although atomoxetine, which is available in the United States, is a similar substance), have been evaluated for their efficacy in addressing aggression, impulsivity, and hyperactivity. Buproprion was evaluated in an open-label pilot study (Riggs, 1998). Thirteen boys with CD and ADHD diagnoses in a residential treatment program were administered buproprion for five weeks. Outcome measures included Conners' Hyperactivity Index and Daydream Attention scores. The data showed a decrease in symptoms, suggesting buproprion may be useful in adolescents with CD and comorbid ADHD. Likewise, Mozes (2005) evaluated reboxetine for efficacy in treating aggression in CD and hyperactivity. An open-label trial was conducted with 15 children (ages 5 to 14) in inpatient treatment. Twelve patients completed the 12-week trial. This study showed significant reduction in symptoms by week eight. While reboxetine was well tolerated, adverse effects such as drowsiness, decreased appetite, bed-wetting, and hair loss were reported among the participants.

In summary, the studies of antidepressant use for the treatment of CD are promising, but there remains the need for larger randomized double-blind placebo-controlled trials. Many of the current studies are small open-label trials that have provided good preliminary data on their specific samples but whose generalizability to larger populations is limited. It should also be noted that side effects for antidepressant medications may include initial increases in suicidal thoughts as well as varying degrees of anxiety, changes in sleep patterns, agitation, nausea, and weight fluctuations. While the potential for adverse effect with antidepressants is less significant that with antipsychotics or mood stabilizers, as with all medications, clinicians must carefully weigh clinical benefits versus risks of side effects.

Stimulants

Stimulants comprise another class of psychotropic medications that have been used to treat CD. Stimulant medications have historically been used to address hyperactive and impulsive behavior; however, early research has shown benefits with aggressive behavior as well. Eisenberg (1963) examined the efficacy of dextroamphetamine in a double-blind placebo-controlled study of 28 institutionalized boys with delinquent behavior. The results demonstrated improvement in symptoms according to teachers, observers, and peers. Decades later, beginning in 1990, studies of the stimulant methylphenidate have demonstrated similar decreases in aggressive behavior. Kaplan (1990) documented a pattern of less aggressive behavior during methylphenidate treatment than in the placebo state. For example, they conducted a seven-week crossover study with nine adolescents (ages 13 to 16) with ADHD and CD and found a significant decrease in total scores on the Adolescent Antisocial Behavior Checklist.

Similarly, Klein (1997) examined the efficacy of methylphenidate in a randomized controlled trial of 83 children with CD. Children aged 6 to 15 were assigned to the methylphenidate or the placebo group for five weeks, and over this period their behavior was rated by parents, teachers, and clinicians and through direct classroom observations. The results indicated that the children's behaviors that were specific to CD decreased significantly with methylphenidate treatment. The researchers concluded that the effects of methylphenidate on symptoms of CD were not a function of the severity of ADHD symptoms because the positive medication effects remained after researchers statistically controlled for the severity of ADHD. Although stimulants may be effective (especially with comorbid ADHD), side effects may include headache, upset stomach, increased blood pressure, decreased appetite, weight loss, nervousness, sleep problems, and emotional instability.

Antihypertensives

Antihypertensives (especially alpha-adrenergic agonists) have also been used to treat aggressive behaviors arising from CD. Kemph (1993) investigated the effectiveness of clonidine in treating aggressive behavior in a pilot study with 17 children and adolescents (ages 5 to 15). After a mean of 5.2 months, 88% of the participants had significantly improved in their emotions and behavior. A more recent study by Hazell (2003) evaluated the effects of clonidine when added to psychostimulant therapy in children diagnosed with ADHD and either CD or ODD. This randomized placebo-controlled study involved 60 children between the ages of 6 and 14. The outcome measure, on Conners' Rating Scales, demonstrated a greater reduction in symptoms in the clonidine group. Adverse effects including drowsiness and dizziness were reported in the clonidine group, but these were noted to be transient. Common side effects may also include dry mouth, bowel-movement difficulties, drowsiness, dizziness, and low energy levels, and subjects may feel weak, especially upon the onset of treatment or after a dose increase.

Benefits and Limitations of Pharmacotherapy as Sole Treatment

Medication can be an effective treatment modality for CD. Psychotropic medications used to treat individuals with CD have included antipsychotics, antidepressants, mood stabilizers, stimulants, and antihypertensives that have demonstrated efficacy in reducing symptoms associated with CD. But physicians and patients need to fully understand the reasons for using a medication, and both its therapeutic benefits and its possible adverse effects. A comprehensive psychological and medical evaluation is usually warranted to minimize any potential risks. It is also critical that physicians and patents discuss the initial use as well as the criteria for continuation or termination of any of the psychotropic medications mentioned above. When taken appropriately, medications may reduce symptoms and improve the quality of life for children and families. But more studies that include larger samples are needed in order to provide additional information on the mechanisms of these medications and on generalizability onto diverse groups of children and young adults.

Psychological Solitary Treatments

Pardini and Frick (2013) indicated that it could be beneficial to individualize treatments for children with CD based on the different developmental pathways of their problem behaviors. Treatment that emphasizes anger management and works to decrease harsh parenting, for instance, might be helpful for children with anger problems and emotional dysregulation issues (Lochman & Wells, 2004). On the other hand, interventions based on enhancing the parent–child relationship might help children with CD and callous-unemotional traits (Thomas & Zimmer-Gembeck, 2007). Kolko and Pardini (2010) further noted that empirically based interventions are helpful in assisting children with CD (Somech & Elizur, 2012). The following section will describe several empirically validated psychosocial interventions designed to address the needs of individuals with CD.

Problem-Solving Skills Training

Psychosocial treatments for CD may focus on the individual youth, the parents, the family system, and the community. Some treatments focus on only one of these aspects, while others include a more comprehensive set of modalities. Cognitive therapy has been used especially to teach adolescents with CD and problem-solving skills, for example, reducing their aggressive behaviors. In other cases, adolescents with CD may fail to recognize alternative interpretations of social situations and may often make negative attributions regarding the motivations of others. They may also have difficulty understanding how others view them and understanding the consequences of their own actions (Kazdin, 2002). Problem-Solving Skills Training (PSST; Kazdin, 2003) addresses this by teaching interpersonal problem-solving skills, and adolescents are encouraged to take a step-by-step approach to social situations and to focus on all aspects of a situation before deciding how to respond. Therapists use in-session modeling of prosocial behavior, role-playing, corrective feedback, and social reinforcement. Several meta-analytic reviews of the effectiveness of PSST have supported its usefulness. One review of 36 studies using participants between the ages of 4 and 17 found that the effectiveness of self-statement modification, modeling, and problem-solving training exceeded that of the placebo and attention-control groups (Baer & Nietzel, 1991). Research using randomized clinical trials also suggested particular benefit to children aged 11 and older (Durlak et al., 1991). Overall, these studies showed reduced aggressive and antisocial behavior at home, at school, and in the community at the end of treatment and at a one year follow-up (Kazdin, 2002).

Parent Management Training

Parent Management Training (PMT) is also an effective and empirically supported treatment for CD (Kazdin, 2005). In PMT, parents are taught to modify their adolescents' behavior in the home using social learning principles. Children learn basic principles regarding reinforcement and consequences, and they learn alternative strategies for using these to manage their adolescents' behavior. Adolescents are also brought into the therapy for behavioral contracting. Basic characteristics of PMT include having parents identify, define, and observe problem behavior; target specific behaviors for change; implement social learning principles, and provide contingent consequences (Kazdin, 2005).

Parent Management Training is considered one of the most empirically validated treatments for CD. For instance, Brestan and Eyberg (1998) examined 82 studies and suggested that 20 interventions had a significant probability of meeting criteria for efficacious treatment for youth identified as conduct disordered. The results of these studies showed that adolescents with parents who had participated in PMT showed marked improvement in behavior as reported by parents and teachers and in school and police reports. Many of the behavioral improvements could be directly connected to parental behavior and practices, and these treatment gains were maintained for up to 14 years (Long et al., 1994). McCart et al. (2006) conducted a more recent meta-analysis of parent training effectiveness. Their results suggested that parent management training was effective in reducing aggressive behavior, and also significantly reduced the parents' own psychosocial distress.

Parent–Child Interaction Therapy

Parent–Child Interaction Therapy is an evidence-based intervention approach for young children with emotional and behavioral disorders that works on improving the quality of the parent–child relationship and dyadic patterns. In fact, many parent training programs based on Parent–Child Interaction Therapy and Webster-Stratton's Parent Training Program (1990) have been repeatedly shown to have empirical support in comparison to control groups, although these studies have generally only looked at children under the age of 10. Research has suggested that adolescents appear to respond less well to parent management techniques than children (Dishion & Patterson, 1992). In 2008, for example, Eyeberg et al. (2008) conducted a study to examine well-established and efficacious treatments for CD. Their review identified two evidence-based multicomponent treatment approaches for adolescents with significantly delinquent behavior, both of which included both parent and child training components. These were multisystemic therapy (MST) and multidimensional treatment foster care (MTFC).

Multisystemic Therapy

Multisystemic therapy (Henggeler & Bordiun, 1990) is a family-systems-based approach that considers adolescent delinquent behavior as it is embedded within the family, school, community, and peer system. Therefore MST interventions combine cognitive–behavioral approaches, behavior therapies, parent training, and pragmatic family therapies. Strong evidence in support of MST has come from multiple randomized controlled clinical trials involving youth with disruptive behaviors. For example, male adolescents who had committed criminal offenses or were on probation showed significant treatment gains and lower recidivism under MST than members of the control groups (Henggeler et al., 2009). In addition, efficacy trials for MST among violent and chronic juvenile offenders have shown improved family relations, decreased youth behavior problems, and decreased recidivism when compared to individual counseling after a four-year follow-up (Borduin et al., 1995). Similar results have been found with juvenile sex offenders. When compared to those in individual counseling, for example, adolescent sex offenders participating in MST demonstrated a 93% lower rate of sexual reoffending and 72% lower rate of other criminal offending (Borduin et al., 1990). When compared to "usual" sex offender services, MST has also shown decreased out-of-home placements, decreased delinquency, and improved family relations for juvenile sex offenders (Borduin et al., 2009).

Multidimensional Treatment Foster Care

Multidimensional treatment foster care (Chamberlain & Smith, 2003) is a community-based program originally developed as an alternative to institutionalization for youth with severe and chronic delinquent behavior. During treatment, youths are placed in a foster home for six to nine months and undergo intensive support and treatment. In addition, the foster parents receive a 20-hour parent management training course in which they learn to implement basic social learning principles. After their training, the foster parents implement a daily token-reinforcement system in which the youth receives points for engaging in appropriate and positive behaviors and loses points for negative behaviors. In addition to the parent management component, each youth participating in MTFC meets weekly with an individual therapist who provides support and works with them on problem-solving skills, anger management, social skills, and educational or vocational planning. The adolescent also meets weekly with a behavior support specialist trained in applied behavior analysis who focuses on teaching prosocial behaviors through one-on-one interactions within the community setting. Many research studies have demonstrated positive outcomes for this approach. For example, Rhoades et al. (2013) found that adolescent girls showed significant decreases in delinquent behaviors after participating in this type of intervention.

Functional Family Therapy

Research on family-based treatments of CD and delinquency in adolescents has also focused on two other interventions: functional family therapy (FFT) and brief strategic family therapy (Henggeler & Sheidow, 2012). FFT (Alexander et al., 1994) integrates systems, behavioral, and cognitive approaches to therapy. Overall, FFT focuses on the functions that various behaviors serve and requires that a functional analysis be conducted prior to intervention. FFT considers how the behavior of each family member functions within the family system. The therapy's treatment goals are to increase reciprocity and positive reinforcement among family members. Early research using randomized trials showed that FFT was more effective than three other comparison conditions at improving family interactions and decreasing recidivism for statutory offenses, but not for criminal offenses (Alexander & Parsons, 1973). More recent research using a randomized efficacy study with substance-abusing youth did not find FFT to be more effective than the comparison groups (Waldron et al., 2001). Overall, though, research indicated that adolescents participating in FFT had better results than those participating in client-centered family groups or psychodynamically oriented family therapy as well as those receiving no treatment (Alexander et al., 1994).

Brief Strategic Family Therapy

Brief strategic family therapy (BSFT; Szapocznik et al., 2003), initially developed for use with Hispanic youth in the Miami, Florida area, is another emerging approach for treating adolescent conduct problems. As with most treatments discussed herein, BSFT also views adolescent behavior problems in terms of family dysfunction, and BSFT is therefore problem focused and attempts to alter the interaction patterns among family members (Kazdin, 2002). Therapy is generally delivered in a weekly format, either at a clinic or in the family's home, for a duration of 8 to 24 sessions depending on family needs. Two randomized trials with adolescents referred for treatment showed more posttreatment reduction in conduct symptoms among youth who completed BSFT than among youths in the control group (Coatsworth et al., 2001). Youth completing BSFT also had greater improvement in behavior problems posttreatment than those in a participatory learning condition (Santisteban et al., 2003).

Benefits and Limitations of Psychotherapy as Sole Treatment

Overall, a number of psychosocial treatments for CD have shown promise in research trials. Because the etiology of CD may include psychological and sociological aspects such as disordered cognitions, deviant peer groups, and dysfunctional family systems, these treatments may work because they address those factors. According to Kazdin (2002), familial criminal behavior, family relational difficulties, harsh punishment and permissive parenting, and low levels of affection, emotional support, acceptance, and attachment all contribute to conduct problems. Therefore interventions that focus on those parent, youth, and family characteristics that contribute to or maintain the child's conduct problems are directly focusing on causal factors of the disorder. But there are limitations to using solely psychosocial treatment methods. For example, treatments with a parent training component tend to have high dropout rates. In addition, these treatments require that families learn and implement social learning principles, which may be difficult in many family circumstances. When the adolescent's problems are more severe, their parents may also find it more difficult to implement these strategies. Many of the treatment programs are also intensive. For example, MST requires cognitive treatment for the adolescent, PMT, intervention with the school, community interventions when necessary, and therapists who are readily available.

Access to care may pose further limitations, for example, among adolescents who are adjudicated or who do not reside in areas with convenient access to mental health care. Even if treatment agencies are reasonably close, they may not deliver empirically supported treatments or have adequately trained therapists. Financial considerations may also limit access to psychological care on an outpatient basis. Although research has suggested that implementing small-group parent management training in neighborhoods is a highly cost-effective way to deliver therapy (Cunningham et al., 1995), most communities still do not have such treatments available and parents still find it difficult to access these services, especially if they are not referred through outside sources (e.g., court).

Combination Treatments

Conduct disorder has been considered difficult to treat, with decades of research making only small steps in identifying successful interventions

(Burke et al., 2004). Within the last two decades, cognitive and behavioral therapies have been the most researched for children and adolescents with CD, while pharmacological therapies continue to be amongst those least studied (Mpofu, 2002). Even among psychosocial treatments for CD youth, many have proven to be ineffective as a result of their failures to incorporate factors linked to the development of CD (Frick, 2001). Despite their promise for treating youth with CD, combined treatments have not been well researched for children and adolescents, and few studies have evaluated the effects of combined psychosocial and pharmacological treatment protocols for children with CD (Brown et al., 2008). When considering treatment options, it is important to target the processes that research has demonstrated to contribute to the development and maintenance of CD. These include biological factors (predispositions), functional factors (child temperament, academic performance, impulsivity, social cognition, etc.), and psychosocial factors (parenting methods, child abuse, peer effects, socioeconomic stresses, trauma, life stressors, ability to cope, etc.) (Burke et al., 2004).

The identification of effective treatments for children and adolescents with CD has a twofold significance, namely, significance at an individual level and at a systemic level. At an individual level, many youths with CD show significant psychosocial impairments, including low educational achievement, poor social relationships, conflict with parents and teachers, involvement with the legal system, and high emotional distress (Frick, 2001). Clinical data and outcomes from longitudinal studies have demonstrated that the prognosis for CD youths is relatively poor and that uninformed and ill-conceived treatments for youth CD can do more harm than good. According to the author, intervention programs for children with CD need to be implemented with caution, as some approaches might be harmful to children. Given this poor prognosis and the detrimental effects of subpar treatments for CD youth, it is crucial to identify treatments that have strong empirical support for effectiveness and positive outcomes. At a systemic level, it is important for schools and communities to identify effective treatments of CD youth as part of a comprehensive approach to decreasing violence in schools and in the community. School violence continues to occur and to threaten the physical, psychological, and emotional well-being of students and school staff (National Association of School Psychologists, 2006). Given the aggressive nature of students with CD, targeting this population for intervention may be an important step in the effort to reduce violence.

As early as 1974, Maletzky evaluated dextroamphetamine in a double-blind placebo-controlled study of 28 teenagers with antisocial behavior. When dextroamphetamine was added to ongoing therapy, there was a significant reduction in antisocial behavior in these teenagers. Other studies also indicated a positive outcome for combined therapies for children and youngsters with CD. When adolescents between the ages of 15 and 19 were placed for 16 weeks into either a fluoxetine group with cognitive-behavioral therapy (CBT), a CBT-only group, or a placebo group, for example, the fluoxetine-and-CBT group had greater efficacy and gains on one but not both depression measures than either the placebo group or the CBT-only group, and was not associated with greater decline in self-reported substance use or CD symptoms (Riggs, 2007).

Brown et al. (2008) reviewed a randomized placebo-controlled study that examined separate and incremental effects of methylphenidate and behavior modification in 16 children with ADHD and ODD. The results revealed that both treatment modalities showed positive effects when the treatment was a standalone rather than combined approach. The authors also discussed the Multimodal Treatment of Attention-Deficit Hyperactivity Disorder (MTA) study, which included 579 children randomly assigned either to routine community care (CC) or to one of three study-delivered treatments, each lasting 14 months. The three MTA treatments consisted of monthly medication management (usually methylphenidate), intensive behavioral treatment, and the combination. According to Brown et al. (2008), the MTA study found that children with ADHD and ODD/CD responded well to stimulant medication alone, while children with ADHD and other disorders responded well to a combined treatment of medication and psychosocial interventions.

Benefits and Limitations of Combined Treatments

There are potential benefits of using a combined pharmacological and psychotherapeutic approach when treating children and adolescents with CD. These may include having a more comprehensive and individualized approach that is wider in scope and one that may be more likely to target the wide array of risk factors linked to the development and maintenance of CD symptoms for each individual child. The few studies that reviewed combined pharmacological and psychological treatments for youth with CD revealed inconsistent results, however, and the studies have many limitations. As previously discussed, there are few studies on the efficacy of combined interventions for youth with CD, so further research is warranted. To assist in this effort, research for combined approaches may begin with interventions, both psychological and pharmacological, that possess empirical data supporting their effectiveness as unimodal treatment approaches and, in the case of psychological treatments, interventions that target factors that have been linked to the development and maintenance of CD. Data detailing and comparing the cost effectiveness of combined and unimodal treatment approaches might also be worth exploring.

Summary and Recommendations

With the myriad factors contributing to CD, it is logical to assume that targeting many of these factors may require more than one intervention, as any single modality will not generally suffice to treat these multidimensional problems (Burke et al., 2004). In addition to a multimodal approach, there is evidence showing that interventions must be individualized and tailored to the unique needs of each child and adolescent with CD (Frick, 2001). These needs vary depending on the specific mechanisms underlying each subject's cognitive, emotional, and behavioral disturbances. Given the complexity and multidimensional nature of CD, combined approaches may hold real promise for treating children and adolescents with this disorder.

Combined treatments may involve integrating various psychosocial treatments, such as MST and FFT, both of which focus on the interaction of systems, environments, and cognitive and behavioral interventions (Kazdin, 1997). Combined approaches may also involve a combination of pharmacological and psychotherapeutic modalities. For instance, medications may be used to treat maladaptive, impulsive, or dangerous symptoms as part of a comprehensive treatment plan, while cognitive or behavioral interventions are incorporated to enhance effective coping mechanisms. One benefit of adding pharmacological interventions to psychosocial interventions is that the pharmacological intervention may enhance the child or adolescent's responsiveness to the psychological interventions. Stimulant medication, for example, has been shown to reduce conduct problems in children with ADHD and comorbid CD. It has also been shown to decrease the rate of disruptive classroom behaviors, including verbal and physical aggression, teasing, destruction of property, and cheating (Frick, 2001).

If children with CD are able to reduce their aggression through the use of medication, then they may be better able to take active part in interventions aimed at building and practicing social skills. A child with conduct disorder taking stimulant medication may also be better able to reduce verbal aggression toward adults, and consequently may be more receptive to and capable of engaging in psychotherapy aimed at developing coping skills to deal with anger. As disruptive behaviors decrease and children develop a repertoire of alternative socially acceptable behaviors, they may begin to experience success in interactions with others and consequently experience a more rewarding quality of life.

The following vignette offers a case example of a student with severe emotional disturbance who was initially nonresponsive to traditional counseling and interventions over more than six months of treatment. This youth had a significant psychiatric history with treatment in a variety of different mental health settings. But after a combined treatment with counseling and psychotropic medication— along with the dedication and persistence of a community of caring teachers, physicians, and mental health professionals—his outcome was excellent.

Mark, age 17, had rocky beginnings after enrolling in a self-contained special day-class program for students with severe emotional disturbance. He immediately presented himself as impulsive, saying anything that came to mind, however inappropriate: he used disrespectful language toward staff members and peers, and made negative sexual comments toward others. He engaged in property destruction such as purposefully urinating on the bathroom floor and writing gang names on the school walls. He also engaged in frequent fights with peers and teaching staff. He had difficulty staying in class for an entire period and would often run away from his class and wander around the school campus. He would use illegal substances on school grounds whenever he had the opportunity to do so; he would sometimes arrive at school hung over or under the influence of marijuana after smoking it at home.

Mark did not want to be at school and did not like following the school rules. He resisted participating in his counseling and psychotherapy sessions, which were often cut short. Academically, Mark was behind in credits needed to graduate. He had been diagnosed with ADHD and CD when he was 13 years old and had a significant history of substance abuse and alcohol abuse, including using marijuana, heroin, cocaine, and methamphetamine. On two occasions, his behaviors became so severe that they resulted in police involvement and involuntary psychiatric hospitalizations. Given the severity of his psychiatric conditions, Mark qualified for free outpatient psychotherapy and psychiatric services through the county mental health program as well as for school-based services, but he repeatedly refused to access these services even though all the service providers tried hard to engage him in treatment.

Mark was the third oldest of nine siblings, five of whom still lived at home. He lived in an economically disadvantaged and violent urban area. His neighborhood was in constant distress and disarray, with frequent drive-by shootings, robberies, homicides, and other violent crimes. Drugs, gangs, and prostitutes were also prevalent on the streets nearby. Although his own family was relatively stable in terms of living and financial situation, their home was crowded and Mark lacked emotional support from his family. On the few occasions that he talked to his therapist, he mentioned growing up in a household where arguing, bickering, and fighting would happen on a daily basis. Although there was no reported child abuse, Mark's therapist suspected that he suffered from emotional abuse and trauma. Mark also did not have the greatest relationship with his siblings—they had limited contact, and everybody just went about their own business. In general, the idea that Mark would not make it in the world was impressed upon him from a young age. For example, his family had little confidence that he would graduate from high school, and they often expressed this to him. He once remarked that he would probably end up in jail or die at a young age. Throughout his educational career, Mark struggled academically and would not follow directions from teachers or complete his homework. Standardized cognitive and academic tests showed he was functioning within the average range, and learning disabilities were ruled out. Later in elementary school, he began to fight with other children and cut classes. He eventually started to use drugs and hang out with friends who had gang affiliations.

For the first two years of high school, Mark was enrolled in the special day-class program and began to receive weekly school-based psychotherapy services with an assigned school psychologist as well as daily "check-ins," weekly drug counseling, and daily participation in the school's extended-day program to make up the credits he needed to graduate. Mark's engagement in therapy was "minimal," and he was described as "nonresponsive." His school psychologist utilized multiple approaches and therapeutic methods to try to build a therapeutic relationship; however, these efforts were unsuccessful. His school psychologist tried the person-centered approach, the psychodynamic method, solution-focused therapy, and cognitive behavioral therapy to no avail during the first few months. He also reached out to Mark's family through phone calls and attempted to help them understand the importance of providing Mark with the emotional support he needed if he was to believe in his abilities to graduate and to succeed in life.

When other treatment modalities showed limited impact, a psychiatrist prescribed medications. Initially, Mark was resistant. But after multiple conversations with school staff and community-based providers, though still reluctant, he became more open to medications. During his psychiatric evaluation, he reported smoking a pack of cigarettes per day and being mildly overweight. He also had sleep problems, a decreased appetite, concentration difficulties,

(continued)

(continued)

and his weight had fluctuated. Mark admitted that he had suffered for many years from depression, and that this had been followed on and off by his therapist for the past few years. His willingness to seek help for it had decreased, however, and he finally refused any form of assistance from professionals.

Mark had a history of suicidal ideation, with multiple suicide attempts by overdose, cutting himself, and reckless driving when he was younger. He indicated that he had no history of mania, nor was there a family history of bipolar disorder, depression, anxiety, or psychotic disorders. Additionally, Mark noted that he had been on lithium for a while. He was now taking citalopram for depression and anxiety, and had tried fluoxetine, sertraline, paroxetine, and bupropion for depression in the past. He had found that these medications did not work for him. He did not report any other significant medical histories. His psychiatrist decided to start him on a regimen of antipsychotics. Mark initially reported side effects such as dizziness, nausea, tiredness, and blurred vision. With careful titration, he reported fewer side effects. His treatment team also carefully monitored his suicidality, given his past suicide attempts and hospitalization.

Although Mark was initially resistant to any form of treatment, with the patience and perseverance of staff, over time Mark began to warm up to the idea of medication and slowly started to show signs of improvement. He was prescribed aripiprazole and became open to taking his medication consistently. His medication helped him to keep calm and focused. He learned to self-manage and cope with restlessness and impulsivity by asking his teacher for permission to take short walks instead of eloping from class. He noted that the medication calmed him down. As a result, he attended classes more frequently and fully participated in his counseling and therapy sessions during the latter part of the school year. During his one-on-one therapy sessions, he learned the basics of cognitive behavioral therapy. He was able to identify his distorted cognition and thinking patterns. He acquired skills that helped him challenge his negative and pessimistic thoughts and change his inappropriate feelings and unproductive behaviors. He gradually became skilled at recognizing and connecting his thoughts, emotions, and actions. During this time, parent education and family therapy were also offered to Mark's family, but their participation was limited. Although he had periodic relapses, he was sober for longer periods of time. He admitted that the growing process was difficult, but he enjoyed the self-actualization and improvement. He revealed that he had to maintain a "tough guy" facade in order to survive in the school setting and on the street. If people found out that he was receiving therapy, he felt he would be in big trouble. Finally, he was able to create and form meaningful relationships with other less troubled peers in school and began to engage in school-based activities. Moreover, he enjoyed the connections that he had with his therapist and teacher. Mark eventually set for himself the goal of graduating from high school, which gave him a sense of purpose. By June, he proved to himself, his family, and the community of caring adults supporting him that he was capable of accomplishing his goal of earning his high school diploma.

References

Alexander, J. F., & Parsons, B. V. (1973). Short-term behavioral intervention with delinquent families: Impact on family process and recidivism. *Journal of Abnormal Psychology, 81,* 219–255.

Alexander, J. F., et al. (1994). The process and outcome of marital and family therapy research: Review and evaluation. In A. E. Bergin & S. L. Garfield (Eds.), *Handbook of behavior therapy and behavior change* (4th ed., pp. 595–630). New York: Wiley.

Armenteros, J. L. (2002). Citalopram treatment for impulsive aggression in children and adolescents: An open pilot study. *Journal of the American Academy of Child and Adolescent Psychiatry, 41,* 522–529.

Baer, R. A., & Nietzel, M. T. (1991). Cognitive and behavioral treatment of impulsivity in children: A meta-analytic review of the outcome literature. *Journal of Clinical Child Psychology, 20,* 400–412.

Blair, D. D. (1992). Extrapyramidal symptoms are serious side-effects of antipsychotic and other drugs. *Nurse Practitioner, 17*(11), 62–64.

Borduin, C. M., et al. (1990). Multisystemic treatment of adolescent sexual offenders. *International Journal of Offender Therapy and Comparative Criminology, 35,* 105–114.

Borduin, C. M., et al. (1995). Multisystemic treatment of serious juvenile offenders: Long-term prevention of criminality and violence. *Journal of Consulting and Clinical Psychology, 63,* 569–578.

Borduin, C. M., et al. (2009). A randomized clinical trial of multisystemic therapy with juvenile sexual offenders: Effect on youth social ecology and criminal activity. *Journal of Consulting and Clinical Psychology, 77,* 26–37.

Brennan, L. M., & Shaw, D. S. (2013). Revisiting data related to the age of onset and developmental course of female conduct problems. *Clinical Child and Family Psychology Review, 16,* 35–58.

Brestan, E. V., & Eyberg, S. M. (1998). Effective psychosocial treatments of conduct-disordered children and adolescents: 29 years, 82 studies, and 5,272 kids. *Journal of Clinical Child Psychology, 27,* 180–189.

Brown, R. T., et al. (2008). Oppositional defiant and conduct disorders. In *Childhood mental health disorders: Evidence base and contextual factors for psychosocial, psychopharmacological, and combined interventions.* Washington, DC: American Psychological Association. doi:10.1037/11638-003

Buitelaar, J. V. K. (2001). A randomized controlled trial of risperidone in the treatment of aggression in hospitalized adolescents with subaverage cognitive abilities. *Journal of Clinical Psychiatry, 62*(4), 239–248.

Burke, J. D., et al. (2004). Oppositional defiant disorder and conduct disorder: A review of the past 10 years: II. *Focus: The Journal of Lifelong Learning in Psychiatry, 11*(4), 558–576.

Campbell, M. A. (1995). Lithium in hospitalized aggressive children with conduct disorder: A double-blind and placebo-controlled study. *Journal of the American Academy of Child and Adolescent Psychiatry, 34*(4), 445–453.

Chamberlain, P., & Smith, D. K. (2003). Antisocial behavior in children and adolescents: The Oregon Multidimensional Treatment Foster Care Model. In A. E. Kazdin & J. R. Weisz (Eds.), *Evidence-based psychotherapies for children and adolescents* (pp. 282–300). New York: Guilford Press.

Coatsworth, J. D., et al. (2001). Brief strategic family therapy versus community control: Engagement, retention, and an exploration of the moderating role of adolescent symptoms severity. *Family Process, 40*, 313–332.

Conner, D. F. (2008). Randomized controlled pilot study of quetiapine in the treatment of adolescent conduct disorder. *Journal of Child and Adolescent Psychopharmacology, 18*(2), 140–156.

Cunningham, C. E., et al. (1995). Large group school-based courses for parents of preschoolers at risk for disruptive behaviour disorders: Utilization, outcome, and cost effectiveness. *Journal of Child Psychology and Psychiatry, 36*, 1141–1159.

Dishion, T. J., & Patterson, G. R. (1992). Age effects in parent training outcomes. *Behavior Therapy, 23*, 719–723.

Donovan, S. S. (1997). Divalproex treatment of disruptive adolescents: A report of 10 cases. *Journal of Clinical Psychiatry, 58*(1), 12–15.

Durlak, J. A., et al. (1991). Effectiveness of cognitive-behavioral therapy for maladaptive children: A meta-analysis. *Psychological Bulletin, 110*, 204–214.

Eisenberg, L. L. (1963). A psychopharmacologic experiment in a training school for delinquent boys. *American Journal of Orthopsychiatry, 33*, 431–437.

Eyeberg, S. M., et al. (2008). Evidence-based psychosocial treatments for children and adolescents with disruptive behavior. *Journal of Clinical Child and Adolescent Psychology, 37*(1), 215–237.

Farrington, D. P. (2004). Conduct disorder, aggression, and delinquency. In R. M. Lerner & L. Steinberg (Eds.), *Handbook of adolescent psychology* (2nd ed.). Hoboken, NJ: John Wiley & Sons.

Findling, R. K. T. (2009). An open-label study of aripiprazole: Pharmacokinetics, tolerability, and effectiveness in children and adolescents with conduct disorder. *Journal of Child and Adolescent Psychopharmacology, 19*(4), 431–439.

Frick, P. (2001). Effective interventions for children and adolescents with conduct disorder. *Canadian Journal of Psychiatry, 46*, 597–608.

Greenhill, L. S. (1985). Molindone hydrochloride treatment of hospitalized children with conduct disorder. *Journal of Clinical Psychiatry, 46*(8), 20–25.

Hazell, P. S. (2003). A randomized controlled trial of clonidine added to psychostimulant medication for hyperactive and aggressive children. *Journal of the American Academy of Child and Adolescent Psychiatry, 42*(8), 886–894.

Henggeler, S. W., & Borduin, C. M. (1990). *Family therapy and beyond: A multisystemic approach to teaching the behavior problems of children and adolescents.* Pacific Grove, CA: Brooks/Cole.

Henggeler, S. W., & Sheidow, A. J. (2012). Empirically supported family-based treatments for conduct disorder and delinquency in adolescents. *Journal of Marital and Family Therapy*, *38*(1), 30–58.

Henggeler, S. W., et al. (2009). *Multisystemic therapy for antisocial behavior in children and adolescents* (2nd ed.). New York: Guilford Press.

Hinshaw, S. P., et al. (1993). Issues of taxonomy and comorbidity in the development of conduct disorder. *Developmental Psychology*, *20*, 1120–1134.

Howard, R., et al. (2012). Adolescent-onset alcohol abuse exacerbates the influence of childhood conduct disorder on late adolescent and early adult antisocial behavior. *Journal of Forensic Psychiatry and Psychology*, *23*, 7–22.

Kafantaris, V. C. G. (1992). Carbamazepine in hospitalized aggressive conduct disorder children: An open pilot study. *Psychopharmacology Bulletin*, *28*(3), 220.

Kaplan, S. B. (1990). Effects of methylphenidate on adolescents with aggressive conduct disorder and ADHD: A preliminary report. *Journal of the American Academy of Child and Adolescent Psychiatry*, *29*(5), 719–723.

Kaplan, S. S. (1994). Prescribing practices of outpatient child psychiatrists. *Journal of the American Academy of Child and Adolescent Psychiatry*, *33*, 35–44.

Kazdin, A. E. (1997). Practitioner review: Psychosocial treatments for conduct disorder in children. *Journal of Child Psychology and Psychiatry*, *38*(2), 161–178.

Kazdin, A. E. (2002). Psychosocial treatments for conduct disorder in children and adolescents. In P. E. Nathan & J. M. Gorman (Eds.), *A guide to treatments that work* (2nd ed.). New York: Oxford University Press.

Kazdin, A. E. (2003). Problem-Solving Skills Training and parent management training for conduct disorder. In A. E. Kazdin & J. R. Weisz (Eds.), *Evidence-based psychotherapies for children and adolescents* (pp. 241–262). New York: Guilford Press.

Kazdin, A. E. (2005). *Parent management training: Treatment for oppositional, aggressive, and antisocial behavior in children and adolescents*. New York: Oxford University Press.

Kemph, J. D. (1993). Treatment of aggressive children with clonidine: Results of an open pilot study. *Journal of the Academy of Child and Adolescent Psychiatry*, *32*(3), 577–581.

Khanzode, L. S. (2006). Efficacy profiles of psychopharmacology: Divalproex sodium in conduct disorder. *Child Psychiatry and Human Development*, *37*, 55–64.

Kimonis, E. R., & Frick, P. J. (2010). Oppositional defiant disorder and conduct disorder grown up. *Journal of Developmental and Behavioral Pediatrics*, *31*(3), 244–254.

Klein, R. A. (1997). Clinical efficacy of methylphenidate in conduct disorder with and without attention deficit hyperactivity disorder. *Archives of General Psychiatry*, *54*(12), 1073–1080.

Kolko, D. J., & Pardini, D. A. (2010). Odd dimensions, ADHD, and callous-unemotional traits as predictors of treatment response in children with disruptive behavior disorders. *Journal of Abnormal Psychology*, *119*, 713–725.

Lahey, B. B., & Loeber, R. (1994). Framework for a developmental model of oppositional defiant disorder and conduct disorder. In D. K. Routh (Ed.), *Disruptive behavior disorders in childhood* (pp. 139–180). New York: Plenum.

Lochman, J. E., & Wells, K. C. (2004). The Coping Power Program for preadolescent aggressive boys and their parents: Outcome effects at the 1-year follow-up. *Journal of Consulting and Clinical Psychology*, *72*, 571–578.

Loeber, R., et al. (2002). What are adolescent antecedents to antisocial personality disorder? *Criminal Behaviour and Mental Health*, *12*, 24–36.

Long, P., et al. (1994). Does parent training with young noncompliant children have long-term effects? *Behaviour Research and Therapy, 32,* 101–107.

Maletzky, B. (1974). d-Amphetamine and delinquency: Hyperkinesis persisting. *Diseases of the Nervous System, 35*(12), 543–547.

Masi, G. M. (2006). Olanzapine treatment in adolescents with severe conduct disorder. *European Psychiatry, 21*(1), 51–57.

McCart, M. R., et al. (2006). Differential effectiveness of behavioral parent-training and cognitive-behavioral therapy for antisocial youth: A meta-analysis. *Journal of Abnormal Child Psychology, 34*(4), 527–573.

Mozes, T. M.-A. (2005). Reboxetine as an optional treatment for hyperkinetic conduct disorder: A prospective open-label trial. *Journal of Child and Adolescent Psychopharmacology, 15*(2), 259–269.

Mpofu, E. (2002). Psychopharmacology in the treatment of conduct disorder children and adolescents: Rationale, prospects, and ethics. *South African Journal of Psychology, 32*(4), 9–21.

National Association of School Psychologists. (2006). *School violence* (Position Statement). Bethesda, MD: Author.

Odgers, C. L., et al. (2007). Prediction of differential adult health burden by conduct problem subtypes in males. *Archives of General Psychiatry, 64,* 476–484.

Pardini, D., & Frick, P. J. (2013). Multiple developmental pathways to conduct disorder: Current conceptualizations and clinical implications. *Journal of the Cnadian Academy of Child and Adolescent Psychiatry, 22*(1), 20–25.

Rhoades, K. A., et al. (2013). MTFC for high-risk adolescent girls: A comparison of outcomes in England and the United States. *Journal of Child and Adolescent Substance Abuse, 22,* 435–449.

Rifkin, A. K. (1997). Lithium treatment of conduct disorders in adolescents. *American Journal of Psychiatry, 154,* 554–555.

Riggs, P. L. (1998). An open trial of bupropion for ADHD in adolescents with substance use disorders and conduct disorder. *Journal of American Academy of Child and Adolescent Psychiatry, 37*(12), 1271–1278.

Riggs, P. M.-G. (2007). A randomized controlled trial of fluoxetine and cognitive behavioral therapy in adolescents with major depression, behavior problems, and substance use disorders. *Archives of Pediatric Adolescent Medicine, 161*(11), 1026–1034.

Sanders, L. M., & Schaechter, J. (2007). Conduct disorder. *Pediatrics in Review, 28*(11), 433–343.

Santisteban, D. A., et al. (2003). Efficacy of brief strategic family therapy in modifying Hispanic adolescent behavior problems and substance use. *Journal of Family Psychology, 17,* 121–133.

Soller, M. K. (2006). Psychopharmacologic treatment of juvenile offenders. *Child and Adolescent Psychiatric Clinics of North America, 15,* 477–499.

Somech, L. Y., & Elizur, Y. (2012). Promoting self-regulation and cooperation in pre-kindergarten children with conduct problems: A randomized controlled trial. *Journal of the American Academy of Child and Adolescent Psychiatry, 51,* 412–422.

Steiner, H. P. (2003). Divalproex sodium for the treatment of conduct disorder: A randomized controlled clinical trial. *Journal of Clinical Psychiatry, 64*(10), 1183–1191.

Szapocznik, J., et al. (2003). *Brief strategic family therapy for adolescent drug abuse.* NIH Publication No. 03-4751. Bethesda, MD: National Institute on Drug Abuse.

Tcheremissine, O. L., & Lieving, L. M. (2006). Pharmacological aspects of the treatment of conduct disorder in children and adolescents. *CNS Drugs, 20*(7), 549–565.

Thomas, R., & Zimmer-Gembeck, M. J. (2007). Behavioral outcomes of Parent-Child Interaction Therapy and Triple P—Positive Parenting Program: A review and meta-analysis. *Journal of Abnormal Child Psychology, 35,* 475–495.

Van Bellinghem, M. D. (2001). Risperidone in the treatment of behavioral distur-bances in children and adolescents with borderline intellectual functioning: A double-blind, placebo-controlled pilot trial. *Journal of Child and Adolescent Psychopharmacology, 11*(1), 5–13.

Waldron, H. B., et al. (2001). Treatment outcomes for adolescent substance abuse at 4 and 7 month assessments. *Journal of Consulting and Clinical Psychology, 69,* 802–813.

Wu, T. (2011). Conduct disorder. In S. Goldstein & J. Naglieri (Eds.), *The encyclopedia of child behavior and development.* New York: Springer.

Zubieta, J. K., & Alessi, N. E. (1992). Acute and chronic administration of trazadone in the treatment of disruptive behavior disorders. *Journal of Clinical Psychophar-macology, 12,* 346–351.

8 Tourette's Disorder and Other Tic Disorders

*Loran P. Hayes, Michael B. Himle,
Krishnapriya Ramanujam, and
David Shprecher*

The fifth edition of the *Diagnostic and Statistical Manual of Mental Disorders* (DSM-5) defines tic disorders as childhood-onset neuropsychiatric disorders characterized by involuntary motor or vocal tics (American Psychiatric Association, 2013). Tics are defined as sudden, recurrent, and nonrhythmic movements (motor tics) or vocalizations (vocal tics) that typically fluctuate in form, frequency, and intensity over time. Tics can be further characterized as simple or complex. Simple tics are rapid, meaningless, discrete movements or sounds such as eye blinking, face twitching, sniffing, or throat clearing. Complex motor tics appear more purposeful, such as hand gestures, patterned touching or tapping, and orchestrated patterns of multiple simple tics. Complex vocal tics include uttering words, phrases, or complete sentences.

Many individuals also report the presence of premonitory urges, which are unpleasant somatic sensations that occur prior to the tic occurrence (Leckman et al., 1993). Premonitory urges are often described as a sensation of pressure, itching, burning, or a "not just right" feeling that is often localized to the area of the tic. Most patients who experience premonitory urges describe them as aversive signals of an upcoming tic that increase in intensity, especially upon attempts to suppress the tics, and are alleviated when the tic is performed (Kwak et al., 2003). In fact, many report that their tics are "semi-volitional" responses that are performed, at least in part, to reduce the urge (Kwak et al., 2003).

Diagnostic Considerations

The DSM-5 recognizes three primary tic disorders: persistent motor or vocal tic disorder, Tourette's disorder, and provisional tic disorder. Persistent motor or vocal tic disorder involves single or multiple motor or vocal tics, but not both, that are present for at least one year. Tourette's disorder (TD) involves both multiple motor and one or more vocal tics that occur for at least one year. Provisional tic disorder involves single or multiple tics (motor or vocal) for less than one year since initial onset. Severity is determined on the basis of tic frequency, intensity, complexity, and interference resulting from the tics.

Large international samples have suggested that up to 85% of individuals with a tic disorder meet criteria for at least one comorbid psychiatric disorder, with most experiencing multiple comorbidities. The most common comorbid conditions include attention-deficit/hyperactivity disorder (ADHD), which occurs in 50%–75% of cases, and obsessive compulsive disorder (OCD), which occurs in 27%–40% of cases. In addition to ADHD and OCD, tic disorders are also associated with increased risk for mood and anxiety disorders, impulse control problems (e.g., rage attacks), and learning and sleep problems (Freeman et al., 2000).

Although some individuals report little or no impairment associated with their tics, others report substantial disability and diminished quality of life, including social withdrawal, difficulty making and keeping friends, social ridicule, and occupational problems (Woods et al., 2007). In many cases, however, comorbid conditions contribute more to functional impairment than the tics themselves (Wand et al., 1993).

Prevalence and Course

Prevalence estimates for tic disorders vary considerably. Studies have shown that transient tics are common, occurring in 4%–24% of school-aged children (Robertson, 2008). Estimates for chronic tic disorders, including TD, range from 0.1% to 3%, with best estimates suggesting a lifetime prevalence of 1% (Robertson, 2008). Tic disorders occur more commonly in males than females by a ratio of 4:1 in general school-age populations and 6:1 in clinical populations (Kadesjo & Gillberg, 2000).

Tics typically start in childhood, with mean age of onset at 7 years (Robertson, 2008). Motor tics usually precede vocal tics, and simple tics generally precede complex tics (Bloch & Leckman, 2009). Tics generally take a waxing and waning course, usually peak in severity at a mean age of 10 (Leckman et al., 1998) and then decrease in severity through adolescence and early adulthood. Most adults report at least moderate tic improvement (Leckman et al., 1998). In addition to natural waxing and waning, tics are idiosyncratically influenced by contextual factors such as stress, mood states, social situations, and fatigue (Silva et al., 1995).

Pharmacological Solitary Treatments

Though TD was originally thought to have a psychogenic origin, it is now clear that tic disorders have a developmental neurobiological basis. Abnormal density of inhibitory basal ganglia neurons—together with nuclear imaging evidence for reduced GABA receptor density, excessive dopamine release with amphetamine challenge, and increased density of striatal dopaminergic nerve terminals—support the continued study and clinical use of drugs that inhibit dopamine and enhance inhibitory neurotransmission within the basal ganglia (Felling & Singer, 2011).

Given the known neurobiological origin of tics, pharmacotherapy has historically been considered the first-line intervention for TD. While there have been few large randomized placebo-controlled trials examining the efficacy of pharmacotherapy for the treatment of TD (especially in children), small randomized controlled trials (RCTs), quasi-experimental studies, and open-label trials provide substantial empirical support for the efficacy of several tic-suppressing agents. Those with adequate empirical support include the typical and atypical neuroleptics and alpha-2 agonists.

Typical neuroleptics are the most potent medications for reducing tics and have the strongest empirical support. Consistent with findings suggesting dysregulation of dopamine in the etiology of tics, these agents are believed to be effective because they directly block postsynaptic dopamine type 2 receptors. Reports of successful treatment of tics with haloperidol date back over 50 years (Seignot, 1961). Since then, several controlled and uncontrolled trials have supported the tic-reducing properties of both haloperidol and pimozide. For example, Shapiro et al. (1989) conducted a randomized placebo-controlled crossover trial comparing haloperidol and pimozide in 57 children and adults with tics and found that both medications were more effective than placebo, with haloperidol slightly more effective than pimozide on a clinician rating scale of tic severity. More recently, Sallee et al. (1997) conducted a similar randomized double-blind placebo-controlled crossover trial, again comparing haloperidol to pimozide, this time with 22 children and adolescents with chronic tic disorders. This study found pimozide (40% tic reduction) to be more effective than haloperidol (27% tic reduction). In addition, pimozide was associated with fewer serious side effects and fewer dose-limiting side effects compared to haloperidol. Fluphenazine, a typical neuroleptic that has also been shown to be effective for tics in open-label (Goetz et al., 1984) and small controlled trials (Borison et al., 1982), is considered the best-tolerated conventional antipsychotic. In a retrospective study (mean treatment duration 2.6 years), there were no cases of tardive dyskinesia, but 122 of 268 patients discontinued, including 28 who discontinued owing to lack of efficacy alone and 51 who discontinued because of side effects alone (drowsiness, weight gain, akathisia, acute dystonic reactions, or depression; Wijemanne et al., 2014). While tardive dyskinesia is rare in treatment of TD (Müller-Vahl et al., 2011), up to 84% of patients experience adverse side effects that limit use of typical neuroleptics (Sallee et al., 1997).

For this reason, attention has turned to atypical neuroleptics. Of this class, risperidone (Waldon et al., 2013) and aripiprazole have the most empirical support. Several small open-label studies and two randomized controlled trials have shown risperidone to be as effective as (or better than) pimozide for reducing tics, but with fewer side effects (e.g., Gilbert et al., 2004). In addition, Gaffney et al. (2002) conducted a small double-blind randomized comparison trial. They found risperidone and clonidine were equally efficacious for reducing tics in children with "pure" TD. But risperidone was more efficacious for reducing tics in children with TD and comorbid OCD (Gaffney et al., 2002). Efficacy and safety of aripiprazole are supported by one RCT of 61 pediatric subjects (Yoo et al., 2013) as well as additional case and open-label studies (Harrison et al., 2007).

The evidence for other atypical neuroleptics is mixed. While ziprasidone has shown promise in case studies and small open-label trials, clozapine and quetiapine appear less effective (see Harrison et al., 2007, for a review). A recent meta-analysis compared risperidone, pimozide, haloperidol, and ziprasidone and found these medications (as a group) to be more beneficial than placebo, without significant individual differences in efficacy (Weisman et al., 2013). One double-blind crossover trial found olanzapine to be more effective than low-dose pimozide for reducing tics (Onofrj et al., 2000). Sulpiride and tiapride, atypical antipsychotics of the benzamide class (used as first-line treatment in Europe), have shown efficacy in several uncontrolled trials (Robertson et al., 1990) and at least one small placebo-controlled trial (Eggers et al., 1988). While weight gain is common with all antipsychotics, atypical neuroleptics are generally viewed as having more unfavorable effects on metabolic indices of glycemia, triglyceridemia, and cholesterolemia. This requires further study specifically in TD, where a single head-to-head pediatric trial found significant increases in hyperglycemia with pimozide and cholesterolemia with aripiprazole (Rizzo et al., 2012).

Alpha-adrenergic agonists (alpha-2 agonists) have the broadest evidence base outside of neuroleptics supporting their use for tic disorders. Alpha-2 agonists reduce central noradrenergic activity, which has indirect effects on serotonergic and dopaminergic neurotransmission (Carpenter et al., 1999). Although generally less effective in reducing tics than the neuroleptics (e.g., Weisman et al., 2013), they are often used in first-line treatment owing to their relatively favorable side-effect profile and improvement of comorbid ADHD symptoms (Tourette Syndrome Study Group, 2002). Within this class, clonidine and guanfacine have the most empirical support. To date, at least two RCTs have shown clonidine to be superior to placebo for reducing tics (Leckman et al., 1991), and at least one study (Tourette Syndrome Study Group, 2002) has shown clonidine to be superior to placebo for reducing ADHD symptoms in children with TD plus ADHD. Guanfacine has been shown superior to placebo for tic suppression in mild TD (Cummings et al., 2002) as well as comorbid ADHD symptoms (Scahill et al., 2001). Guanfacine and clonidine have not been directly compared, and both pose practical challenges because of short half-lives and potential for sedation and hypotension; however, tolerability and convenience of dosing may be improved through the use of guanfacine extended-release tablet or clonidine patch systems. A recent meta-analysis concluded that alpha-2 agonists are beneficial for reducing tics (compared to placebo) but are generally less effective than neuroleptics. In this meta-analysis, ADHD moderated the efficacy of alpha-2 agonists, with trials enrolling subjects with ADHD plus TD showing a moderate-to-large effect and trials excluding ADHD showing a small nonsignificant effect, suggesting that alpha-2 agonists might have little benefit for TD patients without comorbid ADHD (Bloch and Leckman, 2009).

In addition to the medications described above, the dopamine depleter tetrabenazine has shown sustained, often dramatic benefit for tics in open-label studies (e.g., Jankovic & Beach, 1997). Side effects of fatigue, depression, anxiety, akathisia, insomnia, and Parkinsonism require careful titration and may require dose reduction or discontinuation. Topiramate was shown to be effective over placebo (at a maximum tolerated mean dose of 118 mg/day) for tic suppression in a small RCT of 29 patients (Jankovic et al., 2010), as well as in several small head-to-head trials against haloperidol (Yang et al., 2013). Side effects of topiramate in these trials included drowsiness, cognitive slowing, loss of weight/appetite, diarrhea, and nephrolithiasis.

Numerous other pharmacological agents have been evaluated for use in tic disorders. Use of botulinum toxin for focal motor tics was supported by one small RCT of 10 patients with motor tics, as well as a handful of open-label and case studies for patients with severe vocal tics (reviewed in Simpson et al., 2008). One small RCT showed delta-9-tetrahydrocannabinol effective over placebo for tic suppression (Müller-Vahl et al., 2003), though there are legal barriers to its use and study in the United States. Clinicians should screen patients regarding self-medication with cannabis, which is not uncommon in our clinical experience. Because of failure (or weak treatment effects) in RCTs, baclofen, levetiracetam (Lyon et al., 2010), and dopamine agonists have fallen out of favor for treatment of tic disorders (Kurlan et al., 2012).

Benefits and Limitations of Pharmacotherapy as Sole Treatment

Scientific evidence of the effective pharmacological management of TD reveals that several agents have been shown to be effective, including typical and atypical antipsychotics (especially haloperidol and pimozide) and alpha-2 agonists (clonidine and guanfacine). But significant adverse effects (especially for antipsychotics) often lead to medication discontinuation and limit the benefits patients derive from these medications. For this reason, these medications are best reserved for severe cases where tics have significant adverse impacts on the patient's adaptive functioning and behavioral treatments have failed to provide adequate relief. Medications with more favorable side-effect profiles have also been investigated, and some have shown promise for suppressing tics, but response is often idiosyncratic and incomplete, and therefore it is difficult to accurately anticipate patients' responses to those agents. Furthermore, comorbidity is common in TD and often complicates pharmacological management.

Psychological Solitary Treatments

While it is clear that tics have a biological origin, there is evidence that they are influenced by psychosocial factors. Rather than offering an explanation for the underlying cause of tics, the behavioral model emphasizes how psychosocial factors can lead to variability in tic expression and how the environment can be modified to reduce the overall severity of tics. The underlying assumption of this model is that psychosocial factors can make tics more or less likely to occur within a particular context and can shape their form, frequency, and intensity (Woods et al., 2008).

To understand how the environment influences tics, the behavioral model considers two primary variables: antecedents and consequences. Antecedents are contextual variables that precede tics and function to make tics better or worse. Several studies have shown that external antecedents, such as the presence of particular people (e.g., a parent, teacher, or peer), specific places (e.g., home, school, quiet places), and activities (e.g., social activities, watching television, talking about tics) are commonly associated with tic fluctuation (Silva et al., 1995). Consequence variables are outcomes or reactions that occur contingent upon tics that make them more or less likely to occur and shape how they are expressed. Common examples of tic-contingent consequences include attention (e.g., sympathy, teasing, people staring, or looking) and disruption of ongoing activities (e.g., being sent out of the room during a difficult academic task). In some instances, these consequences can reinforce the tic, thereby making it more frequent or intense. Identification and modification of these factors can, in some cases, minimize tic exacerbation and reduce overall tic severity.

Internal antecedents and consequences are also believed to affect tics. Examples of internal antecedents that have been associated with tic exacerbation include premonitory urges, mood states, and specific cognitions (Steinberg et al., 2013). Of particular importance to the behavioral model is the role of the premonitory urge. As noted earlier, studies have shown that most individuals report that aversive premonitory urges precede at least some of their tics and that performance of the tic alleviates these urges (Leckman et al., 1993). The behavioral model proposes that there is a functional relationship between premonitory urges and tics such that tics are strengthened (i.e., become more frequent and forceful) through negative reinforcement because they reduce the unpleasant urges (Evers & van de Wetering, 1994). Theoretically, if an individual learns strategies to prevent the tic from occurring when the premonitory urge strikes, the urge will habituate and the tic will no longer produce relief, resulting in a reduction in the frequency and intensity of the tic. The model also suggests that other internal antecedents that worsen tics, such as anxiety or boredom, can be addressed with behavioral procedures even if they are not linked to specific antecedent-consequence contingencies.

Based on the behavioral model, several efficacious psychosocial interventions have been developed and tested. Of these, the interventions with the most empirical support are habit reversal training (HRT), an extended version of HRT referred to as comprehensive behavioral intervention for tics (CBIT), and exposure and response prevention (ERP). Each of these treatment approaches, along with the research supporting their efficacy, is described below.

To date, the psychosocial intervention with the most empirical support is HRT. As the name implies, HRT was based on the "habit model" originally proposed by Azrin and Nunn (1973). The rationale for HRT was based on two primary hypotheses. First, it was proposed that because tics are performed with such high frequency, they become overlearned (and thus are performed largely outside of the individual's awareness) and are incorporated into normal ongoing behavior through behavioral chaining. Second, when tics are exhibited, they are shaped and strengthened by the automatic negative reinforcement (e.g., urge reduction) and external social reinforcement contingencies described above.

Based on this conceptualization, Azrin and Nunn (1973) developed HRT. The goals of HRT are to (1) help the individual become more aware of discrete instances of tics; (2) to break the link between tics and other ongoing behavior; (3) to break the link between tics and premonitory sensations, thereby allowing urge habituation; and (4) to differentially reinforce active tic management while extinguishing social reinforcement for tics. To accomplish these goals, HRT uses three primary techniques: awareness training (AT), competing response training (CRT), and social support. The purpose of AT is to help patients to become more aware of each discrete occurrence of their tic(s). After becoming able to recognize most occurrences of the targeted tic, the patient learns to engage in a competing response (CR) that is directly incompatible with the performance of the tic, thereby breaking the association between the tic and other ongoing behavior and also breaking the negative reinforcement cycle by allowing urge habituation. Finally, a social support person is recruited to prompt the patient to use the CR if observed ticcing and to reinforce the correct use of the CR (e.g., provide praise) while otherwise ignoring the performance of the tic. Within the HRT procedure, each tic is targeted systematically, typically one tic per session.

Because HRT was developed within the field of applied behavior analysis, much of the early evidence for its efficacy came from small studies utilizing small-N (single subject) designs. In general, these studies support the efficacy of HRT, with tic reduction ranging from 38% to 96% (see Himle et al., 2006, for a review). More recently, a series of small randomized controlled trials have shown HRT to be more effective than wait-list (Azrin & Peterson, 1990) and supportive psychotherapy (e.g., Deckersbach et al., 2006), and a review concluded that HRT meets criteria for a "well-established treatment" according to guidelines outlined by the American Psychological Association's Task Force on Promotion and Dissemination of Psychological Procedures (Cook & Blacher, 2007).

Additional evidence supporting the efficacy of HRT comes from recent research examining CBIT, an expanded treatment package (Woods et al., 2008). The primary therapeutic activity used in CBIT is HRT; however, the CBIT package also includes several additional therapeutic activities to address tic-exacerbating antecedents and consequences, including psychoeducation, relaxation training (RT), and a function-based assessment and treatment (FBAT) protocol. The goal of psychoeducation is to eliminate potentially negative social consequences that may be inadvertently reinforcing tics as well as to reduce shame, anxiety, and worry, which have been shown to worsen tics in many individuals (Silva et al., 1995). Similarly, the purpose of RT is to reduce stress and anxiety, which are known to exacerbate tics in many individuals (Peterson & Azrin, 1992). Although RT has not generally been shown to be an effective stand-alone treatment for tics (Bergin et al., 1998), it has been shown to be effective for reducing tics in some individuals, especially in the short term (Peterson & Azrin, 1992). Finally, FBAT techniques are employed to identify and modify contextual variables that may be worsening tics (Himle et al., 2014). The FBAT protocol involves a semistructured functional assessment interview designed to identify antecedents and consequences associated with tic exacerbations. This information is then used to develop function-based treatment strategies to reduce or eliminate tic-exacerbating factors.

The efficacy of CBIT was recently demonstrated in two large randomized controlled trials (a child trial and an adult trial) comparing CBIT to a supportive psychotherapy control condition (Piacentini et al., 2010; Wilhelm et al., 2012). In both trials, participants received 10 sessions of treatment, and a masked independent evaluator assessed outcomes. Results of the child trial ($N = 126$ children and adolescents, ages 9 to 17) revealed that 53% of participants receiving CBIT were characterized as treatment responders, as opposed to 19% in the control condition. In addition, there was a 31% reduction in tic severity on the Yale Global Tic Severity Scale (YGTSS; Leckman et al., 1989) following CBIT as opposed to a 14% reduction for the control group (effect size = 0.68), and treatment gains were maintained at a six-month follow-up (Piacentini et al., 2010). Similar results were observed in the adult trial (N = 122), with 38% of CBIT participants showing a clinically significant response, compared to 6.4% in the control group, with 26% reduction in tic severity (on the YGTSS) for CBIT, compared to an 11% reduction for supportive psychotherapy (effect size = 0.57; Wilhelm et al., 2012).

A final treatment that has shown promise in the treatment of tics is an adapted version of ERP. ERP is based on the negative-reinforcement hypothesis whereby tics are reinforced by removal of an aversive premonitory urge. The process of ERP for tics involves exposing patients to premonitory urges and antecedent sensations of tics, and then preventing the tic through general resistance or suppression. Similar to HRT, this approach is believed to facilitate urge habituation (Verdellen et al., 2008). One of the main advantages cited for the ERP approach is that it targets all tics at once (rather than the tic-by-tic approach used in HRT).

Preliminary research on ERP for TD has shown promise. Verdellen et al. (2004) compared ERP to HRT in a randomized controlled study of 43 patients with TD (age range 7–55). The study found that both ERP and HRT produced clinically significant reduction in tic severity on the YGTSS, with a slight (though nonsignificant) advantage for ERP (33% reduction vs. 18% reduction for ERP and HRT, respectively). In addition, both groups maintained clinical gains at three months posttreatment. In a follow-up analysis of participants who received ERP, the researchers also found that premonitory urges reduce in severity over the course of ERP, suggesting that habituation to the premonitory urge may be the mechanism underlying the efficacy of ERP for tics (Verdellen et al., 2008).

Benefits and Limitations of Psychotherapy as Sole Treatment

Behavior therapy has been shown to be effective for reducing tics, especially when clinicians administer specific treatments described in detailed procedural manuals (e.g., Woods et al., 2008). Although there are historical concerns about behavior therapy having iatrogenic side effects (i.e., worsening of tics, symptom substitution), large RCTs have not found evidence to support these concerns (Piacentini et al., 2010; Wilhelm et al., 2012). Most effective treatments require specifically trained providers, however, and those clinicians may not be widely available, especially in rural areas. In addition, time, effort, and cost associated with behavioral treatment, as well as lingering misperceptions about treatment, are additional barriers (Scahill et al., 2013). As with pharmacological treatments, comorbidity (e.g., ADHD) often complicates treatment, and clinicians must appropriately and effectively address comorbid conditions when providing psychological treatment for patients with TD.

Combined Treatments

To date, no head-to-head studies have examined the relative efficacy of behavior therapy, pharmacotherapy, or their combination. But some inferences can be drawn from psychosocial treatment studies. In the aforementioned CBIT trials, 38% of children and 25% of adults receiving CBIT entered the study on a stable dose of tic-suppressing medication. Both trials found that medication status did not moderate outcome within either treatment group, but there was a trend for lower CBIT response rates among adults receiving tic-suppressing medication (vs. no tic-suppressing medication). Unfortunately, no studies have thus far examined whether a combination of medication and behavior therapy enhances outcomes.

In addition to integrated pharmacological and psychosocial treatment to specifically target tics, management of common comorbidities (e.g., ADHD) is also of concern. ADHD and other behavioral symptoms may interfere with a patient's compliance and ability to benefit from behavior therapy. Although no studies have yet examined whether comorbid symptoms moderate treatment outcome, Deckersbach et al. (2006) did report that adults with greater deficits in response inhibition responded "less well" to HRT. Although the sample size in this study was small ($N = 15$), which limits the generalizability, these findings are consistent with our clinical impression for both adults and children receiving HRT and CBIT. While there is some evidence that disruptive behaviors can be effectively treated with behavior therapy in children with TD (Sukhodolsky et al., 2009), given the lack of transdiagnostic treatments for tic disorders and comorbid conditions (particularly ADHD), careful pharmacological management of ADHD symptoms should be considered in order to maximize likelihood of a positive response to behavior therapy. As noted above, alpha-2 agonists have been shown to reduce both tics and ADHD symptoms, so this may be a logical first-line approach. Additionally, atomoxetine (a selective norepinephrine reuptake inhibitor) has been shown to reduce ADHD symptoms in children with comorbid TD in a double-blind placebo-controlled study (Spencer et al., 2008). Finally, although there has historically been much concern that psychostimulants may worsen tics, this conventional wisdom has been called into question by two meta-analyses examining pharmacological treatments in for ADHD in children with a comorbid tic disorder, which found that most psychostimulants, in correct dosages, effectively treat ADHD symptoms without worsening tics (Pringsheim & Steeves, 2012).

Benefits and Limitations of Combined Treatments

Although to date no research has examined the benefits or drawbacks of combined treatments for tic disorders, much can be inferred from available research about each modality. At least theoretically, combined treatments hold the promise of integrating the benefits of each type of treatment, and therefore combined treatment should counteract at least some of the limitations of each approach used in isolation. Psychotherapeutic approaches teach patients skills to help them address urges to tic, and those changes are likely to benefit individuals in the long run, regardless of whether they ultimately remain on medications. Psychosocial approaches also help patients learn to manage stress, a major precipitant of tics. Conversely, adding pharmacotherapy can help address greater severity of tics, and the onset of improvement is likely to be faster than with psychotherapy alone.

Combined treatments, however, come with their own set of challenges. In most cases, patients need treatment with two providers, and access to both forms of treatment may be more difficult, as well as costlier and more time consuming.

Summary and Recommendations

Both pharmacological and psychosocial treatments have been shown to be effective for reducing tics; however, side effects often limit the use of the most effective tic-suppressing medications. In addition, comorbid symptoms are common and often contribute to functional impairment, emphasizing the need to address both tics and comorbid symptoms. When considering a treatment regimen, it is important that clinicians first conduct a careful assessment to determine which target symptoms (i.e., tics vs. comorbid symptoms) are most responsible for functional impairment. For patients with mild to moderate tic symptoms or for patients whose comorbid symptoms are not contributing to functional impairment, nonpharmacological interventions are the preferred initial treatment approach. But when tics are severe and cause functional disability, or when significant comorbid symptoms are present, a combination of pharmacological and psychosocial treatments to address both tics and comorbid symptoms is preferred. Further pharmacological options may be considered after examining response to first-line treatments.

Jack is a 10-year-old boy diagnosed with Tourette's disorder and ADHD (combined subtype). His tics began at age 5 with simple motor and vocal tics and took the typical waxing-and-waning course. Until recently, his tics caused minimal disruption and impairment and, as such, his parents had not sought prior treatment. His parents reported that his tics had been gradually increasing in frequency and intensity for the past year, with a marked increase when Jack was transitioned to a new school. At the time he presented for treatment,

Jack exhibited numerous motor and vocal tics that ranged from simple (e.g., eye blinking, throat clearing, grunting, head jerking) to complex (e.g., "sniffing" his fingers, coprolalia [i.e., swearing]). In addition, Jack reported that many of his tics were preceded by a sense of building pressure inside his body (localized to the area of his tics) that was briefly alleviated by tic behavior, only to return almost immediately. Consistent with clinical observation, his parents noted that his tics occurred almost constantly and that he rarely went more than a few minutes without any tics. Although his tics were frequent, he reported minimal interference with ongoing behavior or speech. He did note that his tics occasionally drew unwanted attention, however, especially from teachers and one particular peer.

Prior to beginning treatment, Jack underwent a physical exam and received a structured clinical interview, several parent- and self-report forms to assess tic and comorbidity presence and severity, and the YGTSS (Leckman et al., 1989). As expected, he scored in the clinical range on a measure of ADHD symptoms. His score on the YGTSS (total tic score = 26/50) placed him in the moderate range of tic severity.

Based on Jack's clinical assessment results, it was recommended that he receive a combination of CBIT and medication to treat his tics. But because his ADHD would likely interfere with his full participation in therapy, it was recommended that treatment be administered sequentially, beginning with a six-week trial of guanfacine prior to initiating CBIT. Guanfacine was chosen as the first-line agent because of its effectiveness for reducing ADHD symptoms and tics, as well as its tolerable side-effect profile. Jack was started on 0.5 mg at night, titrated slowly (0.5 mg every 7 days) to 2 mg at night. Because symptom response only lasted for the first two hours of the school day, treatment was titrated to 3 mg/day (1 mg in the morning, 2 mg at night). Further titration was limited by side effects (i.e., sedation and dizziness). After six weeks at this dose, Jack returned to the clinic for reassessment. The assessment determined that Jack's tics, especially his vocal tics, had improved modestly both in terms of intensity and frequency (YGTSS total tic score = 22/50). As is common in TD, however, a new tic (a complex motor-vocal combination) had recently emerged and was causing significant problems in the classroom. In addition, both Jack and his parents noticed a moderate improvement in his ADHD symptoms.

Based on his response to guanfacine, it was recommended that he continue on his current dose and begin a course of CBIT. As per standardized protocol (Woods et al., 2008), Jack received 10 sessions of CBIT over the course of 12 weeks. To monitor treatment

(continued)

(continued)

progress, Jack's parents completed the Parent Tic Questionnaire (PTQ; Chang et al., 2009) at each session, and the YGTSS was readministered at posttreatment.

Review of self-report forms and a clinician's assessment revealed several targets for function-based intervention. For example, one of Jack's peers at school frequently mimicked his tics, which in turn led to tic exacerbations. In addition, because his vocal tics were disruptive to his classmates, the teacher frequently sent Jack out of the room (to the gymnasium) for "tic breaks" so that he could "get his tics out." Although Jack enjoyed going to the gym, being asked to leave class resulted in him needing to complete more of his schoolwork at home. Jack's mother also reported that Jack often came home from school stressed out and anxious, which led to considerable tic exacerbation. As a result, he was usually allowed to watch television until he calmed down and his tics lessened, which resulted in him not having enough time to complete his homework. To address these factors, a plan was developed in conjunction with Jack's schoolteachers to educate his peers about TD, to reduce teasing, and to minimize tic breaks. When tic breaks were deemed necessary (e.g., if vocal tics were disruptive during an exam), Jack was sent to a support room (rather than the gym), where he completed his schoolwork. Jack was also taught relaxation techniques, including diaphragmatic breathing and progressive muscle relaxation, to reduce stress and anxiety, and he was instructed to practice these exercises at home after school (rather than watching television).

Habit reversal training began with the most bothersome tic on Jack's hierarchy (coprolalia). First, Jack was taught to become more aware of each occurrence of his tic using standardized awareness training procedures (see Woods et al., 2008). In particular, he was taught to recognize and detect pre-tic warning signs, including the pressure feeling in his abdomen (i.e., the premonitory urge). After he was able to detect the tic with 80% accuracy in session, he was taught to engage in a CR to prevent the tic from occurring. The CR chosen for his coprolalic vocal tic involved a controlled breathing procedure (see Woods et al., 2008). He was instructed to use the CR whenever he felt the urge to tic and immediately after he caught himself performing the tic (if he failed to detect the warning sign) and to hold the CR for one minute or until the urge to tic subsided (whichever was longer). Finally, Jack's parents were taught to appropriately prompt the correct use of the CR if they witnessed a tic and were instructed to provide praise if they observed Jack using the CR on his own. After practicing the use of the CR in session, Jack and his parents were asked to practice HRT on their own throughout the week, especially during "high-risk" times (e.g., when Jack came home from school).

Sessions progressed through the same protocol weekly, with a new tic targeted each week (progressing from most to least bothersome). Between each session, Jack and his family monitored each of the tics targeted in previous sessions, implemented HRT, and monitored for additional tic-exacerbating antecedents and consequences. At the end of treatment, two additional biweekly sessions were conducted. These sessions focused on problem solving, relapse prevention, and the development of a plan to address any new tics that may emerge.

At the end of CBIT, Jack was reassessed using the YGTSS. Results of the follow-up assessment revealed that Jack's tics had reduced markedly (YGTSS total tic score = 12/50). Clinical improvement was also observed on the PTQ (65% reduction in overall tic severity from pre- to posttreatment). Jack reported that his coprolalia tic was practically eliminated and that, although his vocal tics still occurred on occasion, they were markedly reduced in intensity and volume. Similar results were also observed for his motor tics with the exception of eye blinking, which was still frequent but not bothersome. In addition, Jack noted that his classmates no longer mimicked his tics and he was no longer being sent out of the classroom for tic breaks. Tic exacerbations at home were also infrequent. Medication discontinuation was considered, but because the medication was well tolerated and improved both his tics and ADHD, his current medication regimen was continued.

References

American Psychiatric Association. (2013). *Diagnostic and statistical manual of mental disorders* (5th ed.). Washington, DC: Author.

Azrin, N. H., & Nunn, R. G. (1973). Habit-reversal: A method of eliminating nervous habits and tics. *Behaviour Research and Therapy, 11,* 619–628.

Azrin, N. H., & Peterson, A. L. (1990). Treatment of Tourette syndrome by habit reversal: A waiting-list control group comparison. *Behavior Therapy, 21,* 305–318.

Bergin, A., et al. (1998). Relaxation therapy in Tourette syndrome: A pilot study. *Pediatric Neurology, 18,* 136–142.

Bloch, M. H., & Leckman, J. F. (2009). Clinical course of Tourette syndrome. *Journal of Psychosomatic Research, 67,* 497–501. doi:10.1016/j.jpsychores.2009.09.002

Borison, R. L., et al. (1982). New pharmacological approaches in the treatment of Tourette syndrome. *Advances in Neurology, 35,* 377.

Carpenter, L. L., et al. (1999). Pharmacological and other somatic approaches to treatment. In J. F. Leckman & D. J. Cohen (Eds.), *Tourette's syndrome—Tics, obsessions, compulsions: Developmental psychopathology and clinical care* (pp. 370–397). New York: John Wiley & Sons.

Chang, S., et al. (2009). Initial development and psychometric properties of a brief parent-report measure for assessing tic severity in children with chronic tic disorders. *Child and Family Behavior Therapy, 31,* 181–191.

Cook, C. R., & Blacher, J. (2007). Evidence-based psychosocial treatments for tic disorders. *Clinical Psychology: Science and Practice, 14,* 252–267.

Cummings, D. D., et al. (2002). Neuropsychiatric effects of guanfacine in children with mild Tourette syndrome: A pilot study. *Clinical Neuropharmacology, 25,* 325–332.

Deckersbach, T., et al. (2006). Habit reversal versus supportive psychotherapy in Tourette's disorder: A randomized controlled trial and predictors of treatment response. *Behaviour Research and Therapy, 44,* 1079–1090.

Eggers, C. H., et al. (1988). Clinical and neurobiological findings in children suffering from tic disease following treatment with tiapride. *European Archives of Psychiatry and Neurological Sciences, 237,* 223–229.

Evers, R. A., & van de Wetering, B. J. (1994). A treatment model for motor tics based on a specific tension-reduction technique. *Journal of Behavior Therapy and Experimental Psychiatry, 25,* 255–260.

Felling, R. J., & Singer, H. S. (2011). Neurobiology of Tourette syndrome: Current status and need for further investigation. *Journal of Neuroscience, 31,* 12,387–12,395.

Freeman, R. D., et al. (2000). An international perspective on Tourette syndrome: Selected findings from 3,500 individuals in 22 countries. *Developmental Medicine and Child Neurology, 42,* 436–447.

Gaffney, G. R., et al. (2002). Risperidone versus clonidine in the treatment of children and adolescents with Tourette's syndrome. *Journal of the American Academy of Child and Adolescent Psychiatry, 41,* 330–336.

Gilbert, D. L., et al. (2004). Tic reduction with risperidone versus pimozide in a randomized, double-blind, crossover trial. *Journal of the American Academy of Child and Adolescent Psychiatry, 43,* 206–214.

Goetz, C. G., et al. (1984). Fluphenazine and multifocal tic disorders. *Archives of Neurology, 41,* 271.

Harrison, J. N., et al. (2007). Medical management of Tourette syndrome and co-occurring conditions. In D. W. Woods, J. C. Piacentini, & J. T. Walkup (Eds.), *Treating Tourette syndrome and tic disorders: A guide for practitioners* (pp. 113–153). New York: Guilford Press.

Himle, M. B., et al. (2006). Brief review of habit reversal training for Tourette syndrome. *Journal of Child Neurology, 21,* 719–725.

Himle, M. B., et al. (2014). Variables associated with tic exacerbation in children with chronic tic disorders. *Behavior Modification, 38*(2), 163–183. doi:10.1177/0145445514531016

Jankovic, J., & Beach, J. (1997). Long-term effects of tetrabenazine in hyperkinetic movement disorders. *Neurology, 48,* 358–362.

Jankovic, J., et al. (2010). A randomised, double-blind, placebo-controlled study of topiramate in the treatment of Tourette syndrome. *Journal of Neurology, Neurosurgery and Psychiatry, 81,* 70–73.

Kadesjo, B., & Gillberg, C. (2000). Tourette's disorder: Epidemiology and comorbidity in primary school children. *Journal of the American Academy of Child Adolescent Psychiatry, 39,* 548–555. doi:10.1097/00004583-200005000-00007

Kurlan, R., et al. (2012). A multicenter randomized placebo-controlled clinical trial of pramipexole for Tourette's syndrome. *Movement Disorders, 27,* 775–778.

Kwak, C., et al. (2003). Premonitory sensory phenomenon in Tourette's syndrome. *Movement Disorders, 18,* 1530–1533.

Leckman, J. F., et al. (1989). The Yale Global Tic Severity Scale: Initial testing of a clinician-rated scale of tic severity. *Journal of the American Academy of Child and Adolescent Psychiatry, 28,* 566–573.

Leckman, J. F., et al. (1991). Clonidine treatment of Gilles de la Tourette's syndrome. *Archives of General Psychiatry, 48,* 324.

Leckman, J. F., et al. (1993). Premonitory urges in Tourette's syndrome. *American Journal of Psychiatry, 150,* 98–102.

Leckman, J. F., et al. (1998). Course of tic severity in Tourette syndrome: The first two decades. *Pediatrics, 102,* 14–19.

Lyon, G., et al. (2010). Tourette's disorder. *Current Treatment Options in Neurology, 12,* 274–286.

Müller-Vahl, K. R., et al. (2003). Delta-9-tetrahydrocannabinol is effective in the treatment of tics in Tourette syndrome: A 6-week randomized trial. *Journal of Clinical Psychiatry, 64,* 1–7.

Müller-Vahl, K. R., et al. (2011). Does Tourette syndrome prevent tardive dyskinesia? *Movement Disorders, 26,* 2442–2443.

Onofrj, M., et al. (2000). Olanzapine in severe Gilles de la Tourette syndrome: A 52-week double-blind cross over study vs. low-dose pimozide. *Journal of Neurology, 247,* 443–446.

Peterson, A. L., & Azrin, N. H. (1992). An evaluation of behavioral treatments for Tourette syndrome. *Behaviour Research and Therapy, 30,* 167–174.

Piacentini, J., et al. (2010). Behavior therapy for children with Tourette disorder: A randomized controlled trial. *Journal of the American Medical Association, 303,* 1929–1937. doi:10.1001/jama.2010.607

Pringsheim, T., & Steeves, T. (2012). Cochrane Review: Pharmacological treatment for attention deficit hyperactivity disorder (ADHD) in children with comorbid tic disorders. *Evidence-Based Child Health: A Cochrane Review Journal, 7,* 1196–1230.

Rizzo, R., et al. (2012). Metabolic effects of aripiprazole and pimozide in children with Tourette syndrome. *Pediatric Neurology, 47,* 419–422. doi:10.1016/j.pediatr-neurol.2012.08.015

Robertson, M. M. (2008). The prevalence and epidemiology of Gilles de la Tourette syndrome: I. The epidemiological and prevalence studies. *Journal of Psychosomatic Research, 65,* 461–472. doi:10.1016/j.jpsychores.2008.03.006

Robertson, M. M., et al. (1990). Management of Gilles de la Tourette syndrome using sulpiride. *Clinical neuropharmacology, 13,* 229–235.

Sallee, F. R., et al. (1997). Relative efficacy of haloperidol and pimozide in children and adolescents with Tourette's disorder. *American Journal of Psychiatry, 154,* 1057–1062.

Scahill, L., et al. (2001). A placebo-controlled study of guanfacine in the treatment of children with tic disorders and attention deficit hyperactivity disorder. *American Journal of Psychiatry, 158,* 1067–1074.

Scahill, L., et al. (2013). Current controversies on the role of behavior therapy in Tourette syndrome. *Movement Disorders, 28,* 1179–1183.

Seignot, M. J. N. (1961). A case of the syndrome of tics of Gilles de la Tourette controlled by R 1625. *Annales Médico-Psychologiques, 119,* 578–579.

Shapiro, E., et al. (1989). Controlled study of haloperidol, pimozide, and placebo for the treatment of Gilles de la Tourette's syndrome. *Archives of General Psychiatry, 46,* 722.

Silva, R. R., et al. (1995). Environmental factors and related fluctuation of symptoms in children and adolescents with Tourette's disorder. *Journal of Child Psychology and Psychiatry, 36,* 305–312.

Simpson, D. M., et al. (2008) Botulinum neurotoxin for the treatment of movement disorders. *Neurology, 70,* 1699–1706.

Spencer, T. J., et al. (2008). Atomoxetine treatment of ADHD in children with comorbid Tourette syndrome. *Journal of Attention Disorders, 11,* 470–481.

Steinberg, T., et al. (2013). Tic-related cognition, sensory phenomena, and anxiety in children and adolescents with Tourette syndrome. *Comprehensive Psychiatry, 54,* 462–466.

Sukhodolsky, D. G., et al. (2009). Randomized trial of anger control training for adolescents with Tourette's syndrome and disruptive behavior. *Journal of the American Academy of Child and Adolescent Psychiatry, 48,* 413–421.

Tourette Syndrome Study Group. (2002). Treatment of ADHD in children with Tourette syndrome: A randomized controlled trial. *Neurology, 58,* 527–536.

Verdellen, C. W., et al. (2004). Exposure with response prevention versus habit reversal in Tourettes's syndrome: A controlled study. *Behaviour Research and Therapy, 42,* 501–511. doi:10.1016/s0005-7967(03)00154-2

Verdellen, C. W., et al. (2008). Habituation of premonitory sensations during exposure and response prevention treatment in Tourette's syndrome. *Behavior Modification, 32,* 215–227. doi:10.1177/0145445507309020

Vincent, D. A. (2008). Botulinum toxin in the management of laryngeal tics. *Journal of Voice, 22,* 251–256.

Waldon, K., et al. (2013). Trials of pharmacological interventions for Tourette syndrome: A systematic review. *Behavioural Neurology, 26,* 265–273.

Wand, R. R., et al. (1993). Tourette syndrome: Associated symptoms and most disabling features. *Neuroscience and Biobehavioral Reviews, 17,* 271–275.

Weisman, H., et al. (2013). Systematic review: Pharmacological treatment of tic disorders—Efficacy of antipsychotic and alpha-2 adrenergic agonist agents. *Neuroscience and Biobehavioral Reviews, 37,* 1162–1171.

Wijemanne, S., et al. (2014). Long-term efficacy and safety of fluphenazine in patients with Tourette syndrome. *Movement Disorders, 29,* 126–30.

Wilhelm, S., et al. (2012). Randomized trial of behavior therapy for adults with Tourette syndrome. *Archives of General Psychiatry, 69,* 795–803.

Woods, D. W., et al. (2007). Management of social and occupational difficulties in persons with Tourette syndrome. In D. W. Woods, J. C. Piacentini, & J. T. Walkup (Eds.), *Treating Tourette syndrome and tic disorders* (pp. 265–277). New York: Guilford Press.

Woods, D. W., et al. (2008). *Managing Tourette syndrome: A behavioral intervention for children and adults.* New York: Oxford University Press.

Yang, C., et al. (2013). Topiramate for Tourette's syndrome in children: A meta-analysis. *Pediatric Neurology, 49,* 344–350.

Yoo, Y. K., et al. (2013). A multicenter, randomized, double-blind, placebo-controlled study of aripiprazole in children and adolescents with Tourette's disorder. *Journal of Clinical Psychiatry, 74,* 772–780.

9 Intermittent Explosive Disorder

Edward F. Hudspeth, Dawn Wirick, and Kimberly M. Matthews

Since intermittent explosive disorder (IED) became a diagnostic category in the third edition of the *Diagnostic and Statistical Manual of Mental Disorders* (DSM-III; American Psychiatric Association [APA], 1980) the exclusionary criteria combined with the vague operational definitions within the IED category made diagnosis and research difficult (Coccaro, 2003b). More recently, DSM-5 (APA, 2013) included a criterion for verbal aggression (rather than just physical aggression), allowing for inclusion of additional individuals into the diagnostic category (Coccaro, 2013).

Specifically, IED is the DSM-5 diagnostic category utilized to classify individuals who engage in repetitive patterns of impulsive aggression that are markedly disproportionate to stimuli that provoke the reaction and cannot be better accounted for by substances, medical conditions, or other psychological disorders (McCloskey et al., 2012). Additionally, IED is the sole disorder in the DSM-5 that puts affective aggressive behavior at the forefront of the diagnosis.

Diagnostic Considerations

A full medical examination should precede any diagnosis of IED, including physical and neurological examinations as well as a thorough review of one's medical record (Olvera, 2002). In addition, consultation with a neurologist is essential in many cases, because it is necessary to assist with exclusionary diagnoses such as head injury, memory loss, or seizures. A structured or semistructured diagnostic interview ensuring that comorbid and preexisting conditions will be given central consideration should also be employed. Robins and Navaco (1999) suggest that individuals with severe anger may not be accurate representatives of their actual behavioral patterns of aggression. Therefore it is recommended that clients' families and other corroborating resource persons be an integral part of the diagnostic process.

Because there is a high level of comorbidity between IED and other psychiatric disorders, one of the greatest challenges facing clinicians is clinically determining whether another mental health diagnosis better accounts for the aggression. Because the DSM contains many diagnoses that contain an element of aggression, concerns about limitations of the DSM diagnostic criteria for IED influenced the development of a set of alternative integrated research IED (IED-IR) criteria (McCloskey et al., 2012). The IED-IR criteria provide an objective definition of minimal aggression frequency as either twice-weekly verbal aggression for four consecutive weeks or three acts of physical aggression within a one-year period (Coccaro, 2003a). The IED-IR criteria also require the aggressive acts to be primarily affective in nature (acting out anger), and to result in clinically significant distress or impairment. In addition, the IED-IR criteria exclude borderline and antisocial personality disorders from this group of disorders, because IED is believed to more effectively explain aggressive behavior. In sum, the IED-IR was created in an attempt to more accurately assess and diagnose IED and to help differentiate it from other mental disorders that might better account for the affective explosiveness.

No published diagnostic assessment tools have been designed specifically to diagnose IED, perhaps because of diagnostic challenges, the use of multiple criteria to diagnose the disorder, and the relative absence of IED research (as compared to most other disruptive disorders). However, two unpublished instruments have been created to help diagnose IED.

The Intermittent Explosive Disorder Module (IED-M; Coccaro, unpublished instrument, as cited in Olvera, 2002; Olvera et al., 2001) is a 20- to 30-minute structured diagnostic interview created to acquire comprehensive information needed to arrive at a diagnosis of IED by using both DSM-5 and IED-IR criteria. The IED-M includes quantitative information about lifetime and current verbal aggression, aggression against property, and physical aggression (McCloskey et al., 2012). Descriptions of the three most serious instances of each type of aggression during the one-year period in which the aggression occurred most frequently (e.g., "What were the consequences of this outburst?") provide information about how proportionate the aggressive response is to the situation at hand. Additional information about aggressive acts is also obtained, including—but not limited to—age of onset, each type of aggression, the effects of aggressive behaviors on relationships with family and friends, subjective level of distress, emotions, physical symptoms before and after an outburst, and substance use during aggressive outbursts. The IED-M has been utilized in at least one published study (Coccaro et al., 2004), providing evidence of the instrument's construct validity. In particular, individuals diagnosed as having IED were more aggressive on both self-report and behavioral measures than comparison groups within this study. This study also provided evidence that the IED group reported higher levels of lifetime verbal and physical aggression than community control groups (Olvera et al., 2001).

Similarly, the Intermittent Explosive Disorder Diagnostic Questionnaire (IED-DQ; McCloskey, unpublished instrument, as cited in Coccaro & McCloskey, 2010) is a seven-item self-report measure that is designed to diagnose IED according to either the DSM-5 or the IED-IR diagnostic criteria. The IED-DQ includes items that assess aggression frequency and severity, distress associated with aggressive behavior, and mental health or medical diagnoses that must be excluded in order to diagnose IED (McCloskey et al., 2012). Results from an initial developmental study utilizing the IED-DQ indicate that the instrument has satisfactory psychometric properties with sufficient interrater reliability, test-retest reliability, and construct validity in differentiating subjects with IED from controls on self-report measures of anger and aggression (McCloskey et al., 2012).

Prevalence and Course

Historically, IED was thought to be quite rare, but recent clinical and epidemiological findings have pointed to the notion that it is an under-diagnosed disorder with lifetime prevalence rates ranging from 4% to 7% (Coccaro & McCloskey, 2006). Coccaro (2012) summarizes worldwide prevalence rates and places North America at the top, followed by South America, Europe, Asia, the Middle East, and Africa. But there is a great deal of variation in reported prevalence rates; for example, Fincham et al. (2009) places Africa at the top, reporting a 9.5% prevalence rate.

Intermittent explosive disorder usually begins during childhood (Coccaro, 2000) and is linked to significant impairments in interpersonal and occupational functioning, which are related to workplace difficulties, problematic relationships, and involvement with legal systems (McElroy et al., 1998). These components are further heightened when this chronic disorder is left untreated (Kessler et al., 2006). Finally, IED is associated with medical problems that include coronary artery disease, hypertension, and stroke (McCloskey et al., 2010).

Pharmacological Solitary Treatments

Though there are numerous medications utilized to treat aggression associated with IED, currently there are no medications that carry the specific indication for IED treatment. In reviewing the available research, readers will find that medications are often classified according to their usefulness in treating impulse control disorders (ICDs) in general (Schreiber et al., 2011), resistant or refractory IED (Coccaro, 2013), impulsive repetitive aggression (Jones et al., 2011), and agitation and violence (McElroy, 1999). Medication choice may also reflect the presumed neurobiological origins of symptoms or IED as a disorder. Coccaro (2012), for example, described "neurobiological support for the presence of serotonergic abnormalities globally and specifically in areas of the limbic system (the anterior cingulate) and in the orbitofrontal cortex" (p. 585). With this in mind, the medications are utilized to treat these dysfunctions within the neurotransmitter systems and the brain regions involved.

Of the medications prescribed to treat IED and symptoms associated with IED, antidepressants (especially antidepressants such as selective serotonin reuptake inhibitors, or SSRIs), mood stabilizers (anticonvulsants, atypical antipsychotics, and lithium), and antihypertensives (beta blockers and alpha-2 agonists) are among the most researched and utilized.

Selective Serotonin Reuptake Inhibitors

Dysfunction within the serotonin system (lower levels of serotonin) is associated with impulsivity and aggressiveness. An SSRI selectively prevents the reuptake of serotonin by the presynaptic neuron, thus allowing it to remain in the synapse and produces its effect. Utilizing a SSRI therefore allows more serotonin to remain in the synapse, increasing its effect on control over aggressive impulses.

Of the SSRIs, fluoxetine has been researched most frequently. Two studies provide evidence that fluoxetine is beneficial in treating IED. In a small study of patients with IED and personality disorders, Coccaro and Kavoussi (1997) noted a reduction of aggressive symptoms in those taking fluoxetine as compare to those taking a placebo. Likewise and more recently, in a larger 14-week double-blind study, Coccaro et al. (2009) reported a significant reduction in the frequency and severity of impulsive aggression as well as a reduction in irritability. Since 2009, other studies have replicated the findings of these two studies.

Coccaro (2013) notes that lower doses of fluoxetine are used for first-line treatment and higher doses for resistant IED. Coccaro and Kavoussi (1997) recommend a three-month minimum trial to produce desired effects. Side effects may include sleep disturbances, sexual dysfunction, and headache (Ferguson, 2001).

Anticonvulsant Mood Stabilizers

In the antiepileptic or anticonvulsant class, valproate/divalproex, carbamazepine oxcarbazepine, and phenytoin have been studied frequently. Carbamazepine, oxcarbazepine, and phenytoin produce their effect by blocking sodium channels and thus stabilizing neuronal membrane excitation, while valproate/divalproex stabilizes neuronal membranes through gamma-aminobutyric acid (GABA). Simplistically, anticonvulsants reduce neuronal excitability, thus improving mood stability.

Two studies provide evidence for the effectiveness of valproate/divalproex in patients exhibiting aggressive behaviors. In a small double-blind placebo-controlled study of children and adolescents with explosive tempers and mood liability, Donovan et al. (2000) reported significant improvements in mood stability and a reduction in outbursts. Similarly, Hollander et al. (2003), in a large multicenter randomized double-blind placebo-controlled study demonstrated a reduction in impulsive aggression, irritability, and overall severity in a group of cluster B personality disorder patients with comorbid IED.

Thirty years ago, Mattes (1984) reported that carbamazepine reduced aggressiveness in individuals with rage outbursts. In this study, although all patients had multiple diagnoses, almost half had been diagnosed with IED. More recently, Stanford et al. (2005), in a double-blind placebo-controlled parallel-group-design study of men with impulsive aggression, showed significant reduction in impulsive aggression for those taking carbamazepine, phenytoin, or valproate.

Oxcarbazepine has been the recent focus of aggression treatment studies as well. Mattes (2012) provided a rational for its use in the prison population and in a 10-week double-blind placebo-controlled study. Mattes (2005) demonstrated that oxcarbazepine significantly reduced impulsive aggressiveness when compared to placebo.

Stanford et al. (2001), in a six-week double-blind placebo-controlled crossover study, explored the effects of phenytoin on individuals with impulsive aggression. The authors reported a significant reduction in impulsive-aggressive behaviors for those taking phenytoin. Also, as noted earlier, Stanford et al. (2005), in a study comparing the effectiveness of carbamazepine, phenytoin, and valproate in men with impulsive aggression, showed a significant reduction in impulsive aggression for those on either of the medications.

According to Coccaro (2013), phenytoin, oxcarbazepine, and carbamazepine may be used in conjunction with an SSRI in resistant IED. Refractory IED may be treated with valproate/divalproex and newer antiepileptics such as lamotrigine (see Tritt et al., 2005) or topirimate (see Nickel et al., 2005). Side effects may include sedation, decreased cognition, lethargy, and weight gain (Swann, 2001).

Atypical Antipsychotics

Atypical antipsychotics are a newer addition to the treatment spectrum of IED. Atypical antipsychotics have a multipronged mechanism of action affecting numerous neurotransmitters (viz., serotonin, norepinephrine, dopamine, etc.), thus improving multiple dysfunctional neurotransmitter systems and stabilizing mood. Side effects include sedation, cognitive deficits, lethargy, and weight gain (Sharif, 2003).

Of those studied, risperidone was explored most often. To a lesser extent, clozapine and olanzapine have also been studied. Buitelaar et al. (2001), in a predominantly male group, studied the effectiveness and safety of risperidone in a six-week double-blind randomized parallel-group-design study. All participants had subaverage intelligence and were hospitalized for various disorders that included aggressiveness. The authors reported that risperidone use was associated with a reduction in severe aggression.

Lithium

Lithium has been utilized for decades to treat aggression. According to a recent meta-analytic review, "There was evidence for significant reductions in aggression for those taking phenytoin, lithium, carbamazepine/oxcarbazepine, but not for valproate or levetiracetam" (Jones et al., 2011, p. 96). In an older study exploring the usefulness of lithium to treat impulsive aggression, Sheard et al. (1976) conducted a double-blind placebo-controlled trial with prisoners who were nonpsychotic. The authors noted a significant reduction in aggressiveness and made the recommendation that lithium be a viable option for nonpsychotic impulsive-aggressive individuals. Other studies have supported the efficacy of lithium in aggressive clients; however, many are specific to clients diagnosed with conduct disorder (see Campbell et al., 1995).

Individuals taking lithium are required to monitor their diet in order to prevent toxicity. Specifically, patients should limit their sodium intake and be sure to drink plenty of water. With the development of newer medications that are free of dietary restrictions and provide a better safety profile, lithium is not considered a typical first-line treatment for IED. Coccaro (2013) recommends that lithium be utilized only for adult individuals with refractory IED.

Beta Blockers

Beta blockers are antihypertensives that have shown usefulness in treating IED. Propranolol and pindolol have been studied and utilized most frequently. These medications produce their effect through blockade of beta receptors, possibly in the brainstem, thus affecting norepinephrine and reducing sympathetic nervous system stimulation. Side effects include depression, hypotension, lethargy, and sexual dysfunction (Muzyk & Gagliardi, 2010).

Greendyke et al. (1986) explored the efficacy of propranolol in a small double-blind placebo-controlled crossover study of individuals with organic brain disease and violent behavior. The authors reported a significant reduction in assaultive behaviors. Similarly, in a small double-blind placebo-controlled crossover study of individuals with organic brain disease, Greendyke and Kanter (1986) researched the use of pindolol for impulsive-explosive behaviors. Pindolol produced significant behavioral benefits.

Alpha-2 Agonists

Alpha-2 agonists are another class of antihypertensives that may be useful in treating IED aggression. Of these medications, clonidine is the most used; however, guanfacine is often interchanged. Many research studies simply refer to the use of alpha-2 agonists rather than differentiate between the two. The mechanism of action of alpha-2 agonists is believed to arise from the inhibitory nature (i.e., inhibits norepinephrine release) of alpha-2 receptors in the brainstem. Norepinephrine is associated with stress and arousal; therefore, by inhibiting norepinephrine, aggressiveness and impulsivity may be reduced. Side effects include sedation, hypotension, lethargy, and mild depression (Ming et al., 2008).

Ming et al. (2008), in an open-label retrospective study, explored the efficacy of clonidine in children diagnosed with autism spectrum disorder who exhibited, among other things, mood disorder and aggressive behaviors. Participants were predominantly boys. The outcome showed that clonidine was effective at reducing mood instability and aggressiveness.

Benefits and Limitations of Pharmacotherapy as Sole Treatment

Ample neuroscience research has highlighted the neurotransmitters and brain regions involved in IED. Therefore, when medications are utilized to improve the function of dysfunctional neurotransmitter systems or brain regions, clients experience a reduction of symptoms. Pharmacological management of IED may also be a more cost-effective method for treating IED and any comorbid symptom.

As a solitary approach, pharmacological management of IED is limited by the overall efficacy of medications in ameliorating all symptoms of IED. Some symptoms may improve or remiss; however, others remain relatively unchanged. With all things considered, there is a need for continued research in the area of pharmacotherapy for treatment of IED, especially randomized controlled clinical trials that focus specifically on the symptoms cluster within IED.

Psychological Solitary Treatments

Although multiple interventions (both pharmacological and psychological) have been utilized to treat anger and aggression with differing efficacy, little research has specifically examined the effectiveness of treating IED. However, the effectiveness of psychological interventions in treating anger dysregulation has been the subject of extensive research (Beck & Fernandez, 1998). Cognitive-behavioral therapy (CBT) interventions such as relaxation training, social skill training, and multicomponent treatments have been shown to have moderate to large effects in the treatment of anger. CBT has also been shown to reduce aggression (McCloskey et al., 2012), especially when specific CBT treatment manuals are utilized. Individual compliance and adherence to CBT treatment were monitored, and results revealed increases in positive behaviors as well as consistent decreases in aggression. Consequently, it is suggested that clinicians choose structured interventions that are delivered in an individualized format (McCloskey et al., 2012).

Two published studies examined treatments of individuals diagnosed with IED. The first revealed efficacy of a brief (four 90-minute sessions) CBT program for aggressive drivers. Additional analyses revealed that drivers who had been diagnosed with IED tended to improve less than drivers not diagnosed with IED; thus, implying that individuals diagnosed with IED may require a longer, more intensive therapy schedule than those without IED (Galovski & Blanchard, 2002). Therefore it is essential to recognize that, although CBT has been shown to work with anger dysregulation, those diagnosed with IED may require a longer course of CBT treatment.

The second study compared a 12-week multicomponent CBT intervention delivered in an individual format to those meeting IED diagnostic criteria. The counseling intervention, based upon the Cognitive, Relaxation, and Coping Skills Training (CRCST) anger management manual (Deffenbacher & McKay, 2000), was composed of three primary components. The primary focus of the first two sessions consisted of increasing awareness of physiological cues and teaching relaxation (e.g., progressive muscle relaxation, guided imagery). During the third session, clients were provided a rationale for the application of time-outs to prevent impulsive-aggressive behaviors. During the fourth and fifth sessions, the rationale for cognitive restructuring was introduced through the A-B-C cognitive model. Six types of cognitive distortions were introduced and explicated (e.g., misattribution, overgeneralization, labeling, blaming, demanding/commanding, and magnifying/catastrophizing), with examples and strategies for assisting in reduction of each cognitive distortion. The second half of the treatment focused on implementing and generalizing previously learned relaxation and cognitive skills through practice and imagined exposure. The final session also consisted of relapse prevention strategies (McCloskey et al., 2012). The treatment was delivered in individual or group sessions. The participants demonstrated a higher reduction in anger and aggressive behaviors when compared to subjects in the wait-list, control group. Specifically, clients diagnosed with IED decreased their aggressive behavior from pretreatment to posttreatment by over 55% in the group CBT assignment and by over 75% in the individual CBT assignment (McCloskey et al., 2012). In addition, the treatment gains were maintained at a three-month follow-up. Clients in the individual CBT assignment also reported a greater decrease in hostile thoughts and a larger improvement in quality of life as compared to waitlist clients. In sum, almost half (7 of 15) of the clients in the individual CBT condition achieved remission status (e.g., no physical aggression in the past two weeks) at the end of treatment. Comparatively, only two of the subjects in the group CBT condition and one of the subjects in the waitlist condition met the remission criteria.

Behavioral management therapy, social skills training, cognitive-behavioral therapy (with an emphasis on anger management), group therapy, and family therapy have also been shown to be useful for controlling aggressive behavior (Olvera, 2002). Because anger is a multidimensional concept, clinicians must consider the antecedents, behavioral response dimensions, cognitive dimensions, physiological responses, and subjective experience of the emotion. An example of a therapeutic modality that addresses the multidimensional aspects of anger is social skills interventions (Olvera, 2002). This treatment includes social skills training with a cognitive-behavioral element using both individual and group formats. The sessions begin with a primary focus on social problem solving, such as identifying and defining key anger issues. In therapy, clients learn increased awareness of anger and physiological arousal as cues with which to begin problem solving. Additional training focuses on reducing impulsive reactions, considering consequences, and implementing alternative behaviors. Cognitive techniques include the use of self-statements and reframing perceptions of stressful situations. Additional behaviorally based training focuses on adjusting body language in social settings and learning how to negotiate interpersonal wants and needs. Controlled studies of this treatment used with aggressive children have reported improvement on a variety of measures (Olvera, 2002), but decreases in aggression as an outcome variable were solely found in aggressive socially rejected children.

Benefits and Limitations of Psychotherapy as Sole Treatment

Psychosocial treatment has been shown to improve many of the core features and symptoms of IED. As a treatment approach, CBT-based treatment, regardless of the disorder, can lead to improvements in both the thinking patterns and exhibited behaviors of individuals. As a part of a CBT-based approach, teaching clients to act rather than react produces noticeable effects. Also, as clients develop new coping skills and implement these skills, they improve.

As a solitary approach, psychosocial treatment may not produce improvements quickly enough to address the severity of IED symptoms. Many clients need rapid stabilization, with medication, before they can benefit from psychotherapy.

Overall, research findings suggest that CBT-based treatment shows promise in treating symptoms for IED, but some of the obtained results have been inconsistent, and further research is needed to outline the process that leads to aggression reduction in clients with IED. Randomized clinical trial studies have not been conducted, yet they have been recommended. Future research needs to focus upon the layered nature of the symptoms and their outward behavioral manifestations in order to apply accurate differential diagnoses.

Combined Treatments

There is a paucity of research on combined treatment of IED; this section reviews research that suggests these treatments may be effective although benefits have not yet been confirmed through controlled studies. The majority of that literature is extrapolated from the more widely researched comparable area of impulsive aggression.

Adolescents and Adults

Coccaro (2013) suggests that a comprehensive approach to treating patients with IED may combine pharmacotherapy with CBT. He reported that evidence exists that each treatment alone provides benefits, but he cautions that to date the literature is lacking research comparing a combined approach to CBT or pharmacotherapy alone. In a combined treatment paradigm, therapists should begin with a thorough biopsychosocial intake interview with the client and preferably outside observers. Olvera (2002) recommends that therapists interview several observants, especially those closest to the individual, because IED clients struggle with objectivity regarding their symptoms. The goal of the interview is to determine the potential of underlying or comorbid disorders or organic causes leading to appropriate psychiatric or neurological referrals (Olvera, 2002). To determine if the client's aggression is better explained by another diagnostic category, Olvera suggests utilizing a diagnostic timeline to differentiate the sequential course of aggressive and comorbid symptoms.

Working with IED clients can be challenging for therapists who struggle with maintaining empathy during limit setting (Ng & Mejia, 2011). Another challenge for therapists that might occur is transference or countertransference during the client's angry outburst (Ng & Mejia, 2011). But combining CBT and medication reduces the frequency of angry outbursts by raising the triggering threshold and teaching the client to anticipate and manage triggering stimuli in a healthier fashion (Coccaro, 2013). Coccaro suggests that clients may be resistant to drug therapy or CBT, making them poor candidates for these therapies. For resistant clients, he suggests reassessing motivation and working with these clients if they return for assistance. If the client is resistant but remains in the therapeutic environment, therapists might want to consider motivational interviewing strategies. McCloskey et al. (2008), for example, conducted a randomized clinical trial (pilot study) comparing individual and group CBT to a waitlist control group. Overall, they found that clients within the individual and group treatments experienced a decrease in aggression and anger in comparison to the control group. Additionally, clients who engaged in individual therapy experienced less hostility. Coccaro recommends that CBT therapy includes cognitive restructuring, relaxation training, coping skills training, and relapse prevention, all of which are therapeutically sound techniques to consider as part of a combined approach. So CBT may be a good first step to IED treatment for clients initially resistant to medications, and it may be beneficial when combined with an appropriate medication (for clients who may benefit from it and become more receptive to this treatment modality).

Children

While working with IED adults might be challenging, working with children can be even more so. Children can receive an IED diagnosis as early as age 6, and children with severe impulsivity or aggression may be medicated in order to improve symptoms and address safety concerns. Sweeney and Tatum (1995) note that antipsychotics have been found to be effective in children in lowering aggression, but caution that because of their side effects they should only be considered after exploring all other treatment options.

Combining pharmacology and play therapy is beneficial when the alternative of not medicating the child limits the chances for a successful therapeutic outcome (Sweeney & Tatum, 1995). The play therapy setting is conducive to countering some of the negative aspects of taking medications. For example, children often experience self-concept or self-esteem issues related to the stigma of having to take medication. Play therapy offers medicated children the opportunity to process the above issues to regain a sense of control and mastery over their immediate environment.

Beyond the therapeutic benefits of play therapy for the medicated child, therapists also play a central role in advocacy for their clients and monitoring treatment response (both desired and adverse effects). Child therapists must know how to obtain information about treatment response from children who have not yet developed significant verbal skills, and must work in concert with the prescribing physicians to inform them about the children's response to the medications. In addition, therapists are able to differentiate children who legitimately need psychiatric care from those currently medicated for "biologically-based symptoms when in fact the child is behaviorally responding to an emotional trauma or inappropriate parenting" (Sweeney & Tatum, 1995, p. 55). For these reasons, psychotherapists and play therapists working with children have "an obligation to his or her child clients to be educated on issues of child psychopharmacology" (Sweeney & Tatum, 1995, p. 55).

Benefits and Limitations of Combined Treatments

A combined approach to treating IED offers synergy between psychotherapy and medication. For the most part, medications set the stage for improvement as psychotherapy provides the tools for success. Medications thus provide initial stabilization, improving clients' engagement in their psychotherapy. In a combined approach, therapists can process with their clients the potential costs versus benefits of pharmacotherapy, leading to more positive treatment outcomes and improved medication compliance. Also, therapists are a first line of defense for identifying deleterious side effects that may have gone unnoticed if a client was solely receiving pharmacotherapy.

It is important for therapists to understand that a combined treatment approach for IED clients, while potentially beneficial, also complicates the therapist's job, for it adds additional goals that must be addressed in therapy. Therapists must also become familiar with the potential side effects of medication and be capable of differentiating the manifestation of pharmacotherapy side effects from other symptoms. Finally, coordinating treatment between two providers may be a challenge, and it is likely to require more time and effort by the therapist, the prescriber, and the client.

Summary and Recommendations

Although IED has been a DSM diagnosis for over 20 years, there is relatively scarce research about treating clients diagnosed with IED. This dearth may be due in part to limitations inherent in the DSM diagnostic criteria. Although there are no specific IED treatments that meet the criteria for empirically validated treatments (McCloskey et al., 2012), evidence from some studies reveals that behavioral and cognitive-behavioral interventions have been effective in reducing anger and aggression and in improving social skills. Research exploring IED treatment with medication is limited as well; however, there is evidence of medication efficacy for many of the symptoms associated with IED. Although it can be expected that combined treatments may offer the benefits of each modality, research on combined treatment for IED is almost nonexistent, and further study is required in this area. All in all, however, it is reasonable to expect that unless symptoms are severe and the clients exhibit danger to themselves or others, psychotherapy (especially cognitive and behavioral interventions) should be utilized as first-line approaches, and when improvement is not sufficient or symptoms are severe enough to require faster stabilization, a combined approach seems most sensible.

This case vignette demonstrates the course of treatment for an adolescent client. The client's treatment began with a solitary psychosocial approach that proved helpful but failed to remiss some symptoms. As a result, the client's psychosocial treatment was supplemented with pharmacological treatment. The resulting combined approach proved to remiss more symptoms and support better outcomes.

Brian, a 16-year-old white male, was referred to the local community mental health agency through the family court system. His case plan required him to engage in (1) individual counseling for a minimum of 10 weeks, (2) family counseling for 10 weeks, (3) individual anger management classes for 12 weeks, and (4) anger management group for 12 sessions.

In his intake session, Brian's mother explained that the first time Brian "exploded" was after playing a video game with his stepfather. When Brian's stepfather began celebrating that he won the game, Brian stood up, began yelling obscenities at his stepfather, and then punched him in the jaw. Brian then proceeded to pick up lamps, tables, a chair, and throw them at his stepfather, younger brother, and mother. Brian's mother reported that this incident occurred when he was 12, and that the family attributed this outburst to his frustration about his mother recently giving birth to his youngest sister.

The second incident occurred at age 13, when Brian lost a basketball game in their backyard. Brian hurled the basketball through the family room window, breaking it. Brian then wrestled one of his friends to the ground and began punching him repeatedly. When two of Brian's friends attempted to pull Brian off, he began punching them as well. When Brian's stepfather attempted to pull him off the other boy, he began punching his stepfather as well. The stepfather reported that he needed physical assistance from a neighbor to pull Brian off the victim. No charges were pressed at this time,

(continued)

(continued)

but the boy's father threatened to press assault charges if anything remotely similar reoccurred. Brian stated that he did not remember throwing the objects, but did remember becoming extremely angry, and believed he could have killed the boy who taunted him about not making the game-winning shot. He stated that he could not remember how he found himself on the ground punching the other teen, but did remember that his anger came on suddenly and that he wanted to hurt someone. He also shared that during this sudden onset he believed he could have taken down the other five teen boys who were there. Once he started punching and hitting, he explained, it became a situation he could not stop.

In the most recent episode, at the age of 15, Brian attacked his younger brother. He and his younger brother were discussing an upcoming vacation, and Brian's younger brother reminded Brian that if he did not improve his grades, he would not be able to go. Brian began verbally attacking his younger brother, suddenly punched him in the face, and continued to punch him in the face and broke his nose. At this point, the stepfather entered the room and attempted to break up the fight. Brian then began punching the stepfather in the face. Brian's mother called the police as the stepfather struggled to pull Brian off of his 11-year-old brother. When the police arrived, Brian's mother decided that she needed to take action, so she reported prior destruction of property (Brian had been punching holes in the walls of the home for about one year) and pointed out that she believed her younger son's nose had been broken. The paramedics confirmed that her son's nose was broken, and they were concerned about a broken jaw as well. The stepfather did not have any broken bones but had suffered significant bruising.

As a result of the police being called, Brian entered the juvenile justice system. He was not sentenced to serve any juvenile jail time, but he was placed on probation for one year. Part of his probation was to undergo a psychiatric evaluation and engage in the previously mentioned case plan. He also was required to complete 100 hours of community service. Because of his angry outbursts at his mother, threatening her with physical harm when she attempted to send him to school, he missed a considerable amount of schoolwork. As a result, Brian was required to repeat the tenth grade.

Brian admitted that he was becoming angrier every day, and that everything and everyone around him feared him. He shared that he found himself increasingly fascinated with weapons, namely, rifles. Brian reported that he had been studying various guns on the Internet and expressed an interest in joining a local gun club in his community, as he wanted to meet others with shared interests. Brian also found himself missing more school and having issues with maintaining sleep. He admitted to having vivid, violent dreams that would awaken him.

At the time of his intake interview, he looked his stated age and was dressed casually in jeans and a t-shirt. His mood was angry, which appeared congruent with his affect. His thoughts were focused upon his preoccupation with physical violence, and how using a gun would show that he could not be threatened. Despite these thoughts, he demonstrated a high level of insight into his condition. He had never hurt animals, and expressed remorse about unintentionally hurting his brother when he punched him in the nose. His suicide risk appeared low.

Although Brian was initially resistant to counseling, he agreed to keep a "thinking, feeling, doing" journal. In this journal, he was asked to record his thoughts, feelings, and behaviors before he began to engage in acts that would involve yelling, hitting, throwing, and the like. He was assigned this journaling exercise in between sessions to arrive at a baseline. Between the second and third sessions, he claimed to forget about the assignment. But between the third and fourth session he did complete a daily journal. The journal revealed that when he perceived that others were verbally attacking him, he automatically began to engage in physical violence. Therapy also involved utilizing "thought-stopping" techniques to cue him visually to environmental factors that would precipitate or encourage him to yell, hit, scream, or throw objects. Brian created a "stop sign" to hold in front of himself before he began to yell, hit, or scream. He created this visual cue in session so that he could create it the way he wanted it to look. He was required to share each week how well this visual cue worked for him, and if it did not work, to create a visual cue that would be effective in visually directing him to refrain from violent behaviors. Because Brian appeared to be a visual learner, the journal assignment and thought-stopping stop sign appeared to work well for him.

At the end of Brian's tenth individual session, the therapist met with his mother to discuss his progress. The mother noted positive changes yet was concerned that he remained "easy to set off." It seemed evident that therapy alone was not enough, and so the therapist referred Brian to a local child psychiatrist for a medication consult. After seeking consent, the therapist prepared a summary report, to send to the child psychiatrist, describing her concerns. Based on the therapist's report and his clinical judgment, the child psychiatrist prescribed 20 mg of fluoxetine daily.

(continued)

(continued)

Brian continued in therapy, and his therapist proceeded with CBT techniques and activities to continue to change his negative interpretations of triggering situations and utilize thought- and behavior-stopping techniques to improve self-control. After a few weeks, Brian's mother reported he became less irritable and less reactive. But Brian reported having more vivid dreams and continued sleep disturbances that caused him to wake up suddenly. Subsequently, Brian made another visit to the child psychiatrist. Because of his vivid dreams, Brain was tapered off of the fluoxetine and was prescribed 150 mg of oxcarbazepine daily.

Therapy continued as before, and Brian tolerated the new medication better. Over time, he reported a decrease in sleep disturbance, irritability, and reactiveness. His mother corroborated the improvement, and Brian's violent outbursts stopped. It is at this point that the therapy was terminated, but Brian and the family were encouraged to continue utilizing the techniques that were learned during the course of therapy.

References

APA. American Psychiatric Association. (1980). *Diagnostic and statistical manual of mental disorders* (3rd ed.). Washington, DC: Author.

APA. American Psychiatric Association. (2013). *Diagnostic and statistical manual of mental disorders* (5th ed.). Washington, DC: Author.

Beck, R., & Fernandez, E. (1998). Cognitive behavioral therapy in the treatment of anger. *Cognitive Therapy and Research, 22*(1), 62–75.

Buitelaar, J. K., et al. (2001). A randomized controlled trial of risperidone in the treatment of aggression in hospitalized adolescents with subaverage cognitive abilities. *Journal of Clinical Psychiatry, 62*(4), 239–248.

Campbell, M., et al. (1995). Lithium in hospitalized aggressive children with conduct disorder: A double-blind and placebo-controlled study. *Journal of the American Academy of Child and Adolescent Psychiatry, 34*(4), 445–453.

Coccaro, E. F. (2000). Intermittent explosive disorder. *Current Psychiatry Reports, 2*(1), 67–71.

Coccaro, E. F. (2003a). Intermittent explosive disorder. In E. F. Coccaro (Ed.), *Aggression: Psychiatric assessment and treatment* (pp. 149–199). New York: Marcel Dekker.

Coccaro, E. F. (2003b). Intermittent explosive disorder: Taming temper tantrums in the volatile, impulsive adult. *Current Psychiatry, 2*(7), 42–60.

Coccaro, E. F. (2012). Intermittent explosive disorder as a disorder of impulsive aggression for DSM-5. *American Journal of Psychiatry, 169*(6), 577–588. doi:10.1176/appi.ajp.2012.11081259

Coccaro, E. (2013). Intermittent explosive disorder in adults: Treatment and prognosis. *Up to Date.* Retrieved from http://www.uptodate.com/contents/intermittent-explosive-disorder-in-adults-treatment-and-prognosis.

Coccaro, E. F., & Kavoussi, R. L. (1997). Fluoextine and impulsive aggressive behavior in personality disordered subjects. *Archives of General Psychiatry, 54,* 1081–1088.

Coccaro, E. F., & McCloskey, M. S. (2006). Hothead Harry, gnome assassin: Combined treatment of intermittent explosive disorder. In R. L. Spitzer, M. B. Williams, & J. B. W. Gibbon (Eds.), *DSM-IV-TR casebook.* Washington, DC: American Psychiatric Publishing.

Coccaro, E. F., & McCloskey, M. S. (2010). Intermittent explosive disorder: Clinical aspects. In E. Aboujaoude & L. M. Koran (Eds.), *Impulse control disorders.* New York: Cambridge University Press.

Coccaro, E. F., et al. (2004). Lifetime and 1-month prevalence rates of intermittent explosive disorder in a community sample. *Journal of Clinical Psychiatry, 65*(6), 820–824.

Coccaro, E. F., et al. (2009). A double-blind, randomized, placebo-controlled trial of fluoxetine in patients with intermittent explosive disorder. *Journal of Clinical Psychiatry, 70*(5), 653–662. doi:10.4088/JCP.08m04150

Deffenbacher, J. L., & McKay, M. (2000). Overcoming situational and general anger. Oakland, CA: New Harbinger.

Donovan, S. J., et al. (2000). Divalproex treatment for youth with explosive temper and mood lability: A double-blind, placebo-controlled crossover design. *American Journal of Psychiatry, 157*(5), 818–820. doi:10.1176/appi.ajp.157.5.818

Ferguson, J. M. (2001). SSRI antidepressant medications: Adverse effects and tolerability. *Primary Care Companion to the Journal of Clinical Psychiatry, 3*(1), 22–27.

Fincham, D., et al. (2009). Intermittent explosive disorder in South Africa: Prevalence, correlates, and the role of traumatic exposures. *Psychopathology, 42*(2), 92–98. doi:10.1159/000203341

Galovski, T., & Blanchard, E. B. (2002). The effectiveness of a brief psychological intervention on court-referred and self-referred aggressive drivers. *Behaviour Research and Therapy, 40*(12), 1385–1402.

Greendyke, R. M., & Kanter, D. R. (1986). Therapeutic effects of pindolol on behavioral disturbances associated with organic brain disease: A double-blind study. *Journal of Clinical Psychiatry, 47*(8), 423–426

Greendyke, R. M., et al. (1986). Propanolol treatment of assaultive patients with organic brain disease: A double-blind crossover, placebo controlled study. *Journal of Nervous and Mental Disease, 174*(5), 290–294.

Hollander, E., et al. (2003). Divalproex in the treatment of impulsive aggression: Efficacy in cluster B personality disorders. *Neuropsychopharmacology, 28*(6), 1186–1197.

Jones, R. M., et al. (2011). Efficacy of mood stabilizers in the treatment of impulsive or repetitive aggression: Systematic review and meta-analysis. *British Journal of Psychiatry, 198*(2), 93–98. doi:10.1192/bjp.bp.110.083030

Kessler, R. C., et al. (2006). The prevalence and correlates of DSM-IV intermittent explosive disorder in the National Comorbidity Survey Replication. *Archives of General Psychiatry, 55*(4), 137–141.

Mattes, J. A. (1984). Carbamazepine for uncontrolled rage outbursts. *Lancet, 324*(8412), 1164–1165.

Mattes, J. A. (2005). Oxcarbazepine in patients with impulsive aggression: A double-blind, placebo-controlled trial. *Journal of Clinical Psychopharmacology, 25*(6), 575–579.

Mattes, J. A. (2012). Medications for aggressiveness in prison: Focus on oxcarbazepine. *Journal of the American Academy of Psychiatry and the Law, 40*(2), 234–238.

McCloskey, M. S., et al. (2008). Cognitive-behavioral therapy for intermittent explosive disorder: A pilot randomized clinical trial. *Journal of Consulting and Clinical Psychology, 76*(5), 876–886. doi:10.1037/0022-006X.76.5.876

McCloskey, M. S., et al. (2010). Unhealthy aggression: The association between intermittent explosive disorder and negative health outcomes. *Health Psychology, 29*(3), 324–332. doi:10.1037/a0019072

McCloskey, M. S., et al. (2012). Assessment and treatment of intermittent explosive disorder. In J. E. Grant & M. N. Potenza (Eds.), *The Oxford handbook of impulse control disorders* (pp. 344–352). New York: Oxford University Press.

McElroy, S. L. (1999). Recognition and treatment of DSM-IV intermittent explosive disorder. *Journal of Clinical Psychiatry, 60*(Suppl. 15), 12–16.

McElroy, S. L., et al. (1998). DSM-IV intermittent explosive disorder: A report of 27 cases. *Journal of Clinical Psychiatry, 59*(4), 137–141.

Ming, X., et al. (2008). Use of clonidine in children with autism spectrum disorders. *Brain and Development, 30*(7), 454–460. doi:10.1016/j.braindev.2007.12.007

Muzyk, A. J., & Gagliardi, J. P. (2010). Do beta blockers cause depression? *Current Psychiatry, 9*(5), 50–55.

Ng, W. K., & Mejia, J. (2011). Intrusive thoughts in a boy: A review of intermittent explosive disorder. *McMaster University Medical Journal, 8*(1), 77–79.

Nickel, C., et al. (2005). Topiramate in treatment of depressive and anger symptoms in female depressive patients: A randomized, double-blind, placebo-controlled study. *Journal of Affective Disorders, 87*(2–3), 243–252.

Olvera, R. L. (2002). Intermittent explosive disorder: Epidemiology, diagnosis, and management. *CNS Drugs, 16*(8), 517–526.

Olvera, R. L., et al. (2001). Validation of the Interview Module for Intermittent Explosive Disorder (M-IED) in children and adolescents: A pilot study. *Psychiatry Research, 101*(13), 259–267.

Robins, S., & Navaco, R. M. (1999). Systems conceptualization and treatment of anger. *Journal of Clinical Psychology, 30*(1), 279–287.

Schreiber, L., et al. (2011). Impulse control disorders: Updated review of clinical characteristics and pharmacological management. *Frontiers in Psychiatry, 2*(1), 1–11. doi:10.3389/fpsyt.2011.00001

Sharif, Z. A. (2003). Overview of safety and tolerability of atypical antipsychotics used in primary care. *Primary Care Companion to the Journal of Clinical Psychiatry, 5*(Suppl. 3), 14–21.

Sheard, M. H., et al. (1976). The effect of lithium on impulsive aggressive behavior in man. *American Journal of Psychiatry, 133*(12), 1409–1413.

Stanford, M. S., et al. (2001). A double-blind placebo-controlled crossover study of phenytoin in individuals with impulsive aggression. *Psychiatry Research, 103*(2–3), 193–203.

Stanford, M. S., et al. (2005). A comparison of anticonvulsants in the treatment of impulsive aggression. *Experimental Clinical Psychopharmacology, 13*(1), 72–77.

Swann, A. C. (2001). Major system toxicities and side effects of anticonvulsants. *Journal of Clinical Psychiatry, 62*(Suppl. 14), 16–21.

Sweeney, D. S., & Tatum, R. J. (1995). Play therapy and psychopharmacology: What the play therapist needs to know. *International Journal of Play Therapy, 4*(2), 41–57. doi:10.1037/h0089304

Tritt, K., et al. (2005). Lamotrigine treatment of aggression in female borderline-patients: A randomized, double-blind, placebo-controlled study. *Journal of Psychopharmacology, 19*(3), 287–291.

Part III

Disorders With Disruptive Behaviors as Commonly Associated Features

10 Intellectual Disability and Autism Spectrum Disorder

Robert W. Heffer, Brandi L. Chew,
Robert Perna, Sonia C. Izmirian,
Michael S. L. Ching,[1] Ashlee R. Loughan,
Ivette M. Calles, and Vincent P. Aguirre

According to the fifth edition of the *Diagnostic and Statistical Manual of Mental Disorders* (DSM-5; American Psychiatric Association [APA], 2013) intellectual disability (ID) and autism spectrum disorder (ASD) are neurodevelopmental disorders with onset occurring from birth to early childhood. Three criteria define a diagnosis of ID: (1) deficits in intellectual functioning (e.g., reasoning, problem solving, planning, abstract thinking, judgment, academic learning, and learning for experience) confirmed by both clinical assessment and individualized standardized intelligence testing; (2) deficits in adaptive functioning that result in failure to meet developmental and sociocultural standards for personal independence and social responsibility and limit functioning in one or more activities of daily life across multiple environments, such as home, school, work, and community; and (3) onset of intellectual and adaptive deficits during the developmental period (prior to the age of 18). Four levels of ID severity (mild, moderate, severe, and profound) are delineated on the basis of adaptive functioning rather than IQ scores, within three domains (conceptual, social, and practical). Detailed examples/criteria descriptions of the ID severity level by adaptive functioning domain matrix are provided by APA (2013, Table 1, pp. 34–36).

Autism spectrum disorder is characterized by developmental deficits in reciprocal social communication and interaction and limited repetitive patterns of behaviors, interests, or activities (APA, 2013). Deficits in social communication involve verbal and nonverbal communication, developing, maintaining and understanding relationships, reciprocal communication, sharing interests or affect with others, and adjusting social contexts. Limited repetitive behaviors can range from abnormally intense or focused interests, inflexibility in routine, ritualized patterns of verbal or nonverbal behavior, stereotyped or repetitive patterns of speech or motor movement, and unusual sensitivity to sensory environmental stimuli. Symptoms must be evident in early childhood and lead to impairment in daily functioning. ASD may be specified with accompanying intellectual impairment, language impairment, medical, genetic, or environmental factors, catatonia, and other neu-rodevelopmental, mental, or behavior disorders. Three diagnostic levels of severity exist that vary by degree of impairment in social com-munication ability *and* restrictive repetitive behaviors: (1) requiring support, (2) requiring substantial support, and (3) requiring very sub-stantial support.

Diagnostic Considerations

Disruptive behavior patterns in ID and ASD often include irritability, aggression, emotional dysregulation, behavioral outbursts, and noncom-pliance/defiance with rules and expectations. Common disorders comorbid with ID include attention-deficit/hyperactivity disorder (ADHD), depres-sive and bipolar disorders, anxiety disorders, ASD, stereotypic movement disorder, impulse control disorders, and major neurocognitive disorders (Maulik et al., 2011). ASD may be comorbid with varying severities of ID and structural language disorders (APA, 2013). Psychiatric symptoms beyond the scope of ASD result in 70% of diagnosed individuals having a comorbid diagnosis and 40% of diagnosed individuals having two or more comorbid diagnoses. ASD is frequently comorbid with internalizing problems, ADHD, and developmental coordination disorder. Disruptive behavior problems may be concurrent with ASD and are an emphasis in interventions. In a population-derived sample of children with ASD, for example, Simonoff et al. (2008) reported 28% comorbidity with opposi-tional defiant disorder.

Prevalence and Course

Both ID and ASD are lifelong disabilities that occur in about 1% of the general population (APA, 2013). Risk factors for ID include genetic conditions (e.g., Down syndrome, Fragile X syndrome, Williams syndrome, phenylketonuria, and Prader-Willi syndrome); prenatal exposure to alco-hol and other drugs or toxins; perinatal events during labor and delivery; and postnatal events such as injury, infections, intoxications, or severe and chronic social deprivation (Fletcher-Janzen & Reynolds, 2003; Raymond & Tarpey, 2006). Prevalence rates for disruptive behaviors—including aggression, harm to others, and property destruction—have been reported between 11% and 27% among people with ID, with higher rates (38%) in institutional settings (Harris, 1993). Disruptive behaviors co-occurring with ASD are ubiquitous across the life span (Farmer & Aman, 2011) and may include verbal and physical aggression, emotional-behavioral outbursts, bullying, stealing, defiance, intimidation, inappro-priate sexual behavior or touching, self-mutilation, general emotional dysregulation, and property destruction.

Pharmacological Solitary Treatments

Although controversial, the use of psychotropic medications for individuals with ID or ASD remains high (Elvins & Green, 2010; Sharma & Shaw, 2012; Young & Hawkins, 2002). In institutions without drug monitoring programs, for example, psychotropic medication use typically ranges from 30% to 40%, and in community settings, use ranges from 19% to 29%, with reports as high as 50% in various clinical settings (de Kuijper et al., 2010; Gralton at al., 1998; Holden & Gitlesen, 2004). To date, disruptive behaviors continue to be a primary reason for pharmacological interventions for individuals with ID and ASD.

Intellectual Disability

Aggressive behavior is the most common reason for psychiatric referrals in persons with ID (Janowsky et al., 2006). Antipsychotic medications are frequently used as a primary treatment of such aggression, although federal and state guidelines encourage less use of these medications (Janowsky et al., 2006).

Two broad categories of antipsychotic medications exist: typical (first generation) and atypical (second generation). Because of the risk for extrapyramidal symptoms (EPS) and sometimes permanent movement disorders (i.e., tardive dyskinesia), typical antipsychotic medications are used more often in emergency psychiatric situations or cases where other medications have not been successful.

Currently, atypical antipsychotic medications are frequently prescribed for disruptive behaviors. Although they pose lower risk for EPS, these medications increase risks of weight gain and concomitant diabetes, hypercholesterolemia, and metabolic syndrome. Retrospective data suggest that persons with ID are at higher risk of sedation and weight gain than the general population (Simeon et al., 2002). Common baseline and regularly scheduled measures of relevant lab tests may include fasting glucose or hemoglobin HbA_{1c}, cholesterol, triglycerides, prolactin (in youth), vital signs, weight, height, waist circumference (in adults), and body mass index (BMI). A review of 195 studies (117 typical antipsychotics and 78 atypical antipsychotics) indicated that atypical antipsychotics are the first choice for treatment of schizophrenia in people with ID (La Malfa et al., 2006). Specifically, a number of studies demonstrated the efficacy of risperidone in the treatment of disruptive behaviors, especially aggression.

Randomized controlled trials (RCTs) investigating the use of antipsychotics in individuals with ID across the life span have shown beneficial results. Snyder et al. (2002) investigated the use of risperidone in 110 children (ages 5–12 years; IQ range 36–84) with disruptive behavior disorders during a six-week double-blind study. Using the Nisonger Child Behavior Rating Form (NCBRF) Conduct Problem subscale, changes from baseline were significantly greater in the risperidone group compared to the placebo group. Aman et al. (2002), in a replication of Snyder et al. (2002) with 118 children, reported similar results, suggesting risperidone to be about twice as effective as placebo. Gagiano et al. (2005) investigated 77 adults (ages 18–59 years; IQ range 35–85) comparing risperidone (dose range 1–4 mg/day) versus placebo. Results revealed the risperidone group had a 21.5% greater improvement on a study-specific behavior checklist, a 23.5% improvement on the Clinical Global Impression Scale, and favorable results on the Behavior Problem Inventory. Comparable results are evident across other risperidone treatment investigations (Deb et al., 2001; Shedlack et al., 2005).

Olanzapine has also been shown to significantly reduce self-injurious and aggressive behavior in adults with ID (Janowsky et al., 2003a). This retrospective study involved 20 adults with intellectual disability who had significant aggressive, destructive, or self-injurious behaviors. Participants received multiple psychotropic medications at baseline, and when olanzapine (mean daily dose of 9.1 mg) was added to their medication regime, concurrent dosage reductions of conventional antipsychotic medications were made. Results revealed a significant decrease in the targeted aggressive, destructive, and self-injurious behaviors and in global challenging behaviors. During the first six months of treatment, however, individuals experienced significant weight gain and other side effects such as sedation and constipation.

Although some studies support the efficacy of risperidone and other antipsychotics in the treatment of aggressive behavior, efficacy across studies varies significantly. Rana et al. (2013) conducted a systematic review of published research on the efficacy of various psychotropic medications on self-injurious behaviors in adults with ID and concluded "weak evidence" exists that any medications had benefits over placebo. A thorough review of relevant research suggests that, for maximal efficacy, medication should be utilized in the context of a comprehensive behavior management plan (Scahill et al., 2012).

Autism Spectrum Disorder

Similar to the ID literature, ASD individuals with significant aggressive behavior or irritability patterns are often prescribed psychotropic medications. Although other medication classes (e.g., stimulants, tricyclics, selective serotonin reuptake inhibitors, and alpha-adrenergics) have been studied with mixed results, antipsychotic medications have the best empirical support for reducing disruptive behaviors. Prescribing for behavior management often results in off-label medication use, however. The US Food and Drug Administration (FDA) has approved all antipsychotics for a variety of adult indications (e.g., schizophrenia, bipolar disorder) and some for children, including aripiprazole for both children (ages 6–17 years) and adults, risperidone for children (age 5 and older) and adults, and iloperidone for adolescents and adults. In October 2006, the FDA approved risperidone for the treatment of irritability, aggression, self-injury, and tantrums in children and adolescents (ages 5–16 years) with ASD (Malone & Waheed, 2009). Whether prescribed on- or off-label, close monitoring is highly recommended, especially in individuals who have difficulty reporting adverse effects.

A meta-analysis of 22 studies (16 open-label studies and 6 placebo-controlled studies) found antipsychotic medications to have significant effects in improving irritability and aggression in children with ASD. Specifically, the mean treatment effect size was one standard deviation across studies (Sharma & Shaw, 2012). Haloperidol is the most critically studied typical antipsychotic for use in the treatment of ASD (Malone & Waheed, 2009). Double-blind and placebo-controlled trials of haloperidol have been reported, showing short- and long-term efficacy and safety. For example, Remington et al. (2001) investigated haloperidol (dose range 1–1.5 mg) versus clomipramine, a tricyclic antidepressant (dose range 100–150 mg), in the treatment of 36 individuals (ages 10–36 years) with ASD. Of interest were not the overall treatment effects, but the premature termination rates for each group. Only 37.5% of the clomipramine group (vs. 69.7% of the haloperidol group) completed the study, with reasons reported as adverse side effects and behavioral problems. When analyzing completed trials, both haloperidol and clomipramine proved effective and superior to baseline in reducing behavioral problems.

The Research Units on Pediatric Psychopharmacology Autism Network (RUPPAN) conducted an eight-week double-blind placebo-controlled study of 101 children (ages 5–17 years) to evaluate the efficacy of risperidone (RUPPAN, 2005). The risperidone group revealed statistically significant clinical improvement compared to the placebo group (69% vs. 12%) on the Aberrant Behavior Checklist (ABC) Irritability Scale and the Clinical Global Impressions-Improvement Rating (CGI-I). Significant improvement was also noted on both the ABC Stereotypy and Hyperactivity Scales. Of 63 participants, 51 continued to show a positive response during a four-month follow-up phase. Similarly, Shea et al. (2004) conducted an eight-week double-blind placebo-controlled trial of risperidone in 79 children (ages 5–12 years) and showed significant decrease in symptoms compared to the placebo group (64% vs. 31%) in irritability, along with hyperactivity, inappropriate speech, lethargy/social withdrawal, and stereotypical behavior. As an example of emerging evidence requiring further study, Ghanizadeh and Moghimi-Sarani

(2013) completed a double-blind placebo-controlled RCT examining the efficacy and safety of *n*-acetylcysteine added to risperidone for treating irritability in 40 children (ages 3.5–16 years) with ASD. The ABC Irritability Scale revealed a significant difference showing reduced behavioral problems with *n*-acetylcysteine added. Common adverse effects with this medication combination included constipation (16.1%), increased appetite (16.1%), fatigue (12.9%), nervousness (12.9%), and daytime drowsiness (12.9%). Although shown to be relatively safe, studies of risperidone with children with ASD (Findling et al., 2004) also show a relatively high incidence of certain adverse effects: somnolence (33%), headache (33%), rhinitis (28%), and weight gain (21%).

Benefits and Limitations of Pharmacotherapy as Sole Treatment

Typically, medications should be prescribed after trials of nonpharmacological strategies. Although recommended across all age groups, this approach is especially salient for youth to avoid risk to their developing brain. Moreover, many medications used to ameliorate behavioral problems in adults are not FDA approved for children. Fine-tuning pediatric dosages is complicated owing to adult–child differences in pharmacokinetics. Pediatric research suggests that some behavioral interventions may be equally as effective as medications without the risk of adverse effects (Horner et al., 2002). Medication may be necessary as a first-line approach when behavioral problems include severe aggression toward self or others (e.g., family/peers).

Although psychotropic medications are considered a second-line approach following ineffective behavioral intervention, they may not always be necessary or helpful. In fact, when reviewing research to decide on medication options, comparing medication efficacy to other treatments (not only comparisons with placebo) is important. "Safe practices" when prescribing for individuals with ID and ASD, such as "start lower and go slower," are recommended for the starting dosage and titration compared to dosages used in individuals without ID or ASD (Hässler & Reis, 2010). Individuals with ID may be at risk for overmedication with antipsychotics, resulting in sedation, social withdrawal, and loss of cognitive function (Ahmed et al., 2000).

An important consideration is adherence, especially in light of estimates of 40% nonadherence with antipsychotics (Robinson, 1999). Serum levels may help determine adherence and dosing, although clinical status and response should always take precedence. When nonadherence is an issue, long-acting injectable risperidone dosed every two weeks or longer is an option.

When using pharmacotherapy, routine laboratory studies may be added to the primary monitoring of clinical efficacy/status to identify side effects, track the need for dosage changes, and make decisions to add medications for symptoms not being well managed on the current regime. No universal algorithm exists for medication treatment of aggressive behavior, which is typically a pattern caused by issues specific to the individual and circumstances in which the pattern is embedded.

In addition, individual differences emerge in efficacy of medications versus behavioral strategies, and multiple reasons may lead clinicians to opt for one treatment modality over another. For example, a clinician may opt for medications other than a second-generation antipsychotic if the patient has a history of adverse reactions to those medications, long QT syndrome (a heart rhythm disorder), metabolic syndrome, liver disease, concomitant use of drugs known to cause elevated glucose, or lack of enzymes to metabolize risperidone (de Leon et al., 2005, 2009). Because psychotropic medications present medical risks, many clinicians opt for a trial of behavioral strategies (especially in youth) before considering medications. Further, pharmacotherapy alone does not teach the individual to improve coping, self-monitoring, or other skills helpful in the long term.

Psychological Solitary Treatments

Published treatment guidelines regarding evidence-based treatments for disruptive behaviors may be applied to persons with ID or ASD (Charlop-Christy et al., 2002; Durand, 1990; Eyberg et al., 2008; Fisher et al., 2011; Forgatch & Patterson, 2010; Walker & Gresham, 2013). In addition, published treatment guidelines that cut across the intervention categories we use below are available specifically for individuals with ID or ASD. For example, guidelines for youth and adults with ID are described in Odom et al. (2007), Peacock et al. (2010), Sturney and Didden (2014), Taylor et al. (2013), Tsakanikos and McCarthy (2014), Wehmeyer et al. (2007), and Wodrich and Schmitt (2006). Chedd and Levine (2012) describe ASD treatment planning, and Goldstein and Naglieri (2013) and Reichow et al. (2010) provide guidelines for ASD evidence-based treatment.

Studies described in the following sections have demonstrated the efficacy of psychological interventions in reducing disruptive behaviors in individuals with ID and ASD. Implementation of these interventions varies from intensive one-on-one approaches to educational programs focused on individuals and their support systems. The most commonly used interventions are categorized as behavioral interventions, social skills training, parent–caregiver training/education (PT/E), preventive interventions, and adult interventions. In these sections, interventions for ID and ASD are described together on account of their similarities in implementation.

Behavioral Interventions

Substantial research supports behavioral interventions to manage disruptive behaviors in youth with ASD and ID. Horner et al. (2002) found that implementing behavioral interventions reduced the severity of problem behaviors in children with ASD by 80%–90%. Applied behavior analysis (ABA) procedures are most commonly used to treat a variety of disruptive and aggressive behaviors associated with ASD and ID (Matson, 2009; Matson et al., 2005). ABA approaches are categorized as package procedures or functional analyses. Package procedures apply traditional ABA interventions designed to ameliorate problem behaviors across a range of contexts by manipulating behavioral contingencies and focusing on social reinforcement of appropriate behaviors, token economy, choice making, and punishment procedures. Functional assessment is used to assess the function and purpose of behaviors in need of change, and results are used to tailor package procedures to particular contexts.

Randomized controlled trials examining ABA have led to its classification as an evidence-based intervention for individuals with ASD (Rogers & Vismara, 2008). Although substantial empirical data support ABA to improve communication and adaptive skills for individuals with ASD, inconsistent evidence exists for its efficacy in reducing problem behaviors, with some studies suggesting a lack of reduction in severity of problem behaviors (Smith et al., 2000). A meta-analysis on behavioral interventions for disruptive behaviors in young children with ASD (Horner et al., 2002) indicated improved outcomes when positive behavioral supports (e.g., functional behavior analyses and functional communication interventions) supplemented behavioral models. This converges with the literature's emphasis on gathering data to aid in understanding *functions* of behaviors prior to implementing treatment strategies and teaching functional communication skills to aid in behavioral regulation (Didden et al., 1997).

Social Skills Training

Research on social skills training has supported its effectiveness in enhancing prosocial skills and reducing challenging behaviors in individuals with developmental disabilities (Alavi et al., 2013; Laugeson et al., 2012). Nevertheless, other research suggests that social skills training has minimal effectiveness, poor generalizability, and limited maintenance (Bellini et al., 2007; Kokina & Kern, 2010). Frankel et al. (2010) conducted an RCT using the Children's Friendship Training Program and found that, although parents reported decreased peer conflict, both parents and teachers did not observe significant reductions in the children's externalizing behaviors or levels of aggression.

Parent or Caregiver Training/Education (PT/E)

Because disruptive behaviors frequently occur across settings, interventions should include a PT/E component (Rogers & Vismara, 2008). Matson et al. (2009) describe this as "a treatment approach that uniquely positions the therapy model toward a goal of generalization [from the clinic] to other relevant community settings" (p. 962). PT/E interventions typically teach parents how to apply behavioral modification concepts to the home and other naturalistic settings and to improve the parent–child relationship (Brookman-Frazee et al., 2006). For example, Feldman et al. (1999) taught basic child-care skills to mothers with ID via self-learning pictorial-parenting manuals. Results indicated that many parents with ID may improve their child-care skills without intensive training and that self-instruction may be an easy and cost-effective way of reducing the risk of child neglect resulting from parenting skill deficiencies. Although most research on disruptive behaviors in ID or ASD emphasizes treating young children, some support exists for the use of multisystemic therapy to treat older children with ASD (Wagner et al., 2013).

Randomized controlled trials examining PT/E interventions have revealed decreases in problem behaviors in children with Asperger disorder (Sofronoff et al., 2004) and significant reductions in disruptive behaviors in children with developmental delays (McIntyre, 2008). Building the capacity of family members and caregivers can be an effective intervention across various demographics. The Triple P—Positive Parent Program, for example, was effective in significantly reducing disruptive behaviors and parenting stress for Chinese parents of preschoolers with a developmental disability (Leung et al., 2013). In addition, Singh et al. (2006) compared intensive behavior management training for group home staff to behavior management followed by mindfulness. They observed a significant reduction in aberrant behaviors by adult residents after the latter training.

Preventive Interventions

Another avenue for managing disruptive behaviors in individuals with ID or ASD focuses on preventive changes to an individual's environment to address *antecedents* of disruptive behaviors. These interventions often result in significant decreases in disruptive behaviors, reductions in using physical restraints, and enhancement in the efficacy of other treatments (Brosnan & Healy, 2011; Heyvaert et al., 2012; Williams, 2010). In addition, some evidence exists for mindfulness to reduce aggression in adolescents with high-functioning ASD (Singh et al., 2011).

Adult Interventions

A disproportionate number of child versus adult studies focus on psychological interventions for managing behavior problems in individuals with developmental disabilities. In addition, frequent overlap emerges in the literature on managing behavioral problems in adults with ASD and ID. In a recent review, Vereenooghe and Langdon (2013) found favorable outcomes for cognitive-behavioral treatment (CBT) as an effective treatment for managing anger and aggression in adults with ID, especially when treatment was individualized. One such CBT intervention successfully taught anger management skills to men with mild-moderate ID and a history of aggression living in secure settings (Taylor et al., 2005).

An RCT (Hassiotis et al., 2009) found that supplementing a standard hospital multidisciplinary treatment team with behavioral specialists was effective in reducing problem behaviors in adults with developmental disabilities. In addition, the cost of the behavioral therapists was comparable to the standard treatment team. Exploratory analyses (Van Bourgondien et al., 2003) revealed significant reductions in problem behaviors when implementing the evidence-based Treatment and Education of Autistic and Related Communication Handicapped Children (TEACCH) model in an adult residential program.

Benefits and Limitations of Psychotherapy as Sole Treatment

Significant support exists for psychological interventions in managing behavior problems in individuals who have ASD or ID without psychotropic medications. Despite strong empirical support, however, psychological interventions can be expensive and labor and time intensive. Another concern is that clinicians sometimes combine components from various curricula, treatment protocols, and programs. Reviews of psychological and behavioral interventions for children with ASD, for example, discourage this eclectic approach to implementation (Rogers & Vismara, 2008) because of its decreased efficacy. But these studies primarily focus on interventions aimed at the core symptoms of ASD and less on challenging disruptive behaviors.

Combined Treatments

Relatively few RCTs have studied combined psychological and pharmacological interventions to manage challenging behaviors in individuals diagnosed with ID and ASD. Limited evidence suggests, however, that integrating pharmacological and psychological treatments may be of greater benefit than implementing either alone.

Intellectual Disability

Compared to literature on solely psychopharmacological or psychological interventions, few empirical investigations exist on the effectiveness of combined approaches for disruptive behaviors in individuals with ID. The literature consists primarily of pharmacological studies in which patients were permitted to participate in behavioral therapy during medication trials. For example, Aman et al. (2002) allowed youth diagnosed with ID to continue behavioral therapy through the course of a clinical trial of risperidone. In this semicombined treatment approach study, risperidone was superior to placebo in decreasing severe problem behaviors (e.g., aggression, hyperactivity, self-injurious behavior), supporting the effectiveness of a combined approach to treat disruptive behaviors in children with ID. Case studies also suggest that the combination of stimulant medication with behavioral strategies in children with ID may be effective at reducing disruptive behavior (Blum et al., 1996).

Rigorous evidence is lacking for combined interventions for adults with ID. Through retrospective data analysis, however, some examination has occurred on the effectiveness of combining medications (e.g., serotonergic antidepressants and topiramate) with behavior therapy in the treatment of aggressive, self-injurious, and disruptive behaviors (Janowsky et al., 2003b; Janowsky et al., 2005). These two studies found that both medications were effective in decreasing disruptive behaviors while clients received behavior therapy. Although these studies did not control for behavior therapy, results suggest that combining psychological and pharmacological treatments may be effective in treating disruptive behavior in adults with ID.

In addition, Devapriam et al. (2008) used a multidisciplinary treatment approach in specialized psychiatric inpatient units for adults with ID. They found that patients' aggressive behaviors improved when using levomepromazine while concurrently receiving speech and language therapy for communication problems and psychological interventions for behavior management problems. Although this study was not randomized for the psychological interventions, the results indicated that combined treatment approaches may be effective in treating challenging behaviors in adults diagnosed with ID.

Autism Spectrum Disorder

Aman et al. (2009) conducted one of the few RCTs examining the effects of combining behavioral interventions and risperidone. From the 124 families of children with ASD, 75 were randomized to the combined treatment approach (PT/E and risperidone) and 49 were placed in the risperidone-only approach. The PT/E sessions were based on a parent manual, customized for each family, and included antecedent-prevention strategies, positive reinforcement, compliance training, and instructional methods for teaching new skills. After 24 weeks, the combined group was prescribed significantly less risperidone, exhibited significantly less noncompliant behaviors, and experienced significantly less irritability, stereotypic behavior, and hyperactivity/noncompliance than the medication-only group. The combined group also had larger improvement in adaptive behavior including socialization, communication, and noncompliance (Scahill et al., 2012).

Handen et al. (2013) examined behavioral changes observed among these same families across four conditions: free play, social attention seeking, demands, and tangible rewards restriction. Parents in the combined group used fewer restrictive statements (e.g., "no" and "stop") and more reinforcement (e.g., high-fives, hugs, praise) in some of these conditions compared to the medication-only group. Overall, results suggested that combined treatment approaches were more effective in reducing disruptive behavior than the medication-only condition. Despite promising findings, a one-year follow-up of participants suggested poor maintenance of the improvements (Arnold et al., 2012). At follow-up, the children's noncompliance regressed back to baseline, with a larger deterioration occurring in the combined group, and no difference was found in risperidone dosage between the combined group and medication-only group. However, 94% of parents in the combined group were using behavior management techniques, compared to only 53% in the medication-only group. Families in the combined group reported that the most helpful techniques remained behavioral principles, daily schedules, planned ignoring, and reinforcement.

In addition to RCTs, retrospective studies suggest that combined treatment is effective. Frazier et al. (2010) examined combined therapy in the treatment of aggression in children with ASD and found a combination of behavioral treatment and antipsychotic medication was more effective than behavioral treatment alone. Qualitative information from psychiatric hospitals suggests that a combined approach (i.e., ABA and pharmacotherapy) with large multidisciplinary treatment teams can be used to treat aggression, self-injurious behavior, property destruction, and emotional dysregulation in children with ASD (Siegel & Gabriels, 2014). But one caveat in referencing psychiatric hospitalization data is that the information is largely retrospective and uncontrolled.

Other studies have examined the efficacy of pharmacotherapy while participants continued their behavioral therapy not associated with the study. Shea et al. (2004) found risperidone to be effective in treating disruptive behaviors in children with ASD when participants were allowed to continue behavior therapy throughout the medication trial, providing evidence that pharmacological treatments can be beneficial for those who have prior experience with behavioral therapies.

Benefits and Limitations of Combined Treatments

An integrated treatment approach may promote greater improvements in target behaviors through increased collaboration among professionals, which is essential when individualizing a treatment plan that combines medication and psychological approaches. Several models describe a collaborative approach to treatment planning among medical, psychological, and educational providers that strongly emphasize data collection to inform the team of the individual's progress and the next steps of treatment (Ellis et al., 2007).

True collaboration, however, requires time, resources, and organizational support. Treatment team members must dedicate adequate time to consult with each other. A high degree of collaboration is required to ensure coordinated changes in behavioral or pharmacological approaches. To create a functional and collaborative treatment model, Mohr et al. (2002) suggest a few key elements: a shared understanding of different models, effective communication, respect for team members, multidisciplinary input, ability to resolve dynamic tensions, and adequate resources. Although combining treatment approaches requires more effort, researchers and practitioners should continue to scientifically evaluate the efficacy of such integrated care.

Summary and Recommendations

Overall, more published evidence-based treatment protocols for youth and adults with ID or ASD are needed. In the meantime, some evidence-based treatment protocols for children with disruptive behaviors may be applied to youth with ID or ASD. For example, Eyberg et al. (2008) emphasized parent training to be first priority for treating young children. Some evidence-based treatments for parent training include Parent–Child Interaction Therapy (PCIT; Zisser & Eyberg, 2010) and the Parent Management Training-Oregon Model (Forgatch & Patterson, 2010). In addition, the Picture Exchange Communication System (PECS; Charlop-Christy et al., 2002) can provide reduction in problem behaviors for children through aids in communication.

Further research is needed on differential effectiveness of medications in specific subgroups (e.g., responders vs. nonresponders, ID, ASD, chronic vs. episodic pattern) with aggression. Also, long-term research is urgently needed to determine the optimal approach for management of aggressive behavior and to compare groups treated with and without medications. If research controlling for severity symptoms can make this long-term comparison, patients and treating clinicians could make more well-informed treatment decisions *before* the initiation of treatment. Currently, insufficient research is available to determine how much behavior will improve, how long that will take, and how long psychotropic medications will be needed for ID and ASD subgroups.

Given the breadth of psychological treatment research discouraging an eclectic (as opposed to manualized) approach, further studies should determine whether these recommendations apply to interventions for disruptive behaviors in individuals with ASD and ID. In addition, researchers should continue to examine the efficacy of psychological interventions in *adults* with developmental disabilities.

Owing to the lack of research comparing combined treatment methods to psychological or pharmacological approaches alone, future studies should include a combined condition. This methodology would provide more information about which psychological treatments work well in combination with pharmacological treatments and whether the benefits of combined treatments are maintained for both children and adults with ID or ASD. Furthermore, although theoretical and practical recommendations exist to guide professionals in collaborating on a multidisciplinary team, research should study the optimal levels with which these teams should collaborate. For example, research should examine the method (e.g., presentation of objective data) and frequency with which treatment teams need to communicate to maintain a strong collaboration.

Our overarching conceptual model for this evidence-based practice case vignette was the Bioecological Model of Human Development (Bronfenbrenner & Morris, 2006), which was applied using the Therapeutic Family Assessment Model described by Heffer et al. (2003). A contextual systems orientation is foundational to the Bioecological Model that maps how a person's biology fuels development within the interwoven and transactional context of proximal and distal layers of influence, such as the family, community, culture, and society. The Therapeutic Family Assessment Model evaluates influences proposed in the Bioecological Model specific to an individual's or immediate family's cognitive, affective, behavioral, structural/developmental, and communication/ interpersonal domains of functioning. Assessment information across domains is gathered using multiple assessment strategies, including both formal and informal and self-report or observational techniques. Initial assessment defines treatment goals and ongoing assessment refines treatment and clarifies appropriate and socially valid treatment outcomes.

Tony, the eldest of three children in his home, was a 13-year-old Hispanic male with ASD and borderline intellectual functioning and moderately low adaptive behavior levels. Tony's parents were professionals with a college education. Spanish and English were spoken in the home. Family, community, and church support were important aspects of this family. Cultural characteristics of *familismo* and *respeto* (i.e., importance of the extended family in making decisions about treatment/support and emphasis on being respectful toward people based on age or educational authority, respectively) were obvious in Tony's nuclear and extended family. Overall, a collaborative-consultative approach with Tony and his parents considered family values, goals, dual-language/cultural emphases, developmental needs, family time and obligations, and sibling concerns/roles.

The Special Education (SPED) team at Tony's school determined him eligible for services as an Individuals with Disabilities Education Act–defined student with autism when he was a preschooler and subsequently developed consecutive iterations of an individualized education plan (IEP) for him. Triennial SPED reevaluations tracked Tony's levels of intellectual and adaptive behavior functioning; ASD-related and other behavioral–emotional patterns; formal and classroom-based academic skills; social and interpersonal skills; and response to academic, social skill, and behavioral–emotional focused interventions. IEP goals and patterns/levels of functioning also were tracked and modified via annual, and more frequently when needed, IEP review meetings that included Tony's parents.

During the first few weeks of Tony's transition to the seventh grade on a middle school campus (the previous academic year he was on a fifth- and sixth-grade intermediate school campus), his parents and teachers noted behavioral changes. He became more disruptive and inattentive at school, more oppositional at home, and seemed more resistant to changes in his routine, and he increased the frequency, duration, and intensity of his emotional outbursts at home and school. Tony's parents met with his developmental–behavioral pediatrician about these behavioral changes, and she referred them back to a community-based psychologist who had provided services to them on and off throughout Tony's development. It became clear to the psychologist that these behavioral changes were a function of a common developmental trajectory of ASD (with borderline intellectual functioning) interacting with aspects of changes in Tony's maturation, school campus, and family (e.g., his parents were challenged by how best to respond to Tony's experiences in early adolescence and developmental changes and coping responses of his younger siblings). In addition, the psychologist learned that Tony's problematic behavior pattern extended to his after-school appointments at a local rehabilitation center and decided that a team approach to evidence-based assessment and treatment was needed. Communication and coordination of

(continued)

(continued)

services occurred between Tony's psychologist, physician, parents, school psychologist and teachers, and local rehabilitation center personnel (i.e., speech–language pathologist, occupational therapist, and ABA autism specialist).

A functional behavior analysis (FBA) conducted in the home, school, and rehabilitation center by the psychologist, school psychologist, and autism specialist revealed problematic behavior patterns of (1) frequent disruptive vocal/verbal outbursts accompanied by emotional dysregulation, (2) frequent inattention/distractibility, (3) occasional hand flapping, and (4) occasional noncompliance with instructions from adults. The "core" treatment team (i.e., psychologist, school psychologist, and autism specialist) consulted by phone conference to review FBA data and then continued every week for a month to evaluate change over time and design/monitor treatments. The "full" treatment team (i.e., parents, psychologist, rehabilitation center staff, and school staff) then met to review the FBA data and develop a behavior intervention plan (BIP) for his IEP, which was also adapted to nonschool settings. The full treatment team then met in October and December of the Fall semester, including some by phone conference, to collaborate, coordinate services, monitor progress, and design/modify interventions.

A changing criterion design (Gresham, 2014) was used to evaluate baseline levels of each of the four targeted behaviors across each of the three settings and then to identify behavioral changes once interventions were implemented. The psychologist, school psychologist, and autism specialist conducted regular (weekly initially and then, after four weeks, monthly) treatment integrity checks to ensure that adults at home, school, and the rehabilitation center were consistently, accurately, and uniformly implementing the interventions. The psychologist conducted in-session observations of the parents implementing the interventions with Tony and provided feedback to the parents to refine their approach. Similar integrity checks were conducted by the school psychologist with Tony and school staff and by the autism specialist with Tony and the rehabilitation center personnel.

Vocal/emotional control was targeted first (owing to the severity and chronicity of the behavior and interruption of Tony's and his peers' activities), and focused attention, appropriate use of hands, and looking at adults and complying with instructions were subsequently targeted, in the listed order. Behavioral and PT/E interventions were developed in the school BIP (and applied to rehabilitation and home settings) based on the FBA. Specifically, for Tony's classrooms, rehabilitation center appointments, and time at home, a token economy system (Walker & Gresham, 2013) that included social reinforcement of appropriate behaviors and a picture exchange communication system (Charlop-Christy et al., 2002) was developed. The psychologist, school psychologist, and autism specialist provided training for parents, school staff, and rehabilitation center staff, respectively. In addition, the psychologist provided the parents with PT/E interventions gleaned from the Parent Management Training-Oregon Model (Forgatch & Patterson, 2010) and further informed by guidelines in Chedd and Levine (2012) and Goldstein and Naglieri (2013). Essential components included antecedent-prevention strategies, positive reinforcement, planned ignoring, daily scheduling/structure, compliance training, and instructional methods for teaching new skills.

Improvements were observed across the four problem areas, but levels remained problematic and disruptive. For example, Tony's levels of compliance with adult instructions (once his attention to the instructions was fully obtained) improved substantially across all three settings. In addition, his hand flapping was reduced to once or twice per school week, no incidents at rehabilitation center appointments, and only several times per week at home. Even so, adults continued to need to redirect and refocus Tony because of his distractibility and inattentiveness. In addition, although the duration of Tony's vocal/verbal outbursts reduced from 15 to 5 minutes at home and from 15 to 2 minutes at school and the rehabilitation center, the frequency (twice per rehabilitation appointment, four to five times per day at school and at home on weekends) and intensity remained problematic. School staff needed to remove students from the classroom for safety and disruption reasons, for example, until Tony regained emotional control, and the rehabilitation staff could not reliably complete Tony's appointments that included social skill and peer interaction components.

At the parents' request and authorization, the psychologist consulted with the physician and provided a summary from the core treatment team to accompany her medication evaluation appointment with Tony and his parents. Based on this clinical information, she decided to add risperidone to the behavioral treatment plan. The core treatment team continued to monitor and implement nonpharmacological interventions, and the physician monitored his response to medications, including possible adverse reactions.

(continued)

(continued)

The combined treatment approach resulted in acceptable levels of functioning across the four problems targeted, such that problem behaviors decreased further and reached appropriate levels for a youth with ASD. Specifically, the addition of risperidone resulted in slight weight gain, but also further reductions of hand flapping to one to two occurrences per week across settings and reductions of vocal/verbal outbursts to one to two occurrences per week across settings. Typical duration of the vocal/verbal outbursts was reduced to 0.5–1 minute, and the intensity levels did *not* necessitate removal of others nearby for safety and disruption reasons. Further, school and rehabilitation staff much more effectively accomplished Tony's social skill and peer interaction skills training, with positive behavioral results for Tony after two months of his risperidone use. Compliance with adult instructions continued to remain at improved levels, and adults' need to redirect and refocus Tony as a result of his distractibility and inattentiveness improved even further following use of risperidone.

The core team continued to consult regularly, and the full team met twice in the school Spring semester to monitor and coordinate services. The last meeting was at the end of the Spring semester and focused on generalization and maintenance of treatment effects and planning for the next school year and for summer activities at home and the rehabilitation center.

Note

1 The views expressed in this publication are those of the authors and do not reflect the official policy or position of the Department of the Army, Department of Defense, or the US Government.

References

Ahmed, Z., et al. (2000). Reducing antipsychotic medication in people with a learning disability. *British Journal of Psychiatry, 176,* 42–46.

Alavi, S. Z., et al. (2013). The effect of social skills training on aggression of mild mentally retarded children. *Social and Behavioral Sciences, 84,* 1166–1170. doi:10.1016/j.sbspro.2013.06.720

Aman, M. G., et al. (2002). Double-blind, placebo-controlled study of risperidone for the treatment of disruptive behaviors in children with subaverage intelligence. *American Journal of Psychiatry, 159*(8), 1337–1346. doi:10.1176/appi. ajp.159.8.1337

Aman, M. G., et al. (2009). Medication and parent training in children with pervasive developmental disorders and serious behavior problems: Results from a randomized clinical trial. *Journal of the American Academy of Child and Adolescent Psychiatry, 48*(12), 1143–1154. doi:10.1097/CHI.0b013e3181bfd669

American Psychiatric Association. (2013). *Diagnostic and statistical manual of mental disorders* (5th ed.). Washington, DC: Author.

Arnold, L. E., et al. (2012). Research Units of Pediatric Psychopharmacology (RUPP) autism network randomized clinical trial of parent training and medication: One-year follow-up. *Journal of the American Academy of Child and Adolescent Psychiatry, 51*(11), 1173–1184. doi:10.1016/j.jaac.2012.08.028

Bellini, S., et al. (2007). A meta-analysis of school-based social skills training interventions for children with autism spectrum disorders. *Remedial and Special Education, 28*(3), 153–162. doi:10.1177/07419325070280030401

Blum, N. J., et al. (1996). Separate and combined effects of methylphenidate and a behavioral intervention on disruptive behavior in children with mental retardation. *Journal of Applied Behavior Analysis, 29*(3), 305–319. doi:10.1901/jaba.1996.29-305

Bronfenbrenner, U., & Morris, P. A. (2006). The bioecological model of human development. In W. Damon & R. M. Lerner (Eds.), *Handbook of child psychology* (Vol. 1). *Theoretical models of human development* (6th ed., pp. 793–828). New York: John Wiley.

Brookman-Frazee, L., et al. (2006). Parenting interventions for children with autism spectrum and disruptive behavior disorders: Opportunities for cross-fertilization. *Clinical Child and Family Psychology Review, 9*(3–4), 181–200.

Brosnan, J., & Healy, O. (2011). A review of behavioral interventions for the treatment of aggression in individuals with developmental disabilities. *Research in Developmental Disabilities, 32,* 437–446. doi:10.1016/j.ridd.2010.12.023

Charlop-Christy, M. H., et al. (2002). Using the picture exchange communication system (PECS) with children with autism: Assessment of PECS acquisition, speech, social-communicative behavior, and problem behavior. *Journal of Applied Behavior Analysis, 35*(3), 213–231.

Chedd, N., & Levine, K. (2012). *Treatment planning for children with autism spectrum disorders: An individualized, problem-solving approach.* Hoboken, NJ: Wiley.

Deb, S., et al. (2001). Mental disorder in adults with intellectual disability: Prevalence of functional psychiatric illness among a community-based population aged between 16 and 64 years. *Journal of Intellectual Disability Research, 45*(6), 495–505.

de Kuijper, G., et al. (2010). Use of antipsychotic drugs in individuals with intellectual disability (ID) in the Netherlands: Prevalence and reasons for prescription. *Journal of Intellectual Disability Research, 54*(7), 659–667.

de Leon, J., et al. (2005). The dosing of atypical antipsychotics. *Psychosomatics, 46,* 262–273.

de Leon, J., et al. (2009). Practical guidelines for the use of new generation antipsychotic drugs (except clozapine) in adult individuals with intellectual disabilities. *Research in Developmental Disabilities, 30,* 613–669.

Devapriam, J., et al. (2008). Use of levomepromazine in the management of aggression in adults with intellectual disability. *British Journal of Developmental Disabilities, 54*(106), 11–17. doi:10.1179/096979508799103305

Didden, R., et al. (1997). Meta-analytic study on treatment effectiveness for problem behaviors with individuals who have mental retardation. *American Journal of Mental Retardation, 101,* 387–399.

Durand, V. M. (1990). *Severe behavior problems: A functional communication training approach.* New York: Guilford Press.

Ellis, C. R., et al. (2007). Physician collaboration involving students with autism spectrum disorders. *Psychology in the Schools, 44*(7), 737–747. doi:10.1002/pits.20262

Elvins, R., & Green J. (2010). Pharmacological management of core and comorbid symptoms in autistic spectrum disorder. *Advances in Psychiatric Treatment, 16,* 349–360. doi:10.1192/apt.bp.108.005538

Eyberg, S. M., et al. (2008). Evidence-based psychosocial treatments for children and adolescents with disruptive behavior. *Journal of Clinical Child and Adolescent Psychology, 37*(1), 215–237.

Farmer, C. A., & Aman, M. G. (2011). Aggressive behavior in a sample of children with autism spectrum disorders. *Research in Autism Spectrum Disorders, 5*(1), 317–323.

Feldman, M. A., et al. (1999). Using self-instructional pictorial manuals to teach child-care skills to mothers with intellectual disabilities. *Behavior Modification, 23,* 480–497.

Findling, R. L., et al. (2004). Long-term, open label study of risperidone in children with severe disruptive behaviors and below average IQ. *American Journal of Psychiatry, 161,* 677–684.

Fisher, W. W., et al. (Eds.). (2011). *Handbook of applied behavior analysis.* New York: Guilford Press.

Fletcher-Janzen, E., & Reynolds, C. R. (Eds.). (2003). *Childhood disorders diagnostic desk reference.* Hoboken, NJ: Wiley.

Forgatch, M. S., & Patterson, G. R. (2010). Parent Management Training-Oregon Model: An intervention for antisocial behavior in children and adolescents. *Evidence-Based Psychotherapies for Children and Adolescents, 2,* 159–178.

Frankel, F., et al. (2010). A randomized controlled study of parent-assisted children's friendship training with children having autism spectrum disorders. *Journal of Autism and Developmental Disorders, 40*(7), 827–842. doi:10.1007/s10803-009-0932-z

Frazier, T. W., et al. (2010). Effectiveness of medication combined with intensive behavioral intervention for reducing aggression in youth with autism spectrum disorder. *Journal of Child and Adolescent Psychopharmacology, 20*(3), 167–177. doi:10.1089/cap.2009.0048

Gagiano, C., et al. (2005). Short- and long-term efficacy and safety of risperidone in adults with disruptive behavior disorders. *Psychopharmacology, 179*(3), 629–636.

Ghanizadeh, A., & Moghimi-Sarani, E. (2013). A randomized double blind placebo controlled clinical trial of n-acetylcysteine added to risperidone for treating autistic disorders. *BMC Psychiatry, 13,* 196–202.

Goldstein, S., & Naglieri, J. A. (Eds.). (2013). *Interventions for autism spectrum disorders: translating science into practice.* New York: Springer.

Gralton, E., et al. (1998). Antipsychotic medication, psychiatric diagnosis and children with intellectual disability: A 12-year follow-up study. *Journal of Intellectual Disability Research, 42,* 49–57.

Gresham, F. M. (2014). Quantitative research methods and designs in consultation. In W. P. Erchul & S. M. Sheridan (Eds.), *Handbook of research in school consultation* (2nd ed., pp. 79–102). New York: Routledge.

Handen, B. L., et al. (2013). Use of a direct observational measure in a trial of risperidone and parent training in children with pervasive developmental disorders. *Journal of Developmental and Physical Disabilities, 25,* 355–371. doi:10.1007/s10882-012-9316-y

Harris, P. (1993). The nature and extent of aggressive behaviour amongst people with learning difficulties (mental handicap) in a single health district. *Journal of Intellectual Disability Research, 37,* 221–242.

Hassiotis, A., et al. (2009). Randomized, single-blind, controlled trial of a specialist behavior therapy team for challenging behavior in adults with intellectual disabilities. *American Journal of Psychiatry, 166*(11), 1278–1285. doi:10.1176/appi.ajp.2009.08111747

Hässler, F., & Reis, O. (2010). Pharmacotherapy of disruptive behavior in mentally retarded subjects: A review of the current literature. *Developmental Disability Research Review, 16*(3), 265–272.

Heffer, R. W., et al. (2003). Therapeutic family assessment: A systems approach. In K. Jordan (Ed.), *Handbook of couple and family assessment* (pp. 21–47). New York: Prentice-Hall.

Heyvaert, M., et al. (2012). A multilevel meta-analysis of single-case and small-n research on interventions for reducing challenging behavior in persons with intellectual disabilities. *Research in Developmental Disabilities, 33*(2), 766–780. doi:10.1016/j.ridd.2011.10.010

Holden, B., & Gitlesen, J. P. (2004). Psychotropic medication in adults with mental retardation: Prevalence and prescription practices. *Research in Developmental Disabilities, 25*(6), 509–521.

Horner, R. H., et al. (2002). Problems behavior interventions for young children with autism: A research synthesis. *Journal of Autism and Developmental Disorders, 32,* 432–446.

Janowsky, D. S., et al. (2003a). Olanzapine for self-injurious, aggressive, and disruptive behaviors in intellectually disabled adults: A retrospective, open-label, naturalistic trial. *Clinical Journal of Psychiatry, 64*(10), 1258–1265.

Janowsky, D. S., et al. (2003b). Effects of topiramate on aggressive, self-injurious, and disruptive/destructive behaviors in the intellectually disabled: An open-label retrospective study. *Journal of Clinical Psychopharmacology, 23,* 500–504. doi:10.1097/01.jcp.0000088906.24613.76

Janowsky, D. S., et al. (2005). Serotonergic antidepressant effects on aggressive, self-injurious and destructive/disruptive behaviours in intellectually disabled adults: A retrospective, open-label, naturalistic trial. *International Journal of Neuropsychopharmacology, 8*(1), 37–48. doi:10.1017/S146114570400481X

Janowsky, D. S., et al. (2006). Relapse of aggressive and disruptive behavior in mentally retarded adults following antipsychotic drug withdrawal predicts psychotropic drug use a decade later. *Clinical Journal of Psychiatry, 67*(8), 1272–1277.

Kokina, A., & Kern, L. (2010). Social story interventions for students with autism spectrum disorders: A meta-analysis. *Journal of Autism and Developmental Disorders, 40,* 812–826. doi:10.1007/s10803-009-0931-0

La Malfa, G., et al. (2006). Reviewing the use of antipsychotic drugs in people with intellectual disability. *Human Psychopharmacology: Clinical and Experimental, 21*(2), 73–89.

Laugeson, E. A., et al. (2012). Evidence-based social skills training for adolescents with autism spectrum disorders: The UCLA PEERS program. *Journal of Autism and Developmental Disorders, 42,* 1025–1036. doi:10.1007/s10803-011-1339-1

Leung, C., et al. (2013). The effectiveness of a group Triple P with Chinese parents who have a child with developmental disabilities: A randomized controlled trial. *Research in Developmental Disabilities, 34,* 976–984. doi:10.1016/j.ridd.2012.11.023

Malone, R. P., & Waheed, A. (2009). The role of antipsychotics in the management of behavioral symptoms in children and adolescents with autism. *Drugs, 69*(5), 535–548.

Matson, J. (2009). Aggression and tantrums in children with autism: A review of behavioral treatments and maintaining variables. *Journal of Mental Health Research in Intellectual Disabilities, 2*(3), 169–187.

Matson, J. L., et al. (2005). Assessing and treating aggression in children and adolescents with developmental disabilities: A 20-year review. *Educational Psychology, 25*(2–3), 151–181. doi:10.1080/0144341042000301148

Matson, J. L., et al. (2009). Parent training: A review of methods for children with developmental disabilities. *Research in Developmental Disabilities, 30,* 961–968. doi:10.1016/j.rasd.2009.02.003

Maulik, P. K., et al. (2011). Prevalence of intellectual disability: A meta-analysis of population-based studies. *Research in Developmental Disabilities, 32,* 419–436.

McIntyre, L. L. (2008). Parent training for young children with developmental disabilities: A randomized controlled trial. *American Journal of Mental Retardation, 113*(5), 356–368. doi:10.1352/2008.113:356-368

Mohr, C., et al. (2002). Collaboration—Together we can find the way in dual diagnosis. *Issues in Mental Health Nursing, 23,* 171–180. doi:10.1080/0161 28402753542794

Odom, S. L., et al. (2010). Evaluation of comprehensive treatment models for individuals with autism spectrum disorders. *Journal of Autism and Developmental Disorders, 40,* 425–436.

Peacock, G. G., et al. (Eds.). (2012). *Practical handbook of school psychology: Effective practices for the 21st century.* New York: Guilford Press.

Rana, F., et al. (2013). Pharmacological interventions for self-injurious behaviour in adults with intellectual disabilities. *Cochrane Database Systemic Review, 30*(4), CD009084.

Raymond, F. L., & Tarpey, P. (2006). The genetics of mental retardation. *Human Molecular Genetics, 15,* R110–R116. doi:10.1093/hmg/ddl189

Reichow, B., et al. (Eds.). (2010). *Evidence-based practices and treatments for children with autism.* New York: Springer.

Remington, G., et al. (2001). Clomipramine versus Haloperidol in the treatment of autistic disorder: A double-blind, placebo-controlled, crossover study. *Journal of Clinical Psychopharmacology, 21*(4), 440–444.

Robinson, D., et al. (1999). Predictors of relapse following response from a first episode of schizophrenia or schizoaffective disorder. *Archives of General Psychiatry, 56*(3), 241–247.

Rogers, S., & Vismara, L. A. (2008). Evidence-based comprehensive treatment for early autism. *Journal of Clinical Child and Adolescent Psychology, 37*(1), 8–38. doi:10.1080/15374410701817808

RUPPAN. Research Units on Pediatric Psychopharmacology Autism Network. (2005). Risperidone treatment of autistic disorder: Longer-term benefits and blinded discontinuation after 6 months. *American Journal of Psychiatry, 162,* 1361–1369.

Scahill, L., et al. (2012). Effects of risperdone and parent training on adaptive functioning in children with pervasive developmental disorders and serious behavior problems. *Journal of the American Academy of Child and Adolescent Psychiatry, 51*(2), 136–146. doi:10.1016/j.jaac.2011.11.010

Sharma, A., & Shaw, S. R. (2012). Efficacy of risperidone in managing maladaptive behaviors for children with autistic spectrum disorder. *Journal of Pediatric Healthcare, 26*(4), 291–299.

Shea, S., et al. (2004). Risperidone in the treatment of disruptive behavioral symptoms in children with autistic and other pervasive developmental disorder. *Pediatrics, 114*(5), 634–641. doi:10.1542/peds.2003-0263-F

Shedlack, K. J., et al. (2005). Assessing the utility of atypical antipsychotic medication in adults with mild mental retardation and comorbid psychiatric disorders. *Clinical Journal of Psychiatry, 66,* 52–62.

Siegel, M., & Gabriels, R. (2014). Psychiatric hospital treatment of children with autism and serious behavioral disturbance. *Child and Adolescent Psychiatric Clinics of North American, 23*(1), 125–142. doi:10.1016/j.chc.2013.07.004

Simeon, J., et al. (2002). A retrospective chart review of risperidone use in treatment-resistant children and adolescents with psychiatric disorders. *Progress in Neuropsychopharmacology and Biological Psychiatry, 26,* 267–275.

Simonoff, E., et al. (2008). Psychiatric disorders in children with autism spectrum disorders: Prevalence, comorbidity, and associated factors in a population-derived sample. *Journal of the American Academy of Child and Adolescent Psychiatry, 47*(8), 921–929.

Singh, N. N., et al. (2006). Mindful staff increase learning and reduce aggression in adults with developmental disabilities. *Research in Developmental Disabilities, 282,* 545–558. doi:10.1016/j.ridd.2005.07.002

Singh, N. N., et al. (2011). A mindfulness-based strategy for self-management of aggressive behavior in adolescents with autism. *Research in Autism Spectrum Disorders, 5,* 1153–1158.

Smith, T., et al. (2000). Randomized trial of intensive early intervention for children with pervasive developmental disorder. *American Journal on Mental Retardation, 105,* 269–285.

Snyder, R., et al. (2002). Effects of risperidone on conduct and disruptive behavior disorders in children with subaverage IQs. *Journal of the American Academy of Child and Adolescent Psychiatry, 41*(9), 1026–1036.

Sofronoff, K., et al. (2004). Parent management training and Asperger syndrome: A randomized controlled trial to evaluate a parent based intervention. *Autism, 8*(3), 301–317. doi:10.1177/1362361304045215

Sturney, P., & Diddler, R. (Eds.). (2014). *Evidence-based practice and intellectual disabilities.* Hoboken, NJ: Wiley-Blackwell.

Taylor, J. L., et al. (2005). Individual cognitive-behavioural anger treatment for people with mild-borderline intellectual disabilities and histories of aggression: A controlled trial. *British Journal of Clinical Psychology, 44,* 367–382.

Tsakanikos, E., & McCarthy, J. (Eds.). (2014). *Handbook of psychopathology in intellectual disability: Research, practice, policy.* New York: Springer.

Van Bourgondien, M. E., et al. (2003). Effects of a model treatment approach on adults with autism. *Journal of Autism and Developmental Disorders, 33*(2), 131–140. doi:10.1023/A:1022931224934

Vereenooghe, L., & Langdon, P. E. (2013). Psychological therapies for people with intellectual disabilities: A systematic review and meta-analysis. *Research in Developmental Disabilities, 34*(11), 4085–4102. doi:10.1016/j.ridd.2013.08.030

Wagner, D. V., et al. (2013). Multisystemic therapy for disruptive behavior problems in youths with autism spectrum disorders: A progress report. *Journal of Marital and Family Therapy, 40*(3), 319–331. doi:10.1111/jmft.12012

Walker, H. M., & Gresham, F. M. (Eds.). (2013). *Handbook of evidence-based practices for emotional and behavioral disorders.* New York: Guilford Press.

Wehmeyer, M. L., et al. (2007). *Promoting self-determination in students with intellectual and developmental disabilities.* New York: Guilford Press.

Williams, D. E. (2010). Reducing and eliminating restraint of people with developmental disabilities and severe behavior disorders: An overview of recent research. *Research in Developmental Disabilities, 31*(6), 1142–1148. doi:10.1016/j. ridd.2010.07.014

Wodrich, D. L., & Schmitt, A. J. (2006). *Patterns of learning disorders: Working systematically from assessment to intervention.* New York: Guilford Press.

Young, A. T., & Hawkins, J. (2002). Psychotropic medication prescriptions: An analysis of the reasons people with mental retardation are prescribed psychotropic medication. *Journal of Developmental and Physical Disabilities, 14*, 129–142.

Zisser, A., & Eyberg, S. M. (2010). Treating oppositional behavior in children using parent-child interaction therapy. In A. E. Kazdin & J. R. Weisz (Eds.), *Evidence-based psychotherapies for children and adolescents* (2nd ed., pp. 179–193). New York: Guilford Press.

11 Mood and Personality Disorders

Mimi Sa

The dynamic of overwhelming urges that surpass an individual's ability to control them is the theoretical origin of disruptive behaviors. As discussed in prior chapters, lack of self-control can be caused by biologic factors (such as reduced levels of serotonin levels, as reported by Worbe et al., 2014), developmental events (such as childhood abuse, as discussed by Brodsky and Stanley, 2008), or a combination of both. Poor self-control can lead to impulsive behaviors. Such individuals frequently fail to predict negative outcomes for their behavior and are poor at delaying gratification (Barkley, 1997). Impaired self-control can also lead to deficits in regulation of emotion, a fundamental element of most mood and personality disorders. Dysregulation of emotion coupled with impulsivity are key ingredients in behaviors that defy social norms (as seen in antisocial personality disorder) and cause significant impairment in functioning (prevalent in both mood and personality disorders).

Impulsive individuals tend to have elevated motor activity/agitation, pay less attention to their surroundings, and fail to plan ahead. Krahe (2013) asserts that lack of self-control and aggression are frequently prevalent in impulsive individuals. She defines aggression as a behavior that is intended to harm or injure another living being. As discussed below, aggression is frequently a primary therapeutic target when working with major depressive disorder (MDD), bipolar disorder (BD), borderline personality disorder (BPD), and antisocial personality disorder (ASPD).

Disruptive impulsive urges are associated with more aggressive and violent behaviors, more legal infractions, higher rates of relapse, and higher rates of suicide attempts and completions. According to Moeller et al. (2001), impulsivity is more prevalent in individuals with mood and personality disorders than other psychiatric patients or healthy controls, making those diagnostic categories particularly important for discussion when considering treatment of disruptive behaviors. Moeller et al. (2001) add that any treatment of mood and personality disorders should expressly focus on treatment of impulsivity for maximum symptom reduction and treatment response.

Mood Disorders Characterized by Disruptive Behaviors

The most catastrophic yet preventable disruptive behavior is suicide, and depression is the most common underlying disorder of suicidal behaviors (Centers for Disease Control and Prevention, National Center for Injury Prevention and Control, 2012). Suicide is one of the leading causes of death and is a major public health concern worldwide. Impulsivity and aggression are more prevalent in depressed individuals who attempt and complete suicide (Corruble et al., 2003; Oquendo et al., 2004) than those who do not. In their 2005 study of males who had completed suicide, Dumais et al. (2005) found that younger depressed suicide victims (ages 18–40) were more impulsive and aggressive than same-age depressed nonsuicidal controls or older suicide victims. Also, the younger suicide victims used more violent means of taking their life than the older victims. While the authors do not theorize as to the cause of this finding, biological differences (such as higher levels of testosterone and underdeveloped prefrontal cortex, which manages impulse control) between younger and older subjects seem plausible. The authors also reported the risk for suicide in depressed subjects increased with the presence of comorbid aggressive/impulsive personality disorders and alcohol abuse/dependence.

Corruble et al. (2003) looked at the effects of impulsivity on rates of suicide. They identified three dimensions of impulsivity: behavioral loss of control, nonplanning, and cognitive impulsivity. The authors found a positive correlation between recent suicide attempts with elevated behavioral loss of control and cognitive impulsivity.

Swann et al. (2005) found that impulsivity in bipolar subjects contributed to the risk for suicidal behavior, and subjects with the most lethal suicide attempts had the highest impulsivity scores. In their follow-up study, Swann et al. (2009a) found that impulsivity as a trait is more prevalent in bipolar subjects than nonbipolar subjects. Similarity, Swann et al. (2009b) found the severity of impulsivity is positively correlated with early onset of symptoms, more frequent manic or depressive episodes, and more suicide attempts. Impulsivity includes impairments in attention and response inhibition, and individuals with bipolar disorder were impaired in both aspects, leading to difficulties with delaying rewards and resulting in more disruptive acts. Moreover, severity of the illness directly correlates with the degree of impairment in response inhibition.

Diagnostic Considerations

Major depressive disorder in the United States is the number one cause of disability, reduced productivity, and costs of health care (Greenberg et al., 2003). Individuals with this disorder are characterized by feelings of sadness/depression for most of the day and anhedonia for at least two weeks. They experience significant impairment in functioning in major areas of their life such as social interactions, professional performance, or self-care. Additional presence of irritability and impulsivity is negatively associated with prognosis. It is most highly comorbid with anxiety disorders, as identified in the 2005 National Comorbidity Survey (Kessler et al., 2005). Significant correlations were as follows: generalized anxiety disorder, or GAD ($r = 0.62$), agoraphobia ($r = 0.52$), and posttraumatic stress disorder ($r = 0.50$). Alcohol dependence was significant at $r = 0.37$ and drug dependence at $r = 0.40$.

Bipolar I disorder is the most severe of the cycling mood disorders. People with this diagnosis experience extreme mood states that fluctuate between depression and mania, sometimes experiencing both at the same time. Mania is associated with a decreased need for sleep, high energy levels, feelings of grandiosity, hyper-goal-driven behaviors, and, most importantly, impulsive high-risk behaviors (such as sexual promiscuity, gambling, substance abuse, or aggression toward self and others). The depressive episodes in BD are similar to those of major depression. Individuals may also exhibit a mixed-mood state (a combination of major depression and manic features), which is potentially more dangerous because increased psychomotor energy may result in impulsive/violent acts. Similar to MDD, BD is most highly comorbid with anxiety. For this disorder the highest correlations are as follows: agoraphobia ($r = 0.52$), panic disorder ($r = 0.51$), and GAD ($r = 0.49$).

A new diagnosis, disruptive mood dysregulation disorder (DMDD), has been identified in the fifth edition of the *Diagnostic and Statistical Manual of Mental Disorders* (DSM-5) to capture children who have severe nonepisodic irritability and hyperarousal similar to that seen in mania and hypomania, but who lack the clearly defined manic and depressive episodes characteristic in bipolar disorder. The diagnosis was created in part to address a controversy over the dramatic increase in the number of children being diagnosed with bipolar disorder over the past 15 years, and the common practice of treating these children with mood-stabilizing medications, many of which have significant potential for dangerous side effects. Leibenluft (2011) in her literature review argued that nonepisodic irritability in children is a separate phenotype from the more classic bipolar disorder seen in children with clearly delineated mood episodes. In the longitudinal studies she reviewed, nonepisodic irritability in children was relatively common and positively correlated with an increased risk for developing anxiety and unipolar depression in adulthood, but not bipolar disorder. She also found that familial rates of bipolar disorder were highly elevated for those children with classic bipolar symptoms but no more elevated than the general population for children with nonepisodic irritability. Leibenluft (2011) defined severe mood dysregulation as the presence of irritability with outbursts of anger that are extreme and enduring, interspersed with episodes of sadness, and reported that the impairments children suffer from these symptoms (which essentially constitute DMDD as defined in DSM-5) are equally as severe as symptoms of bipolar disorder.

Prevalence and Course

Based on data from the National Comorbidity Survey replication of 2005 (Kessler et al., 2005), the lifetime prevalence of MDD is 16.6% of the adult population, but DSM-5 reports a lower 12-month prevalence of 7% (American Psychiatric Association [APA], 2013). These differences may be due to the age segment studied—prevalence of MDD in the 18–29 age group is three times higher than among those age 60 or older (APA, 2013). Untreated depressive episodes can last from 6 to 18 months, but average is about 8 months. Treated episodes typically last from six weeks to three months. In depression treated with medications, episodes tend to return, especially when antidepressants are discontinued prematurely. The average age of onset is 14.5 years of age.

Bipolar symptoms usually appear during the late adolescent years, but they can emerge at any time from early childhood into one's 50s. According to a study by Brotman et al. (2006), the lifetime prevalence for bipolar disorder ($N = 1,420$) was 0.1%, and DSM-5 reports a 12-month prevalence of 0.6% (APA, 2013). For a small number of people diagnosed with bipolar disorder, symptoms will improve with medication to the point that medications will no longer be necessary, but it is more typical for manic and depressive episodes to reoccur. The chances of having a second manic episode are virtually 100% (Kessler et al., 2005), but with treatment the risk drops to 50%. A high percentage (82.9%) of bipolar patients are classified as severe and often require inpatient treatment. At least half of the cases start before age 25. Individuals with bipolar disorder have higher rates of arrest and incarceration than individuals with no mental illness and are overrepresented in jails and prisons. They have more work-related disruption and more interpersonal conflicts.

Information about the prevalence and course of DMDD is not yet available, as it is a new disorder first listed in DSM-5. Brotman et al. (2006) previously reported lifetime prevalence of DMDD-like symptoms ($N = 1,420$) to be 3.3%. DSM-5 estimated 6- to 12-month prevalence to fall in the 2%–5% range and suggested that symptoms of the disorder are likely to diminish as children transition into adulthood (APA, 2013).

Personality Disorders Characterized by Disruptive Behaviors

The impulsivity, aggression, and irritability prevalent in personality disorders are considered to be stable traits that are more resistant to therapeutic interventions than symptoms in other disorders (Moeller et al., 2001). In order for the individuals to meet criteria for a personality disorder, they must display "an enduring pattern" of internal experience and behaviors that are significantly impaired relative to their culture and must display impairment in at least two of the following four areas: distorted cognitions, emotional dysregulation, impaired impulse control, and poor interpersonal functioning. These traits must be present independent of the individuals' mood state. BPD and ASPD are the two personality disorders most associated with disruptive behaviors, and the only personality disorders in which disruptive behaviors are listed as core symptoms (APA, 2013).

Lawrence et al. (2010) closely examined the role of impulsivity in BPD by dividing impulsivity into two categories: preference for immediate gratification and rejection of longer-term rewards. They found that subjects with BPD had a tendency toward immediate gratification and rejection of longer-term rewards, independent of negative emotion and feelings of rejection. The authors concluded that the impulsivity inherent in BPD is a trait that is characteristic rather than reactionary. This finding has important implications for treatment planning and prognosis.

The difference between impulsive and nonimpulsive behaviors is most salient in ASPD. In their study, Moeller et al. (2001) divided inmates with ASPD into two categories: those who had committed impulsive acts of aggression and those who had committed premeditated acts of aggression. They found a strong biologic marker in the impulsive subjects, but not in those who planned their crime. Specifically, impulsive inmates had inferior verbal skills and lower peak P300 evoked-potential amplitude levels. Furthermore, antiepileptic medications dramatically reduced the aggressive behaviors of impulsive inmates, while the aggressive behaviors of the premediated actors did not decline. Similarly, Coccarro et al. (1989) found reduced levels of 5HT in individuals with mood and personality disorders who displayed suicidal and impulsive/aggressive behaviors. Moeller et al. (2001) assert that treatments for ASPD must include screening for impulsivity and consideration of possible underlying biologic substrates.

In an effort to clarify the role of impulsivity in antisocial behaviors, Swann et al. (2010) compared male subjects on parole with ASPD to males with no psychological disorder. Impulsivity was broken down into inability to evaluate a situation thoroughly before responding (rapid-response impulsivity) and inability to delay response despite a larger reward (reward-delay impulsivity). The authors found that the ASPD subjects were impaired in rapid-response impulsivity, and the more severe the ASPD, the more impulsive they were.

Diagnostic Considerations

Antisocial personality disorder and BPD are grouped in Cluster B (known as the "dramatic, emotional, erratic cluster") of personality disorders and account for the largest prevalence of disruptive behaviors among personality disorders (Moeller et al., 2001). The correlation between personality disorders and other psychological diagnoses is higher for Cluster B than either Cluster A or C disorders (Lenzenweger et al., 2007).

Individuals with ASPD typically do not feel remorse for their behaviors, but they can at times pretend to show regret and empathy when it is in their best interest to do so (such as in front of a judge). Such individuals often pursue gratification of their needs with disregard of the rights of others; they tend to be impulsive, irritable, and aggressive. The socially deviant behaviors of this disorder must be present by age 15, must be enduring in nature, and cannot be better accounted for by another psychological disorder.

Borderline personality disorder is one of the most widely researched of the personality pathologies, perhaps owing to the often violent, disruptive, and impulsive nature of the behaviors common in this disorder. Individuals with BPD tend to have intense and unstable emotions and thus impaired relationships with others. They are often afraid of being abandoned and can respond in violent, dramatic ways when they feel slighted by others. They tend to see the world in black and white and will often swing from overvaluing to undervaluing those around them. They have an unstable sense of self and have difficulty maintaining a solid, consistent lifestyle. Such individuals commonly harm themselves and punish those around them.

Linehan (1993) explains that, unlike major depressive disorder, individuals with BPD are not depressed at baseline but often exhibit bursts of "affective instability" that can last anywhere from a few hours to a few days and do not meet criteria for a mood disorder. Individuals with BPD struggle with regulation of emotions and can have brief flare-ups of sadness, anxiety, or anger. They also tend to be impulsive behaviorally and prone to self-injury, mutilation, and suicide attempts. Linehan (1993) explains that many individuals with BPD have adopted extreme behaviors in order to obtain the desired validation when their environment fails to respond to less extreme behaviors.

Prevalence and Course

According to Lenzenweger et al. (2007), the prevalence rate for ASPD among adults in the United States is 0.6%, and rates are higher in males than females (about 3:1). In one study, Alegria et al. (2013) found that women with ASPD reported more frequent childhood emotional neglect and sexual abuse and parent-related adverse events during childhood. The women in their study displayed less violent antisocial behaviors than men but had higher rates of aggressiveness and irritability. The women also reported higher rates of being victimized, were more functionally impaired, and had less social support than their male counterparts. The authors argued that because there are gender differences in origin and expression of antisocial behaviors, there should be gender-specific treatment programs. ASPD is highly prevalent among incarcerated individuals and is characterized by ongoing participation in illegal activities, hostility toward others, dishonesty, and recklessness. The course of the disorder tends to be chronic and is negatively related to early onset of antisocial behaviors and substance abuse (Loeber et al., 1993).

Although it is commonly believed that BPD is more prevalent in women, in an analysis of the Wave 2 National Epidemiologic Survey data, Grant et al. (2008) found no statistically significant gender differences (overall rate at 5.9%, males at 5.6%, and females at 6.2%), although there was a numerically larger rate of females identified in treatment. Native American males, younger adults, and single adults (whether separated, divorced, or widowed), and those with lower incomes and education were overrepresented. Jovev et al. (2013) found childhood abuse (specifically sexual abuse and neglect) to be a significant predictor of BPD. They also found a positive correlation between severity of abuse and severity of behavioral symptoms. The expected outcome for people with BPD is more positive than previously believed. Recent studies report that up to 88% of people with the disorder experience significant improvement over time (Grant et al., 2008).

Comorbidity of Mood and Personality Disorders

The mood and personality disorders discussed herein are characterized by aggression and impulsivity, and the co-occurrence of these disorders increases the likelihood of disruptive symptoms. For example, Soloff et al. (2000) found that the comorbidity of BPD with a major depressive episode increased the number and seriousness of suicide attempts as well as hopelessness, while impulsive aggression specifically increased the risk of suicidal behavior. Although the impulsivity characteristic of BPD was not by itself a predictor of more attempts or increased lethality, the combination of the static trait of impulsivity with depression and the corresponding hopelessness increased severity and frequency of suicide attempts.

There are compelling correlates between the disruptive behaviors common in ASPD and BD, especially with relation to impulsivity. Barzman et al. (2007) found high rates of illegal acts (53%) among adolescents who had recently been diagnosed with BD, and early onset of BD was positively correlated with antisocial behaviors in juveniles, with an increased likelihood of incarceration. Accordingly, Barzman et al. (2007) asserted that there is a higher prevalence of incarcerated individuals with BD than in the general population. Swann et al. (2010) found that impulsive behaviors such as abuse of substances and suicide attempts were more likely in individuals with comorbid ASPD and BD than with either disorder alone.

Swann et al. (2010) investigated the effects of what they called "trait impulsivity" on severity of illness in subjects with BD, ASPD, and the two disorders combined. They viewed impulsivity as both trait-like (a stable characteristic of an individual's behavior often seen in ASPD) and state-like (such as precipitated by the increased noradrenergic release during a manic episode). The two can co-occur and compound the severity of each other. Swann et al. found subjects with BD alone or ASPD alone were more impulsive than nonpathological controls, and subjects with BD, regardless of whether they had comorbid ASPD, were more impulsive than individuals with ASPD alone. They concluded that the compounding of BD on top of ASPD is negatively associated with prognosis because of increased impulsivity. Interestingly, Swann et al. found that impulsivity was not associated with severity of the crime for subjects with ASPD. They concluded that premeditation is associated with severity of the crime and is more characteristic of the calculating nature found in ASPD.

Solitary Pharmacological Treatments for Mood Disorders

Many studies have investigated the effectiveness of antidepressant and mood-stabilizing medications for symptom reduction in mood disorders, and some of those specifically reviewed the benefits of using medications to reduce aggressive and impulsive symptoms. Grunebam et al. (2013), for example, compared the selective serotonin reuptake inhibitor (SSRI) paroxetine to the norepinephrine-dopamine reuptake inhibitor (NDRI) buproprion and their effects on suicidal behaviors and thoughts. They found paroxetine to be statistically superior ($p < 0.001$) to buproprion in reducing suicidality in subjects with MDD who had made prior suicide attempts or current suicidal ideation.

Similarly, Zisook et al. (2011) compared the effectiveness of escitalopram, buproprion, mirtazapine, and venlafaxine in addressing suicidality among subjects with MDD. For those subjects who began the study with suicidal ideation, all treatment conditions reduced suicidal thought (with the escitalopram plus buproprion condition showing superiority after 12 weeks). In depressed subjects with no baseline suicidal ideation, however, no one treatment condition prevented suicidal thought better than another. By contrast, the mirtazapine plus venlafaxine condition resulted in four subjects with no prior history of suicidal ideation attempting suicide. The authors therefore cautioned against the combination of mirtazapine with venlafaxine.

All antidepressants can potentially increase suicidal thought (Breggin, 2003), and serotonin agents in particular can increase suicidal/homicidal ideation, violence, hypomania/mania, and insomnia, constituting the very symptoms that may lead to disruptive behaviors and severe functional impairment. Thus antidepressants must be used with caution, especially in BD. It is recommended that BD be ruled out before SSRIs are started.

As seen in the STAR*D study, as many as 60% of patients do not obtain remission from their symptoms from one antidepressant (Berman et al., 2007). Aripiprazole is an effective adjunct to standard antidepressant medications, and it has been shown to produce significantly superior remission of depression symptoms when used in conjunction with an antidepressant versus placebo plus antidepressant. Aripiprazole may be effective in treating refractory unipolar depression owing to its mood-elevating serotonin and dopamine partial-agonism, coupled with the anger-modulating properties of its weak stimulation of the D2 receptor that is less activating than endogenous dopamine.

Leibenluft (2011) argued that because DMDD appears to be a separate phenotype from BPD, and because children with DMDD are most likely to develop unipolar depression or anxiety in adulthood, then first-line treatments for DMDD should include SSRIs or stimulants. She suggested that stimulants should be considered because of their effectiveness in the treatment of impulsivity and asserted that, unlike in BPD, SSRIs and stimulants are not likely to cause mania or mood dysregulation in DMDD because of its diagnostic uniqueness from BPD. A current clinical trial is comparing treatment of DMDD in children with citalopram plus a stimulant versus a stimulant plus placebo (clinicaltrials.gov identifier NCT00794040).

According to the Canadian Network for Mood and Anxiety Treatments (CANMAT) by Yaltham et al. (2013), the first-line treatments for BPD in Canada are lithium, lamotrigrine, valproate, olanzapine, quetiapine, aripiprazole, and risperidone long-acting injection. Lurasidone alone or in combination with lamotrigrine is the new second-line treatment, and asenapine is the new third-line treatment.

Lithium has long been a treatment of choice for BPD patients worldwide. It is lauded for its neurogenerative properties and antidepressant effects, and it is well established as being effective in reducing aggression. Of great importance is its superior effectiveness in reducing suicidality, as reported by Gonzalez-Pinto et al. (2006). In their study, these authors found only 2 in 100 subjects who adhered to their lithium treatment attempted suicide, while 11.4 in 100 subjects who stopped their lithium treatment attempted suicide (a fivefold increase in suicide attempts when lithium was discontinued). Although effective, lithium often causes severe side effects, and common reasons for discontinuation include renal damage (Tredget et al., 2010) and thyroid abnormalities (Gyulai et al., 2003). Gyulai et al. (2003) found that subjects with rapid-cycling BD were more likely to have thyroid abnormalities, a condition likely unmasked during a lithium trial, owing to the robust effect of lithium on the reduction of serum thyroxine. In their study, Lazarus et al. (2009) found that subjects had up to 40% chance of goiter and 20% chance of hypothyroidism in bipolar lithium users. Gyulai et al. (2003) suggest initially checking thyroxine levels and performing an ultrasound to measure thyroid size at baseline and then annually after that for patients using lithium chronically, especially for patients with a family history of thyroid disorders.

Lamotrigrine is being used with increased frequency for stabilization of BD. It has been found to improve stabilization in rapid-cycling BD and is more effective in treating the depressive episodes of the disorder than the other antiepileptic drugs (Bowden et al., 2004; Muzina et al., 2005). Lamotrigrine appears less useful in the treatment of acute mania. It is appealing for its side-effect profile (less weight gain and metabolic concerns per Morrell et al., 2003) but does have the rare potential to cause the life-threatening Stevens–Johnson syndrome. Bowden et al. (2004) report 0.1% incidence among adults for this syndrome. According to Bowden et al., lamotrigrine was well tolerated and should not be avoided as a treatment choice because of this rare risk (which starts as a rash). They found the highest predictor of a serious rash from lamotrigrine was a serious rash in response to other antiepileptics.

Valproate has a great deal of evidence for its utility in the reduction of aggression, impulsivity, and suicidality of BD. In a recent study, Woo et al. (2014) found valproate to be superior to lithium when both were paired with an antipsychotic in preventing rehospitalization during the first year after discharge. Valproate can cause weight gain and metabolic abnormalities, Chang et al. (2010) found that it caused higher insulin, triglyceride, and body mass index and lower glucose and high-density lipoprotein cholesterol versus controls, and is also known for causing agranulocytosis. Rahman et al. (2009) found up to 26% of participants in his study developed the white blood cell disorder with much higher incidence for African Americans—44% of those with the disorder versus Caucasians at 29% and Latinos at 11%.

With the advent of second-generation antipsychotics (SGAs), and their improved side-effect profile, many prescribers have turned to them for use in both the acute and maintenance treatment of disruptive behaviors in BD. While all of the SGAs have proven effective in the reduction of disruptive behaviors in BD (Singh et al., 2013), the medications vary significantly in their side-effect profile (specifically metabolic concerns), which can be an essential component to choosing the appropriate medication.

Rummel-Kluge et al. (2010) compared the metabolic side effects of SGAs. They found olanzapine caused the most weight gain, then clozapine and risperidone. Quetiapine led to the highest increase in cholesterol, and olanzapine produced the highest increase in glucose. Boyda et al. (2013) looked at two novel SGAs (asenapine and iolperidone), compared them to olanzapine, and found that asenapine produced negligible metabolic changes, while iolperidone caused substantial metabolic liability comparable to olanzapine. Of all SGAs studied, Citrome et al. (2014) found that aripiprazole was associated with the lowest risk of metabolic abnormalities. It is most associated with movement disorders (i.e., akathesia) and gastrointestinal disturbances. These studies should be used as a guide for the prescriber to consider when choosing a mood-stabilizing agent.

Interestingly, Romo-Nava et al. (2014) in their randomized controlled trial (RCT) showed that 5 mg of melatonin significantly attenuated the negative metabolic effects of SGAs used in BD patients. The melatonin reduced diastolic blood pressure, weight gain, and fat mass versus placebo to a highly significant degree. The authors concluded that melatonin may be a cost-effective option for mitigating the unwanted metabolic effects of SGAs.

To date, no treatments have been approved by the US Food and Drug Administration (FDA) that can resolve depression or suicidal behaviors within hours of administration. In one study, Zarate et al. (2012) found that a single infusion of ketamine (0.5 mg/kg) administered on two days, two weeks apart, reduced depression and suicidal ideation within 40 minutes of each infusion in 79% of subjects, while 0% responded to placebo. They reported that the only significant side effect was dissociation. The authors conclude that ketamine produces a rapid, safe, and effective response to depression and suicidal ideation in individuals with BD.

A novel treatment for bipolar depression is modafinil or armodafinil. These medications are FDA approved for narcolepsy but have been shown to significantly reduce depression without triggering mania in two RCTs (Calabrese et al., 2010; Frye et al., 2007).

Because medications used to treat disruptive symptoms often pose significant risks of medical complications and serious side effects, herbal approaches have been considered. Hallahan et al. (2007) looked at the effects of omega-3 fatty acids on subjects who had committed repeated acts of self-harm that included impulsive, aggressive, and hostile behaviors. They reported that 1.2 g of omega-3 significantly improved mood and overall well-being, and suicidal thought was greatly reduced. The supplement did not reduce levels of impulsivity and self-injurious behavior, but the authors suggest that further studies should look at whether higher doses of the fatty acid could provide even more benefit for the treatment of impulsive and disruptive behaviors. Because most patients tolerate these compounds with few (if any) risks and adverse effects, further potential benefits of this approach should be investigated.

Benefits and Limitations of Pharmacotherapy as Sole Treatment

One of the main benefits of using medications for the treatment of mood disorders is the speed with which beneficial effects usually take place (especially in the case of ketamine). In the acutely manic, severely disruptive, or suicidal patient, immediate response to treatment is critical. Because many different types of health-care providers (including general physicians) can prescribe psychotropics, access to these medications often is easier than access to psychotherapists. Also, the cost may be less of a burden, especially as insurance coverage of medication treatments can be superior to coverage of psychotherapy treatment. The investment of time is also less significant; once patients are stabilized on medications, they usually require periodic follow-up, whereas active psychotherapy requires regular office visits. On the other hand, psychotropic medications in some patients cause significant adverse effects, and this is especially true in mood-stabilizing agents. Because these medications are often hard to tolerate, many patients discontinue them, further limiting their utility.

Solitary Psychological Treatments for Mood Disorders

Psychotherapy is recommended for depressed individuals who have significant psychosocial stress, interpersonal conflict, a comorbid personality disorder, have access to psychotherapy providers or who prefer therapy over medications. APA guidelines list cognitive-behavioral therapy (CBT), interpersonal psychotherapy (IPT), and psychodynamic therapy as evidence-based psychosocial interventions for depression (APA, 2010), and many of these treatments specifically address disruptive behaviors and symptoms.

In a randomized controlled study, for example, Brown et al. (2005) showed that CBT is an effective intervention for the prevention of suicide attempts in individuals who have already attempted. In a fairly brief amount of time (about eight sessions), they were able to reduce suicide attempts by 50%. Psychodynamic therapy has also been shown to be beneficial. Maina et al. (2005) found that psychodynamic therapy was superior to placebo in the remission of depressive symptoms and had longer-lasting effects than supportive psychotherapy at six months follow-up.

Alavi et al. (2013) found that weekly outpatient CBT reduced suicidal ideation and hopelessness in depressed adolescents who had attempted suicide within the past three months. They compared outcomes to subjects in a wait-list control condition and found a significant reduction in suicidal ideation (54%–77% reduction). This finding is particularly important because suicide is the number one cause of death for adolescents, in part because of their increased impulsivity and reduced amount of coping skills.

On the other end of the age spectrum, Heisel et al. (2014) found that a 16-session course of IPT reduced suicidal ideation, thoughts of death, and depressive symptom severity and also improved perceived meaning in life, social adjustment, perceived social support, and psychological well-being in geriatric patients. This finding is particularly important in that geriatric individuals complete suicide every 97 minutes in the United States, and older white males have the highest rates of suicide completions among all segments of the population. Geriatric patients also exhibit greatest risks of significant adverse effects from psychotropic medications, and therefore effective reduction in suicidality via psychotherapy is uniquely important in this population.

Miklowitz (2006) reports that, in his review of studies, he did not find evidence for superior efficacy of one psychotherapeutic modality over another in the treatment of mood disorders. However in an interesting study by Kwan et al. (2010), the authors examined patient preference as a relevant factor in response to treatment. They found that preference for modality affected how much patients engaged in treatment, including whether they started treatment, stayed in treatment, attended appointments, and formed positive therapeutic rapport. Those factors ultimately influenced treatment outcomes and reduced depressive symptoms when preference was adhered to. The authors concluded that it is therefore important to consider the patients' beliefs, knowledge, and opinions about different treatments when selecting the therapeutic approach, as ignoring those factors could alienate the patients and reduce treatment compliance.

Similarly, Givens et al. (2007) found that ethnicity significantly affected preferences for depression treatment. In their study, African Americans, Asian Americans, and Latinos were more likely to prefer psychotherapy to pharmacology in the treatment of depression, as the majority did not believe depression is biologic in origin and that antidepressants are addictive. Instead, the subjects expected counseling and prayer to be more effective.

Because DMDD is a new diagnosis, there are currently no psychotherapies that have been found to be effective in evidence-based clinical research. Previously, Leigh et al. (2012) found CBT to be helpful in the reduction of irritability and for the regulation of mood in children with similar symptoms to DMDD. A current clinical trial involves a pilot RCT looking at a customized form of dialectical behavior therapy (DBT) designed to help children reduce the irritability and impulsivity characteristic of DMDD (clinicaltrials.gov identifier NCT01862549).

Bipolar disorder more commonly requires treatment with medications, especially in cases where more severe symptoms are evident, and psychotherapy is often used as an adjunct to medication treatment. But some research about effectiveness of psychotherapy, especially for disruptive symptoms of BD, is beginning to emerge. In a small study by Van Dijk et al. (2013), for example, DBT was found to be effective in the treatment of BD, and subjects improved their affective control (thus reducing suicidality), had fewer emergency room visits, and fewer mental health–related admissions in the six months following treatment. In another study, Ives-Deliperi et al. (2013) found that mindfulness-based cognitive therapy increased the ability of subjects with bipolar disorder to regulate their emotions. There are similarities between mindfulness-based cognitive therapy and DBT, both of which teach the individual to regulate their emotions and reduce impulsivity.

Benefits and Limitations of Psychotherapy as Sole Treatment

Psychotherapy is a process of learning strategies to overcome symptoms (including aggressive and impulsive tendencies), and therefore it inherently produces longer-lasting results than pharmacotherapy. Psychotherapy is intended to continue until the patient has gained the skills needed to maintain remission of symptoms, thus aiding the prevention of future episodes. By contrast, the benefits of medications usually end when patients stop taking them.

Psychotherapy is also noninvasive and does not introduce compounds into the body that may produce adverse effects. This is particularly important in the treatment of children, geriatric patients, pregnant women, or patients with comorbid medical conditions. Similarly, some psychotropic medications can be lethal if taken in high doses, which can be a crucial factor in choice of intervention for the suicidal patient. For example, the introduction of antidepressant medications has been reported to initially increase suicidal thoughts in certain patients, especially in children and adolescents, and consequently these medications carry a black box warning.

Conversely, the benefits of psychotherapy usually require some length of time to take effect—often weeks or months—which may not be an option for the acutely suicidal patient. Similarly, individuals in acute manic episodes are less likely to respond to therapy and may require immediate pharmacological intervention for their personal safety (Frank et al., 2005). Psychotherapy also necessitates a larger investment of time and money, as most psychotherapies require 10–26 weekly or biweekly sessions, each lasting an hour. By contrast, the use of medications usually requires an initial appointment with the prescriber and perhaps two to three follow-up appointments over the next several months. For some individuals, pharmacotherapy is more cost and time effective.

Combined Treatments for Mood Disorders

Combination treatment may conceptually offer the benefits of both monotherapies, but relatively little research has examined combination treatments for mood disorders that specifically address disruptive symptoms. Wiles et al. (2013) looked at adults with treatment-resistant depression and found CBT to be effective when combined with medication at reducing symptoms of depression, including associated disruptive features. They found that the benefits of this therapeutic combination met the higher standard of symptom remission (rather than only treatment response), and benefits lasted over 12 months.

Schramm et al. (2007) compared the combination of IPT with pharmacotherapy versus pharmacotherapy with clinical management for inpatients with MDD. They found that patients who received IPT with medications had superior response rates (71% vs. 51%), higher remission rates (49% vs. 34%), and retained greater treatment gains at three months follow-up (including reduced rates of disruptive behaviors) than subjects who received medication with clinical management. The authors conclude that these findings should have implications for the design of inpatient treatment programming for patients with MDD.

De Jonghe et al. (2004) compared the efficacy of treatment of MDD between psychotherapy alone and in combination with antidepressants. The authors found that both treatment modalities significantly reduced depressive symptoms (using three different standardized instruments), but the combined treatment modality was significantly more effective than psychotherapy alone. However, there were several subjects who dropped out of the study because they initially wanted only psychotherapy but were placed in the combination group. The authors concluded that while combination therapy did prove to be more effective in the treatment of depression over 24 weeks, patient preference for treatment is an important factor in effectiveness.

In some cases, patients initially fail to respond to either monotherapy, and clinicians may need to consider whether pharmacotherapy should be added to psychotherapy (or vice versa). Dekker et al. (2013) randomly assigned subjects with moderate depression into either a short-term psychodynamic therapy group or treatment with an antidepressant. Those patients with less than 30% symptom improvement after eight weeks were offered combined treatment. Interestingly, 40% of patients wanted to continue with their monotherapy in spite of poor response. By the end of treatment, those patients who had started with psychodynamic therapy had improved more than those initially receiving antidepressants. However, Dekker et al. (2013) also found significant improvement when subjects who had been poor responders to monotherapy received combination therapy. The authors concluded that starting with psychotherapy may be preferable in mild to moderately depressed individuals (given the superior response) and that, once again, patient preference is an important factor when choosing treatment strategies.

Leibenluft (2011) argues that, because DMDD appears to be on a continuum with unipolar depression, the treatment protocol for DMDD should parallel that of MDD. Therefore, as mentioned above, the combined treatment of antidepressants with psychotherapies that focus on reduction of impulsivity and disruptive behaviors (such as CBT and DBT) is recommended.

In addition to unipolar depression, CBT combined with mood stabilizers has been shown to be more effective clinically and more cost efficient in the treatment of BD than medication alone. Lam et al. (2005) selected nonacute outpatients with BD who were having frequent mood relapses (including disruptive behaviors) in spite of taking prescription mood stabilizers. They found that subjects who completed CBT spent 110 fewer days over 30 months in a bipolar episode (defined as meeting criteria for major depressive, hypomanic, or manic episodes) reported significantly better mood and social functioning ratings, and were better at managing their bipolar symptoms than subjects who took medications alone.

Miklowitz et al. (2007) compared the effectiveness of IPT to brief collaborative care in conjunction with pharmacotherapy in treatment of bipolar depression. They found that patients in the IPT group had higher recovery rates by the end of one year and shorter time to recovery than patients in the collaborative care cohort. Patients in the IPT group were also 1.58 times more likely to be asymptomatic during any month in the study than those in collaborative care ($p = 0.003$). The authors concluded that IPT was superior as an adjunct to pharmacotherapy than brief treatment for enhancing stabilization from bipolar depression.

Benefits and Limitations of Combined Treatments

As seen in the above studies, the benefits of using combined treatments include superior treatment outcomes (such as fewer hospitalizations for impulsive behaviors and reduced suicide rates), as well as responses that are both faster (via medications) and more enduring (through psychotherapy). The superior efficacy of combined treatments are especially compelling in light of large studies such as the STAR*D trial, which showed response rates around 30% to first-line medications, and studies showing response rates around 50% to psychotherapy alone. The faster response rates to medications can improve patients' receptivity to psychotherapy as well as their motivation for change, while psychotherapy is important in strengthening medication compliance, reducing stigma of treatment for mental illness, engaging family support, and gaining insight into the destructive nature of impulsive behaviors. Psychotherapy can assist the patient in creating a healthy response style to stressors, while medication can help reduce the perceived sensation of sadness, hopelessness, irritability, anger, and suicidality.

On the other hand, limitations to utilizing both modalities include the cost, time commitment, and in some cases the increased difficulty of accessing two different treatment providers. Also, as mentioned above, pregnant women, children, and geriatric patients may not be able to safely tolerate many psychotropic medications, while other patients may have cultural or personal beliefs against medications or psychotherapy. Language can be a greater barrier in psychotherapy than medications, as communication is an essential component and adequate interpretive services are often unavailable, too expensive, or inappropriate when conducting psychotherapy. Non-English-speaking patients tend to come from low socioeconomic status; further reducing many of their options for accessing or affording either treatment modality.

Solitary Pharmacological Treatments for Personality Disorders

Second-generation antipsychotics have shown significant promise in the reduction of impulsivity in BPD and ASPD. Zanarini et al. (2004) in their preliminary randomized trial found that in patients with BPD, olanzapine either alone or combined with fluoxetine was superior to fluoxetine alone in reducing impulsive aggression. While Nickel et al. (2006) found that aripiprazole was significantly effective in reducing patients' scores on the SCL-90, HAM-D, HAM-A, and State-Trait Anger Expression Inventory compared to placebo, and they concluded that aripiprazole is effective in reducing the volatile and aggressive behaviors common in BPD.

In their open-label study, Rocca et al. (2002) found risperidone to significantly reduce aggression and improve overall global functioning in BPD subjects when given an average of 3.27 mg/day, and the side-effect profile was reportedly well tolerated. Villeneuve and Lemelin (2005) also conducted an open-label study of 23 outpatients with BPD and found that low doses of quetiapine (250 mg +/–50 mg) significantly improved impulsivity and hostility as well as social and global functioning. Walker et al. (2003) found that quetiapine significantly reduced irritability, impulsivity, and aggressiveness in four patients with ASPD referred to a maximum-security psychiatric facility.

With regard to antiepileptics, Pinto and Akiskai (1998) found lamotrigine to be effective in attaining remission of the disruptive symptoms of BPD in patients who had been previously unresponsive to medication trials. At one year follow-up, all participants no longer met criteria for BPD. Hollander et al. (2003) in their placebo-controlled double-blind trial found that divalproex significantly reduced impulsive aggression in subjects with BPD.

Topiramate had an inverted U-shape effect on the reduction of aggression in antisocial subjects in a study by Lane et al. (2009). The authors found that acute doses (>400 mg/day) were effective in the reduction of aggression, but smaller doses (100–300 mg, peaking at 200 mg) actually led to an increase in aggression. The authors concluded that, similar to the effects of alcohol on gamma-aminobutyric acid-A (GABA-A) receptors, a lower level of stimulation on the GABA-A receptor can lead to aggression, while a higher level can lead to reductions in irritability and aggression.

In a case study, Newman and McDermott (2011) found that 40 mg of propranolol taken twice daily significantly reduced the aggressive, impulsive, and violent behaviors of a man with ASPD. The man also stated that he felt better able to control his emotions, less frustrated, and less irritable on the medication. His caseworker concurred. This individual had been erroneously diagnosed with bipolar disorder, had not responded well to treatment with mood stabilizers and antipsychotics, and had been hospitalized over 50 times because of his disruptive behaviors.

In their review, Rosenbluth et al. (2012) concluded that when selecting medications for the treatment of personality disorders, it is important to focus on symptom relief versus resolution of the disorder. To that end, the authors suggest that for treatment of depressive symptoms SSRIs are a good choice, whereas mood stabilizers and antipsychotics are the medications of choice for aggression, hostility, and impulsivity. Another consideration in choice of psychotropic for patients with personality disorders is safety. Medications that can be lethal if taken in overdose (such as tricyclics and some benzodiazepines) should be avoided in impulsive personality-disordered individuals with a history of self-harm or depression.

Benefits and Limitations of Pharmacotherapy as Sole Treatment

While medications may be effective in the reduction of aggression and impulsivity, they only work as long as the patient is compliant with treatment. The benefit of medications is that subjects quickly obtain reductions in impulsivity, which in some cases could save lives. Medications are often more cost effective and more accessible than psychotherapy, as all prescribers can usually provide them. Also, compliance in long-term psychotherapy is often poor in individuals with personality disorders.

The drawback is that in most cases, once the medication is terminated, so is the benefit. Pharmacotherapy may reduce symptom acuity (in some cases) but does not teach the psychosocial skills needed for long-term adaptive functioning. Also, suicide attempts are prevalent in BPD, and alcohol and drug abuse are more common in both BPD and APD, making the potential lethality of some psychotropic medications an essential clinical consideration. Much care should be taken when selecting medications to treat patients who exhibit significant impulsive behaviors, suicidality, and drug abuse/dependence, symptoms that are common in individuals with these personality disorders.

Solitary Psychological Treatments for Personality Disorders

Unlike mood disorders, personality disorders are considered to be characterological in nature and tend to present as chronic and pervasive while causing considerable interpersonal dysfunction and psychological distress. They are considered by many to be more difficult to treat than most other disorders, in part because these individuals often do not seek mental health treatment, and those who do drop out about 70% of the time (Dingfelder, 2004).

Borderline personality disorder is the most studied of all personality disorders (perhaps because of patients' extremely volatile, disruptive, and often life-threatening behaviors), and the most researched psychotherapeutic intervention for this disorder is DBT, developed by Marsha Linehan (1987). Since the inception of DBT, several other empirically validated therapeutic modalities for treatment of BPD have emerged, including two psychodynamic psychotherapies, transference-focused psychotherapy (Clarkin & Kemberg, 2004) and mentalization-based therapy (Bateman & Fonagy, 2009), and another cognitive-behavioral therapy called schema-focused therapy (Giesen-Bloo et al., 2006).

In a study by Linehan et al. (2006), the authors compared the effectiveness of DBT versus psychotherapy that was nonbehavioral in treating suicidal behaviors and overall psychological functioning in BPD subjects. The authors found that DBT produced superior results to the contrasted therapeutic modality. Specifically, the DBT participants were half as likely to attempt suicide ($p = 0.005$), required fewer hospitalizations due to suicidal ideation ($p = 0.004$), were less likely to drop out of treatment ($p < 0.001$), had fewer psychiatric hospitalizations ($p = 0.007$), and had fewer visits to the emergency department ($p = 0.04$) than participants who received the alternate intervention.

Mentalization-based treatment (MBT) was compared to structured clinical management (SCM) for subjects with BPD in a study by Bateman and Fonagy (2009). The results of this study showed that both groups had improved outcomes from their disruptive symptoms, but participants in the MBT group showed more dramatic declines in both self-reported and clinically reviewed problems, including suicide attempts and hospitalizations. The authors assert that the benefit to this modality is the simplicity of the training process, thereby making the intervention more accessible in health-care facilities and across different providers.

Giesen-Bloo et al. (2006) directly compared schema-focused therapy (SFT) to transference-focused psychotherapy (TFP) in the treatment of BPD. Their findings showed that both modalities were effective in reducing the disruptive symptoms of BPD, but SFT was superior to TFP for all measures, and dropout rates for TFP participants were higher. After three years of treatment, participants in the SFT group were more likely to recover (p = 0.04) or display clinical improvement (p = 0.009) than those from the TFP group. Also, SFT participants reported a larger improvement in quality of life than TFP patients ($p < 0.001$).

With regard to ASPD, a 2012 study by Cullen et al. (2012) examined male inpatients in a secure forensic setting who had committed antisocial acts. They found that their rehabilitative cognitive skills program reduced violence, verbal aggression, and disruptive behaviors in inmates with impaired impulse control. The program was not effective for inmates who had committed premeditated antisocial acts, again underscoring the need for clear psychological differentiation between impulsive versus calculated antisocial behaviors. This finding creates important implications for future treatment designs and raises the question of a possible need to subtype the disorder (impulsive vs. calculating).

Gerhart et al. (2013) implemented a 14-week cognitive-behavioral program for violence reduction using subjects with Cluster B personality disorders. They found that individuals who were ready to change had better outcomes to treatment than those who were resistant to change. Both ASPD and BPD subjects (who were motivated to change) had higher responsiveness to their program than subjects with narcissistic personality features (who were not motivated to change). ASPD subjects responded to treatment at a rate similar to subjects with no personality disorder, while subjects with BPD responded at faster rates. Because BPD subjects had the highest willingness to change, they were the best candidates for this treatment program.

Benefits and Limitations of Psychotherapy as Sole Treatment

Because of the chronicity of disruptive behaviors common in the above-mentioned personality disorders, learning coping skills, de-escalation techniques, management of triggers, and practice of good self-care in particular are critical to long-term treatment gains. Interpersonal conflict is such a common source of psychic distress in BPD that improvements in interpersonal skills and affect regulation techniques (including self-soothing and ability to tolerate being alone) are likely to bring about a significant reduction in impulsive behaviors and overall distress. Similarly, teaching individuals with ASPD methods of expressing anger and getting their needs met without violence are likely to dramatically reduce incidences of impulsive violence.

Lethality and acute symptom exacerbations are also common in these disorders, and must be quickly addressed to improve safety. In those cases, psychosocial treatments may not act quickly enough, and medications may be essential. Deeply violent individuals must be immediately subdued, and in those cases medications (along with physical restraints) may be the only recourse. Learning to avoid triggers and gaining skills to modulate anger often takes many months to years. Whenever the provider is faced with the immediate safety of the patient or others around the patient, psychosocial treatments alone are usually not sufficient.

Combined Treatments of Personality Disorders

There are limited studies that examine combination therapies for personality disorders, but some research findings are beginning to emerge. Vaslamatzis et al.'s (2014) naturalistic study compared combined therapy versus psychotherapy only for treatment of severe impulsivity and suicidality in personality-disordered inpatients. They found that psychodynamic psychotherapy alone was effective in reducing impulsivity, while combined treatment was more effective for reducing suicidality rather than impulsivity. In another small study, Bellino et al. (2010) showed that treating BPD subjects with a combination of IPT with fluoxetine was superior in the reduction of disruptive behaviors to the use of fluoxetine alone.

There are some studies that assess mono versus combined therapies of comorbid mood and personality disorders. For example, Kool et al. (2003) found that subjects with comorbid mood and personality disorders in the combined treatment group exhibited reductions in the severity of both personality pathology and depression, whereas subjects in the medication-only group revealed reductions only in severity of depression. In another study, Kool et al. (2007) compared combined therapy (medications with psychodynamic psychotherapy) to pharmacotherapy only for depressed patients with or without comorbid personality disorders. They found that combined therapy was significantly superior in reducing depressive symptoms in patients with comorbid personality disorders, while combined treatment was no more efficacious than pharmacotherapy only in patients without added personality disorders.

Swartz et al. (2005) compared subjects with BD to those with BD and BPD combined. They found that the BD group responded much better to a combination of mood stabilizers with weekly psychotherapy (74% response rate) versus the BD–BPD subjects (25% response rate). The BD–BPD group also required significantly higher doses of mood-stabilizing medications and had a higher dropout rate. But the authors concluded that even though the comorbid subjects were inherently much more difficult to treat and took longer to respond, they did have a significant amount of good responses to the combination treatment and recommended combination treatment for these co-occurring disorders.

Benefits and Limitations of Combined Treatments

When using combined treatment in BPD and ASPD (especially with comorbid mood disorders), safety and stabilization (including reductions in impulsivity and aggression toward self or others) can often be achieved more quickly and effectively with medications, while long-term coping skills, improved medication compliance, and global functioning are better addressed in psychotherapy. The combination may therefore provide both quick and lasting positive effects. Once the medication is eliminated, however, in most cases so is the benefit. Therefore adding cognitive reframing of interpersonal conflicts, gaining the skill of self soothing, and learning to de-escalate anger and aggression are all essential skills that must be addressed in psychotherapy to help people with these disorders gain significant long-term improvement of their disruptive and destructive behaviors.

On the other hand, it may not be feasible for an individual to participate in both modalities. Many individuals with BPD and ASPD deny that they have a personality disorder and blame other causes for their interpersonal problems. In addition, these individuals often have difficulties maintaining employment and thus obtaining insurance, which can be a major obstacle in obtaining mental health treatment (especially psychotherapy). Even if they start psychotherapy, individuals with these disorders often have trouble building rapport with a therapist. Thus attrition from psychotherapy is high, further limiting the likelihood of deriving benefits from psychological treatments.

Summary and Recommendations

Poor regulation of emotion coupled with high rates of impulsive behaviors (such as suicide attempts, self-injurious behavior, and violence toward others) are highly prevalent among individuals with the more severe mood disorders (MDD and BD) and those with ASPD and BPD. Impulsivity is even more prevalent when BD is comorbid with a personality disorder. The combination of both pathologies is negatively associated with severity of symptoms and prognosis. Among the studies reviewed, there was consensus that regulation of emotion, improved self-control, and reduction of impulsivity are critical to the successful treatment of severe mood disorders and the abovementioned personality disorders.

Treatments for those disorders should (1) evaluate the individual's initial levels of impulsivity and self-control and (2) target improvement of those behaviors in treatment. In patients who are appropriate candidates for combination treatment, the combination of psychotherapy with pharmacotherapy appears clearly superior to either modality alone. Pharmacotherapy is essential for providing a faster stabilization of impulsivity/aggression and mood, while psychotherapy helps individuals gain an understanding of their disorder and its etiology as well as how to effectively cope and manage symptoms. Psychotropics assist with biologic stability, while psychotherapy is enduring and improves long-term functioning.

While the combined treatments are often superior, there are times when both modalities either cannot or should not be jointly implemented.

For example, some patients may not accept biological treatments, and no amount of psychoeducation may alter their perspective. In other cases, such as in pregnant females, geriatric patients already taking multiple medications, or young children, medication may be contraindicated.

In selecting the modality of psychotherapy, the provider must consider the needs and symptom presentation of the patient. While, on the whole, research findings do not reveal much statistical difference in effectiveness between modalities, some studies show superiority of CBT in reducing suicidality in adults with BD or unipolar depression, and superiority of DBT in managing the impulsive and violent behaviors common in BPD. Psychodynamic therapy appeared most appropriate when interpersonal conflicts were a relevant factor in symptom presentation.

Just as some patients may not be good candidates for treatment with medications, others may not be willing or able to dedicate the time needed for psychotherapy and may prefer medications. Some patients live in areas with few psychotherapists, and have greater access to medications through midlevel or primary care prescribers, while others may not be able to afford the cost of psychotherapy or may choose medications first, as they tend to provide faster onset of at least some improvement.

When selecting appropriate psychotropics, the provider must consider safety and lethality first. If the patient is acutely suicidal, tricyclic antidepressants, benzodiazepines, and antiepileptics should be used with caution. Comorbid substance-use disorders (or when other family members in the home have chemical addictions), metabolic concerns, or other health issues should also be evaluated for possible risks of certain psychotropics.

Whether medications, psychotherapy, or both modalities are most appropriate for patients with mood or the abovementioned personality disorders, the literature is clear that specifically targeting impulsive, disruptive, and violent behaviors should be paramount. The research findings reviewed above should provide clinicians with a guide for treatment selection in a variety of clinical situations.

This case study provides an example of optimal utilization of combined treatments for a male with bipolar disorder whose illness was characterized by a cluster of disruptive, impulsive, and destructive behaviors. The approach included a diagnostic evaluation to guide treatment selection as well as cultural assessment to better understand the patient's beliefs about his disorder and preferences for treatment and to comprehensively ascertain what treatments had been tried and failed with him in the past.

(continued)

(continued)

This 29-year-old Native American homosexual male from a remote part of the United States exhibited a long history of chemical abuse, prostitution for drugs and money, extreme violence, incarceration, and a series of severely high-risk behaviors. His parents divorced when he was young, and he reportedly did not bond well with either of them. He bounced back and forth between the homes of his parents, both of whom were severely chemically dependent. He dropped out of school around age 13 and ran away from home. He eventually ended up living on the streets in a major US city, quickly falling into a lifestyle of drugs and prostitution. The lifestyle he led was dangerous, often getting into serious fights or ending up in jail.

Because of his tribal affiliation, he was able to receive free health care. As part of a probation requirement, he agreed to complete chemical dependency inpatient treatment. While he learned a great deal about abuse and addiction issues, he found that being sober only unmasked his mental illness. During his sobriety, he realized he had periods of time where he had trouble sleeping and felt like he was high on stimulant drugs (his friends thought he was too), while at other times he became so hopeless and depressed he wanted to die. The patient quickly relapsed with alcohol and heroin to help him sleep and stimulants when he was depressed. His cycle of prostitution, fighting, and drugs resumed.

He was again incarcerated and ordered to complete chemical and mental health treatment after his jail term was completed. He was diagnosed with depression and polysubstance addiction and treated with 150 mg of buproprion bid. The patient stated initially that the medication lifted his mood, but then he became violently manic and went out on a rampage of sex, drugs, and violence that led to him being severely beaten and hospitalized. Then he had to face more serious charges and served three years in prison. During that time he was able to remain sober but continued with promiscuous and violent sexual behaviors and wildly labile moods. He attempted to hang himself at one point and was put on suicide watch after that. While incarcerated, the prison doctor tried him on a series of SSRI medications, only to cause more severe lability and irritability.

When his moods permitted, he studied and read a great deal, with a particular interest in pharmacology. It was his dream to become a pharmacy technician. He was discharged from prison and hitchhiked his way across the United States until he ended up on a random Indian reservation. There he met a woman who was very nurturing but morbidly obese. She promised to take care of him if he would stop his promiscuity and drugs. The patient enjoyed the safety of being in her home and with her family, and so he and the woman married. But his moods continued to cycle, and when he was manic he would go to other cities and have sex with strange men and do drugs. His wife's family found out about his behaviors, and he had many physical altercations with her brothers as a result.

He decided to seek mental health treatment again, and this time he met with a psychiatrist who again treated him for depression using medications such as mirtazapine, venlafaxine, and duloxetine. He discontinued the mirtazapine after one month because of excessive weight gain and a general feeling of lethargy. Venlafaxine made him agitated, as did duloxetine, so he stopped both of those medications as well and then discontinued seeing the psychiatrist owing to the lack of a positive response to his treatments.

After some more legal infractions and a threat from his wife that she would divorce him and leave him homeless if he did not stop his impulsive and destructive behaviors, he sought treatment with a psychologist. After completing in-depth assessment, the psychologist diagnosed him with bipolar I disorder. The patient was started on 25 mg of lamotrigine for mood stabilization and was slowly brought up to 200 mg/day. He reported noticing no serious side effects from the medication and felt less depressed and much less angry and volatile on the medication. He fought less with his wife, but still longed for sexual contact with men.

He then began psychotherapy with the psychologist. He explored his sexuality and whether it was fair to his wife to remain with her when he was attracted to men (he was only rarely sexually active with his wife, preferring instead acts of mutual masturbation). It was a long and difficult process, as the patient had low self-esteem from the years of rape and violence he had endured and the humiliation from harassment for being gay (which can be particularly humiliating for a Native American male owing to the common rejection of homosexuality in their culture). The thought of being on his own was frightening, as each time he had been independent in the past, he had ended up homeless or in prison. But this time he went back to school to become a pharmacy technician, and because of his stabilized mood he was able to refrain from abusing drugs and alcohol. He eventually became able to satisfy his homosexual urges by talking to men online, and his wife tolerated that.

Several times throughout his treatment, the patient decided he did not have bipolar disorder and discontinued his medication.

(continued)

(continued)

Each time that happened, the consequences of his impulsive behaviors were significant. He relapsed into alcohol abuse and drove to another city to have anonymous gay sex. He either got into physical fights with his wife's brothers or became violent with his homosexual partners. During those periods he discontinued psychotherapy. These episodes lasted anywhere from weeks to months.

Finally, the patient decided he was tired of his chaotic lifestyle and of being in a loveless marriage. He returned to psychotherapy and was restarted on lamotrigine. But this time it did not have the same mood-stabilizing effects as it had previously. Therefore 5 mg daily of aripiprazole was added, and the patient reported a significant reduction in his lability, insomnia, anger, and desire for high-risk behaviors. His depression became well controlled as well. He completed his training as a pharmacy technician, but instead decided he wanted to become a chemical dependency counselor for Native Americans, with a particular focus on dual diagnoses. He left his wife and moved to another city. There he completed his training and earned a license as an alcohol and drug counselor and soon after found a job in that field. He later reported he was in a committed relationship with a man, was satisfied with his new career, and was maintaining his medication regime. He stated that with his moods stabilized, he no longer desired multiple sexual partners, drugs or alcohol, and had no physical altercations with others.

The critical element of this patient's treatment was starting with the correct diagnosis and not becoming distracted by his chemical abuse and illegal behaviors. Although he did abuse drugs and alcohol, that was a symptom rather than a primary disorder. His cycle of destructive, disruptive, and high-risk behaviors could only stop once his mood was stable. His intellect and desire to help others were considerable strengths and elevated him to a high level of functioning once his mood was stable and he was able to think and feel clearly. To maintain sobriety without treating his mood disorder would have likely been impossible. Medications were chosen that were tolerable to him, and once he felt better he quickly became able to build rapport with his provider, which further advanced his progress. Respect and consideration for his ethnicity was critical, as was an understanding of his sexual orientation. A collaborative and nonjudgmental approach helped strengthen his self-esteem and turn his dangerous lifestyle into one that was healthy and productive.

References

Alavi, A., et al. (2013). Effectiveness of cognitive-behavioral therapy in decreasing suicidal ideation and hopelessness of the adolescents with previous suicidal attempts. *Iranian Journal of Pediatrics, 23*(4), 467–472.

Alegria, A., et al. (2013). Sex differences in antisocial personality disorder: Results from the national epidemiological survey on alcohol and related conditions. *Personality Disorders: Theory, Research, and Treatment, 4*(3), 214–222.

APA. American Psychiatric Association. (2010). *Practice guideline for the treatment of patients with major depressive disorder* (3rd ed.). Washington, DC: Author.

APA. American Psychiatric Association. (2013). *Diagnostic and statistical manual of mental disorders* (5th ed.). Washington, DC: Author.

Barkley, R. A. (1997). *ADHD and the nature of self-control.* New York: Guilford Press.

Barzman, D., et al. (2007). Rates, types, and psychosocial correlates of legal charges in adolescents with newly diagnosed bipolar disorder. *Bipolar Disorders, 9*(4), 339–344.

Bateman, A., & Fonagy, P. (2009). Randomized controlled trial of outpatient mentalization-based treatment versus structured clinical management for borderline personality disorder. *American Journal of Psychiatry, 166*(12), 1355–1364.

Bellino, S., et al. (2010). Adaptation of interpersonal psychotherapy to borderline personality disorder: A comparison of combined therapy and single pharmaco-therapy. *Canadian Journal of Psychiatry, 55*(2), 74–81.

Berman, R., et al. (2007). The efficacy and safety of aripiprazole as adjunctive therapy in major depressive disorder: A multicenter, randomized, double-blind, placebo-controlled study. *Journal of Clinical Psychiatry, 68*(6), 843–853.

Bowden, C. L., et al. (2004). Safety and tolerability of lamotrigine for bipolar disorder. *Drug Safety, 27*(3), 173–184.

Boyda, H., et al. (2013). Metabolic side effects of the novel second-generation antipsychotic drugs asenapine and iolperidone: A comparison with olanzapine. *PLoS One, 8*(1), e53459.

Breggin, P. (2003). Fluvoxamine as a cause of stimulation, mania, and aggression with a critical analysis of the FDA-approved label. *International Journal of Risk and Safety in Medicine, 14,* 71–86.

Brodsky, B., & Stanley, B. (2008). Adverse childhood experiences and suicidal behavior. *Psychiatric Clinics of North America, 31*(2), 223–235.

Brotman, M., et al. (2006). Prevalence, clinical correlates, and longitudinal course of severe mood dys-regulation in children. *Biological Psychiatry, 60,* 991–997.

Brown, G., et al. (2005). Cognitive therapy for the prevention of suicide attempts: A randomized controlled trial. *Journal of the American Medical Association, 294,* 563–570.

Calabrese, J., et al. (2010). Adjunctive armodafinil for major depressive episodes associated with bipolar I disorder: A randomized, multicenter, double-blind, placebo-controlled, proof-of-concept study. *Journal of Clinical Psychiatry, 71*(10), 1363–1370.

Centers for Disease Control and Prevention, National Center for Injury Prevention and Control. (2012). Web-based Injury Statistics Query and Reporting System (WISQARS). Retrieved from www.cdc.gov/ncipc/wisqars.

Chang, H., et al. (2010). The role of valproate in metabolic disturbances in bipolar disorder patients. *Journal of Affective Disorders, 124*(3), 319–323.

Citrome, L., et al. (2014). A review of real-world data on the effects of aripiprazole on weight and metabolic outcomes in adults. *Current Medical Research and Opinion, 30*(8), 1629–1641.

Clarkin, J., & Kemberg, O. (2004). The Personality Disorders Institute/Borderline Personality Disorders Research Foundation randomized controlled borderline personality disorder: Rational, methods and patient characteristics. *Journal of Personality Disorders, 18*(1), 52–72.

Coccaro, E., et al. (1989). Serotonergic studies in patients with affective and personality disorders. *Archives of General Psychiatry, 46*, 587–599.

Corruble, E., et al. (2003). Understanding impulsivity in severe depression? A psychometrical contribution. *Journal of Affective Disorders, 27*(5), 829–833.

Cullen, A., et al. (2012). A multisite randomized trial of cognitive skills program for male mentally disordered offenders: Violence and antisocial behavior outcomes. *Journal of Consulting and Clinical Psychology, 80*(6), 1114–1120.

de Jonghe, F., et al. (2004). Psychotherapy alone and combined with pharmacotherapy in treatment of depression. *British Journal of Psychiatry, 185*, 37–45.

Dekker, J., et al. (2013). What is the best sequential treatment strategy in the treatment of depression? Addigin pharmacotherapy to psychotherapy or vice versa? *Psychotherapy and Psychosomatics, 82*(2), 89–98.

Dingfelder, S. (2004). Treatment for the "untreatable": Despite the difficult-to-treat reputation of personality disorders, clinical trials of treatments show promise. *APA Monitor, 35*(3), 46.

Dumais, B., et al. (2005). Risk factors for suicide completion in major depression: A case-control study of impulsive and aggressive behaviors in men. *American Journal of Psychiatry, 162*, 2116–2124.

Frank, E., et al. (2005). Two-year outcomes for interpersonal and social rhythm therapy individuals with bipolar I disorder. *Archives of General Psychiatry, 62*(9), 996.

Frye, M., et al. (2007). A placebo-controlled evaluation of adjunctive modafinil in the treatment of bipolar depression. *American Journal of Psychiatry, 164*(8), 1242–1249.

Gerhart, J., et al. (2013). The moderating effects of Cluster B personality traits on violence reduction training: A mixed-model analysis. *Journal of Interpersonal Violence, 28*(1), 45–61.

Giesen-Bloo, J., et al. (2006). Outpatient psychotherapy for borderline personality disorder: Randomized trial of schema-focused therapy vs transference-focused psychotherapy. *Archives of General Psychiatry, 63*(6), 649–658.

Givens, J., et al. (2007). Ethnicity and preferences for depression treatment. *General Hospital Psychiatry, 29*(3), 182–191.

Gonzalez-Pinto, A., et al. (2006). Suicidal risk in bipolar I disorder patients and adherence to long-term lithium treatment. *Bipolar Disorders, 8*(5.2), 618–624.

Grant, B., et al. (2008). Prevalence, correlates, disability, and comorbidity of DSM-IV borderline personality disorder: Results from the Wave 2 National Epidemiologic Survey on Alcohol and Related Conditions. *Journal of Clinical Psychiatry, 69*(4), 533–545.

Greenberg, P., et al. (2003). The economic burden of depression in the United States: How did it change between 1990 and 2000? *Journal of Clinical Psychiatry, 64*, 1465–1475.

Grunebaum, M., et al. (2013). SSRI versus bupropion effects on symptom clusters in suicidal depression: Post hoc analysis of a randomized clinical trial. *Journal of Clinical Psychiatry, 74*(9), 872–879.

Gyulai, L., et al. (2003). Thyroid hypofunction in patients with rapid-cycling bipolar disorder after lithium challenge. *Biological Psychiatry, 53*(10), 899–905.

Hallahan, B., et al. (2007). Omega-3 fatty acid supplementation in patients with recurrent self-harm: Single-centre double-blind randomised controlled trial. *British Journal of Psychiatry, 190*, 118–122.

Heisel, M., et al. (2014). Adapting interpersonal psychotherapy for older adults at risk for suicide. *American Journal of Geriatric Psychiatry, 40*(2), 156–164.

Hollander, E., et al. (2003). Divalproex in the treatment of impulsive aggression: Efficacy in Cluster B personality disorders. *Neuropsychopharmacology, 28*(6), 1186–1197.

Ives-Deliperi, V., et al. (2013). The effects of mindfulness-based cognitive therapy in patients with bipolar disorder: A controlled functional MRI investigation. *Journal of Affective Disorders, 150*(3), 1152–1157.

Jovev, M., et al. (2013). Temperament and maltreatment in the emergence of borderline and antisocial personality pathology during early adolescence. *Journal of the Canadian Academy of Child and Adolescent Psychiatry, 22*(3), 220–229.

Kessler, R., et al. (2005). Prevalence, severity, and comorbidity of 12-month DSM-IV disorders in the National Comorbidity Survey Replication. *Archives of General Psychiatry, 62*(6), 617–627.

Kool, S., et al. (2003). Efficacy of combined therapy and pharmacotherapy for depressed patients with or without personality disorders. *Harvard Review of Psychiatry, 11*(3), 133–141.

Kool, S., et al. (2007). Treatment of depressive disorder and comorbid personality pathology: Combined therapy versus pharmacotherapy. *Tijdschrift voor Psychiatrie, 49*(6), 361–372.

Krahe, B. (2013). *The social psychology of aggression* (2nd ed.). New York: Psychology Press.

Kwan, B., et al. (2010). Treatment preference, engagement, and clinical improvement in pharmacotherapy versus psychotherapy for depression. *Behavior, Research and Therapy, 48*(8), 799–804.

Lam, D., et al. (2005). Relapse prevention in patients with bipolar disorder: Cognitive therapy outcome after 2 years. *American Journal of Psychiatry, 162*(2), 324–329.

Lane, S., et al. (2009). Acute topiramate differentially affects human aggressive responding at low vs. moderate doses in subjects with histories of substance abuse and antisocial behavior. *Pharmacology and Biochemical Behavior, 92*(2), 357–362.

Lawrence, K., et al. (2010). Impulsivity in borderline personality disorder: Reward-based decision-making and its relationship to emotional distress. *Journal of Personality Disorders, 24*(6), 785–799.

Lazarus, J. (2009). Lithium and thyroid. *Best Practice and Research Clinical Endocrinology and Metabolism, 23*(6), 723–733.

Leibenluft, E. (2011). Severe mood dysregulation, irritability, and the diagnostic boundaries of bipolar disorder in youths. *American Journal of Psychiatry, 168,* 129–142.

Leigh, E., et al. (2012). Mood regulation in youth: Research findings and clinical approaches to irritability and short-lived episodes of mania-like symptoms. *Current Opinions in Psychiatry, 25*(4), 271–276.

Lenzenweger, M. F., et al. (2007). DSM-IV personality disorders in the National Comorbidity Survey Replication. *Biological Psychiatry, 62*(6), 553–564.

Linehan, M. (1987). Dialectical behavior therapy for borderline personality disorder: Theory and method. *Bulletin of the Menninger Clinic, 51*(3), 261–276.

Linehan, M. (1993). *Cognitive-behavioral treatment of borderline personality disorder.* New York: Guilford Press.

Linehan, M., et al. (2006). Two year randomized controlled trial and follow-up of dialectical behavior therapy vs therapy by experts for suicidal behaviors and borderline personality disorder. *Archives of General Psychiatry, 63*(7), 757–766.

Loeber, R., et al. (1993). Developmental pathways in disruptive child behavior. *Developmental Psychopathology, 5,* 103–133.

Maina, G., et al. (2005). Randomized controlled trial comparing brief dynamic and supportive therapy with waiting list condition in minor depressive disorders. *Psychotherapy and Psychosomatics, 74*(1), 43–50.

Miklowitz, D. (2006). A review of evidence-based psychosocial interventions for bipolar disorder. *Journal of Clinical Psychiatry, 67*(11), 28–33.

Miklowitz, D., et al. (2007). Psychosocial treatments for bipolar depression: A 1-year randomized trial from the Systematic Treatment Enhancement Program. *Archives of General Psychiatry, 64*(4), 419–426.

Moeller, F., et al. (2001). Psychiatric aspects of impulsivity. *American Journal of Psychiatry, 158*(11), 1783–1793.

Morrell, M., et al. (2003). Higher androgens and weight gain with valproate compared with lamotrigine for epilepsy. *American Journal of Psychiatry, 54*(2–3), 189–199.

Muzina, D., et al. (2005). Lamotrigine and antiepileptic drugs as mood stabilizers in bipolar disorder. *Acta Psychiatra Scandia, 426,* 21–28.

Newman, W., and McDermott, B. (2011). Beta blockers for violence prophylaxis: Case reports. *Journal of Clinical Psychopharmacology, 31*(6), 785–787.

Nickel, M., et al. (2006). Aripiprazole in the treatment of patients with borderline personality disorder: A double-blind, placebo-controlled study. *American Journal of Psychiatry, 163*(5), 833–838.

Oquendo, M., et al. (2004). Prospective study of clinical predictors of suicidal acts after a major depressive episode in patients with major depressive disorder or bipolar disorder. *American Journal of Psychiatry, 161,* 1433–1441.

Pinto, O., and Akiskai, J. (1998). Lamotrigine as a promising approach to borderline personality: An open case series without concurrent DSM-IV major mood disorder. *Journal of Affective Disorders, 51*(3), 333–343.

Rahman, A., et al. (2009). Evaluating the incidence of leukopenia and neutropenia with valproate, quetiapine, or the combination in children and adolescents. *Annals of Pharmacotherapy, 43*(5), 822–830.

Rocca, P., et al. (2002). Treatment of borderline personality disorder with risperdone. *Journal of Clinical Psychiatry, 63*(3), 241–244.

Romo-Nava, F., et al. (2014). Melatonin attenuates antipsychotic metabolic effects: An eight-week randomized, double-blind, parallel-group, placebo-controlled clinical trial. *Bipolar Disorders, 16*(4), 410–421.

Rosenbluth, M., et al. (2012). The Canadian Network for Mood and Anxiety Treatments (CANMAT) task force recommendations for the management of patients with mood disorders and comorbid personality disorders. *Annals of Clinical Psychiatry, 24*(1), 56–68.

Rummel-Kluge, C., et al. (2010). Head to head comparisons of metabolic side effects of second generation antipsychotics in the treatment of schizophrenia: A systematic review and meta-analysis. *Schizophrenia Research, 123*(2–3), 225–233.

Schramm, E., et al. (2007) An intensive treatment program of interpersonal psychotherapy plus pharmacotherapy for depressed inpatients: Acute and long-term results. *American Journal of Psychiatry, 164*, 768–777.

Singh, V., et al. (2013). Relative effectiveness of adjunctive risperidone on manic and depressive symptoms in mixed mania. *International Journal of Clinical Psychopharmacology, 28*(2), 91–95.

Soloff, P., et al. (2000). Characteristics of suicide attempts of patients with major depressive episode and borderline personality disorder: A comparative study. *American Journal of Psychiatry, 157*, 601–608.

Swann, A., et al. (2005). Increased impulsivity associated with severity of suicide attempt history in patients with bipolar disorder. *American Journal of Psychiatry, 162*(9), 1680–1687.

Swann, A., et al. (2009a). Increased trait-like impulsivity and course of illness in bipolar disorder. *Bipolar Disorders, 11*(3), 280–288.

Swann, A., et al. (2009b). Severity of bipolar disorder is associated with impairment of response inhibition. *Journal of Affective Disorders, 116*(1–2), 30–36.

Swann, A., et al. (2010). Trait impulsivity and response inhibition in antisocial personality disorder. *Journal of Psychiatric Research, 43*(12), 1057–1063.

Swartz, H., et al. (2005). Acute treatment outcomes in patients with bipolar I disorder and co-morbid borderline personality disorder receiving medication and psychotherapy. *Bipolar Disorders, 7*(2), 192–197.

Tredget, J., et al. (2010). Effects of chronic lithium treatment on renal function. *Journal of Affective Disorders, 126*(3), 436–440.

Van Dijk, S., et al. (2013). A randomized, controlled pilot study of dialectical behavior therapy skills in a psychoeducational group for individuals with bipolar disorder. *Journal of Affective Disorders, 145*(3), 386–393.

Vaslamatzis, G., et al. (2014). Is the residential combined (psychotherapy plus medication) treatment of patients with severe personality disorder effective in terms of suicidality and impulsivity? *Journal of Nervous and Mental Disease, 202*(2), 138–143.

Villeneuve, E., and Lemelin, S. (2005). Open-label study of atypical neuroleptic quetiapine for treatment of borderline personality disorder: Impulsivity as main target. *Journal of Clinical Psychiatry, 66*(10), 1298–1303.

Walker, C., et al. (2003). Treating impulsivity, irritability and aggression of antisocial personality disorder with quetiapine. *International Journal of Offender Therapy and Comparative Criminology, 47*(5), 556–567.

Wiles, N., et al. (2013). Cognitive behavioural therapy as an adjunct to pharmacotherapy for primary care based patients with treatment resistant depression: Results of the CoBalT randomised controlled trial. *Lancet, 381*(9864), 375–384.

Woo, Y., et al. (2014). One-year rehospitalization rates of patients with first-episode bipolar mania receiving lithium or valproate and adjunctive atypical antipsychotics. *Psychiatry and Clinical Neurosciences, 68*(6), 418–424.

Worbe, Y., et al. (2014). Serotonin depletion induces "waiting impulsivity" on the human four-choice serial reaction time task: Cross-species translational significance. *Neuropsychopharmacology, 39*(6), 1519–1526.

Yatham, L., et al. (2013). Canadian Network for Mood and Anxiety Treatments (CANMAT) and International Society for Bipolar Disorders (ISBD) collaborative update of CANMAT guidelines for the management of patients with bipolar disorder: Update 2013. *Bipolar Disorders, 15*(1), 1–44.

Zanarini, M., et al. (2004). A preliminary, randomized trial of fluoxetine, olanzapine, and the olanzapine-fluoxetine combination in women with borderline personality disorder. *Journal of Clinical Psychiatry, 65*(7), 903–907.

Zarate, C., et al. (2012). Replication of ketamine's antidepressant efficacy in bipolar depression: A randomized controlled add-on trial. *Biological Psychiatry, 71*(11), 939–946.

Zisook, S., et al. (2011). Effect of antidepressant medication treatment on suicidal ideation and behavior in a randomized trial: An exploratory report from the combining medications to enhance depression outcomes study. *Journal of Clinical Psychiatry, 72*(10), 1322–1332.

12 Neurocognitive Disorders and Delirium

Benjamin D. Hill, Channing Sofko,
Lia Billington, and Heather Kirkpatrick

Estimates are that 48.1 million individuals worldwide will have a diagnosis of dementia by 2020, and projections rise to 90.3 million by 2040 (Prince et al., 2013). Dementia is a neurodegenerative change in cognitive functioning resulting in functional impairment. Verbal outbursts and physical agitation are common as dementia progresses and sometimes lead to aggressive behaviors (Lyketsos et al., 2011). Disruptive behaviors may occur in 90% of individuals with dementia during the course of illness (Chiu et al., 2006). These behaviors are associated with an increase in institutionalization and contribute to caregiver burden (Chung & Cummings, 2000).

Compared to dementia—a chronic encephalopathy—delirium can be considered an acute encephalopathy. Delirium is a common complication in hospitalized older adults and prevalence increases with age, reaching 14% for those over the age of 85 (Inouye, 2006). The behavioral disturbances seen in delirium can result in increased medical problems, and hallucinations or delusions experienced during periods of delirium can result in homicidal or suicidal behavior (Cole, 2004). Older adults who experience delirium are at three times greater risk of institutionalization and have higher rates of functional decline (American Psychiatric Association [APA], 2013). The prevalence and associated disruptive behaviors of both dementia and delirium place significant demands on both the health-care system and informal caregivers.

The behavioral disturbances affecting individuals with dementia or delirium also affect their caregivers. Caregiver burden is the cumulative impact of physical, psychological, emotional, social, and financial stressors associated with caregiving (Kasuya et al., 2000). Langa et al. (2001) found that older adults without cognitive impairments required 4.6 hours per week of informal care, while those with mild dementia required an additional 8.5 hours, moderate dementia an additional 17.4 hours, and severe dementia an additional 41.5 hours of care per week.

Diagnostic Considerations

Dementia

The fifth edition of the *Diagnostic and Statistical Manual of Mental Disorders* (DSM-5; APA, 2013) has replaced the diagnosis of dementia with a new diagnostic terminology of either mild or major neurocognitive disorder. Both new diagnoses have cognitive impairment as a core aspect, with the differentiating component being that everyday functioning (also known as instrumental activities of daily living, or IADLs) is impaired in major neurocognitive disorder but preserved in mild neurocognitive disorder. Mild neurocognitive disorder is analogous to the prior concept of mild cognitive impairment (MCI) that has developed over the past 20 years. While dementia is a change in cognition sufficient to impair functioning, MCI can reflect a prodromal stage of dementia. Major neurocognitive disorders have the following criteria: (1) significant cognitive decline in at least one domain based on informant or patient report, or neuropsychological testing; (2) the cognitive deficits interfere with IADLs; (3) these deficits occur outside of delirium; and (4) the deficits are not better explained by another psychiatric disorder. Mild neurocognitive disorders share the same criteria with the exception of criterion (2).

Delirium

The DSM-5 classifies delirium based on the following criteria: (1) impaired attention and awareness; (2) the disturbance is acute and fluctuates; (3) at least one additional cognitive domain is affected; (4) the attention/awareness and other cognitive domain change are not better explained by another condition; and (5) the disturbance is not due to another medical condition such as intoxication or withdrawal, toxin exposure, or a combination of etiologies.

Prevalence and Course

Alzheimer disease (AD) accounts for 60%–80% of cases and is the most common dementia presentation. Prevalence of the disease in the United States is 5.4 million cases, and incidence increases with age. Early clinical symptoms may include memory difficulties, apathy, and depression, as well as the cardinal symptom of difficulty learning new information (Alzheimer's Association, 2013). As the disease progresses, judgment becomes impaired, there is evidence of executive dysfunction, and behavioral disturbances (wandering and inappropriate activities) are common (Chiu et al., 2006). To a lesser extent, anxiety/phobias and paranoid or delusional ideation may be seen, including phantom boarder syndrome and Capgras syndrome. Some researchers consider apathy, agitation, anxiety, and irritability as the most prevalent symptoms in AD (Mega et al., 1996). Late-life depression with a strong apathetic component is considered to be a risk factor for AD and potentially a prodromal stage.

Vascular dementia can take the form of major hemorrhage, microscopic bleeds, or small vessel ischemic changes and is generally considered to be the second-most common dementia etiology after AD. These two etiologies frequently co-occur, making the exact prevalence of vascular dementia difficult to calculate, but differences exist in clinical presentation. Incidence increases with age. A vascular etiology for dementia is supported when vascular risk factors are present and there is evidence of cortical vascular infarcts. Individuals with vascular dementia may be disinhibited and aggressive, demonstrate paranoid/delusional ideation or anxiety, and have possible sleep disturbance (Chiu et al., 2006). Changes in appetite, depression, irritability, and apathy are common symptoms (Gupta et al., 2013).

The frontotemporal dementias (FTDs) are a rare category of neurodegenerative conditions that primarily affect the frontal and temporal cortices and comprise 5% of dementia cases. FTD often has an earlier onset (before age 65) than AD. Prevalence peaks in the late 60s and early 70s and does not increase with advanced age. There are at least three common types of FTDs, including behavioral-variant FTD, primary progressive aphasia (PPA), and semantic dementia. Clinically, none of these have memory impairment as a primary symptom.

The FTDs have diverse behavioral presentations. The primary behavioral complication of PPA is often related to the significant frustration these individuals feel because of their inability to communicate. Behavioral-variant FTD has executive deficits as a core feature, but these individuals may perform completely normally on neuropsychological testing. There may be significant negative personality changes such as being disinhibited, impulsive, sexually inappropriate with family members, displaying coarse and vulgar humor and language, and being hyperphagic or orally fixated. Activity disturbances dominate the clinical picture of behavioral variant FTD followed by paranoid/delusional ideation. Hyperactivity and lack of social awareness have been noted with aggressiveness and disinhibition being more common in males (Diehl & Kurz, 2002).

Dementia due to Lewy body disease is often unrecognized and may be the most common etiology for dementia after AD. Neocortical Lewy bodies are found in 20%–30% of dementia patients at autopsy. Incidence does not increase with age. The occipital cortex is preferentially involved, leading to characteristic visuospatial deficits and visual hallucinations, leading to a misdiagnosis of psychosis. This is potentially dangerous, as patients with Lewy body disease may have a strong negative reaction to neuroleptic medications (Baskys, 2004). Other common features are a rapidly fluctuating level of alertness, abnormal REM sleep behaviors, anosmia, and muscle rigidity that may appear Parkinsonian. As visual hallucinations may predominate the clinical presentation, aggression may result. A key feature is an abnormal lack of emotional response to the visual hallucination. Individuals describe the visual hallucinations as detailed and animate, which can lead to a variety of emotional reactions from amusement to fear. McKeith (2004) suggested that the persistence of visual hallucination can help distinguish the hallucinations from those seen in other dementias and in delirium.

Delirium can be a common comorbidity in dementia and occurs in 22%–89% of individuals age 65 or older (Flanagan & Fick, 2010). Incidence increases with age. By definition, the course of delirium is waxing and waning in presentation. While cognitive abilities may appear to be globally suppressed in many cases, the main impairment in delirium is attentional in nature. Additionally, visual hallucinations and alterations in consciousness are common.

Solitary Pharmacological Treatments

Pharmacotherapy for disruptive behaviors in both delirium and dementia should be used cautiously, as few high-quality randomized controlled trials (RCTs) exist. It is considered best practice to manage behaviors with psychosocial interventions first. Physiological contributions to behavioral symptoms of delirium and dementia must be systematically ruled out before pharmacotherapy is considered. Examples of physiological contributions are illness/infection, sensory deprivation, polypharmacy, postoperative status, anesthesia, pain, and withdrawal from alcohol and sedatives. Additionally, current medications must be reviewed as benzodiazepines, corticosteroids, H2-receptor antagonists, sedative hypnotics, narcotics, chlorpromazine, thioridazine, meperidine, all tricyclic antidepressants, and all anticholinergic medications may induce or worsen delirium (American Geriatrics Society [AGS], 2012).

Medications for Disruptive Behaviors in Dementia

For the dementias, clinicians are encouraged to target both the patient-specific symptoms and the underlying etiology. Most studies have focused on AD, as this is the most common etiology, so it is uncertain whether findings apply to other types of dementia. Although memory decline can be a primary presentation in AD, other progressive features or co-occurring factors, such as insomnia, may lie at the root of disruptive behaviors. For all medications considered for use in the elderly, the easily accessed Beers criteria of the AGS (2012) should be followed.

When psychosocial modalities are exhausted and the patient is not deemed dangerous, the following types of neuropsychiatric symptoms are sometimes treated with medications: agitation, aggression, paranoid delusions, hallucinations (usually limited to Lewy body dementia), depression, sleep disorders, wandering, and sexually inappropriate behaviors. The classes of medications used to treat these symptoms include the antipsychotics, nontricyclic antidepressants, trazodone, cholinesterase inhibitors, and memantine. Medications that are occasionally used but with limited evidence are the anticonvulsants (carbamazepine, valproate, gabapentin, lamotrigine), benzodiazepines, methylphenidate, melatonin, and hormonal agents that treat sexually inappropriate behavior (Press & Alexander, 2014). The treatment of sexually inappropriate behaviors with medications is understudied, but a review of case reports ($N = 55$) supports serotonergic medications as the first line of treatment, followed by antiandrogens, luteinizing hormone-releasing agonists, and estrogens (Guay, 2008).

Antipsychotics

Antipsychotics are not approved by the US Food and Drug Administration for treatment of behavioral disorders in patients with dementia, may increase all-cause mortality (1%–2% absolute risk), and carry black box warnings. There is a current initiative by Medicare to decrease antipsychotic use in the elderly. The risk of mortality is increased most with haloperidol and least with quetiapine (Huybrechts et al., 2012). When good psychosocial interventions still leave patients with frightening disruptive delusions, paranoia, or hallucinations, an improved quality of life may outweigh the risk of earlier death in an elderly patient.

In a systematic meta-analysis of six first-generation agents (Sink et al., 2005), there was insufficient evidence of efficacy for treating neuropsychiatric symptoms of dementia. But systematic reviews of second-generation antipsychotics (Lee et al., 2004) have found modest and statistically significant benefits with olanzapine or risperidone. A well-designed trial of patients with AD and either aggression, agitation, or psychosis for treatment with either olanzapine, quetiapine, risperidone, or placebo (Schneider et al., 2006) found support for olanzapine or quetiapine. Ballard et al.'s (2006) meta-analysis focusing on dementia found that aggression significantly decreased with risperidone or olanzapine and psychosis improved with risperidone, but they noted a high incidence of serious adverse events.

A 2013 Cochrane meta-analysis (Declercq et al., 2013) of studies withdrawing dementia patients from antipsychotics found that many dementia patients could safely discontinue these medications. In two of nine trials, however, there was significant behavioral deterioration in people with more severe baseline neuropsychiatric symptoms. Interestingly, some studies have found that antidepressants such as

244 Benjamin D. Hill et al.

citalopram or sertraline are as effective as antipsychotics in decreasing psychotic and other behavioral symptoms (Gaber et al., 2001; Pollock et al., 2007).

Benzodiazepines

Benzodiazepines carry significant cautions and should be avoided for treatment of insomnia and agitation in dementia. They are known to increase the risk of accidents in older individuals who metabolize them more slowly and may cause cognitive impairment in this group (AGS, 2012). Tampi and Tampi (2014) conducted a review of five RCTs and did not find support for routine use of benzodiazepines to treat behavioral and psychological symptoms; however, they may be used as a last resort. The five studies included in the review compared the following medications: (1) diazepam and thioridazine; (2) oxazepam, haloperidol, and diphenhydramine; (3) alprazolam and lorazepam; (4) lorazepam and haloperidol; and (5) intramuscular lorazepam, intramuscular olanzapine, and placebo. Significant differences in efficacy were not found for four of the studies; in one study, thioridazine likely had better efficacy than diazepam and no significant differences existed in tolerability.

Anticonvulsants

Anticonvulsant medications decrease neuronal activity and have been historically used to treat mania. The most commonly prescribed anticonvulsants for psychiatric issues (lamotrigine, valproate, carbamazepine, and gabapentin) have Beers criteria cautions to avoid for patients with a history of falls or fractures. Hyponatremia, myelosuppression, or liver function abnormalities are possible and should be monitored. The few studies to examine their efficacy in dementia have found either limited support or have recommended against their use (Dolder & Nealy, 2012; Pinheiro, 2008). The literature regarding the use of this class of medications is equivocal, with skepticism surrounding off-label uses and case studies that support the use for managing sexual disinhibition (Freymann et al., 2005); however, these should be considered only after all other means have been exhausted (Joller et al., 2013).

Medications for Disruptive Behaviors in Delirium

First-generation antipsychotics (usually haloperidol), second-generation/ atypical antipsychotics, and benzodiazepines are typically used to manage delirium. Expert consensus (Trzepacz et al., 2010) suggests that benzodiazepines should only be used when (1) the etiology of delirium is clearly associated with alcohol or sedative withdrawal or (2) when an antipsychotic medication is contraindicated. Antipsychotics are often contraindicated because they can lower the seizure threshold and induce anticholinergic side effects and akathisia. Surveys suggest that benzodiazepines are commonly overprescribed for delirium (Francis, 2014). Generally, the lowest possible dose of benzodiazepine or antipsychotic medication for the shortest amount of time should be used.

Delirium-related psychotic symptoms and severe agitation may respond to low-dose haloperidol (Francis, 2014) and to the newer atypical antipsychotics that appear to have similar efficacy (Parellada et al., 2004; Skrobik et al., 2004). A Cochrane meta-analysis (Lonergan et al., 2007) found three studies that compared high- and low-dose haloperidol with risperidone, olanzapine, and placebo. The efficacy and incidence of adverse effects of low-dose haloperidol was similar to that of risperidone and olanzapine. High-dose haloperidol was associated with increased incidence of extrapyramidal effects in one study. Low-dose haloperidol decreased the severity and duration of delirium (but not incidence) when compared to placebo in postoperative patients. More recently, Yoon et al. (2013) examined haloperidol, risperidone, olanzapine, and quetiapine in a six-day prospective clinical observational study in hospitalized patients who met diagnostic criteria for delirium ($N = 80$). Those with dementia and comorbid psychiatric disorders were excluded from the study. The four medications were found to be equally safe and efficacious in treating delirium. The treatment response rate to olanzapine was poorer in subjects over the age of 75; the response rates to other antipsychotics were not different between the age groups. The researchers posited two explanations for these differential rates: (1) they reasoned that olanzapine may induce more anticholinergic effects through an affinity toward muscarinic receptors and (2) some of the patients may have had dementia that was undiagnosed.

Benefits and Limitations of Pharmacotherapy as Sole Treatment

Many of the medications used to manage disruptive behaviors have cautions, but sometimes the benefits outweigh the risks or no safer substitution exists. But the tricyclic antidepressants are a clear example of medications that should not be used in older adults because of their anticholinergic and orthostatic hypotension effects. In general, medications that have anticholinergic effects (interfere with acetylcholine) can induce symptoms that look like AD, particularly for individuals who are in a prodromal stage of the disease. These medications are surprisingly common (e.g., most over-the-counter sleep aids, antihistamines, urinary incontinence medication, etc.), and physicians sometimes do not recognize their contributions to symptoms.

In general, the older antipsychotics are associated with extrapyramidal side effects and possible tardive dyskinesia, while the newer atypical antipsychotics carry a risk of metabolic syndrome, including obesity, hyperlipidemia, and diabetes as well as agranulocytosis for clozapine. Antipsychotics are contraindicated in Lewy body dementia owing to a 30%–50% risk of life-threatening side effects such as irreversible Parkinsonism and autonomic dysfunction (Hake & Farlow, 2014). Long-term use of antipsychotics in mild to moderate AD is not associated with either a delay in nursing home admission or increased time to death (Lopez et al., 2013). Benzodiazepines and anticonvulsant medications may result in decreased alertness. There are specific caveats with using antidepressants in the elderly. Tricyclic antidepressants are inappropriate with the exception of low-dose doxepin for sleep. Additionally, paroxetine has anticholinergic side effects and should be avoided. As discussed earlier, visual hallucinations and sleep disturbances are prevalent behavioral symptoms in dementia. Ballard (2013) found that cholinesterase inhibitors may be beneficial in reducing neuropsychiatric symptoms in this population, particularly those who experience visual hallucinations, and claimed these medications are generally tolerated well, providing an alternative to antipsychotics.

It is considered best practice for both delirium and dementia to exhaust psychosocial interventions before turning to pharmacotherapy. Corbett et al. (2012) recommend at least four weeks of ongoing assessment and monitoring, addressing underlying medical issues such as infection or pain, and implementing psychosocial treatment before considering pharmacologic therapy. Even when pharmacotherapy is utilized, psychosocial interventions should be continued in order to utilize the smallest effective dose over the shortest period of time. As seen in this section, most of the medications considered for use in the treatment of delirium and dementia carry cautions for serious medication interactions, medical complications, sedation, and falls. Therefore psychosocial interventions are preferred, and all interventions for elderly adults should be informed by the APA's (2014) Guidelines for Psychological Practice with Older Adults.

Solitary Psychological Treatments

Practice guidelines recommend stepped care in treating behaviors that challenge (Brechin et al., 2013). Goals of psychosocial treatment are to prevent, manage, reduce, or eliminate behaviors that challenge. Psychosocial interventions often attempt to address unmet needs or nonverbalized experiences such as pain, boredom, feelings of loneliness or isolation, anger, fear, or depression. While substantial supportive research exists, much of the evidence is limited by poor-quality study design, small sample size, and lack of random assignment.

Clear evidence for specific psychosocial techniques has remained challenging to discern, and intermittent evidence for specific techniques may not fully consider the multifaceted nature of disruptive behaviors (Bird & Moniz-Cook, 2008). One helpful conceptualization—which comes from the Newcastle biopsychosocial model (James, 2011) and takes into account life history, social environment, cognitive abilities, medication, emotions, health, and personality in considering routes to modify behaviors—is the *iceberg analogy*, which includes things caregivers cannot see in the affected individual (e.g., context, beliefs, physical issues, premorbid personality) that may influence behaviors that challenge.

Another useful strategy is the Treatment Routes for Exploring Agitation (TREA) model, a systematic method for individualizing nonpharmacologic interventions. In an RCT of nursing home residents, the TREA intervention group received individualized care in which an unmet need was hypothesized, a treatment category was identified, and a specific treatment was individualized to the resident's need, preferences, and abilities. Caregivers assigned to the control group were given an in-service presentation on causes of agitation and psychosocial methods. Research assistants directly observed agitated behaviors for two weeks. The TREA interventions produced significant declines in agitated behaviors. Effect sizes were moderate for verbal aggression but large for physical nonaggressive behaviors and total agitation (Cohen-Mansfield et al., 2012). These skills can be taught to families as well as nursing home staff.

In general, it is useful to consider psychosocial techniques as being organized into four categories: cognition-oriented, emotion-oriented, behavior-oriented, and stimulation-oriented approaches (American Psychiatric Association Workgroup on Alzheimer's Disease and Other Dementias, 2007).

Cognition-Oriented Therapies

Cognition-oriented therapies generally aim to provide cognitive stimulation for individuals with dementia and are used to address cognitive impairment in dementia. They often are mental exercises such as commercially available computerized brain games. They generally show little efficacy for slowing cognitive decline. Cognitive therapy has shown some limited effect in reducing behavioral symptoms that may reflect underlying depressive or anxiety symptoms that may manifest as agitation or resistance to care (Cipher et al., 2007). No single psychotherapeutic approach has emerged as most appropriate and well validated for patients with dementia, though individual and group interventions have been explored. Most studies utilized a single approach, usually with weak methodology, and reported mixed evidence for efficacy.

Emotion-Oriented Therapies

Emotion-oriented therapies seek to tailor treatment to address an individual's emotional needs. Emotions that are most frequently associated with behaviors that challenge are anxiety, anger, and depression. Often, persons with moderate to severe dementia cannot verbalize these emotions directly. There is insufficient evidence overall to recommend emotion-oriented therapies to reduce behaviors that challenge, but small well-designed studies show some promise for this approach (O'Neil et al., 2011). One common emotion-oriented technique is reminiscence therapy or life review therapy, which encourages the person to use photos and memorabilia to stimulate recollections of the past. Hsieh et al. (2010) conducted an RCT of group reminiscence therapy and found significant effects for reducing depression and apathy in nursing home residents with mild to moderate dementia.

Validation therapy (VT) is another emotion-centered approach that attempts to accept the impaired individual's emotions rather than refute their perceptions as disordered reality. Toseland et al. (1997) conducted a small RCT and found that VT reduced both verbal and physical aggression in nursing home patients with dementia when compared to those receiving usual care. In addition, a small trial demonstrated improved anxiety-related agitation, irritability, and nighttime problem behaviors (Tondi et al., 2007).

Simulated presence therapy is based on attachment theory and utilizes audio or videotapes of loved ones communicating positive shared memories. At least four trials of reasonable methodological design have found simulated presence therapy to reduce agitation and anxiety in persons with dementia, but several other studies have found that this technique can increase agitation (Zetteler, 2008) and may be best suited for mild to moderate levels of dementia. There is still too little evidence to highly recommend simulated presence theory as an intervention for dementia (O'Neil et al., 2011).

Behavior-Oriented Therapies

Behavior-oriented therapies are generally considered to have moderate evidence regarding their efficacy for reducing behaviors that challenge (Livingston et al., 2005). One area of behavior-oriented intervention is addressing environmental factors that contribute to agitation. There is also increasing attention to utilizing functional analyses techniques for behaviors associated with dementia. Analysis of antecedents, behavior, and consequences (the ABC Model) is helpful for determining triggers for behaviors that challenge, particularly when such analysis indicates circular causality (e.g., a caregiver's anxiety precedes agitation in the person with dementia and this agitation in turn increases the caregiver's anxiety). Functional analysis also examines inadvertently reinforced behavior such as an individual with dementia being positively reinforced for wandering behavior by attracting attention. Examination of the function of the behavior allows for appropriate intervention on the part of the caregiver instead of a response that further agitates the patient. Some well-designed RCTs have been conducted examining functional analyses (Cohen-Mansfield & Werner, 1997; Cohen-Mansfield et al., 2007) and found positive effects.

A Cochrane review (Moniz-Cook et al., 2012) examined 18 trials that met rigorous methodological criteria, most within the home setting. Few studies implemented functional analysis alone, as it was typically part of a multimodal intervention. Small reductions in frequency of problem behaviors were noted, but these gains were not maintained at follow-up. A reduction of severity and incidence of problem behaviors was not found. The authors concluded that research examining functional analysis in dementia is still nascent, and there is a general lack of consensus about how to measure behaviors that challenge. With respect to other components of behavior-oriented treatment, interventions such as redirection, distraction, and avoiding stimulants are recommended (Press and Alexander, 2014).

Stimulation-Oriented Therapies

Stimulation-oriented therapies include light, music, massage, and exercise interventions. Stimulation therapies assume that individuals with dementia engage in behaviors that challenge as a result of lack of sensory stimulation. Light stimulation is theorized to affect circadian disturbances in the sleep–wake cycle of individuals with dementia. Two RCTs reported that scheduled bright light exposure reduced nocturnal restlessness, but the studies were small and had methodological issues (O'Neil et al., 2011). Two small RCTs examining the role of hand massage and light touch found positive effects such as reduced agitation (Hansen et al., 2006). Evidence regarding animal-assisted therapy, aromatherapy, and acupuncture is primarily qualitative and not rigorous. Music therapy ranges from listening to recorded music, engaging in group singing, or personalizing music played to the individual. O'Neil et al. (2011) reported that several marginal RCTs have found support for music therapy to reduce aggression, agitation, and wandering during the music activity itself. Exercise has been moderately studied, but evidence for the benefit of exercise remains mixed, with the strongest effect found for improvement of sleep and reduced nocturnal awakenings (Alessi et al., 2005). Information regarding specific dose, intensity, and type of exercise is unclear (Gitlin et al., 2012). Regarding other stimulation-oriented therapies such as aromatherapy, animal-assisted therapy, and acupuncture, there is insufficient evidence of efficacy for managing problematic behaviors.

Benefits and Limitations of Psychotherapy as Sole Treatment

Given clear findings regarding safety concerns for pharmacologic approaches, there is increased attention to psychosocial approaches. Strengths of these interventions are in their generally benign nature, while questions remain about their effectiveness. It should be noted that those approaches most likely to be implemented are ones that can be easily integrated into routine care. Attention to feasibility and cost effectiveness as well as efficacy are critical to successful implementation. Cognitive, emotion, and stimulation-oriented therapies generally have little to no demonstrated efficacy for improving functioning or reducing behaviors that challenge. They appear to often be utilized because they have little potential for harm. Behavioral therapies have more clearly established efficacy. But barriers to implementation relate to demands on caregivers and staff, reallocation of staff time, and flexibility. Concerns about asking staff to implement interventions against falling staff-to-resident ratios and increasingly complex care needs at times can result in prioritizing safety to the detriment of potentially effective treatment (Lawrence et al., 2012). Other limitations of using psychosocial interventions include the need for consistent treatment to maintain gains. Many studies find that positive effects last only briefly after cessation of the interventions. In general, the best interventions are person centered and enable persons with dementia to have meaningful social interaction with their caregivers and others (Lawrence et al., 2012).

Combined Treatments

The different behavioral presentations of the major neurocognitive disorders, in combination with the high prevalence rates and projected increases in diagnosis, suggest a need for examination of combined pharmacological and psychosocial interventions. However, a search of the Cochrane Database and PubMed did not yield any relevant results for such approaches to target behavioral disturbances in those with AD (a search of clincialtrials.gov indicated that this is an area under current investigation). The focus of this section will thus be on multidisciplinary interventions and interventions that involve caregivers. Although these studies do not explicitly manipulate medication use, pharmacological management is typically included.

Large RCTs have examined the effect of targeted problem-solving behavioral approaches among community-dwelling individuals with dementia. These techniques, when used by families and caregivers, were found to significantly reduce behaviors that challenge (Gitlin et al., 2010). A recent meta-analysis of 23 RCTs found a moderate effect size (0.34) for family caregiver interventions in reducing behaviors that challenge (Brodaty & Arasaratnam, 2012).

Gitlin et al. (2010) conducted an RCT within the home based on Advancing Caregiver Training (ACT) conceptualization, which includes patient-based items such as unmet needs and pain, caregiver-based items such as stress and communication style, and environmental-based factors such as clutter and hazards. The ACT intervention involved occupational therapy sessions and nursing sessions. The maintenance phase consisted of brief telephone contacts. Initial sessions involved defining goals, reviewing problem behaviors, reviewing the home environment, and observing interactions between the caregiver and the person with dementia. Subsequent sessions were conducted utilizing the National Institutes of Health REACH II problem-solving approach (Belle et al., 2006). Action plans were developed with caregivers and identified target behaviors, treatment goals, triggers, and management strategies. The management strategies consisted of modifying physical environments, using assistive devices, simplifying communications and tasks, and engaging the individual with dementia in activities. Caregivers received psychoeducation in stress reduction and self-care and completed problem-solving exercises. At the end of the 16-week intervention, there was a significant difference in caregiver report of targeted behavior problems, with intervention caregivers reporting better emotional outcomes and enhanced confidence-managing behaviors.

A search of the Cochrane Database revealed few studies of variable quality that assessed the effect of exercise on caregiver burden (Forbes et al., 2013). The best of these found that caregivers who supervised an individual with dementia during an exercise program experienced reduced burden (Vreugdenhil et al., 2012). The intervention group participated in a home-based exercise program for four months in addition to their usual treatment, while those in the control group continued usual care. The interventions were based on the Home Support Exercise Program (Johnson et al., 2003). The intervention group improved on measures of caregiver burden and cognitive and physical functioning.

Opie et al. (2002) examined the effectiveness of a multidisciplinary approach in nursing home residents with severe behavioral disturbances. Residents with advanced dementia were randomly assigned to either an early intervention group or a delayed intervention group. A consultation team was trained to develop specific behavior management plans for patients in three categories (medical, nursing, and psychological) that were implemented for four weeks and modestly decreased the frequency and severity of behavioral disturbances. The most frequent interventions utilized were medical (changing pain management and commencing psychotropic medication), nursing (changing the timing and approach to activities of daily living and communication/aggression management), and psychological (listening to the radio or audiotapes, making environmental changes, and modifying behavior).

Benefits and Limitations of Combined Treatments

Behavior-oriented therapies have the greatest supporting evidence for efficacy, particularly for addressing problematic behaviors, and multidisciplinary approaches have many benefits over single-modality interventions. First, by including a multidisciplinary team, the amount of knowledge and attention given to a patient increases. Second, having a team approach allows for more thorough problem solving when behavioral problems do arise. Third, by involving a team approach, psychosocial and psychological interventions are used as initial interventions, and these interventions are typically cost effective and have few adverse side effects. On the other hand, combined treatment approaches require multiple individuals to be involved in treatment, and coordination of efforts may pose a challenge. Team members must be in agreement and must consistently follow the plan. Because by definition combined treatment approaches include the use of medications, careful monitoring of adverse effects of medications is required, particularly in a population where risks of adverse effects (and their severity) are more significant.

Summary and Recommendations

This review of the pharmacological, psychosocial, and combined treatment approaches to targeting disruptive behaviors highlights a need for future RCTs to explore the current needs of those with delirium and dementia and the realities of an aging population. Specifically, RCTs should examine combined medication management and behavioral interventions, as high-quality studies combining both approaches are essentially nonexistent. We believe behavioral therapies clearly have the most support at this time and should be the first to be studied in conjunction with pharmacological interventions, followed by cognitive therapies. Additionally, future research in the field should take a preventative approach (in line with the emerging positive psychology movement) to reduce cognitive and functional decline. The cognitive therapies may have more potential in this area.

Although behavioral interventions are considered the first line of treatment for disruptive behaviors associated with dementias, severe disruptive behaviors may require treatment with more immediate results, and in some cases the improvement from behavior approaches alone may not be sufficient. Thus, while we would typically recommend behavioral interventions as a monotherapy and the first line of treatment, severe cases may warrant beginning with a pharmacological intervention and transitioning to behavioral monotherapy when the acutely severe situation has stabilized. Additionally, though low-dose antipsychotic medications are often viewed as a first-line treatment in delirium, introducing an agent that taxes metabolic capacity in such medically vulnerable populations is likely to be risky. Future research should carefully review and weigh beneficial versus adverse effects of medications used to manage disruptive behaviors in dementia and delirium and the incremental benefits that these medications may contribute in comprehensive intervention programs. So far, most research has focused on approaches in isolation that may not accurately reflect the reality of the current health-care model. Research should also examine combined approaches in the context of comorbid medical conditions and simultaneous medication management of these conditions.

Mr. Berry is a 72-year-old gentleman who was accompanied to the emergency department by his wife after she noticed a sudden change in his mental status, severe agitation, and that he appeared to be experiencing visual hallucinations. Mr. Berry had been also experiencing sleep disturbances for approximately a week prior to his emergency department visit and had only slept for seven hours total in the past week. He yelled at and threatened physical aggression toward the nursing staff once he was admitted into the hospital. He also demonstrated challenging behaviors such as throwing his medications on the floor, and frequently complained of individuals being in his hospital room that were not observed by the hospital staff, who believed them to be hallucinations. Mr. Berry had been diagnosed with mild Alzheimer dementia two years prior but declined taking a cholinesterase inhibitor at that time. His wife also reported that Mr. Berry had experienced a steady increase in aggressive behaviors over the last two years, even prior to his recent episode.

Mr. Berry's laboratory results indicated the presence of a current infection. His physician suspected an acute delirium episode due to a urinary tract infection, superimposed on dementia, and exacerbated by sleep deprivation related to his metabolic disturbance. Mr. Berry was started on both an antibiotic and a low dose of haloperidol. His family was encouraged to bring in photos from his home and talk to him in a nonchallenging way about recent events to help reorient him. They were instructed to not challenge him on

(continued)

(continued)

hallucinations or odd verbalizations but instead to gently redirect him to factual events. His sleep improved quickly, his mental status returned to its previous baseline, and his aggressive behaviors began to decline over the course of a week. His haloperidol was discontinued when his aggressive behaviors significantly diminished and he appeared to be oriented for several consecutive days. It was noted that he would resume the medication if his behaviors that challenge remerged, but they remained stable and at baseline levels from that point forward. He was instructed to finish his course of antibiotics.

Mr. Berry was discharged and referred for a comprehensive neuropsychological evaluation to provide an objective measure of cognitive functioning, to evaluate potential emotional contributions, and to compare results from his assessment two years prior. There was some concern about the possibility of Lewy body disease, given his visual hallucinations while hospitalized. The neuropsychological exam found that his memory and executive functioning had significantly declined compared to his previous evaluation, and results were generally inconsistent with Lewy body disease and suggestive of Alzheimer disease as the likely pathology. This was important, as the presence of Lewy body disease would have contraindicated any later use of antipsychotic medications. Mr. Berry's observed cognitive decline corresponded with a decline in his activities of daily living over the last year, resulting in his wife taking more of a caregiver role. He stated that he felt his wife treated him like a child, which resulted in significant frustration for him. Mr. Berry also stated that he felt disconnected from his family, and he struggled to remain independent despite his wife's desire to offer more assistance. Mr. Berry reported feeling as though he no longer served a purpose in his family. He was started on a cholinesterase inhibitor to slow his rate of cognitive decline following the evaluation.

His wife also revealed during the interview for the neuropsychological evaluation that Mr. Berry had become lost while driving, needing to call his wife for assistance, several times over the past year. Mrs. Berry also noted that her husband handled most of their finances, and she was concerned that professional scammers had begun to call regularly and ask for him on the phone. When Mr. Berry was asked about these individuals, he responded that some of them were his friends to whom he enjoyed talking, but he knew better than to give them money. This was thought to reflect a change in social cognition related to his dementia. Mrs. Berry also reported that she was beginning to become frustrated by her husband asking her the same question multiple times during the day, as he did not remember her previous answers.

Based on the results of the evaluation and information obtained during the interview, it was recommended that Mr. Berry have an on-road driving exam with a professional driving evaluator and begin using a GPS device with his home address preprogrammed. Mr. Berry was also referred to a psychologist who consulted at a local senior center to examine behavioral contributions to his presentation. Mr. Berry and his wife presented to the psychologist for appraisal of behavioral aspects of his disturbed sleep and aggressive behaviors. Mr. Berry's frustration related to his perceived loss of autonomy was found to underlie many of his aggressive outbursts. Specifically, a functional analysis of the aggressive behaviors was conducted, and Mr. and Mrs. Berry identified antecedents, behaviors, and consequences. Together with the psychologist, they came to realize that aggressive behaviors within the home often arose when responsibilities were taken away from Mr. Berry. Mr. Berry felt that he was being treated like a child, which led him to exert his autonomy through angry outbursts. As a result of these outbursts, his wife began to take on more of the household responsibilities, as she viewed these outbursts as signs of further decline. This in turn made Mr. Berry feel more isolated, more dependent, and more frustrated, further eroding his relationship with his spouse. The functional analysis also allowed the couple to see that Mr. Berry's outbursts were serving to increase the amount of time Mr. Berry's two adult children spent with him, potentially reinforcing these behaviors. When Mr. Berry had anger outbursts, Mrs. Berry often called her children, and they would visit and speak with their father.

As a result of these analyses, Mr. and Mrs. Berry defined ways for Mr. Berry to maintain his independence, contribute to the household responsibilities, and spend time with his children that were independent of any behaviors that challenge. It was decided that Mr. Berry would increase the amount of household chores he completed, with appropriate supervision, to develop his self-efficacy; this would also help reduce the burden placed on his wife. The psychologist emphasized the likelihood that Mr. Berry would have difficulty with many tasks and that he should receive appropriate help with tasks prior to significant frustration. Mr. Berry was instructed on how to use a small calendar to manage his cleaning schedule. Mrs. Berry contacted the couples' children to set regular visits to decrease the reinforcement obtained by Mr. Berry's anger outbursts. It was also decided that his children would visit and interact with their father (watching sports programs or doing household projects with him) on the weekends to allow his wife to have scheduled respite

(continued)

(continued)

time. Mrs. Berry received information about communicating with Mr. Berry in simple short commands when asking him to complete tasks, and Mr. Berry was instructed to write down his wife's answers to his questions to avoid repeated questioning. The psychologist also recommended moving Mr. Berry's bedtime back one to two hours to decrease onset insomnia and early morning exercise in bright light to help maintain his circadian rhythm.

The psychologist also worked with Mrs. Berry to monitor her husband and determined that boredom at home seemed to increase aggression, while engaging in appropriately stimulating activities at the gerontology center (such as mild exercise, yoga, and games) seemed to lead to calmer afternoons and evenings. Working with the psychologist, Mr. and Mrs. Berry also implemented a plan to change their phone number, as the calls by scammers had increased. Mrs. Berry purchased a cell phone exclusively for Mr. Berry's use, and she programmed the names and numbers of his close family members and friends into it so that Mr. Berry would learn to answer the phone only when a person he knew was calling. With the help of the psychologist, the couple decided that Mr. Berry would be able to continue to manage household finances, but that Mrs. Berry would oversee all transactions and be involved in all financial decisions. Mr. and Ms. Berry arranged for both of their signatures to be required for any large financial transactions.

Concerns surrounding Mr. Berry's eating patterns arose when it was noted that Mr. Berry had lost 40 pounds over the last two years and he was below a normal weight. He reported that food tasted bland to him and had little flavor, a common occurrence in Alzheimer disease, where Alzheimer pathology affects the olfactory bulb. A nutritionist at the senior center recommended using more-intense flavors and spices to stimulate his appetite as well as increasing his consumption of antioxidants and healthy fats to preserve brain health.

Mr. Berry and his wife were able to implement the recommend changes, and his behaviors improved. His ongoing plan was to continue to monitor his physical and cognitive status regularly with annual neuropsychological evaluations and behavioral analyses. He was to continue with regular mild exercise, cognitive stimulation, and improved nutrition in addition to donepezil. Mr. Berry and his wife reported walking approximately one mile almost every day and engaging in nonstrenuous yoga twice a week at the senior center. Mr. Berry also developed a number of friendships with other older individuals at the senior center with whom he regularly played card games and board games. His treatment plan noted that the use of agents such as antipsychotics or benzodiazepines for his aggressive behaviors was to be only considered as a last option if they became significantly problematic again.

References

AGS. American Geriatrics Society. (2012). AGS updated Beers criteria for potentially inappropriate medication use in older adults. *Journal of the American Geriatrics Society, 60*(4), 616–631.

Alessi, C. A., et al. (2005). Randomized, controlled trial of a nonpharmacological intervention to improve abnormal sleep/wake patterns in nursing home residents. *Journal of the American Geriatrics Society, 53*(5), 803–810.

Alzheimer's Association. (2013). Alzheimer's disease facts and figures. *Alzheimer's and Dementia, 9*(2), 1–69.

American Psychiatric Association Workgroup on Alzheimer's Disease and Other Dementias. (2007). Practice guidelines for the treatment of patients with Alzheimer's disease and other dementias. *American Journal of Psychiatry 164*(Suppl. 1), 5–56.

APA. American Psychiatric Association. (2013). *Diagnostic and statistical manual of mental disorders* (5th ed.). Washington, DC: Author.

APA. American Psychiatric Association. (2014). Guidelines for psychological practice with older adults. *American Psychologist, 69*(1), 34–65.

Ballard, C. (2013). Neuropsychiatric symptoms in patients with dementias associated with cortical Lewy bodies: Pathophysiology, clinical features, and pharmacological management. *Drugs and Aging, 30*, 603–611.

Ballard, C. G., et al. (2006). Atypical antipsychotics for aggression and psychosis in Alzheimer's disease. *Cochrane Database of Systematic Reviews, 2006*(1), CD003476. doi:10.1002/14651858.CD003476.pub2

Baskys, A. (2004). Lewy body dementia: The litmus test for neuroleptic sensitivity and extrapyramidal symptoms. *Journal of Clinical Psychiatry, 65*(11), 16–22.

Belle, S., et al. (2006). Enhancing the quality of life of dementia caregivers from different ethnic or racial groups: A randomized, controlled trial. *Annals of Internal Medicine, 145*(10), 727–738.

Bird, M., & Moniz-Cook, E. (2008). *Challenging behaviour in dementia: A psychosocial approach to intervention.* New York: John Wiley & Sons. doi:10.1002/9780470773185.ch33

Brechin, D., et al. (2013). Alternatives to antipsychotic medication: Psychological approaches in managing psychological and behavioural distress in people with dementia. Briefing Paper INF 207. Retrieved from http://www.psige.org/public/files/BPS%20FPoP%20-%20Alternatives%20to%20Anti-Psychotic%20Medication%20-%20report%20-%20March%202013.pdf.

Brodaty, H., & Arasaratnam, C. (2012). Meta-analysis of nonpharmacological interventions for neuropsychiatric symptoms of dementia. *American Journal of Psychiatry, 169*(9), 946–953.

Chiu, M. J., et al. (2006). Behavioral and psychologic symptoms in different types of dementia. *Journal of the Formosan Medical Association, 105*(7), 556–562.

Chung, J. A., & Cummings, J. L. (2000). Neurobehavioral and neuropsychiatric symptoms in Alzheimer's disease. *Dementia, 18*(4), 829–846.

Cipher, D. J., et al. (2007). The effectiveness of geropsychological treatment in improving pain, depression, behavioral disturbances, functional disability, and health care utilization in long-term care. *Clinical Gerontologist: The Journal of Aging and Mental Health, 30*(3), 23–40. doi:10.1300/J018v30n03_02

Cohen-Mansfield, J., & Werner, P. (1997). Management of verbally disruptive behaviors in nursing home residents. *Journals of Gerontology, Series A, Biological and Medical Sciences, 52*(6), 369–377.

Cohen-Mansfield, J., et al. (2007). Nonpharmacological treatment of agitation: A controlled trial of systematic individualized intervention. *Journals of Gerontology, Series A, Biological and Medical Sciences, 62*(8), 908–916.

Cohen-Mansfield, J., et al. (2012). Efficacy of nonpharmacologic interventions for agitation in advanced dementia: A randomized, placebo-controlled trial. *Journal of Clinical Psychiatry, 73*(9), 1255–1261. doi:10.4088/JCP.12m07918

Cole, M. (2004). Delirium in elderly patients. *American Journal of Geriatric Psychiatry, 12*(1), 7–21.

Corbett, A., et al. (2012). Treatment of behavioral and psychological symptoms of Alzheimer's disease. *Current Treatment Options in Neurology, 14,* 113–125.

Declercq, T., et al. (2013). Withdrawal versus continuation of chronic antipsychotic drugs for behavioural and psychological symptoms in older people with dementia. *Cochrane Database of Systematic Reviews, 2013*(3), CD007726. doi:10.1002/14651858.CD007726.pub2

Diehl, J., & Kurz, A. (2002). Frontotemporal dementia: Patient characteristics, cognition, and behavior. *International Journal of Geriatric Psychiatry, 17,* 914–918.

Dolder, C. R., & Nealy, K. L. (2012). The efficacy and safety of newer anticonvulsants in patients with dementia. *Drugs and Aging, 29*(8), 627–637.

Flanagan, N. M., & Fick, D. M. (2010). Delirium superimposed on dementia: Assessment and intervention. *Journal of Gerontological Nursing, 36*(11), 19–23.

Forbes, D., et al. (2013). Exercise programs for people with dementia. *Cochrane Database of Systematic Reviews, 2013*(12), CD006489. doi:10.1002/14651858.CD006489.pub3

Francis, J. (2014). Prevention and treatment of delirium and confusional states. *Up to Date.* Retrieved from http://www.uptodateonline.com.

Freymann, N., et al. (2005). Successful treatment of sexual disinhibition in dementia with carbamazepine: A case report. *Pharmacopsychiatry, 38*(3), 144–145.

Gaber, S., et al. (2001). Sertraline versus small doses of haloperidol in the treatment of agitated behavior in patients with dementia. *Archives of Gerontology and Geriatrics Supplement, 7,* 159–162.

Gitlin, L. N., et al. (2010). Targeting and managing behavioral symptoms in individuals with dementia: A randomized trial of a nonpharmacological intervention. *Journal of the American Geriatrics Society, 58*(8), 1465–1474.

Gitlin, L. N., et al. (2012). Nonpharmacologic management of behavioral symptoms in dementia. *Journal of the American Medical Association, 308*(19), 2020–2029.

Guay, D. R. P. (2008). Inappropriate sexual behaviors in cognitively impaired older individuals. *American Journal of Geriatric Pharmacotherapy, 6*(5), 269–288.

Gupta, M., et al. (2013). The profile of behavioral and psychological symptoms in vascular cognitive impairment with and without dementia. *Annals of Indiana Academy of Neurology, 16*(4), 599–602.

Hake, A. M., & Farlow, M. R. (2014). Clinical features and diagnosis of dementia with Lewy bodies. *Up to Date*. Retrieved from http://www.uptodateonline.com.

Hansen, N. V., et al. (2006). Massage and touch for dementia. *Cochrane Database of Systematic Reviews, 2006*(4), CD004989. doi:10.1002/14651858.CD004989.pub2

Hsieh, C. J., et al. (2010). Reminiscence group therapy on depression and apathy in nursing home residents with mild-to-moderate dementia. *Journal of Experimental and Clinical Medicine, 2*(2), 72–78.

Huybrechts, K. F., et al. (2012). Differential risk of death in older residents in nursing homes prescribed specific antipsychotic drugs: population based cohort study. *British Medical Journal, 2012*, 344. doi:10.1136/bmj.e977

Inouye, S. K. (2006). Delirium in older persons. *New England Journal of Medicine, 354*, 1157–1165.

James, I. A. (2011). *Understanding behaviour in dementia that challenges: A guide to assessment and treatment*. London: Jessica Kingsley.

Johnson, C. S. J., et al. (2003). Outcome evaluation of the Canadian Centre for Activity and Aging's home support exercise program for frail older adults. *Journal of Aging and Physical Activity, 11*, 408–424.

Joller, P., et al. (2013). Approach to inappropriate sexual behaviour in people with dementia. *Canadian Family Physician, 59*, 255–260.

Kasuya, R. T., et al. (2000). Caregiver burden and burnout: A guide for primary care physicians. *Postgraduate Medicine, 108*(7), 119–123.

Langa, K., et al. (2001). National estimates of the quantity and cost of informal caregiving for the elderly with dementia. *Journal of General Internal Medicine, 16*(11), 770–778.

Lawrence, V., et al. (2012). Improving quality of life for people with dementia in care homes: Making psychosocial interventions work. *British Journal of Psychiatry, 201*(5), 344–351.

Lee, P. E., et al. (2004). Atypical antipsychotic drugs in the treatment of behavioral and psychological symptoms of dementia: Systematic review. *British Journal of Medicine, 329*, 75.

Livingston, G., et al. (2005). Systematic review of psychological approaches to the management of neuropsychiatric symptoms of dementia. *American Journal of Psychiatry, 162*(11), 1996–2021.

Lonergan, E., et al. (2007). Antipsychotics for delirium. *Cochrane Database of Systematic Reviews, 18*(2), CD005594.

Lopez, O. L., et al. (2013). The long-term effects of conventional and atypical antipsychotics in patients with probable Alzheimer's disease. *American Journal of Psychiatry, 170*(9), 1051–1058.

Lyketsos, C. G., et al. (2011). Neuropsychiatric symptoms in Alzheimer's disease. *Alzheimer's and Dementia, 7*, 532–539.

McKeith, I. (2004). Dementia with Lewy bodies. *Dialogues in Clinical Neuroscience, 6*(3), 333–341.

Mega, M. S., et al. (1996). The spectrum of behavioral changes in Alzheimer's disease. *Neurology, 46*(1), 130–135.

Moniz-Cook, E. D., et al. (2012). Functional analysis-based interventions for challenging behaviour in dementia. *Cochrane Database of Systematic Reviews, 2006*(2), CD006929. doi:10.1002/14651858.CD006929.pub2

O'Neil, M., et al. (2011). *Non-pharmacological interventions for behavioral symptoms of dementia: A systematic review of the evidence.* Washington, DC: Department of Veterans Affairs. Retrieved from http://www.ncbi.nlm.nih.gov/books/NBK54971/.

Opie, J., et al., (2002). Challenging behaviors in nursing home residents with dementia: A randomized controlled trial of multidisciplinary interventions. *International Journal of Geriatric Psychiatry, 17,* 6–13.

Parellada, E., et al. (2004). Risperdone in the treatment of patients with delirium. *Journal of Clinical Psychiatry, 65,* 348–353.

Pinheiro, D. (2008). Anticonvulsant mood stabilizers in the treatment of behavioral and psychological symptoms of dementia (BPSD). *L'Encéphale, 34*(4), 409–415.

Pollock, B. G., et al. (2007). A double-blind comparison of citalopram and risperidone for the treatment of behavioral and psychotic symptoms associated with dementia. *American Journal of Geriatric Psychiatry, 15,* 942–952.

Press, D., & Alexander, M. (2014). Management of neuropsychiatric symptoms of dementia. *Up to Date.* Retrieved from http://www.uptodateonline.com.

Prince, M., et al. (2013). The global prevalence of dementia: A systematic review and metaanalysis. *Alzheimer's and Dementia, 9,* 63–75.

Schneider, L. S., et al. (2006). Effectiveness of atypical antipsychotic drugs in patients with Alzheimer's disease. *New England Journal of Medicine, 355,* 1525–1528.

Sink, K. M., et al. (2005). Pharmacological treatment of neuropsychiatric symptoms of dementia: A review of the evidence. *Journal of the American Medical Association, 293,* 596–608.

Skrobik, Y. K., et al. (2004). Olanzapine vs haloperidol: Treating delirium in a critical care setting. *Intensive Care Medicine, 30,* 444–449.

Tampi, R. R., & Tampi, D. J. (2014). Efficacy and tolerability of benzodiazepines for the treatment of behavioral and psychological symptoms of dementia: A systematic review of randomized control trials. *American Journal of Alzheimer's Disease and Other Dementias.* doi:10.1177/1533317514524813

Tondi, L., et al. (2007). Validation therapy (VT) in nursing home: A case-control study. *Archives of Gerontology and Geriatrics, 44,* 407–411. doi:10.1016/j.archger.2007.01.057

Toseland, R. W., et al. (1997). The impact of validation group therapy on nursing home residents with dementia. *Journal of Applied Gerontology, 16*(1), 31–50.

Trzepacz, P., et al. (2010). Practice guideline for the treatment of patients with delirium. *Psychiatry Online.* doi:10.1176/appi.books.9780890423363.42494

Vreugdenhil, A., et al. (2012). A community-based exercise programme to improve functional ability in people with Alzheimer's disease: A randomized controlled trial. *Scandinavian Journal of Caring Sciences, 26,* 12–19.

Yoon, H., et al. (2013). Efficacy and safety of haloperidol versus atypical antipsychotic medications in the treatment of delirium. *BMC Psychiatry, 13,* 240–251.

Zetteler, J. (2008). Effectiveness of simulated presence therapy for individuals with dementia: A systematic review and meta-analysis. *Aging and Mental Health, 12*(6), 779–785.